MW00448763

LIFE SLIGHTLY OFF CENTER

BY JACK RAYMOND

Contents

Introduction

Look at me, I'm the retired guy. I never expected to use the R word in reference to me. I was never going to retire. I was having too much fun working and making money. Well, life just caught up with me, and here I am out to pasture—retired, done, finished, career over! But surprise, surprise, I love it! I'm free! I am free of deadlines, meetings, rushing around, and phone calls and chasing the all-mighty buck. I now enjoy letting the day take me wherever it takes me. No schedules. I love riding around in my old pickup truck with the country music cranked up. I swear, I am one chaw of tobacco away from being an official redneck!

Life has definitely slowed down, but it has given me the time to reflect on my life. I now realize what a great ride I have had for all these many years. I have experienced life at it best and life at its worst. It has been funny, sad, exciting, confusing, loving, exhausting, and funny. Oh, I've already said "funny," but I guess funny deserves a double billing because funny is what helps make it so great!

I have been telling my stories for years. I'm the guy at the party telling funny stories and getting lots of laughs. The only thing missing is a lamp shade on my head. My poor wife has suffered through thousands of storytelling sessions and still manages to laugh. Well, maybe not laugh; maybe more of a polite chuckle. The kids just roll their eyes and mumble "Here he goes again!" This is when they usually head for the nearest exit. I have tried to curb myself, tried to be the quiet guy in the corner, but it never works. Telling stories is who I am. This is what I love; this is what connects me!

Many years ago, my wife and I were invited to a party by an acquaintance of mine. I didn't know her that well and didn't know her husband at all. Dianna knew neither. Once we got to the party, we discovered that we didn't know a soul there. These were all PBS television people. There were directors, producers, writers, and cameramen in attendance. We had absolutely nothing in common with this group. I wondered why we were invited to this party. At about this time, the hostess said "Jack, tell everyone the story about the time you erased your son." Oh, I get it, I am the evening entertainment. Since I love an audience to tell my stories to, I went ahead and entertained while the hostess videotaped me. I guess she figured they could use the tape at future parties and not have to invite us again. Come to think of it, we were never invited to another party at their home.

Life Slightly Off Center

I have a good friend Ray who loves to tell my stories. We were invited to a party at his house one evening, and he insisted that I tell some of my stories to his guests. After the storytelling session, a woman came up to me and said "I like the way Ray tells your stories better."

Another time, I was walking through the mailroom at the office and happened upon a gang of people who were having a great laugh. I asked the girl doing all the talking "What is so funny?" She said "I just told them one of your stories!"

Now that I am officially out to pasture, I finally have the time to write down all my stories to share with the world! This book is for everyone I have met, told a funny story to, been slapped on the back, and told "Jack, you should write a book!" So here I am, writing a book. You'll be reading about my wife, kids, grandkids, family, friends, and assorted dogs and cats. All these characters in my life have been great fodder for all my stories. Without them, there would be no stories.

Jack

CHAPTER 1

The Early Years

And in the Beginning

My mother told me this story about the day I was born. It was a warm spring day in April. Mom was at home, which was the downstairs apartment of an old two-story house on Bleaker Street in Scranton, Pennsylvania. The midwife who was to assist in the birth lived upstairs. Mom had a broom next to her bed. When the labor pains got intense, she took the broom handle and knocked on the ceiling above her bed. This was the signal for the midwife to come quickly because things were about to start happening. All went according to schedule, thank God, since there were no emergency plans in the schedule. I was born at 10 AM or thereabout on April 11, 1941. Dad was at work at the time. He drove a delivery truck and was delivering a load of bananas to grocery stores out of town. He was due back in the morning. When he did walk into the house, he found Mom in bed and asked "So what's new?" Mom pulled back the blanket and said "This is new!" I was in the bed next to Mom as she introduced Dad to his new day-old son. I was son number two. I had a brother, Billy, who was four years my senior. I was named John Lionel Raymond. The John was for my mother's brother, John (nickname Jackie), and the Lionel was for her other brother. From that moment on, I was always called Jackie by everyone in the family.

Here are few interesting facts that will give you a scope of what was going on in the world the year I came into it. We were at war with Hitler's Nazi Germany and Franklin D. Roosevelt was president. Japan was to bomb Pearl Harbor that December. You could buy a brand new Nash sedan, which got 25 to 30 miles on a gallon of gas, for the mere price of $745; whitewall tires and bumper guards were extra. A Studebaker pickup truck could be yours for $664. Again the whitewall tires were extra. A Maytag washing machine was only $79.95 and that included the automatic wringer. Pall Mall was the top-selling cigarette. The USS North Carolina was commissioned into the fleet. It was the mightiest fighting ship in the Navy and weighed in at 35,000 tons; Billy Raymond had a new brother weighing in at 6 pounds, 4 ounces.

Me Growing Up

When I recall growing up, I just remember bits and pieces. I guess one of my earliest memories was living on Pollard Avenue in Rochester, New York. Billy was outside on the porch sitting on a little suitcase. He was probably about seven or eight years old. Apparently he had done something really bad to provoke Mom to pack his bag and have him sit on the porch. She said the truck from the orphanage would be coming to pick him up. I recall vividly standing there, looking through glass door, and crying and begging Mom to please let Billy in before the orphanage truck arrived. Mom let him suffer for awhile and then apparently gave in because Billy is still around. In hindsight I should have not argued about him going off to the orphanage. I know my life as a kid would have been a lot less miserable without a big brother to torture me.

Another really early memory is when I was about five years old and in kindergarten. I remember hating going to school. School to me consisted of crying kids, naps, and warm milk. I preferred being left alone in a pile of dirt to play with my toys. Every morning I would stuff my pockets with my miniature cars and trucks and head off to school. We lived close enough to the school so that we were walkers. I'd only go as far as my favorite pile of dirt, stop, and play—I would be there all morning. When I saw the kindergarten kids heading home, I'd dust myself off and head for home, too. Mom never caught on for several months. After so many

Life Slightly Off Center

absences, my teacher finally called my mom and the jig was up. I had to repeat kindergarten. I must be one of the few kids in the history of public education to actually flunk kindergarten!

School was really tough for me. I had a hard time learning how to read; so hard in fact that Mom had to send me to a tutor, which she really could not afford. I was under a lot of pressure to get the job done because it was costing Mom and Dad money that they just didn't have. Math was a disaster, and history and science bored me. Back in grade school, all the really slow kids were sent to Mrs. Brush's class. You did not want to go to Mrs. Brush's class because you would be labeled a dummy and teased by all the kids who were not in her class. Going into Mrs. Brush's class was the worst thing that could happen to you. I can remember lying in bed every night praying "Please God, help me to do good in school, and don't let me get sent to Mrs. Brush's class." With the help of God, I was able to barely pass from one grade to the next.

The only thing I could ever do well was draw. Mom would have me draw something whenever we had company at the house. Mom would say "Jackie, show Mrs. Clapp how you can draw." Boats, birds, dogs, cats, boys, girls, horses—you name it and I could pretty much draw it. I remember my first grade teacher was my biggest fan. She was always praising my drawing and called me her little artist. I went back to visit Mrs. Roach when I was a senior in high school, and she still had some of my drawings tacked to her bulletin board.

My world in the early years consisted of my mom, Dad, brother Billy, and sisters, Kathy and Sally. I can close my eyes and still hear Mother calling us to get up for school. "Billy, Jackie, Kathy, Sally GET UP!" Mom was a very quiet woman until it came time to wake us up for school. That is when her voice went up five octaves and turned into this horrible shrill. It was effective and we were up as if we had been shot from a cannon! Our typical weekday morning would be Sally, Kathy, and me getting up first. We had to be in and out of the bathroom before Billy came downstairs. He had to have a clear path to the bathroom and woe be to the poor soul who got in his way. Mom would knock on the bathroom door and say "Hurry up, Billy is coming down." One bathroom and four kids does nothing for keeping the peace. Billy was such a grouch; we were all afraid of him and learned very early to stay out of his way. Our breakfast consisted of corn flakes and hot chocolate. Billy's breakfast consisted of hot chocolate and five or six pieces of toast slathered with gobs of peanut butter. All during breakfast, it was "Mom, Jackie said this" or "Kathy did that" and "Sally said Jackie was a..." Billy would chime in every so often to yell, "Shut up, you guys!" I'm sure Mother was very happy to see us walk out the door for school and leave her in peace.

BILLY JACKIE KATHY SALLY!

We couldn't leave until one of us ran down the cellar to retrieve Mom's curtain rods at the bottom of the steps. This was Mom's ammunition against the giant rats that lived down there. Mom would throw a couple of them down whenever she had to go into the cellar to do the wash or tend the coal furnace. The noise would scare the rats into hiding so Mom couldn't see them. Now when I say rats, I mean rats as big as a medium-size cat with yellow eyes, yellow teeth, and a long rat tail. Mom was terrified of them.

Years later when Mom got her first automatic washer and had it hooked up in the kitchen, she was in heaven: No more washing in the cellar. Although she still kept her arsenal of curtain rods at the ready because she still had the damned fire to tend to during those long, cold New York winters.

As a kid, I would love to go down in that dark, dank basement and quietly wait for those rats to come out and pop them with my Red Rider BB Gun. I never did any damage, but sure scared the hell out of them! I was the great white hunter.

We lived in a series of apartments in the village of Charlotte near Rochester, New York, starting at about when I was two years old. These apartments were usually on the second floor of a two-story house. Mom was always after us kids to be quiet so we wouldn't disturb the people downstairs. There was this one place that didn't have a bathroom upstairs, forcing us to share the bathroom with downstairs neighbors. One day Dad found a message taped to the toilet "Please do not wet seat." That's all it took to get Dad upset, and we'd be on the move again. We never moved more than a block or two from the last place we lived.

Moving day consisted of everyone grabbing something—a lamp, box, or whatever we could carry—and walking to our new place. I am sure the neighbors must have looked out their windows and commented "Oh boy, there go those Raymonds again!" I think about it now and realize how tough life must have been for Mother. She moved so often with four kids and very little money. One apartment was pretty much like the last one. I guess times were really hard, but as a kid, I never realized it. To me, every move was a new adventure.

At one point we lived in the second floor apartment of my Uncle Francis's two-story house. Downstairs lived Uncle Francis, Aunt Ethel, and their son Skipper. (This was the big old house on Pollard Avenue.) We were all young when television came into being. Uncle Francis had one, and we thought Skipper had to be the luckiest kid in the world to actually have a TV in his house. The really big show for kids back then was the *Howdy Doody Show*. This show was on every weekday afternoon at 4 o'clock. Mom would not allow us to ask Aunt Ethel if we could watch the show. If she happened to invite us, then we could go in, be on our best behavior, and not to forget to thank her. Every day at 3:45 PM, Kathy, Sally, and I sat on the steps leading from our apartment to the hallway outside my aunt's apartment. There we waited, hoping she would invite us in. Sometimes she did, but most times she didn't. When she did, it was such a big deal. Howdy Doody, Buffalo Bob, Clara Bell, and Princess Summer Fall Winter Spring were all there to entertain us. But most days we were left to sit on the steps and listen to the show through my aunt's closed door.

Mom and Dad

Mom once told us the story of her meeting Dad. She said it was love at first sight. "Your Dad was so good-looking, nice and tall, with black wavy hair. All the girls were crazy about Walter Raymond! He was a party boy and always had everyone laughing. Florence, on the other hand, was quiet and shy—not the type of girl Walter would normally go for. So the hard-drinking joker meets the shy little Sunday school teacher and the rest is history. His friends said he was crazy, and her friends said it would never work. But work it did and lasted their whole lives.

Mom and Dad fell in love and secretly married. Back in the day when jobs were scarce, a husband and wife could not both have jobs. Mother needed her job to help support her brothers and sisters, and Dad needed his job to help support his family. They kept their marriage a secret in order to keep their jobs. They both continued to live with their respective families for a year after they married.

All of our family came from Scranton and surrounding areas. My dad broke the cycle of living and struggling in Pennsylvania and made the bold decision of moving his family to Rochester, New York. The family at that time consisted of Mom, Dad, Billy, and me. Our sisters, Kathy and Sally, were born in Rochester.

Dad loved nothing better than hanging out at a bar and having a beer with his buddies. At home, Mom was fixing dinner and wanted Dad home so she would send Billy or me out to go find Dad. He would be at either Hank's Grill or the Horseshoe Tavern. I would jump on my bike and head for Hank's first because that was the closest bar to our house. The bar was owned by my Uncle Francis, who was Dad's half brother.

I'd go into the bar, and it always hit me how dark and smelly it was in there. I couldn't understand why all these guys enjoyed hanging around this place on such a beautiful day. The air was blue with smoke and it was hard to see when you first walked in. I'd find Dad sitting there having a beer and say "Come on, Dad, Mom wants you home for supper." "Okay, kid, let me just finish this beer and we'll go." Then, like it always happened, one of Dad's cronies would say "Hey, Walt, is that your son?" "Sure is, this is Jackie." "Well, bartender, give Jackie a Coke and give Walt another beer!" By the time it was all said and done, I would have five Cokes in front of me and Dad would have five more beers, compliments of his buddies. The Cokes back in the day cost 5 cents, and a glass of beer could be had for 10 cents. The phone would ring, and it would be Mom. Dad would say to Uncle Francis to tell her we just left.

Mom made supper every evening. If Dad was working the day shift, which was 8 AM to 4 PM, he was normally home at dinnertime. After dinner, he and Mom would enjoy a cup of tea. It was at this time that Mother would report to Dad if any of us kids had been bad that day. Here is a sampling of how it would be played out.

"Jackie, stand in front of your father and tell him what you did today." We all knew it was coming because whenever one of us got into trouble, my mom would warn us that we would be standing in front of our father that night.

So if I was the chosen one, I would stand up and stammer and mumble my confession. The punishment was terrible. My father would say something like, "I can't believe you did that, I am so ashamed of you." He would put his head down into his hand, rub his forehead, and just shake his head and say, "Jackie, you've got my heart broken. Go on, get out of here, I don't even want to look at you. Beat it." That was the worse punishment he could have given us. Who wants to be responsible for breaking their father's heart? I'd think to myself, *Oh, come on, Dad, just hit me.* A spanking would be so much better than a broken heart. If the infraction was serious enough, we would get spanked by both Mom and Dad. The real spankings were delivered by Dad with his belt...oh boy, did that hurt. The discipline doled out by Mom and Dad pretty much kept us all in line.

When we were smaller, Dad would take us kids to visit Aunt Anna and Uncle Johnny. Anna was Dad's older sister and lived down the street from us on Stutson Street. Aunt Anna was hard of hearing and Dad loved to get us going while visiting her. He would say, "Hey Aunt Anna, you look great, and it looks like you got yourself a new dress. Looks great!" This was said in a very loud booming voice so she could hear him, and then under his breath and in a very quiet voice, he would say "You look like hell and that dress is really ugly." Well, we would go into fits of giggling.

Aunt Anna, who never had any children and didn't understand them, would look at us on the floor rolling around laughing, and ask "Walter, what is wrong with your kids? What do they find so funny?" The whole visit would go like that, and we usually left exhausted from laughing.

We always left with one of Aunt Anna's amazing homemade chocolate chip cookies. Our Uncle Johnny never took his eyes off the TV. He would just sit in his big overstuffed easy chair, smoke cigarettes, and enjoy the first color TV in the neighborhood. It was so crazy. Uncle Johnny had seen an advertisement on television for this piece of colored plastic. He sent away for it. It was green on the bottom, a neutral color in the center, like a light skin tone, and sky blue on the top.

He taped this to the screen of his TV, and like magic he had himself a colored TV. He thought it was the best thing since sliced bread. Our conversation with Uncle Johnny was "Hi Uncle Johnny" and later, "Goodbye, Uncle Johnny." Ole Uncle Johnny had to be the dullest man on the planet. His occupations so fit his personality. For years, he was an elevator operator and then later in life was the old man who handed out towels in the men's locker room at the YMCA.

Years later, after I had grown up and was home on leave from the Air Force, Dad would insist that I go and visit Aunt Anna and Uncle Johnny. He would stay on my case until I went. Every time I went, Aunt Anna would ask, "Now tell me, Jackie, where are you living now and what college are you teaching at?" She always said I looked like a college professor, therefore I must be one. My reply was "No, no, Aunt Anna," I'd shout, since her hearing was getting worse, "I don't teach, I'm in the Air Force." She'd reply, "Oh that's nice, dear, and are you happy? How are your wife and the children?" Uncle Johnny was still watching his color TV from the same easy chair, but he seemed to be getting lower in it every time I went to visit. He was still smoking his cigarettes. He could smoke a cigarette down to the filter without losing the ash. When he was finished, the ash was as long as the cigarette had been. This always amazed me. Our conversation was still the same as when I was a kid: "Hi Uncle Johnny" and "Goodbye Uncle Johnny."

The best thing about those visits was that I never left without one of Aunt Anna's fantastic home-baked chocolate chip cookies.

Life Slightly Off Center

Stutson Street

HOME SWEET HOME

212 *Stutson Street*

I was about nine or ten years old when Dad bought us our very first house. On the day we moved in, Dad said to us "Okay, you guys can run, jump, shout, make lots of noise, and even pee on the seat if you want, because this is our house and we can do whatever we damn well please!" What a thrill that day was—212 Stutson Street became home for the wandering tribe of Raymonds!

Our new house was in pretty much an all-Italian neighborhood. Dad's first rule was that we were not allowed to play with the little neighbor "ginney" kids on the block. He said for us to go out and find some nice "American" kids to play with. My father was the original Archie Bunker. So here we are living in the little Italy of Charlotte among neighbors with names like Chickatelli, Trabollsi, and Vegatelli, and we couldn't play with their kids.

The house on Stutson Street was a two-story house jammed between houses on either side. The house on the right was so close that you would have to turn sideways to get between them. This is where the Chickatelli family lived. There was Mr. and Mrs. Chickatelli and their two kids. On the other side, there was slightly more room between the houses. This is where Mrs. Tootenhauf lived with her older brother and two yappy dogs. Mrs. Tootenhauf talked with a very thick accent. I think it was Dutch and her brother never, ever said one word in all the time we lived there. Their whole house was surrounded by a shoulder-high chain-link fence. In the back yard there was a half-buried standing bath tub, painted sky blue, with a statue of the Virgin Mary inside. Around the Virgin Mary was a flower garden. We kids thought that was very classy.

Stutson Street was a through street and the traffic was pretty heavy during the day. We had no driveway so we had to park the car on a small gravel area between the sidewalk and the road. This is where Dad spent many afternoons with his head buried under the hood of the car working on it. Because the houses were so close together, the man who delivered the coal had to park his truck on our tiny front lawn and run an extended coal shoot from the truck to the back of the house where the cellar window was located. It took a lot of men to keep our house running back then. We had the coal man, the ash man, the garbage man, the milkman, the mailman, and for a while the ice man. He delivered a block of ice about once a week to be put in the ice box to keep the food cold.

When you entered the front door, you were in the hallway. To the right were steps going up to the three bedrooms and one bathroom. (Actually the bathroom consisted of a toilet that never worked. The only action it ever saw was the time Sally heard a noise coming from inside it and lifted the lid to find a huge rat inside. This sent Sally into screaming hysterics! Believe me, these rats were as big as cats and very scary. I would have screamed, too. But I digress—on with the tour of the estate.) At the top of the stairs was the bedroom Billy and I shared. No closet and no door. The only window overlooked Chickatellis' roof. Across from our bedroom and down the hall just a bit was Mom and Dad's bedroom. They not only had a closet, but also a bedroom door. Farther down the hall was the nonworking bathroom and off that bathroom was the room that Sally and Kathy shared. Again, no closet and no door. Going downstairs to the hallway, you would find the living room to the left. This is where we would hang out in the evening and listen to the radio or in later years watch our black-and-white television, which had a round screen and was actually a piece of very, very heavy furniture.

We kids were not allowed to lie on the couch. If Mom caught us, she would yell at us to get off her couch and would say "Boy, I can't wait until you get married and

Life Slightly Off Center

get a house, so I can come over and lie on your couch! And don't even think about putting your feet up on the coffee table."

The front hall emptied into the kitchen. I think this was the biggest room in the house. The floor had a serious slant to it. If you dropped anything, it would roll to the other end. I close my eyes and I can still see my mother in her favorite place. She would be standing over the register with the heat blowing up. She loved that. King, our faithful dog, was allowed only in the kitchen, and he never ventured beyond that threshold.

I can still see us sitting around that old Formica table having supper. If one of us didn't finish every last morsel, Mom would start her speech about kids in Africa starving to death. My brother and sisters never quite finished their milk, and Mom would say, "Pour whatever is left in your glass into Jackie's glass." The milk was warm and yucky, but I just gulped it down and didn't complain. Mother was happy with empty plates and empty glasses.

The times that Dad didn't make home for supper, Mom would fix him a plate and keep it covered and warm on the stove. Our kitchen window looked directly into the Chickatellis' kitchen. We would always check to see what they were having for dinner. "Ah, looks like the Chickatellis are having linguini for dinner tonight." Mom would snap at us to get away from the window.

Moving on from the kitchen, we go into the back hall. Off this hall to the right was our one and only bathroom. This was probably the busiest room in the house. You almost needed a number to get in. There was no shower, so we had to take tub baths. Saturday night was bath night at the Raymonds'. Mom would fill the tub with hot water; now when I say fill, I mean about 6 inches deep. First Sally would have her bath, then Kathy, and then me. By the time I got in, the water was lukewarm and sort of a gray color. I really didn't enjoy bath night.

Beyond the bathroom was a big room where we hung our coats and other stuff. I guess that was our stuff room. I think Mother used to do her ironing back in that room. Out the backdoor was the porch that Dad had built. Dad wasn't a great carpenter and this back porch was a testament to that. The windows were too high and when you sat down, you couldn't look out over our palatial estate. All you could see was the wall below the windows. I am sure the porch was put together with bits and pieces that Dad was able to get hold of for free from his friends. The porch never got much use and became a storage area for stuff. Guess you could call it our stuff porch.

Oh, I forgot the front porch. That was the place we hung out in the summer time. Mom would listen to the radio while Dad enjoyed a beer and a smoke.

Monday at 212 Stutson Street was wash day. This is when Mom dragged all the clothes from upstairs to the basement to wash and then ring everything out. Then she would haul the baskets of clean clothes up the steps and out to the backyard where she would hang everything up on the clothesline, no matter what the weather. When the clothes were dry, she would take them down, put them into her basket, and haul them back into the house for ironing.

Whew, I get exhausted just telling you about this whole procedure. I guess the only saving grace for Mom was that we didn't have that many clothes.

One of my vivid memories of Dad was his discovery of dark wood paneling. It must have been something new back in the '50s, and he thought it was the greatest thing to ever happen to a home owner. Wood paneling covered flaws in the drywall, and so he proceeded to cover every wall in our house with it. The only room to escape was the kitchen. I think Mom probably said enough when he got near her kitchen with his hammer. Mom had to have her kitchen a bright yellow with frilly starched curtains. I think Dad even did the back porch. He used leftover pieces of paneling to make furniture. He made end tables, a coffee table, and even some shelves with it. None of it went to waste.

The backyard was long and narrow. When I was old enough, it was my job to cut the grass. I loved working out in the yard. I would cut the grass, trim the weeds by the neighbors' chain-link fence, and plant small trees along the border between our yard and the Chickatellis' yard. I would dig trees out of the woods and drag them home. One day Mrs. Tootenhauf gave me some small trees out of her yard. I had the place looking pretty good.

One day I went out in the backyard to cut the grass and to my horror found all my trees cut in half. I don't mean trimmed on one side, but actually had the trunks cut down the middle. Mr. Chickatelli had done it! He explained that he couldn't cut his grass with my trees' branches hanging over on his property. I was madder than I have ever been up to that point in my life and I yelled "Why, you stupid ginney, are you nuts!?" He demanded I get my dad—that he wanted to talk to him about me being so disrespectful.

I stormed into the house and told Dad what had happened. Dad went charging outside and was all over Mr. Chickatelli for what he had done, and ended with "you *are* a stupid ginney!" The one and only tree that didn't get hacked in half was a weeping willow. Many years after I had left that old house on Stutson Street, I went by there and discovered that tree is now about 60 feet tall and covers our old yard and the Chickatellis' as well.

At the end of street, up on the corner of Lake Avenue and Stutson was Master's Market, the corner store. Mother sent me there once a day for milk, bread, and cigarettes. I had to deal with either Tony or Carl. I would get the milk and bread and then ask for a pack of Camels. I'd swallow hard, because I knew what was coming, and say, "Mom says to put it on the bill." That is when Tony or Carl, or sometime the both of them, would jump all over me.

The tirade would go something like this: "When does your mother plan on paying this bill; look at all these charges on this bill; this is it, you tell your mother that if she doesn't pay this by tomorrow, there will be no more credit, do you understand?"

I hated going into that store. Mom would send me up again the next day, and we would do it all over again.

So that was a glimpse into life on Stutson Street. I guess maybe we were sorta poor, but we never knew it.

Our Days at the Beach

It was a hot sunny day in the summer of 1952. Kathy, Sally, and I were on our way to Lake Ontario Beach Park. Our first stop was to pick up our friends Billy and his younger sister, Carol, who had become our good beach buddies. Mom packed us off to the beach about six days a week during the summer, depending on the weather. Cold and cloudy was not a good enough reason not to go. A lightning storm would get us a pass.

My responsibility was to watch after my younger sisters. After awhile, going to the beach had become a job. It was a very boring job. We had a very specific schedule. Leave our house at 9 AM, pick up the Hayes kids and then walk ten blocks to the beach. We would get to the beach pretty much by 10 AM, which is when the beach opened and the lifeguards took to their towers. We were told by Mom to always sit by the center lifeguard so we could keep an eye on the giant clock on the bath house and so that Mom would always know where to find us. We would leave the beach at 4 PM, which got us home in time for supper.

We would enter the bathhouse at about 10 AM. Billy and I would go into the men's locker room, put on our bathing suits, and meet the girls out on the beach. We would wander over to the center lifeguard tower and spread out our blanket.

This would become home base for the day. We took every swim class offered by the park. Lessons usually lasted about an hour, and after a few summers of this routine we became really good swimmers!

We spent hours and hours out in the blazing sun with no sunscreen protection. Kathy and I, being olive-skinned, turned browner and browner while our fair-skinned sister, Sally, and the Hayes kids got redder and redder. They were always in some stage of peeling. In fact, peeling off burnt skin became a favorite pastime. We must have looked like a bunch of baboons picking bugs off one another.

Always with one eye on the giant clock, we were always happy to see it hit 12 noon. Lunchtime! Mom packed the same lunch every day. It was peanut butter and lettuce on white bread. There was one sandwich for each of us. There was usually a fair amount of sand in the sandwich at no extra cost. There was nothing to drink, but of course there was always a water fountain if we got thirsty. Billy and Carol had some pretty good lunches as I recall. Actually, anything other than peanut butter and lettuce would be a real treat. There was no way the Hayes kids would consider swapping lunches with us.

Okay, we got the swim lessons done, lunch finished, and it was probably about 12:30 PM. We had a long, hot afternoon ahead of us. This was about the time Billy and I would wander off. We knew of a hole in the brick of the bathhouse that looked directly into the girls' showers. One of us would act as the lookout while the other peeked into the hole, hoping for a glimpse of a young, pretty, naked girl. I think Billy and I were at the age of puberty and this daily excursion was fuel for the

Life Slightly Off Center

puberty fever we suffered. Nine times out of ten we saw nothing. When we did, it was usually older, fat women and a total disappointment. We would laugh, maybe talk a little dirty, but we would be totally let down. The expectation and raging hormones drove us to make the sojourn every day.

Our sisters never knew what we were doing. This was our little secret and usually the high point of the day, but more often than not, the low point of the day. Our efforts did pay off one red-letter day. There in the shower was a beautiful young girl as naked as naked could be, and we got to see her! Okay, maybe she wasn't beautiful, and yes maybe she was a little chubby, but she was young and to us a wonderful erotic experience. This experience kept us going back to the bathhouse every day for the rest of the summer.

The remainder of the afternoon was spent swimming, walking on the beach, and collecting shells. We would lie around in the sand, build sand castles, and pretty much just kill time waiting for the magic hour of 4 PM. We would pack things up, head for the bathhouse, take showers, and meet out in front. We walked past several custard stands on our way home. A lot of the time we would separate, approach strangers, telling them we had lost our bus fare and lived all the way uptown, and ask them for a dime. We usually did pretty well. A good day would get us enough money to get us each 15-cent custards. This was the really good custard. If we didn't do so well, we would settle for the 10-cent custard. Then we headed home with another day at the beach behind us and yet another one ahead of us tomorrow. Those summers seemed endless.

I remember one day Mom and I were walking to church with Kathy and Sally ahead of us. Mom looked at Kathy and said "Oh my, she looks like a little black girl." I thought to myself, *Do you think 36 hours of beach time a week might have something to do with that?*

Church

Mom insisted we go to church on Sunday mornings. She would get Billy, Kathy, Sally, and me shined up. Just before we were ready to leave, Mom would send me upstairs to wake up Dad and have him tie my tie. He was always grumpy when I did this, and the whole time he was working on my tie, he'd be jerking me around and mumbling about when in the hell was I going learn how to do this myself. Finally, for Christmas one year, I received a clip-on tie, and to me that was the greatest invention ever! No more did I have to wake up Dad from a dead sleep. No more did I have to catch hell for not being smart enough to tie a tie. Yes sir, that ole clip-on tie was my salvation on Sunday mornings!

Mom always made sure our shoes were shined, the girls' hair was curled, and they were in their Sunday dresses. I had my hair all slicked down and wore a white shirt, tie, and dark pants. Mom always looked great heading out the door for church. The Raymonds cleaned up pretty good back in the day.

We went to Lake Avenue Baptist Church. It was about two blocks from the house. It had a very old and very small congregation. I remember it as being very stodgy, stiff, and so boring. First we had to go to Sunday school for an hour, and then we went to church for another hour. It was pure agony!

After church, we walked home and had to stay clean and in our Sunday clothes until we had our Sunday dinner. Sunday was not a great day for me. It just dragged on and on. The high point was dinner, which was always fried chicken wings, mashed potatoes, and green beans. And Mom always had dessert on Sundays!

Christmas Past

With four kids and no extra money for Christmas, the holidays were very lean. Mom somehow managed to pull it all together. We all got something special and were totally thrilled on Christmas morning. There was no gift wrapping. Mom simply put our gifts on a chair or the sofa in the living room. We all knew which spot was ours and went immediately to it. The gifts always consisted of things we needed like socks, underwear, and T-shirts. But there was always one gift for each of us that we had asked Santa for, and like magic there it was. The real magic was Mom!

One evening, many years later, we were sitting around the kitchen table reminiscing about Christmases past. My best recollection from those days was getting our Christmas tree. I recalled how on Christmas Eve, Mom would bundle us all up and we would pull the sled up to Lake Avenue to the parking lot where they sold the

trees. I said "Now that was a great tradition!" At about this time, my sister Kathy piped up "You jerk, that wasn't a tradition, that was when all the trees went on sale and Mom could get a tree for a couple of bucks!"

Mom told us that evening about the Christmas she would never forget. She said "Every year, after checking out all the sales, I would get on the bus and go uptown to do the Christmas shopping. Everything I bought was put on credit. The rest of the next year was spent trying to pay it all off. Back in the day, bill collectors would actually come to the house to collect the money they had coming. When they knocked on the door, she would warn us all to be quiet and to get low so they couldn't see us. By the time I got all the bills paid it was time to start all over again with another Christmas.

"One year I was introduced to the concept of a Christmas club account at the local bank. I was determined to put a small amount of money into my account each week. When December rolled around, I went to the bank to claim my money. What a wonderful feeling it was to get on the bus to town with 60 dollars in my purse. I felt like a millionaire! I remember how much fun I had shopping that year. Two dolls for Kathy and Sally, a paint-by-number set for Jackie, and new shoes for Billy—all paid for in cash! New underwear, socks, and T-shirts all paid in cash. I had only one more gift to buy, a new hat for your Dad. I found the perfect hat and put my bags on the floor while I fished through my purse for the last of the money. I paid the clerk cash, and I was all done and feeling so happy! Shopping finished and everything paid for. Merry Christmas to me! I reached down for my shopping bags and they were not there—they were gone! Oh my God, I thought, they can't be gone! I may have left them in the toy department—no bags there—maybe in the shoe department. I raced all over, retracing my steps, but there were no bags to be found. I was totally exhausted and overcome with such sadness. I had to begin my shopping all over again. When the store clerk asked cash or charge, I wearily replied...charge."

Summer Vacations

Every summer when we were kids, our parents would take us to Scranton, Pennsylvania, for a week, and this was called our summer vacation. I'm sure Scranton is a great place to live, but it sure isn't on the top ten places to take your kids on vacation. We all groaned, just at the thought of going. The older we got, the louder we groaned.

The high point of the six-hour trip was a row of old tires standing up half buried in someone's yard and used as a border. Every year they would be painted a different color. We would all take guesses as to what color they would be. We would dissolve into fits of giggles when they finally came into view. Dad would start teasing us about 50 miles away by saying "I think they're right around the next bend." By the time we reached the row of tires, you could just feel the excitement in the car. I guess those tires were a poor man's Grand Canyon.

The weather was almost always gray and dismal. We would always stay at Aunt Viola and Uncle Bob's house. The house was located behind the other houses on the street. There was just barely enough room to drive our car between the houses. I remember their address was 1320 Van Buren Avenue, Rear.

It was a big old house that was as neat as a pin outside. Inside it was squeaky clean and smelled like Pine Sol. Aunt Viola would welcome us with open arms. She was short and fat and smothered us with her hugs and kisses. She always was amazed how tall we were getting and how dark Kathy was. Uncle Bobby would sort of wave at us, say hello, spit a wad of his tobacco in his bucket, and return his attention to whatever baseball game he was watching on TV.

Bobby, their son, was an adult and lived with them. He was in pretty rough shape. He was born with deformed legs and hands and walked with a serious limp. All the years we made this trip, we would always find Little Bobby and Big Bobby together in the living room watching a ball game on TV. In fact, they would spend the whole week we were there visiting watching and discussing baseball.

Our first meal on the day we arrived was always Whimppies. This was a combination of tomato soup and cooked hamburger poured over mashed potatoes. We kids all loved it, and this was the high point of the whole trip—other than the painted tires, of course.

So there we were for five or six days with absolutely nothing to do. Every morning we would get up and sit around the breakfast table and stare at Little Bobby eating puffed wheat cereal with no milk or sugar on it and then drink the milk from a glass. We all thought this was so odd. After that, we would just sort of wander around the yard if it wasn't raining. One time Little Bobby took us for a walk into town, which was a pretty nice experience. Other than that, we did pretty much nothing. Billy and I may have brought our baseball gloves and played catch. Dad would take off soon after our arrival and go have a beer with his old friends. He was gone pretty much all week. As I recall it, he would come for supper, then go off again.

Mom was perfectly happy to spend the days visiting with Aunt Viola. Although Aunt Viola was only Mom's stepsister, she was more like her mother since she and Uncle Bobby had raised her from the time she was a young girl. In fact, Mom was raised in this very same house, so to her this was coming home.

Mom was very content to be there and pretty much ignored us grumbling about having nothing to do. Most of Mom's brothers and sisters still lived in Scranton. There was always a big reunion of aunts and uncles and cousins. They too were amazed at how tall we were getting and equally amazed at how dark Kathy was!

Well, the week's vacation seemed more like a month, but finally the day came for us to pack up and head for home. YIPPEEEEEEEE!

Mother always cried saying goodbye. Dad was ready to leave, and we kids thought this was the best part about going to Scranton—leaving Scranton. We piled in the car, squeezed between the houses, and hit the open road. Mom and Dad sat up front with Sally between them. Sally always sat up front, and we three always sat in the backseat. There was never any argument about it. The little blond-haired, blue-eyed princess sat with Mom and Dad, while the three ragtag dark-haired kids sat in the back.

On the way home, we again looked forward to seeing our painted tires, but we looked forward the most to seeing our old house on Stutson Street. We just wanted to be home.

There was one summer that we broke the tradition of going to Scranton. Dad had rented a cottage at a nearby lake, and we were going there for a whole week. Oh boy, this was going to be the best vacation ever! The day before we were to leave on our dream vacation, my cousin Gordy, who was going with us, and I were playing down by his house. His house was right across from the railroad tracks and we were busting beer bottles on the tracks. My Dad just happened to be in Sammy's Bar having a beer with Gordy's dad. The bar was down the street from Gordy's house and looked out over the railroad tracks. Dad saw us breaking beer bottles and came out and yelled at us to quit it. Don't forget we're going on vacation tomorrow, and you

Life Slightly Off Center

don't want to get hurt and not be able to go. But I had to throw just one more bottle, and in doing so, I tripped and fell, and my hand landed on the broken glass, giving me a serious cut. I was bleeding like a stuck pig. (I have no idea how much a stuck pig bleeds, but had always heard that saying and felt like it applied here.) I wrapped my hand in my shirt and ran home.

I didn't want Dad to see me, because he would get really mad that I hadn't left when he told me to. By the time I got home, my T-shirt was soaked with blood. Mom tried everything to get the bleeding to stop, but it just didn't. She finally called my dad to come home and take me up to Dr. Ottley's office. I needed five stitches to close the cut, and the doctor instructed Dad not to let me get the cut wet for at least a week. He wrapped my whole hand in gauze, put my arm in a sling, and sent me on my way.

The next day we headed off on our dream vacation. A week at the lake, and I am not allowed to get my hand wet. It was pure torture. My dad kept reminding me that if I did as I was told, I wouldn't be in this predicament. My rotten brother and sisters teased me relentlessly by saying, "Jackie, let's go swimming, Oh, that's right, you can't go, 'cause you can't get your hand wet." The only one to take pity on me was my cousin Gordy.

My week at the lake seemed longer than any week I had ever spent in Scranton.

Billy and Me

When I think of my brother, Billy, back in the day, I think about this incident. He was letting me ride on the handlebars of his bike. This was especially fun for both of us because Mom had absolutely forbidden us from doing such a dangerous thing. For a kid, besides doing something dangerous, feeling that rush of getting away with it just doubles the fun. I was probably about seven years old, and we were cruising down Pollard Avenue. All was going great until my left foot got caught in the spokes. I went flying off the handlebars and landed flat on my face in the middle of the road. I had a gash on my forehead that was bleeding pretty badly. My pants were ripped, and my knees and hands were all scraped up with brush burns. I laid there bawling, while Billy was going nuts. "Take it easy, Jackie, you'll be okay. Oh boy, Mom is going to kill me. We can't let Mom see you like this… oh boy, let me think." Eventually he had it figured out. He hid me in his buddy's garage and warned me not to leave. He would go home for bandages and fix me up. "Remember now, do not leave this garage. I will be right back" he said.

I sat in the corner all huddled up and in agonizing pain. I know I was whimpering some and feeling real sorry for myself. Billy eventually returned with a wet rag and got me cleaned up. He helped me pick the cinders out of my knees and hands. Billy left and again warned me not to leave the garage. So there I sat for most of the day, and this time Billy didn't came back. I'm sure he got to playing with his friends and forgot all about me. I got really hungry and finally headed for home. That was the end of it. Mom never found out; I'm sure I must have told her a lie about how I got the road burns and the gash on the head. I'm sure I told her I fell down and that I was fine. Billy never mentioned it again. I knew better than to ever bring it up again. Whenever I tell this story, Billy says "You're nuts. That never happened." When Bill reads this, he'll get all pissed off.

Through the years, Bill and I have grown to be each other's best friend, but he is still a bit of a grouch.

Rotten Brother Tricks

I was really a bad brother to my two younger sisters, Kathy and Sally. I would have been a rotten brother to my older brother, Billy, but I was too afraid of him ever to cross him. With Billy, my main job was just to stay out of his way.

Sally was usually my main target because she was so easy. She was afraid of everything and especially birds. I took full advantage of this fear when Sally and I were I assigned to wash and dry the supper dishes.

We had a parakeet, who, when allowed to fly around the house, would eventually land on someone's head. We kids all thought it was cute. That is, all of us except Sally. After dinner, if it were our turn, Mom would say "Okay, Sally and Jackie, you have the dishes tonight. Sally, you wash, and Jackie will dry them and put them away" and with that she would leave the kitchen. This is when I went

Life Slightly Off Center

JRAYMOND

into action. I took ole Tweetie bird out of his cage, held him on my finger, and warned Sally that if she didn't wash, dry, and put away the dishes, I would get the bird after her. I could have been pointing a loading gun at her because she was that terrified.

She did the whole job while looking over her shoulder, and she knew better than to call for Mom, or even tell Mom afterward. This method of doing the dishes worked great until poor ole Tweetie died.

My ultimate bird trick on Sally happened as follows: My cousin Gordy and I were out in our rowboat on the Genesee River. It was about 10 at night and we were on a mission. Our mission was to collect about twelve pigeons.

We rowed under the swing train bridge where we knew the birds roosted at night. We had brought a couple of orange crates with us to hold our catch. We would reach up into the underside of the bridge and pull down a sleeping pigeon. We got our twelve and rowed back to shore.

I then took the pigeons to my house to set up my ultimate trick. I let the pigeons free on our enclosed back porch and they flew up into the rafters. That night I could barely sleep just thinking of the fun I would have in the morning. I got up early and was sitting at the kitchen table, having a bowl of cereal, when Sally came down to breakfast. I said "Hey Sally, how about going out on the back porch and getting King's bowl so I can feed him." She said sure and headed for the porch. As she stepped onto the porch, I slammed the door as hard as possible, and the pigeons, startled by the sudden noise, started flapping and buzzing all around poor Sally.

She was terrified and clawing at the door and begging me to let her in. I was having a great time until Mother caught me and put an end to the torture. I don't remember what my punishment was, but whatever it was, it was worth it. Poor Sally still hates birds to this day, and I am sure, on some level, she still hates me. Who could blame her?

JRAYMOND

Kathy was more of a challenge. She wasn't afraid of much, so to get to her, it usually involved pain. Like the time she kept bugging me about shooting my BB gun. I didn't let any girls shoot my gun, but she kept it up.

She said, "You're just afraid to let me try because I can probably shoot better than you!" "Okay, kid, go ahead and give it a try. Try to knock that can off the fence." I handed it to her with the cock open. The cock is the thing you open and close to get the pressure built up in the chamber to shoot out the BB. Kathy took the gun, got into position, aimed and fired, and KABLAM, the cock came up and slammed her fingers! She screamed in agony. Kathy never asked to shoot my BB gun again.

Then there was the time I told Kathy I was going to show her a magic trick. I told her I could make her hand smoke. I poured Draino crystals into her hand, added some water, and told her to squeeze her hand shut as hard as she could—sure enough smoke came out of her clenched fist as she screamed in pain while the Draino burned into her hand. I only knew that trick because I had tried it on myself first. Sort of reminds me of the line from movie *Forrest Gump* "Stupid is as stupid does."

If you are a kid and reading this book, let me warn you:
DO NOT TRY THESE ROTTEN BROTHER TRICKS AT HOME!

Life Slightly Off Center

Paper Route and Working at Vosburgs

I guess maybe I was about twelve years old when I started to deliver the *Rochester Democrat and Chronicle*. It was the afternoon newspaper. I had about 50 customers and would deliver the papers every day after school. There we were: me, my dog, King, and the neighbors' dog, Rusty.

The last stop on the route was the bakery, which was my downfall. I was probably the only kid who had a tab at a bakery. I'd get a brownie every day and say "just put it on my tab." Friday was collection day for me. It was so hard to get people to pay up because most of the time they were not home on Friday afternoon, so I spent most of Saturday collecting. I loved it when someone would tag along with me. I often had to bribe friends to go with me. The usual bribe was a brownie.

I think when everything was said and done, I made about $3.00. I usually owed most of that money to the bakery. I did the paper route for quite awhile, but finally gave it up when I got a job as a gardener for the Vosburgs.

The Vosburgs were our local rich folks who had a big house and the huge yard. My brother, Billy, worked for them at one time, and my mom was their housekeeper for a few years when we rented a house next door to them.

Mrs. Vosburg was the boss, and she was the most particular woman I had ever met. I liked the job okay, but she would drive me nuts with all her rules. The lawn was huge and had to be cut with a hand mower. There were two power lawn mowers under her porch that I was not allowed to use because she was afraid they might leak gas on her precious grass. Another rule was that every week the grass had to be cut in a different direction so it would not bend one way. This meant I cut it up and down one week, the next week cut in the opposite direction and the third week I cut it in a circular direction. And you better believe she knew which direction you were suppose to be cutting it. I also had to trim around all the flower beds, trees, sidewalks, and stepping-stones. Those were the days before weed whackers. All of the trimming was done on my knees with hand clippers. Boy, did I have some giant blisters.

I worked just about every day after school and on Saturdays. In the summer, I was there a lot. Mr. Vosburg was retired and would come out every day at 3 o'clock in his dress pants, starched shirt, and tie and sit in the sun. He loved kidding with me. He would always ask if the girls were treating me good, and how is school going, and did Ma pay you yet? I earned 50 cents an hour. I had to keep track of my hours and show Mrs. Vosburg my time sheet. She would pay me on Saturday. Good ole Mr. Vosburg would catch me later in the day and ask what I had earned that week, and whatever the amount was, he would double it. There was always a warning with this bonus: "Now be sure you don't tell Ma about this." There was no way I was going to tell Mrs. Vosburg because she would put an end to it, I am sure.

I guess the worst time to work for the Vosburgs was in the spring and the fall. That was the time when the storm windows had to either be put up or taken down. Their house must have had 100 windows, and they were big windows. In the fall I had to drag all the windows out of the cellar where they were stored. The basement was a long narrow place, and the windows were stored at the very end. Dragging them all out was a monumental task. Then all the windows had to be washed. This, of course, was done under the watchful eye of Mrs. Vosburg, and believe it or not, I could never get them clean enough on my first try. It was so frustrating. After all the storm windows were gleaming, it was time to put them up. This is when my dad would show up. The windows were too heavy for me to do alone. So up on the porch roof we'd go and start putting in the storm windows. Oh, but wait, we had to wash the regular windows before we put the storm windows in place. Mrs. Vosburg was inside the house and would go from window to window with us to make sure we were getting her windows spotless. Oh boy, did my dad get upset dealing with her. He would mutter the whole time we were putting them up. Under his breath, he'd be saying "You dammed fool, what the hell is wrong with this woman," and on and on he'd go. All the time Mrs. Vosburg was on the other side of the window going, "Walter, you missed a spot," and would indicate the spot by clicking a long fingernail on the spot. Did Dad ever get upset, but not so she knew it. I would be in hysterics at the antics of the two of them. This whole process took several weeks.

Living in upstate New York and dealing with cold and snow all winter, everyone looked forward to the spring. Everyone, that is, except for my dad and me because we knew it would be time to take down the Vosburgs' storm windows and put up the screens. So we would go through the whole exercise again. The regular windows had to be washed again; again Mrs. Vosburg had to supervise each and every window, and again Dad would swear that this woman could drive a saint to drink. After all the storm windows were back on the ground, it was time for me to go into action. Now here is the crazy part. Mrs. Vosburg insisted the windows be washed before storing them in that dingy dark basement for the summer. That job

Life Slightly Off Center

more than any other really pissed me off. It just didn't make any sense and seemed like such a waste of time. But I'd wash them, Mrs. Vosburg would inspect them, and then I would take each one to the far end of the basement to be stored until the fall when I would have to wash them all over again. Dad was long gone before this whole procedure started. He'd walk out the gate, wish me luck, and say he had earned himself a few beers. We did this over and over again for years.

Mrs. Vosburg also employed Betty, the lady from down the street, to tend her rose garden. Betty was such a character. She was old and all bent over and always had her hair in a bun with wisp of hair in her face. She must have been 75 or more and had moles on her face. She had an especially big one on the end of her nose with a hair growing out of it. Betty also had a certain smell about her, which I could never place. If Betty walked up behind me, I could smell her coming. Occasionally Mrs. Vosburg would invite Betty and me into the kitchen for lunch. I always enjoyed that. I felt like a big deal sitting in the kitchen in the big house and eating at their table. Lunch was always the same. Tunafish on white bread with the crust cut off and a cup of instant coffee. I especially liked having the crust cut off my bread. It just seemed like such a classy thing to do. I'm sure that is how Mrs. Vosburg's only son, Sonny, had all his sandwiches prepared.

The job I enjoyed the most was washing the Vosburgs' big Cadillac. It was a beautiful car. It was a two-tone green, four-door sedan with leather seats, big wide whitewall tires, full hubcaps, and fender skirts. I was never was allowed to move the car. To get the rear whitewall clean, I would scrub half and then go get Mrs. Vosburg to move the car about 6 inches. Then I could wash the other half.

Betty and Mrs. Vosburg always had a cigarette hanging out of their mouths. Mrs. Vosburg would constantly be making that sound that one makes when trying to cough up a lugie. My brother, who was off in the Navy, came home one weekend, and I was on my way over to Vosburgs. Billy asked, "Hey Jack, did Mrs. Vosburg ever get that lugie up?"

I guess that about sums up my years at the Vosburgs. I credit the whole experience with my love for being out in the yard to this day. To me there is no better day than a full day out in the yard just dinking around. The best part, there is no Mrs. Vosburg telling me what to do. She was a character, but basically a good person, and I have nothing but good feelings about those crazy days.

Gordy and Me

My cousin Gordy was a big part of my childhood. He was more like a brother to me. He was my best buddy, and we did everything together. One day he called to tell me he was on his way over to the house. My dad, who was a big joker, said "If that's Gordy, tell him to go to Ferguson's Hardware and pick up a gallon of striped paint. Tell them to put it on my bill." Gordy's response to this request was "What color?"

Gordy and his family lived on River Street over a machine shop. The railroad tracks and the Genesee River were right across the street from their apartment. Gordy and I spent a lot of time in and around that ole river. When we were about eleven years old, my brother Bill and his buddies gave us an old rowboat. Don't know where they got it, probably stole it, but we didn't ask any questions. All we cared about was having our very own boat. We scraped it, painted it, filled the holes with tar, and christened it the "Channel Cat." It was an exciting day when we launched that old boat. A whole new world opened up for us. We were free! We spent many hours on that boat and had such great times.

We had the whole summer ahead of us and could do whatever we wanted. All we wanted to do was take the boat out into the lake. Whenever we went out in the boat, one of would row, while the other one sat in an inner tube tied behind. When the rower got tired, we would switch places.

JRAYMOND

This was our routine...we would drag the boat across the street, across the tracks, and down the bank into the river. We would row down the river past the pier and into Lake Ontario. That would cover about three miles. Then we would go right after we cleared the pier and head for Durand Eastman Beach. That was about five miles. We would pull the Channel Cat up onto the beach, grab our fishing poles and bucket, go up the hill, across the railroad tracks, across the highway, and into Durand Eastman Park. Our secret fishing spot was hidden back in the woods. The fishing was great and we would pull in fish as fast as we could bait our hooks. The fish were very small, but that was fine. We put our catch into our bucket of water and carefully get them back to the boat without spilling too much water. We didn't want to do anything to harm the fish because we had big plans for them.

Before we headed back home, we would take a swim in the lake. When we got back to Gordy's house, we would jump on our bikes with the bucket of fish and head for my house, which was about ten blocks away. We dropped our bikes in my back-yard and head for the woods behind my house. There we had our secret stock pond and that is where we would deposit our fish. I have no idea what we had in mind for our stock pond, but it seemed like a good idea at the time.

One day while we were fishing in our secret fishing spot in Durand Park, a man in uniform approached us. He identified himself as a New York State game warden and wanted to know what we were doing. I said "Fishing, sir. This is our favorite spot. It's great! We always catch a bunch of fish!" "Oh, do you now?" he replied. "This is a State Fish Hatchery, and you boys are fishing illegally. You'd better dump those fish back and get out of here now, and don't ever let me catch you here again! Do you understand—never?" "Yes sir!" we replied in unison and with that we were gone, and our fish stocking career was finished!

Another time we took the boat out and ignored the red flag waving at the end of the pier. The red flag was a storm warning flag, and you were not supposed to be on the lake when it was flying. We made our usual trip to the beach and had a great time playing in the high waves. We spent a few hours at the beach and then headed for home. It was really getting rough but we loved it. There was Gordy in the tube, me rowing, and we're laughing as the Channel Cat rode up one huge wave and then come slamming down with the bow going under the water and then come popping up again. The rougher it got, the better we liked it. It was at about this time we noticed a bunch of people along the beach watching us. Some of them even had binoculars. Then we spotted the Coast Guard cutter heading our way and having a tough time in the rough surf. With their blast horn, they yelled "BEACH THAT CRAFT!" I said "hey, Gordy, I think they mean us; how cool is that? They called our boat a craft!" We struggled and finally got the boat to the beach. As we were beach-ing our boat, two angry Coast Guards approached us. They escorted us directly to the commander's office. We only knew he was the commander because of the sign on his door. He gave us hell for taking the boat out when the red flag was flying and even more hell for not wearing life preservers. Our punishment was severe. We could not take our beloved Channel Cat home. We had to leave it at the Coast Guard Station, and from that day forward we would have to ask the commander's permission to take her out. This was pretty much the end of our sailing days. It was great fun while it lasted, but having to walk all the way to the Coast Guard Station to get permission to go out was too much. It just took all the fun out of it.

Gordy and I were always trying to earn spending money. We were too young to get real jobs and neither of us ever got an allowance, so we did whatever we could to make some money. We searched for bottles to take back to the grocery store for a 2 cent deposit, or a nickel if you got the big bottles. We set pins in the local bowling alley. You actually had to sit at the end of the alley, and when the pins got knocked down, you had to jump down and set them up again. Now that was a rough job, and I got hit more than once.

Another way to earn a few bucks was to catch blood suckers, also called leaches. We would sell them to the Lake Avenue Bait Shop for 3 cents each. Our system for getting them was to walk the shallows of the river without shoes on and with our pants rolled up. The blood suckers would latch themselves to our legs and feet and begin to suck our blood. We would go up on the bank, pull the suckers off, put them in a jar, and go back into the river again.

When you look back on some of the stunts we pulled, it is surprising we survived at all. Many nights you would find Gordy and me on the golf course catching night crawlers on the greens. These babies were worth 2 cents each at the bait shop. Easy money!

Our ultimate money-making scheme sort of happened by accident. One day we were cutting through the lumberyard and discovered a pond in the middle of it. We came up with the idea of using all the scrap lumber lying around to build ourselves a raft. We came back the next morning, armed with hammers and nails. We spent several days putting our raft together. It was finally ready to launch. We floated it out into the middle of the pond and jumped aboard. Our raft immediately sank to the bottom. We jumped off and the raft resurfaced and low and behold, it was loaded with small crabs, sometimes known as crawdads. These crabs are used for fishing bait. Gordy and I looked at each other and let out a whoop and slapped hands. We were in business! Our raft had become a crab catcher, and boy, did we catch a lot of crabs. The crabs could earn us 3 cents each! We were RICH!

We went crab catching every day for a week. We were catching these little critters like crazy and would soon be ready to cash them in at the local bait shop. Then, our whole business went up in smoke! A big, burly, mean-looking lumberyard employee showed up at the pond and wanted to know what the hell we thought we were doing! We explained what we were doing and asked if he might be interested in buying some of our crabs. He ran us out of there in a hurry, threatening to drown us if he ever caught us near the pond or even in the lumberyard again. The pond had been stocked with crabs by the employees. They used these crabs for their own fishing. Yet another business had gone south for Jack and Gordy.

Then there was the time my Uncle Francis asked if we would like to earn 60 bucks for painting his house. I said, "60 bucks! Are you kidding? 60 bucks! You bet we'll paint your house, Uncle Francis." He got the paintbrushes and supplied us with the ladders. We spent weeks painting this big two-story house with a detached garage. The damn house needed two coats of paint, which of course, doubled our work. Pretty soon, 60 bucks didn't seem like a whole lot of money. We were almost done, and the house was looking good. We were now starting on the garage, and I

was doing the back. There was a big pile of horse manure behind the garage, and rather than take the extra time to shovel it out of the way, I simply stuck my ladder in it, climbed up, and started painting. We were using oil base paint, so it took a while to dry. I got the whole top half of the back of the garage done, when the ladder began to slip, knocking me off balance. The ladder went flying back sending me into the bushes and flipping gobs of horseshit all over the wet paint. Gordy and I surveyed the damage, groaned at the thought of having to scrape all that crap off the garage, and repaint it. We were just too tired to be bothered. So I did the next best thing. I put the ladder back in place, climbed up, and painted all that horseshit white. If my uncle asked, we would just explain that the paint got really thick and lumpy. But he never asked. That was our first and last painting job. Another career nipped in the bud.

Oh, there is one other story with Gordy that I just thought about. One time we were playing tag down by the river. Gordy jumped a chain-link fence and I followed him. Unknown to us, we were now in the enclosure that housed the sewer processing plant. Gordy ran around the pool containing all that smelly terrible sludge. I thought it was a solid mass and went running across it to tag Gordy. I went in it up to my knees and was sinking fast. Gordy pulled me out and then reached down and pulled out my shoes. Luckily, he was able to get them out before they disappeared forever since they were the only pair of shoes I owned. We went back to Gordy's house down the block. I stank really, really bad. Gordy's mom, my Aunt Dorothy, stopped me at the door and said, "Do you really think you are coming in my house smelling like that?" She made me strip down and she hosed me off.

For many, many years, Gordy and I were pretty much inseparable. We spent a lot of time getting into and out of trouble. When we got to high school, we began to drift apart. He got new friends, I got new friends, and life was never quite the same for us. I look back on our days together as some of my happiest memories.

Starting High School

My prayers were answered. I made it all the way through Number 38 Grade School without any stops in Mrs. Brush's class. Next stop for me was Charlotte Junior/Senior High School. Back in the day, there were no middle schools. I guess the feeling was to throw the little fish in with the big fish, and you either sank or swam. Most of us swam. Going from being a big shot 6th grader to a lower-than-pond-scum 7th grader in junior high was a rude awakening. I held the high position in grade school as a crossing guard. Every time I donned my white safety belt and assumed my position in the road, directing cars to stop and kids to cross, I was given instant respect. I loved it. I used to dream about growing up and one day becoming a professional crossing guard. (How's that for a high pie-in-the-sky career goal?) Near the end of the school year, we 6th graders were treated to a tour of our new school. I was awed at how big it was. It was a beautiful old school with lots of character, lots of rooms and hallways, and a place in which I would find myself lost many times in the coming year. The teacher conducting the tour said "Okay, now let's go take a look at the Olympic-size swimming pool." Swimming pool! Did she say swimming pool? I was just blown away. Not only was I going to get to go to this beautiful school, but I was going to get to go swimming, too! *Wow, I thought, life doesn't get much better than this!* They took us down to the basement, below the water line of the pool, and removed some of the lights. This enabled us to look through the windows into the beautiful blue water. As I pressed my nose up to the glass, what I saw shocked me. There were about forty-five naked boys swimming and splashing around in the pool. Somehow the tour schedule and the boys' swim class had gotten mixed up and we were treated to a real show! One of the boys in the pool swam up to the window to get a closer look, and he and I were eye to eye. When he realized what was happening, his eyes widened, and he went shooting to the surface. One of the girls in our little tour group screamed, and we were quickly hustled out of there. I was completely puzzled as to why a bunch of boys were in a school pool swimming naked. I was about to find out firsthand.

Fast forward to September. It was our first gym class in our new school, and we were scheduled for the pool. Our gym teacher Mr. Murry said "Okay, you guys, strip down, put your things in the lockers, and hit the showers. Take a quick shower, then line up along the edge of the pool.

JRAYMOND

What? Take a shower with all these guys? Guys I went all through grade school with and these other guys I don't even know—and now I had to get bare-ass naked in front of them? We did what we were told to do and didn't ask any questions. Soon enough we were all lined up on the edge of the pool naked with our hands strategically placed and feeling very self conscious. Mr. Murry blew his whistle and said "I know you are all wondering why we don't allow bathing suits in the school pool, right? The reason is quite simply that bathing suits have fibers in them, and we do not want the fibers clogging up the pool filters. Just deal with it; you'll get used to it soon enough."

Well, I guess it made sense, at least until I found out later that the girls were allowed to wear bathing suits. I guess maybe girls' bathing suits don't have fibers. I also found out that on Thursday evenings, they had what they called a Father and Son Swim. They were, of course, allowed to wear suits. Again they must have found those special swim suits that don't contain fibers. My question was where can I get one? You can't fight tradition, and the tradition of boys swimming naked had gone on for years. After awhile, it seemed almost natural to go skinny-dipping with your classmates. Whenever I tell anyone this story, the usual reaction is "You had to swim NAKED?" Looking back, I guess it was kinda weird, but I don't think any of us suffered any permanent damage from the experience.

Life Slightly Off Center

There was one incident that occurred after I had been in the school for awhile. We got a new kid named Phil in swim class. He had transferred from another city. I am sure that his first day in the pool must have been pretty shocking. He and I were underwater when the coach apparently blew his whistle to clear the pool and to hit the showers. When we hit the surface, he and I were the only ones left in the pool. He looked at me and asked "Now what?" I said "We've got to hit the showers." Well, if a new kid asks you which way is the boys' showers, and if there are two doors side by side and one of them leads to the girls' showers, you can't pass up the opportunity to do the wrong thing. You naturally point at the girls' door and stand back and watch the show. Well, ole' Phil went busting through the girls' shower door in all his natural glory, and all you heard was girls screaming. The next thing you know, Phil flew out the door, jumped down four or five steps, and took a running jump into the pool. He came up spitting and swearing, calling me every name in the book. I was hysterical. We went in and showered and got dressed. When he and I were walking past the girl's gym door, we were met by a bunch of the girls and they were pointing and giggling at the new kid. How is that for your first day at a new school?! I don't know why, but Phil and I never did get to be good friends.

Going from Number 38 School to Charlotte High School was a whole new life for me. I remember the first day Mom told Billy to take me to school and show me around. He grunted something and said, "Come on, Jackie, let's go." Once outside he gave me the rules. I was to walk on the opposite side of the street. When he went into his friend's house, I was to wait until they came out and we would move on to his next buddy's house. First we picked up Marshall, then onto Ralph's; by the time

JRAYMOND

I was waiting outside of Jack's house, I got tired of Billy's rules and said to myself the heck with him. I knew the way to school, and I took off on my own. That was the last time Billy and I ever sorta walked to school together.

Another rule Billy had was that I was not to talk to him in school. "Just pretend you don't even know me." Billy was a big shot at school. He was very popular and hung out with the coolest guys, and the girls in his clique were always the hottest girls in the school—the cheerleaders and homecoming queens. He was also a member of the best fraternity. Billy had it all going for him and didn't need his skinny little brother cramping his style. One day, this really good-looking older girl came up to me in school and excitedly asked, "Are you Billy Raymond's brother?" I replied that I was indeed his brother and sort of expected her to say you look just like him. Instead she just squealed "Oh he's so cute" and walked away. I was thinking, *So what am I, chopped liver?* I soon adjusted to this new world of mine. I did my thing while Billy did his, and we happily coexisted in the same school very nicely.

I made new friends and had a whole world of new experiences. I entered the 7th grade knowing nothing about sex. I think I had just given up the idea of Santa Claus the year before. I guess I was sort of slow when it came to worldly things. Dad had never had the big talk with me. So what I learned, I learned from my friends. I remember Mom was pregnant when I was about eleven years old. This should have been the perfect opportunity for our parents to have the big talk, but they didn't. I guess there were certain things that just were not talked about back then. Mother was forty-something and said she was too embarrassed to leave the house in her condition. One evening we were sitting around the supper table. Mom was about seven months along when I asked "Mom, how do women get pregnant?" She was very uncomfortable with this type of conversation, but attempted to explain it to me. Well, a man plants a seed in the woman and from the seed a baby grows. Puzzled, I asked "What kind of seed, like a watermelon seed?" It didn't make any sense to me. "Mom, how does the man plant the seed? Does he just hand it to you and you swallow it and then the baby grows in your belly?" "Enough with the questions, Jackie; you'll find out soon enough."

Well, of course, I did find out eventually from a new friend. He and I were hanging out and just shooting the breeze when I happened to tell him that I had just found out the day before that our minister's wife had twin boys. He said "Wow, I didn't know ministers were allowed to do it!" "It?—what do you mean it?" "You know, have sex." He then went into graphic detail about sex and how babies get made. By the time we got to his house, I pretty much knew what this sex thing was all about. The hardest thing to accept was that my sainted mother would actually do something like that!

The Football Team

I guess I was in about 9th grade when I decided the place to be was on the football team.

Football players seem to have the whole school thing working for them. They had the best-looking girls, and they were just plain cool guys. I wanted to be a cool guy too. I went out for the team and somehow made it. The practices were murder but the glory of just being on the team was worth all the work. I was a linesman. (I may have been a tackle—just don't remember.) On game day we got to wear our jersey in school, and that was good. That automatically gave you cool-guy status, not quarterback or receiver cool-guy status, but you were above the fray. The closer it got to game time, the more nervous I became. By the time 6th period rolled around, my nose would bleed profusely from pure nerves. On the bench, where I spent most of my time, my nose would continue to bleed and get all over my jersey. I could sit on the bench the whole game and still look like I was the roughest, toughest kid on the team. But it was all worth it when I heard the cheerleaders yell "YAY

JACK, YAY RAYMOND, YAY BO, JACK RAYMOND!" The coach came up to me after one of these cheers and yelled, "I don't get it, Raymond, you're one of the laziest kids on the team, and yet the cheerleaders always yell your name first...what is that all about?

I only lasted maybe half the season. It was a good time, but I needed to work, and if I was going to work as hard as the team required me to work, I figured I may as well work and make some money. Also I figured if I lost much more blood from my nose bleeds, I'd wind up dead. So, I went from being a semi-cool guy to a non-cool guy, and everyone lived happily ever after.

Billy, Ellen, and Me

One of my best friends from those early days was a guy named Bill. He was a great kid, and we hit it off right away. We hung out together all the time, and I eventually became almost one of his family. I even called his mother "Ma." Bill and I were always just this side of getting into trouble. Like Ma used to say, "They're not bad kids, just boys being boys." I guess we were about fourteen, and one of our favorite pastimes was hitchhiking just to see how far we could get in a certain time period.

In the fall of the year, we would hitchhike to the different car dealerships around Rochester to check out the new models. We went nuts over these cars and talked constantly about the cars we would own one day. I think maybe the Corvette was at the top of both of our lists.

Once in a while I would spend the night at Bill's house. Often we would get up in the middle of the night, sneak out of the house, and take his sister's car out for a joy ride. We would very quietly push it out of the driveway and then away down the street. When we figured we were far enough away from the house, we'd start it up and take off. We would be gone for hours, but always got back before anyone got up so no one was ever the wiser. This car was a beauty. It was a 1954 Mercury hard-top convertible, with a sunroof. It was probably about 20 feet long with tons of chrome on it. It was a two-tone salmon and white with matching rolled and pleated leather interior, wide whitewall tires, and wire wheels. To top it all off, it had glass-pack

Life Slightly Off Center

dual exhaust so it purred like a kitten. Oh boy, did I love that car!

Another thing worth noting that along with hot cars and cute girls there was pizza. We were there when pizza was introduced as one of the four main food groups for teenagers. Pontillo's Pizzeria opened up in the neighborhood, and we had to go see what all the excitement was about. Bill and I went into Pontillo's and were immediately engulfed in this wonderful smell. We had to have us one of these pizzas. We ordered a cheese pizza and went and sat in a booth until it was ready. Our number was called, and I went up to get it. As I was walking back, I tripped on something, and the pizza went sliding off the tray with a big hunk of bubbling cheese finding its way into Bill's sock! He immediately started jumping around like a mad man and screaming like a little girl about his foot being scalded. When he was able to walk, we left with him limping and muttering about me being an idiot. We both decided we didn't like pizza and couldn't figure out what all the fuss was about. We figured it was just another fad and surely would never last.

Then it happened! It was the winter of 1955, and Bill and I were down near the beach at the skating pond where everyone hung out. It was a great place with a little heated hut where you would change into your skates. The pond was big and provided us all with hours of good times. This particular evening I introduced my best buddy to my friend Ellen and that was it! Bill took a total of maybe 5 minutes to fall head over heels in love. From that night forward, he only had time for Ellen. It was amazing how fast it all happened. He was so in love that he would go to Ellen's and be perfectly happy to sit and watch her do homework.

The next summer Ellen and her family went on vacation to the Thousand Islands. This is a very popular place for people in upstate New York. It is near the Canadian border on the St. Lawrence River. Well ole Bill was just lost without his girl. A whole week without Ellen was more than he could bear. He suggested we hitchhike to the Islands. Sounded good to me. So I lied to my Mom and told her that I was going to spend the weekend at Bill's house and he did the same, saying he would be at my house, and no one was ever the wiser. We took off on our 200-mile adventure.

It took us all day and that night to get there. We were welcomed with open arms by Ellen's family. I had a great time swimming, sunbathing, and eating my fill of their food. Bill had an even better time making out with their daughter.

I don't know how it got started, but Bill and I got into a major food fight. It ended with me being hit in the back of the head with a big gob of butter and Ellen's mother giving us both hell for being so foolish. We spent the rest of the afternoon swimming and working on our tans. Well, that is what I did. Billy and Ellen swam some, sunned some, but spent most of the afternoon making out.

That evening the three of us decided to drive into Cape Vincent to check out the local night life. We wound up at a dance hall with a great band. We were sitting there when the band started playing a favorite song of the day and I asked Ellen to dance. As we drifted across the floor, Ellen looked up at me with those beautiful green eyes and said "Jack, it really smells in here!" I agreed and figured someone had gotten sick and hurled his cookies. I suggest we go to the other end of the dance floor. We did and found it still had this horrible stench. We gave up and went back to our table and Billy. We sat down and Billy says, "What in the hell is that smell?" It was about then that I leaned back in my chair and cupped my hand behind the back of my head. That's when I felt this greasy gob buried in my hair. Oh shit, it's the butter from our food fight, and it had gone rancid! It was me that was responsible for the rotten smell! Ellen went into hysterics, while Billy was totally disgusted. The ride home found me riding shotgun with my head out the window, Ellen still laughing, and Bill muttering and driving really fast, trying to outrun the smell. Bill did a lot of muttering back in those days.

I have to back up here and tell you that Ellen and I were good friends long before Bill came into the picture. Bill was the jealous type of guy and would get very upset at both Ellen and me if he heard we had been together without him. In order to keep the peace, we both made a point of not telling Bill that we had seen each other. Ellen lived a few blocks from me. I would often wander over to her house after supper, and we would shoot the breeze for an hour or so. One evening I was sitting on the front porch with Ellen when she said "Oh shit, here comes Billy!" Sure

Life Slightly Off Center

enough, there was Billy heading down Pollard Avenue. Ellen said "Jack, you better get out of here quick or he'll have a fit!" Say no more; I tore through the house, went through the back door, and jumped off the back porch and over the fence. Ellen told me later that Bill came in all ticked off, demanding to know where Jack was. Ellen very innocently said "Billy, Jack isn't here; why would you think that?" Bill says, "I know he's been here because he left his dog King on the back porch!"

Bill and I continued to be good friends all through high school. It became much easier when I got myself a girlfriend, and the four of us ran around together.

During those days I was hoping to join the Navy after I graduated, and I wanted Billy to join with me on the Buddy Program. This way we could see the world together. I was always bugging Bill about us joining up, but he wanted no part of the Navy or any other thing that would take him away from Ellen. I worked on Bill for a solid year until he finally gave up and went up to the Navy recruiter's office to sign up for the reserves. After filling out a ton of paperwork, we had to take a physical. Bill went one way and I went the other. One of questions on the paperwork we had filled out was if you were a sleep walker. I answered yes because I did occasionally walk in my sleep. The doctor doing my physical was looking over the paperwork and said "I'm afraid you cannot join the Navy, son, because of your sleepwalking. You may just walk off a ship one day." So there I was with my file stamped REJECTED, and here comes Bill with his file stamped APPROVED! Bill had signed

all the necessary paperwork and was now an official member of the United States Naval Reserves. He signed a contract obligating him to go active duty upon graduation. Oh boy, my best buddy was not happy when I explained what had just happened. He was going, and I was staying, and as of that moment, we were not going to see the world together!

Well, time went on and we did graduate from Charlotte. Bill went off to naval training while I joined the Air Force and went to Texas. As luck would have it, Bill got assigned to Antarctica and I got stationed at Hancock Field in Syracuse, New York, about sixty miles from home. This was my big adventure at seeing the world. Bill was not a happy camper when he found out I was so close to home. The poor guy who wanted nothing to do with the military or the adventure of seeing the world was the one actually seeing the world. Our friendship did cool for a few years. All was eventually forgiven, and he was the best man at my wedding and I was the best man at his. He had to travel thousands of miles to get to mine while I had to travel sixty miles to get to his....ain't life strange?

Getting My Driver's License

After I turned sixteen, my main objective in life was to get my license. I got my learner's permit and bugged Dad constantly to take me out to practice driving. He did it, but very reluctantly. I had such a hard time coordinating the clutch while shifting gears. I remember one evening we were practicing in the parking lot down by the beach. Sally had come along for the ride. All was going well until I hit reverse, floored it, and we went flying backward. Dad was yelling "Stop, stop, Jackie, put your foot on the brakes!" Sally was in the back seat praying!

One summer, I had to go to summer school. That meant catching the city bus up to Marshall High. I hated going to summer school and even hated taking the bus more. I casually said, "Hey Dad, can I take the car. I'll be really careful." He said,"You can't drive without a licensed driver, you know that." "Aw, come on, Dad, please. I swear I'll be really careful. You know how good I've been doing lately, please, Dad." I kept bugging him and he was getting really pissed; he finally gave in, threw the keys at me, and said "Go ahead, but if anything happens, don't come crying to me." I was out the door in a shot. This was my first solo drive and I loved it. No one was telling me to slow down, speed up, turn left, turn right, or shift into second. This was so nice, and I was doing great. This is exactly what I needed to build up my confidence. I got to school just fine. On the drive home, I passed a slow moving car in front of me and then back into the right lane. Oh man, look at me, I had just driven into a funeral procession being escorted by two motorcycle policemen! Now what do I do? The police were cruising up and down the procession and spent what seemed like a lot of time right near me.

Life Slightly Off Center

I did what I had to do. I turned on my lights and turned into the cemetery with everybody else. I just could not figure out how to pull out of this without being noticed. We all drove up to the gravesite, and when the other cars were pulling over to park, I slowed down but just kept going. I was shaking at the thought of being caught. I drove out of the cemetery and directly home. Gave the keys back to Dad and told him everything went fine. I never asked to take the car by myself again. By the time I got my driver's license, I had taken five tests and was getting on a first-name basis with some of the employees at the DMV. At one point, the guy giving the test saw me and said, "Oh no, not you again!" Passing that test was one of the biggest events of my young life!

Since there was only one car in the family, I very seldom got to take it out. Maybe I would get it for a special date once in awhile. One day my Dad came to me and asked me to do him a favor.

"Jackie, could you take the car to school tomorrow and after school go up to Wegman's (the grocery store where Mom worked) and pick up your mother's paycheck?" Mom was in the hospital for some surgery, and Dad needed Mom's check. Dad would take the bus to work and told me to pick up Sally at her school so she can ride up with me. "Do you think you can handle that" Dad asked. "Sure, Dad, I can do that. I'll be glad to do that." All the time I'm thinking, *Oh yeah, drive to school, finally!*

The next morning I was up and out the door. Went to meet up with my buddies and off to school we go. At lunch we all went to my car and had lunch and smoked cigarettes. I felt like such a big shot after a day of jingling the keys I had in my pocket to let everyone know that, yes, I had my car keys and, yes, I drove my car to school!

After school, I went over to the grade school and picked up Sally. On our way uptown, we were driving up Dewey Avenue when it started snowing. Okay, I can handle snow, no big deal. We continue on our way and the snow was getting heavier. The car in front of me suddenly stopped, and I didn't. I slammed on the brakes and slid right into the car. I really creamed my Dad's car. The steam was billowing out of the now exposed radiator. I jumped out of the car and ran up to the car I had hit and screamed at old guy driving, "What's wrong with you? Why did you just stop in the middle of the road...are you nuts?" The old guy looked up at me and explained that he had stopped for the school bus in front of him. Oh, you mean you gotta stop for school buses?! I didn't know that. I must have missed that in the driver's manual. The old guy started groaning about his new car. I told him that all I did was break the taillights. He then started groaning about his back. Soon all hell broke loose. Mother's were running out of their houses to make sure their kids were alright, the kids on the bus were sticking out their tongues at me. Soon the police, fire engines, and even the TV cameras arrived.

My sister went up to the old man and was holding his hand while she's crying, saying "You'll be fine, just stay calm," while he was moaning and groaning. Me, I'm dead. When Dad gets hold of me, he is going to kill me! Our car is a mess. It is crushed from the headlights to the windshield.

What a mess! The police came and got me and Sally and put us in the back seat of their patrol car. They started asking us questions. That's when one of the policemen laid it on me by saying "You know this whole incident wouldn't be so bad except for the fact that the old man you hit just happens to be my father, and he just got out of the hospital yesterday after suffering a heart attack!" Oh and one other thing, his dad had just picked up that brand new Chevy from the dealers yesterday! All the time the TV cameras were rolling. I thought I was dead before, but now I was really going to be killed when Dad heard all the details. After everything was done, the cop said "Come on, we'll give you and your sister a ride home." I said, "No, that's okay, I'll just drive my car home." He said "You've gotta be kidding. Son, I think your car is totaled. Come on, we're taking you home." "Oh no, not home; could you take me to my brother's apartment," I pleaded.

We were dropped off at Billy's place. I explained what had happened and ask Billy if he could come home with us and maybe explain to Dad what had happened. At this point I needed a buffer between me and Dad. We got home, and Dad had not gotten there yet. So we sat and waited for him to get home from work. I was ready to throw up I was so nervous. I was actually shaking. I felt so bad. Dad asked me to do him a favor and not only did I screw that up, but I destroyed his car in the process. I was a total loser. I was watching out the window, and here came Dad up the walk. *Oh boy, here we go. If he beats me with his belt, I deserve it.* I suddenly said to Billy, "I'll tell Dad."

Dad walked in and had a puzzled look on his face when he saw us all standing there and no car out in front. He asked "Where's the car? Did you get Mom's check? So what's going on?" I explained what had happened and told him how sorry I was. His response is one I will never forget: "Are you and Sally okay? Did anyone get hurt?" "No, Dad, no one got hurt; we're okay, but I think the car is toast." He said "Don't worry about the car; the car is just a car, and we can always get another one." How was that for a great end to this story? I couldn't believe it.

Dad later found out that the car was indeed totaled and then had to figure out where to get the money to buy another car. I had about $25 saved up and offered it to him, with a promise to give him everything I earned at Vosburgs' to help out. Dad, said "Thanks, but don't worry about it." "Yeaaaaa Dad, you are the BEST!"

The night of the accident I went ice skating with some friends. We stopped for coffee at the local burger joint, and there on TV was my accident on the 11 o'clock news. Look at me! I am suddenly a celebrity!

Stealers Never Win

I was working at the Acme Market after school. I was the stock clerk and enjoyed the job and the people. The boss seemed to like me and gave me as many hours a week that I wanted. One Saturday we were getting ready to close and everyone, I thought, was out back. I was in the front near the cash registers. That is where they kept the cigarettes. I had just gotten my paycheck and don't know whatever possessed me, but I put a pack of cigarettes in my pocket and started to walk away. That's when my boss's booming voice scared the hell out of me, and he said, "Jack, hope you enjoy those smokes, turn in your apron, you are done here." I apologized and told him it would never, ever happen again. "How about giving me one more chance?" He said "No, I can't trust you anymore."

Walking home that day I felt like such a jerk, losing a job over a lousy pack of cigarettes. I was a total loser and so ashamed of myself and swore I would never take anything again. On my way home, I met my cousin Gordy. We got to talking, and he said he was looking for a job and did I know of any openings.

I said "Oh yeah, I hear they are looking for a stock clerk at Acme Market up on Stone Road. Just a word of advice: Don't tell them that your last name is Raymond, and don't use me as a reference. Trust me!"

Dating in High School

High school was great after I got the hang of it. It took awhile, but once I got into my groove, there was no stopping me. I totally enjoyed the whole experience. I guess girls were the biggest treat and also pretty much the most confusing part of the experience.

I got the reputation around school as the guy who never said no. I got asked out to sorority dances, Sadie Hawkins Day dances, and Ladies' Choice-type dances. It was usually some girl I didn't want to be with. Also, I had friends with sisters or girl friends who needed a date for whatever, and ole Jack was always there. I always said yes because I didn't want to hurt their feelings. There was the time a buddy of mine warned me that a certain girl was going to ask me to the sorority's formal dance. *No, not going to do it this time, the answer will be no, forget it, I've had it.* Being the nice guy was costing me a fortune. This formal would cost me a tux, flowers, and dinner and for what? An evening with some girl I don't even like. Well, every time I saw her coming down the hall, I would turn and go the other way. I spent the better part of the week dodging her. Time was running short—just a few more days and it would be too late to ask me. Friday came and she spotted me, I spotted her, and I actually took off running. She lit out in hot pursuit of me and damned if she didn't catch up with me, yelling "Jack, Jack, stop!"

I stopped, and she stopped, and through heavy breathing she asked if I would like to go to the dance with her? Through heavy breathing of my own, I said "Sure, love to go." I beat myself up all the way home for saying yes, trying to figure out how many hours I would have to work at Vosburgs' to pay for this date.

Then, there was the time, a girl came up to me with her teeth wired shut and asked me to go on a hayride with her on Saturday night. I had a hard time understanding her because she couldn't talk so well with her wired mouth, but eventually got it and of course said yes. Thinking to myself, why wouldn't I want to go on a hayride with a girl who could barely talk. Surprisingly we had a great time doing what you do on hayrides, which is making out for two hours or so; we managed to break two or three of her wires. Afterward we went for a burger, only she couldn't have a burger of course so she had a milk shake, which she slurped down with all kinds of sound effects. I learned that she had surgery on her jaw, and that was the reason for her mouth being wired shut. She was really cute and had a great personality. We started dating pretty regularly, and before you know it, the wires came off, and here is this great girl with a great smile.

Jean became my steady girlfriend. One of the great perks of having a steady girl was that it took me off the dating market. Oh yes, my days of dating girls I didn't want to be with were over. Spending my hard-earned money on a girl I didn't even like was over. From then on, I would spend time and money on the girl I was crazy about.

It turns out Jean was a very cheap date. Her mom was very strict and only allowed us to date on Saturday nights. I could pick her up at 8 o'clock and have her home by 11 o'clock. This was hardly time to do much of anything and still have time to park and make out afterward. So we just parked and made out for the entire three hours.

One evening we were parked in the church parking lot down the street from Jean's house. A nun came out and banged on the window and asked what was going on in there. I wiped the steam from the window, and she glared at me, as only nuns can glare, and told us to move on before she called the police. We didn't need any trouble, and we didn't need her mom finding out what we were up to, so we moved on. The next week we were wise enough to park in the Baptist Church parking lot. No nuns wandering around in the dark checking out cars with steamy windows. Jean would always go home with hickies on her neck. When her mother would ask her about them, Jean would lie and say they were from the stiff collars on the jackets she had to wear while working in the grocery store after school.

One sunny, warm Sunday afternoon, we were all taking our girls on a picnic in Hemlock Park. Dad said I could use the car, and I was on my way over to pick up my buddy Denny and his girl, Lorraine, and then onto Jean's house. Jean had worked hard and long on her mother to get permission to actually go on a date with me on a Sunday. We gave up our Saturday night for this, so it was a really big deal! Hemlock Park was known for its beautiful waterways, and everyone who went there usually rented a canoe to really enjoy the park. When I picked up Jean, her mother warned her not to get into a canoe and then waved her finger in my face and said "Jack, do not, and I repeat, do not put my daughter into one of those damned canoes. Do you understand?" "Yes, Ma'am, wouldn't dream of it, Ma'am" I lied.

It took Denny and me the whole way to the park to talk the girls into a canoe ride. By the time we arrived, we had them both convinced that nothing could possibly happen and their folks would never be the wiser.

We met the whole gang there. We rented seven canoes, and we loaded up. Jean had a picnic basket with fried chicken and biscuits. This was going to be one of those days you would remember for a long time! What a picture. It looked like a Norman Rockwell painting. Seven canoes going down the river to a chorus of "Row, row, row your boat, gently down the stream." I don't know what we did wrong, but on the second chorus of "Row, row, row your boat," ours tipped over! In we went, and by the time we got to the surface, Jean' picnic basket with her camera and more important the fried chicken were heading down stream! I came up laughing, Jean came up spitting mad and yelled "Dammit, Jack, do something!" Within minutes, the rescue boat was there and pulled us aboard and soon found our picnic basket. So, all was not lost. As we headed back to the dock, I asked if I could get a refund since we had only used the canoe for about 10 minutes. No refund!

Jean was able to borrow a change of clothes from one of the girls in our group who had brought extra just in case. Well, the girl was fairly big, and Jean was fairly small and looked pretty funny in this outfit. We headed home right after the mishap. Jean's hair was still wet when we pulled into her driveway. Jean's mother met us in the driveway. She took one look at Jean and at Jean's girdle hanging from my radio antenna to dry and very calmly, very seriously, through gritted teeth, said "Jack, go home and don't ever come back here again. Jean, go to your room."

Jean and I continued dating through most of high school. The whole time we were going together, her mother gave her a hard time about dating me exclusively. Jean could never tell her that we were actually going steady. We were madly in love and like most kids at that age, we talked about when we got married and had kids and on and on we would go. I was going to be a great illustrator, and we were going to live happily ever after. But, in the meantime, we would have to be content with our one official date a week, although we did manage to sneak in a date during the week when I would pick up Jean from her sorority meeting. Jean was always under a lot of pressure to date other guys, especially after the canoeing incident. She was a wreck over the whole situation. Then I came up with this brilliant idea. How about if I get one of my buddies to take you out, say, every couple of weeks? He could take you to a movie every now and then. This would make your mother happy and take some of the pressure off of you. Great idea, right? Wrong!

I set Jean up with a friend of mine we'll call Ronnie, mainly because that was his name. Well ole Ronnie and Jean really hit it off, and I mean hit it off big time. Then it was me asking Jean about the marks on her neck, and she would tell me they were from the stiff collars on her work jacket. Ahhhhh, now I was getting a little suspicious. Especially when I would ask her out and she was busy! She and Ronnie fell head over heels in love. Jean broke up with me and eventually married Ronnie and had two sons, which I am sure made Jean's mother very, very happy!

Life Slightly Off Center

Me and My Buddy Chuckie

In about the 8th or 9th grade, Chuck came into my life. He was a great guy, and we had many, many good times together. I became part of his family and spent a lot of time with him and his parents. On weekends I would sometimes spend the night. His bedroom was in the attic. We would go up to bed, but before turning in for the night, we'd sneak a few cigarettes. Chuck had the ashtray hidden under a loose floor board. We thought we were getting away with something until we discovered that his mom was emptying the ashtray when we were not around. His dad would wake us up early on Saturday morning by blasting "Mac the Knife" on their record player. He thought that was real funny. We didn't.

Chuck was pretty much a wild kid. He loved nothing better than to borrow his dad's Oldsmobile and—with me in it—get it up to 100 mph. I don't know if we were really going 100, but it sure scared the hell out of me. The more I told him to slow down, the faster he would go. It is amazing we were not killed.

The big thing with Chuck's family was going up to the Thousand Islands where they had a cottage. I was always invited and loved going there. It got to be a tradition that our first trip up for the season was on Easter weekend. We were all scheduled to go when a huge blizzard hit New York. I remember Chuck's mom had resolved herself and the rest of us that there was no way we were going. She was standing at the stove stirring a pot of spaghetti sauce when Chuck's dad walked in from work, shook the snow off his coat, and said "let's go!" That was it. Things were thrown into the car, along with the pot of sauce, and off we went. The roads were really bad, and we got as far as a little town about halfway to the Islands and could go no further. We stayed the night in the Roxy Hotel, which was great fun. It was my first hotel stay, and Chuck and I got our own room and were awake half the night smoking and talking about girls. The next day we pressed on. The roads were still really bad. The closer we got, the worse the roads got. But we were dealing with tradition here, and nothing was going to stop this crazy family. We got to the bottom of the hill where the cottage was and lugged the supplies the rest of the way. The snow was above our knees. We just about froze that night. It was so cold in the cottage that the bananas sitting on the table froze solid and turned purple!

Most of our trips to the Islands were in the summer and we had really good times. Chuck's dad was great—he let us take the speedboat out by ourselves. If he knew what Chuck did on these excursions, he would have never let us out again. Chuck's favorite trick was to pull his boat up in front of a huge cargo ship and turn off the engine. Then he would see how close the ship would get to us before he took off. I'd be jumping up in down, yelling "Now, Chuck, now!"

He would also get the boat going fast enough that the bow would rise so high out of the water that it was impossible to see where he was going. He did that trick one too many times and wound up landing in a fishing boat and breaking a guy's shoulder. Chuck was probably the first and last person to lose his boating license. There was a big writeup in the paper about this reckless, inconsiderate teenager hotdogging it around the St. Lawrence River in his parents' speedboat. After that incident, my hotdogging buddy was never allowed to take the boat out alone.

I was happy to have survived our boyhood friendship. Chuck and I were great friends all through high school. After graduation, we went our separate ways. He joined the Army while I went into the Air Force. He was stationed over in Germany when he heard about me getting married. He simply went AWOL and flew to New York for our wedding. I know he got into a lot of trouble, but according to Chuck, it was worth it. There was no way he was going to miss Jack's wedding!

Party Time

One Saturday night a bunch of us got together and headed out for a night on the town. We went to a place called Kirby's Bar and Grill. I was the only one who was eighteen and old enough to buy beer. That was because, as you may recall from an earlier story, I was held back in kindergarten. At any rate, Kirby's had a reputation for being easy and not checking IDs. We got there, ordered beer, which was the drink of choice back in the day, and proceeded to have a great time. The place was packed, the music was loud, and the beer was flowing. All of a sudden, we found ourselves in the middle of a raid, and we all got caught. All but one of us got

Life Slightly Off Center

caught. Dave, who just happened to have a broken leg and was in a cast and on crutches, escaped out the bathroom window. The rest of us had our names and the school we attended taken and were told that we would be hearing from them.

A week went by and nothing happened, so we figured the incident had been forgotten. We had gotten away with yet another teenage indiscretion. Then one day I was sitting in class when a kid came in with a message for the teacher. She read it, looked at me, and said "Mr. Raymond, you are wanted in the principal's office." Me? In the principal's office? Back then if the principal wanted to see you, you knew you were in big trouble. I went down to the office and found that ole gang of mine, the gang who got caught in the raid two weeks before. Ellen, who was Miss Goody Two-Shoes, was one of us and also happened to take care of the principal's invalid wife. Now she was in big, big trouble.

The principal gave us one of those looks that only principals know how to give and introduced us to two guys from the New York State Liquor Board. They sat us down and told us that we were being called as witnesses in the case of the state against Kirby's Bar and Grill. They were attempting to have this establishment shut down for serving minors. They gave us each 50 cents that we were to use for bus fare to go uptown to the courthouse. We would be excused from school for the morning of May 23. We were then sent back to our classes. All except for Ellen, and the principal asked her to stay behind.

May 23rd arrived and along with it, the big trial. We arrived on time and were promptly called into the courtroom; each of us had to go forward, sit in the witness chair, and tell the judge what we had been drinking that night. We were all honest and said "beer," and "no, we were not carded." No, we had no trouble getting into the bar. We were all honest except for the last person to testify. That would be Stephanie. The lawyer asked, "And what were you drinking on this date while at Kirby's?" She said "Sir, I was drinking a coke." She batted her eyelashes and just looked so innocent and pure. "And tell me, Stephanie, what were the others at your table drinking?" This is when she really turned up the innocent charm and replied, "I don't know what it was, sir, but it did come in a brown bottle!" Maybe the fact that Stephanie's dad was a judge was a key factor in her saving herself.

Well, the bar was shut down and fined. As we were leaving, we had to pass by the owner of the bar. One of my buddies reached out to shake the owner's hand and said "No hard feelings." The guy just looked at him like, you idiot, no hard feelings? Because of you damned kids, I am ruined. He muttered "No hard feelings, my ass!"

The next afternoon Dad was sitting on the porch reading the paper. The front page headlines read: "WHO IS AT FAULT...THE TEENAGERS, THE PARENTS, OR THE BAR OWNERS?" There it was, the whole story on Kirby's and the raid and the underage drinking. Oh boy, I hoped they didn't put our names in the paper. So far, none of our parents knew anything about the incident. I was standing in front of Dad scanning the story and looking for names. He folded the paper down and said "Have you got a problem? Maybe you could wait until I finish the paper before you start reading it."

"No, sorry, that's okay. I'm just leaving. See you later, Dad." I am happy to say none of our parents ever found out what had happened, and that was lucky for us because heads would have rolled if they did.

Just a post note here: I think Ellen was relieved of her duties of taking care of the principal's wife. How could he trust a beer-drinking teenager with his poor invalid wife?

The Perfect Gift

For my birthday one year, the gang I hung around with had a little bit of a birthday celebration for me. We had a cake with candles, and they insisted I make a wish before I blew them out. One of the gifts given to me by several of the girls was a nice white bathing suit. Great timing because I was in dire need of a new suit. When the weather turned hot, we all got together and went to the beach for a

picnic. There I was in my new white bathing suit and looking good. A couple of my buddies and I decided to take a swim. We splashed around for awhile, then we headed back to the picnic table. Ace looked at me as we walked up the beach and went hysterical, yelling at Chuck to check out Jack's new bathing suit. I looked down to discover the

damn thing was transparent! Everyone on the beach was looking at me, pointing and laughing. Mothers covered their children's eyes. Young girls screamed at the sight. Well, maybe it wasn't quite that dramatic, but there was what God had given me—or maybe not given me—for the whole world to see!

I called for my buddies to help me out. I got Ace to walk directly in front of me, while Chuckie walked directly behind me, leaving no space between the three of us. We must have looked like a scene from an old Charlie Chaplin silent movie. When we got back to our table, I was greeted by giggling girls, the givers of the suit, and they couldn't have been happier.

Raisins

We were in the high school on a Saturday afternoon, decorating the gym for the big school dance. Me and a few buddies got hungry and went in search of something to snack on. We wound up in the Home Ec. classroom and started looking through the cupboards. All we came up with was a huge box of raisins. We ate our fill and still had a half of box left.

Hmmmm, what to do with half a box of raisins? My friends and I were always up to no good and were fast becoming semiprofessional jokers.

One thing led to another and before you know it, we are in one of the main floor girls' bathrooms. We jimmied the lock off the sanitary napkin machine, took all the pads out and filled the machine with raisins!

The next Monday we stationed ourselves outside that bathroom between periods. We roared every time a girl came out with a handful of raisins and a very puzzled look on her face.

MY LAST DIME!

JACK RAYMOND

The Fraternity

Back in high school, the main thing you wanted to do, other than graduate, was to get into a fraternity or a sorority. That was a good measure of your popularity. I remember pledging for Sigma Delta in about 9th or 10th grade along with some of my friends. We had to do goofy things like roll a peanut with our noses down the school's hallway or make sure you always had gum on hand in the event that one of your future frat brothers wanted a piece. Then we would meet at one of the guy's house, in his barn, and get really crazy—like eating worms, which was actually spaghetti, and be paddled with the fraternity paddle that had raised letters on it, which would be transferred to your butt.

I remember the final night of pledging. If you passed this test, you were in, you were a brother. We were told to bring a bottle of maple syrup and a box of corn flakes to the meeting. All pledges were to meet down at the beach. So there we were, standing in a line. The first instruction was to take the syrup and pour it all over yourself, including down your pants. Then we were instructed to roll in the sand and finally pour the box of corn flakes over our heads. By the time we were through, we look like monsters from the black lagoon.

Our next order of business was to get out on the street and all head in different directions looking for a girl. We had to get down on one knee and propose marriage to the first girl we came across. This was usually met with screaming girls, running in the opposite direction.

For the final ritual, we met back in the barn. There we would have a raw egg dropped down the back of our pants and get whacked—I mean a hard whack with the official fraternity paddle. This was known as the golden seal. Then, presto, we were in, and we all had a few beers to celebrate.

I can remember going home that night still covered in sand, syrup, and corn flakes, with an egg down my pants. Mother took one look at me and as usual was completely baffled as to what I was up to. I got a special pass to take a bath that night and it wasn't even Saturday!

I sat there in the tub of hot water with the corn flakes floating around me and thought, *Boy, ain't life grand!*

Life Slightly Off Center

Graduation

Six years in Charlotte High School came to an end all too soon. It was so bittersweet. All those great times were behind us. While we were living them, we probably didn't appreciate them as much as we should have. Going to classes, doing homework, and all the other mundane stuff that made up school left us wishing for it to be all over. We longed to be free, not under our parents' thumbs, not to have teachers on our backs about doing our work.

Our constant saying back then was, "Boy, I can't wait to get out of this place!" I sat there in the school assembly hall in our caps and gowns and heard the names of our friends being called out. As they walked across the stage, my heart sank. I guess in the back of my mind, I knew things would never be quite the same. We would all go in different directions and probably would never know the same deep friendships again.

I smiled when Lorraine walked across the stage, so poised, so beautiful. I smiled because I was thinking about last night at the yearbook banquet and I was sitting next to her. The yearbooks, *The Witan,* were passed out. Everyone quickly opened the books to their own photo to see what had been written below it. Mine read "Why should the Devil have all the fun!" while poor Lorraine's read "I love to dance, I love to sing, I love to do most anything!" She went running out of the banquet in tears.

It is so funny that little tiny incidents like that stick in my mind and still make me chuckle. As I type this, I know that I will treasure the friends I made back then forever.

If I could do it all over again, I think I would start in the 7th grade and relive this high school adventure one more time! Maybe the second time around, I'd take things more seriously and study harder—but then again, probably not.

In June 1960, I left Charlotte High School behind and some of the best times and best friends of my life. I was about to embark on the crooked road called LIFE. This road would wind around and go up and down hills. It has taken me from New York to Florida, to Vietnam, to Massachusetts, Nebraska, Alaska, and finally here to Virginia. I got married, had kids, made great lifelong friends, and met a lot of characters along the way. It has been one hell of a great ride, so hang on because here we go!

First Job

My first real job after high school was working for the Rochester Telephone Company. Since the company was located out in Henrietta, New York, I needed a car. My first car was a 1949 Dodge. I bought it from my buddy Bill for $100. I gave him, I think, $20 down and a promise to pay him $10 a month until I had it paid off. Poor Bill had no need for a car since he was off in the Navy seeing the world. I loved that old car. I had it painted navy blue at this place called Earl Shribe's for $39, and it looked great. I put a set of wide whitewall tires on it, and it was the best-looking car on the block.

My job at the phone company was working in the garage. I'd park trucks, pick up parts from the parts store, fill all the company vehicles with gas, fill batteries with water—you name it, I did it. Each new assignment was usually completed with something other than the desired results. The first truck I parked, which was a giant line truck, resulted in tearing off the mirror and denting the fender of the truck next to it. The first time I went for parts was an experience. My boss told me take the pickup truck, go into the city to our parts supplier, and get a particular part. Little did he know that I couldn't drive a stick shift, and I was not about to tell him. As I pulled out, I hit the gas, popped the clutch, and went squealing out of the garage with the tires smoking. I looked in the rear view mirror to see the boss with his mouth open and just shaking his head.

Well, I got totally lost, and by the time I finally located the parts store and was heading back, it was noon. This meant a lot of traffic downtown. I stopped at an intersection where a cop was directing traffic. He gave me the signal to go ahead, and I stalled the truck. I tried again, stalled again, tried again, and stalled for the third time. Now the people behind me were blowing their horns. Guys were leaning out of their cars, giving me the finger and yelling obscenities at me. The cop finally came over to me and said, "Son, is there something wrong with this truck?" "No, sir," I said, "I'm just not used to driving a stick shift." He said, "I see you work for the phone company." "Yes, sir." "Let me see your driver's license, son." "I don't have it, sir; I left in my jacket pocket back at the shop." "Okay," he says, "I am going to give you just one more chance to get this truck out of here. If you stall it again, I will call for a tow truck and we'll have it towed to the police station. You can explain to your boss what is going on. Do you have that straight?" Talk about pressure. The

Life Slightly Off Center

horns behind me were still blaring as the cop assumed his position in the middle of the intersection and gave me the high sign to go...my knees were shaking, I was sweating, but I went for it. I floored it, popped the clutch, and went tearing through that intersection like I was in the Daytona 500. My tires were smoking like crazy, and as I squealed by the cop, his mouth was open and his whistle had dropped out. Yippee, I made it!

Upon my return to the garage, my boss was waiting for me, and he was really upset. He wanted me to explain why I had taken 3 hours when I should have taken 30 minutes to get there and back.

After many such screw-ups, I was beginning to think that maybe I just was not cut out for this type of work. One day I went to the director's office to see about getting a transfer. My boss could not believe I actually went to the top man in the company. He was fuming and explained that I was supposed to go to him first, and then to two other bosses, but never near the director's office.

Several days after this incident, I was questioning what I should do with my future. I knew it wasn't here at the phone company. I was filling company cars with gas, when a plane flew overhead and it hit me like a ton of bricks—not the plane, but the idea. I would go into the Air Force! I enlisted the next day and got my very first plane ride to Texas and basic training.

Basic Training

Hot, I mean Mississippi hot, and so damned humid is the best way to describe San Antonio, Texas, in September. That is where I found myself in the fall of 1960.

I figured that since my dreams of going into the Navy and seeing the world with my good buddy Bill didn't happen and the phone company job was not what I wanted, maybe a stint in the United States Air Force would be good for me.

All was going great until I, along with a lot of other green recruits, stepped off the bus onto the hallowed grounds of Lackland Air Force Base to begin basic training. This training was to take us from undisciplined boys to highly disciplined men in six short weeks. I am here to tell you that those six weeks turned out to be the longest six weeks of my life! We were met by a mad man in a green uniform, screaming at us to get off the bus, line up, stand at attention, and shut the hell up! We were called losers, misfits, little cry-baby girls, and things that I cannot repeat here.

The experience went downhill from there. The six weeks of hell had begun! I thought to myself, *Maybe this wasn't such a great idea,* and was wondering if I could go home if I didn't like here?

The first couple of days were spent getting uniforms, haircuts, and shots and being yelled at. This, along with constant marching in that Texas heat, was enough to kill you.

The food wasn't bad, but there was never enough of it, and we weren't allowed enough time to eat what was on our tray. Everyone seemed to be in such a big damned hurry.

As I remember it, there were about sixty guys assigned to each barracks. After a long day in the field, we were dismissed and headed back to the barracks. We were allowed a half hour for showers. That is not 30 minutes each, but 30 minutes for all sixty of us. We had to be in and out in the designated half hour. Most nights I was lucky even to get wet! After our invigorating shower, we would spend the rest of the evening shining shoes, pressing uniforms, and studying the rules and regulations we had learned in class that day. Lights out at 10 PM.

After being there for maybe two weeks, one evening this black guy in the bunk next to mine asked to borrow my brush. "Brush?" I said, "I don't have a brush. I have never owned a brush." He got all bent out of shape and said I didn't want to lend him my brush because he was a brother. He then started pushing me around, jabbing me in the chest, saying "You got a problem, white boy?" I pushed him back and before you know it, we were in a knockdown, drag-out fight. He knocked me down onto my bunk and came after me. I put my feet up and caught him in the stomach, sending him flying over his bunk and onto the floor. He was really pissed now and came at me with fists flying. He caught me with a good right hook to the eye. End of fight! I was bleeding like crazy from a cut over my left eye. Now we were both scared because if you got caught fighting in basic, they would send you back to the beginning to start over again. Neither of us wanted that. Now he was begging me not to turn him in. He then spent the next couple of hours running back and forth to the latrine, getting cold wet towels to stop the bleeding. The bleeding didn't stop, and I was getting worried. Finally I got dressed and headed for the base hospital. I had no idea where it was and was stopped by the air police cruising around in a squad car. They wanted to know what I was doing wandering around at 2 in the morning. I explained and they pointed to the direction of the hospital and said it was about two miles. Now you think they would have given me a ride, but they just drove away, leaving me to walk. I finally made it to the hospital and was still bleeding. The doctor on duty sewed me up and then the interrogation began. Who were you fighting with, why were you fighting, and on and on with the questions. I said "No, sir, I was not fighting. I tripped over my footlocker and hit my head." The doctor said "Yeah, sure you did; go on and get out of here before I put you on report!"

I caught hell from the drill instructor the next morning at roll call. You don't show up for roll call with a bandaged head and eye patch and go unnoticed. The drill sergeant was all over me, screaming in my face to tell him exactly what happened and threatening to send my butt back to start basic all over again. I did not relent. I stuck to my story, and he finally gave up. The black guy, whom I now know as Ben, is now my best friend.

I was made squad leader soon after I arrived at basic training. I was the guy who was supposed to set the example. My only qualification for the job was my height. The shortest guys were made road guards and were berated constantly by the drill sergeant.

It was a good time to be tall! But my career as a squad leader was short-lived. After the first major inspection, I, the supreme leader of this group of men, got more demerits than anyone else in the flight. I may have broken a record for the most demerits earned in a single inspection. The drill sergeant announced the results of the inspection. When he got to my name, he said "Your former squad leader, Airman Raymond, is no longer in charge. He is stripped of his duties!" I caught hell for the next couple of weeks for being such a screwup.

Even though I realized early on that military life was not for me, I was determined to get through this training. After the humiliation of the inspection, I promised myself there would be no more screwups. I would follow the rules whether I liked them or not. From that day forward, I did really well. I passed all the inspections with flying colors, aced all my exams, and kept up with everyone out in the field.

Then came the big screwup. I was leaving the base cleaners with my freshly cleaned uniform slung over my right shoulder. A military car drove by me with one-star general flags flying from each front fender indicating that a general officer was aboard. I knew I was required to salute the car. Yet another goofy rule, but hey, when in Rome...so I snapped to attention and gave a sharp salute. The car came to a screeching halt, and a fuming general jumped out. He was in my face screaming at me: "What the hell is the matter with you, Airman, or are you just stupid? Haven't you learned anything here? You do not, and I repeat do not, salute with your left hand!" "But sir," I stammered, "I used my left hand because I was carrying my laundry in my right hand. I am sorry, sir, it will never happen again, sir!" He just gave me a disgusted look, muttered something about me being idiot, climbed back into his car, and drove away. I was thinking how many screwups does a guy have to get before they let him go home.

Somehow I managed to get through the six weeks. Graduation day was one of the happiest days of my life. After the ceremony, we all raced back to our barracks where our orders were to be posted on the bulletin board. We were all anxious to see where in the world the Air Force was sending us. There was a lot of whooping and hollering and also a lot of "Oh shit!" It depended on the assignment you got.

Four other guys and I were not listed. We found out later that our orders were pending, and we would have to wait until we got them before we could leave. We were assigned to a barracks full of rejects and goofballs. These guys were all awaiting discharge from the military. We had to hang out with these misfits until we got our orders.

I was supposed to be home for Thanksgiving, and I had written Mom to tell her when to expect me. Sitting around the barracks one evening, we were all startled when a booming voice came over the loud speaker announcing that Airman Raymond had a phone call.

Whenever you get a phone call, you must stand at attention in front of the loud speaker (aka the squawk box). The first sergeant actually has the phone in his office and relates to you what is being said by the caller for everyone to hear. God forbid that we would actually get to talk on the actual phone and have a private conversation.

There I am, standing at attention in front of the squawk box in my boxer shorts, talking to the drill sergeant while he relates what I am saying to Mom. It started "Jackie, your Mommy wants to know why you didn't come home for Thanksgiving? She is very worried about you. Are you alright, Jackie?" I explained to the sergeant that I was waiting for orders. He in turn explains to Mom and back and forth we go. It was Jackie this and Jackie that, with the emphasis on Jackie. Mom always called me Jackie, and I hated it especially then.

Life Slightly Off Center

After a 10-minute conversation, the Sergeant said "Jackie, your Mommy says good-night and to take care, and she loves you." Then he makes the sound of a big, wet, sloppy kiss! The whole barracks went nuts with laughter. From that night forward, until the day I finally left, every night at lights out, all the guys, about forty of them, would say in unison "one, two, three, GOODNIGHT JACKIE," followed by the sound of a big sloppy kiss!

Classy Lady

I was nineteen and home on leave. I took a chance and called a girl I knew in high school. This girl was so hot that I never had the nerve to ask her out. To my great surprise, she agreed to dinner on Saturday night. We would go to the West-minster Hotel, a very classy restaurant for my very classy lady. It would be expen-sive, but when you take out a girl like Lorraine, you had to go first class. Well, at least almost first class. I had to borrow my brother's car, which is when we lost a lot of the class. It was a 1950 purple Ford convertible with a raggedy top and cardboard in place of a glass back window. I washed it, cleaned out a month's supply of beer cans from the backseat, and hoped for a very dark night.

Saturday night arrived, and I got all dressed up in the gray suit Mom had bought me for my birthday. (What a deal she got—two pairs of pants and a suitcoat for one low price.) I pulled into Lorraine's very well-lit driveway. The house was beautiful, which made the car look that much worse. Lorraine looked fantastic in a white, slinky, floor-length dress, with her beautiful blue-green eyes and that long coal black hair. Damn...she looked like a million bucks! All was going well until she spotted the car. "Jack, you have got to be kidding. We are going to Westminster in this thing?" she asked. I gallantly held her door open and she slid into the front seat and immediately caught her dress on an exposed spring. "Oops," I said, "Sorry about that, Lorraine; you okay? You didn't tear your dress, did you?"

We pulled up in front of the restaurant and the valet helped Lorraine out of the car and then asked me for the keys. I thought that was pretty cool. Lorraine was totally embarrassed, and I am sure she must have looked around to see if

JACK RAYMOND

anyone had seen her exit from "the purple bomb."

We decided to have a few drinks before dinner. My classy lady orders a very expensive scotch on the rocks. When she drank it, she would screw up her face and say "ugh!" "Lorraine, if you don't like it, why order it?" I asked. She explained that she was trying to acquire a taste for it. After several more expensive scotch on the rocks and a lot more faces and "ughs," I said, "Lorraine, while you're out with me, why not try to acquire a taste for beer?"

After a very expensive dinner and yet another scotch, I got the very expensive bill, which totally cleaned me out. Hey, what the hell, I had a very classy lady on my arm, and she was well worth the price.

We got outside, and there was a big puddle in our path to the car. I gallantly offered to carry Lorraine across so she wouldn't get her beautiful white dress muddy. I flipped the cigarette I was smoking in the air, swept Lorraine into my arms, and pressed her against my chest.

That is when I felt a burning pain. I screamed and dropped my classy lady into the puddle! Come to find out, my cigarette had flipped back and found its way inside my suit and burned a hole in my jacket, my shirt, and my chest!

I now have a suit jacket with a hole in it, two pairs of matching pants, and a classy lady who will never see me again!

Life Slightly Off Center

Dianna and Me

My first assignment in the Air Force was at Hancock Field in Syracuse, New York. That is where I met Dianna. She was the cute girl working in the coffee shop in the SAGE building where I worked. We just started sort of kidding around with each other from the start. I nicknamed her McGee. I don't remember why, but it stuck. Every morning I'd go for my coffee and was met by a smiling McGee. It wasn't too long before I asked her out. Our first date was a road trip with a bunch of friends to Niagara Falls. We stopped at one of the friend's parents' house for dinner. We were all sitting around the living room when Dianna started whispering and making strange hand motions. I said "What are you trying to say? Just say it, we're among friends." Dianna got all red in the face and stammered that my fly was open. "Oh, wow, thanks!" I jumped up, zipped up, and said the first thing that came to mind: "Thank God I had on clean underwear!"

Dianna was a great sport and always laughed at my goofy sense of humor. We started going to the movies on base and she would always bring a big bag of fresh popped popcorn. I would meet her inside the theater. My buddy Bill was always with me, so it was not really a date—just friends getting together for a movie. I wasn't ready for any real serious dating since I had recently came out of a rough romance.

One night Bill was sick and couldn't join us at the movies. Dianna told me later she was so happy to see me without Bill. At any rate, the rest is history. We started dating pretty seriously. We always had a great time. We eventually got serious enough for me to take Dianna home to meet the family.

Meeting my family or at least my Dad was not easy. Mom was always there for a buffer. But this trip home found Mom in bed with the flu, and poor Dianna was on her own meeting my Dad. She also got to meet Billy, Kathy, and Sally—everyone was present for the nice dinner Mom had prepared before she collapsed in her sick bed. All was going well, and Dad was behaving himself. By behaving, I mean he wasn't giving Dianna a hard time in his joking way. I could tell the whole gang really liked this girl from Mississippi and they especially enjoyed her lovely Southern drawl. We Yankees were not used to hearing people talk like that. As I said, all was going well, and I began to relax. With dinner over, Dianna and my sisters were at the sink doing the dishes. Dad was still at the table having his cup of tea when he asked, "Dianna, do you have a girdle on?" Dianna's face went crimson, and she told me later she could have died. That was Dad's way of kidding around and giving the new girl a hard time. But it was not the way to kid around with a shy Southern girl home meeting her boyfriend's family for the first time. Dianna soon learned how to handle Dad, and he loved her.

The next day we had a big snowfall and I decided to take Dianna out tobogganing. It was me, Dianna, Billy, Kathy, and Sally. This was Dianna's first time, and she was a bit nervous. We went to our regular place, which was a huge hill on the golf course in Durand Eastman Park. We put Dianna in the front and told her it was the best seat. It is actually the worst seat because you get all the snow in your face. This is where we put all the new people. It is called paying your tobogganing dues. We were a tough crowd. Poor Dianna didn't have a chance. We had a wild ride down the hill and went over a few jumps, the snow was flying, and we wound up in the creek at the bottom of the hill. Dianna was shaken up. She whispered to me through a face full of snow that she had peed her pants all the way down the hill! At this point Dianna should have taken heed and run for the hills, but she was a great sport and kept coming back for more!

Dianna was raised for the most part in Biloxi, Mississippi. After a year of college in Kentucky, she decided to take a break and joined her mom and stepdad in Syracuse where he was stationed. We dated for about three months when her stepdad got orders for an assignment to Otis AFB in Cape Cod, Massachusetts. This meant Dianna would be moving away in January. I wasn't ready for marriage but wasn't ready to let her go either. I figured if I didn't marry her, I'd lose her forever. Finally I realized that I did love her and couldn't let go.

Operation proposal was on. I had to get a ring, which was really difficult when you have no money. I found a jewelry store that would sell me a little diamond on credit. The payment was $25 a month for the next three years. Okay, now I was all set. A few weeks before Dianna was due to move, I took her to dinner. We had a great time, and on the drive home I pulled off to the side of the road and popped the big question!

It was probably the worst proposal ever. I said "How would you like to get married? If you do, I think we should do it right away, like within the next couple of weeks. I just have to do it fast because I have a way of changing my mind...so what do you think?" Dianna was stunned, to say the least. The last thing she expected was a proposal. We had only been dating a few months and had never even discussed marriage. Either the idea of moving to Cape Cod was so bad, or she really loved me and couldn't stand the thought of losing me, but she said "YES!" I like to think it was the love rather than the move that prompted the yes. But yes it was, and

Jack and Dianna were going to get married. Yippeeeeeeee! After a lot of hugging and kissing and planning, I dropped her off at her house.

Dianna excitedly woke her mother to tell her the good news. "Mom, Mom, Jack asked me to marry him, and I said yes, and look at the beautiful ring Jack gave me! He wants to get married right away, like within weeks!" Mom, being older and wiser than either of us, got Dianna to settle down.

"Now sweetheart, I think Jack is a great guy, and I am happy that you two are going to get married, but you will not get married that quickly. You will go with Charley and me to the Cape. You will get a job there and save your money and wait at least six months before you get married. If this is real, and meant to be, you can both wait until you can get it together." Mom was right.

So, off Dianna went to Massachusetts, and we began our long-distance relationship. The letters went flying back and forth, with sap dripping out of them. We loved each other and couldn't wait to be in each other's arms again. Dianna got a job and saved all her money. Me, I wasn't so good at saving money, but I did get some set aside for the big event. We planned on being married in Rochester in June. The months dragged by, and the high point every day—and sometimes the low point—was whether or not I got a letter from Dianna.

Finally June rolled around and the plan was for me to meet Dianna at the train station in downtown Syracuse. We'd jump in the car and drive home to Rochester and get married that next Saturday.

I got to station and started looking for Dianna. It had been six months since we had seen each other. She walked by me, and I didn't even recognize her. It must have been her new hairdo. We had actually walked right past each other!

I stopped, she stopped, and I asked "Dianna, is that you?" She said "Jack?" We were like two strangers meeting for the first time. It was such a strange feeling. Here was the girl I planned to spent the rest of my life with, the girl I was about to marry, and I wasn't even sure who she was. We confirmed that yes, we were who we thought we were. We hugged, kissed, laughed, and walked out of the train station, hand in hand, talking a mile a minute about all the plans!

We jumped in my car and headed for home. Mom had made all the plans for the wedding. We were to be married in the Church of the Master on Lake Avenue and then would have the reception in the backroom of my uncle's beer joint. Hey, not too fancy, but that was the way it was done back in the day.

It was June 14th, two days before the wedding, and Dianna and I were getting to know each other all over again. We were parked behind my old high school, Charlotte, and talking and making out—mostly making out. A cop came up, shinned his flashlight into the car and yelled for us to break it up and to move on. I rolled down the window and said "Officer, this doesn't look so good, but you don't understand—we are actually getting married on Saturday!" He said "Yeah, sure, do you know how many times a week I hear that one? Now get out of here, and don't let me catch you back here again!"

The next day we went to the beach with a bunch of friends. We spent the whole afternoon and had a great time. Then we had to get to the church for the wedding rehearsal. As we are driving to the church, I looked at Diana and said "Can't you do something with your hair?" She went off, "Do something with my hair? We've been at the damn beach all day with the wind, sun, water, and sand, and now you're worried about my hair!" She was mad—I mean, really mad—and said nothing to me for the rest of the evening. We went through the whole rehearsal without a word from her. She, of course, was cordial with everyone else. After the rehearsal, my buddy Chuck dragged me off for my last fling as a free man. Dianna and I parted company with neither of us talking to each other or saying goodbye. Actually, the next words I heard from Dianna was "I do" at the wedding.

My last night as a free man consisted of a lot of beer and lots of laughs and ended with Chuck pouring me into bed that night. Then he got me up the next morning, helped me get dressed, and got me to the church on time. I was standing in the minister's office with my best man, Billy, waiting to get married. This is when Dianna's sister from California came through the door. She introduced herself and then proceeded to walk around me a couple of time and looked me up and down. "So you're Jack. Hmmmm, well, I guess you'll do." As she was leaving, she stopped at the door, and said "Do you know that my kid sister still wets the bed?" With that, she was gone. I thought to myself, *what the hell was I getting myself into?* Too late to wonder—the organ started playing and the show was about to begin.

I have to preface this with a conversation I had had with my Mom the day before. You see, Mom is the official crier at most weddings. I ask her to try to control herself during the ceremony. My sisters, also both criers, were in the wedding, and I knew if Mom started, they would both start, and it would look more like a funeral that a wedding. Mom promised to try really hard not to cry.

Okay, back to the wedding. June 16th arrived warm and sunny and appeared to be the perfect day for our wedding. I was all dressed up in my rented white jacket and black pants tux and was ready to wed. At 2 PM, I walked nervously from the minister's office to the front of the church with my best man nudging me along. As I assumed my position at the altar, I heard this mournful moan behind me, and I thought, *Oh no, there goes Mother*. I turned around and it was Dad, not Mom, crying his eyes out. Now that really touched me. I swallowed hard and tried not to cry, but my emotions got the best of me, and the tears started to flow. This is all the provocation my sisters needed, and they really started to cry. By the time my beautiful bride arrived at the altar, we were a sad sight. Dianna was all smiles, while the blubbering Raymonds were all tears—except my mom.

After the ceremony, the bridal party and immediate family assembled into a receiving line outside in front of the church. I was standing with my mom on one side and Dianna on the other. I asked Mom for a tissue so I could wipe my still wet eyes. She opened her purse, and I saw a tissue and went to grab it. She said, "NO, NO!" and pinched my fingers in her closing purse and slapped my hand away. "But, Mom, I saw a tissue in your purse," I said. "No, you didn't, I don't have a tissue for you," she said. Well, the guests were filing out of the church, and I forgot the whole incident. I later learned from one of my sisters that what I saw in Mom's purse was a sanitary pad wrapped in a tissue. My mother could picture me pulling the tissue out of her purse and having the sanitary pad go sailing into the path of an oncoming guest.

The Honeymoon

The reception in the backroom of my uncle's bar consisted of lots of beer, good food, and music. It was a good time for everyone. We danced our first dance as man and wife, cut the cake, and threw the bouquet. We were on our way. The damned Yankee, as Dianna's family called me, and his beautiful bride were about to start the big adventure! We climbed into a borrowed '56 Ford. I was still in my tux and Dianna was still in her wedding gown.

I turned the key and KABLOOOOM! Some wiseass had put some sort of bomb under the hood as a joke. When the smoke cleared, there was a huge dent in my buddy's hood. I'm guessing the explosive was a little more powerful than the joker had figured. Oh boy, more trouble. We'll have to worry about that later. We drove away with the whole gang waving goodbye. We went back to the house, changed our clothes, and hit the road for the big honeymoon at the Thousand Islands!

The money thing, or should I say the lack of it, was the prime factor in our choice of honeymoon locations. We could only afford a week in the Thousand Islands Air Force Recreation Park. It was not what you would call an exotic, romantic location. It was a bunch of double-wide trailers located on the St. Lawrence River. It was an okay place, but sure not a private place.

The morning after our first night there, we found half the base was filled with people there on vacation. They all knew we were on our honeymoon, and the kidding never let up. One morning we were down on the river sitting among some huge boulders. The sun was shining, and it was a beautiful day. I was fishing, while Dianna, with her hair in curlers, sat there reading a true romance magazine. I thought to myself, *What is wrong with this picture?*

Well, despite the unwanted company, the fishing, the curlers, and the romance magazines, we had a great time! We spent five days at the Islands and then headed for our new home and a whole new life.

We were ready to get started on this Happily Ever After thing.

CHAPTER 2

Phoenix, New York

Our First Home... Phoenix, New York

Dianna and I drove through the small town of Phoenix, New York, heading to the apartment I had rented a few weeks earlier. Dianna was anxious to see our first home. I pulled into a circular driveway and drove past the many giant oaks. The yard was huge and well maintained. At the top of the driveway stood the main house, a big white colonial with green shutters and glassed-in porches on both the first and second levels. It was a very impressive looking house. To the left of the house was a big red barn housing a three-car garage and an apartment above it. The landlord told me, when I rented it, that back in the day it was used as the servants' quarters.

It was a little place with a kitchen, a living room, one bath, and one bedroom. The living-room windows, which were many, looked out over the beautiful yard with the big oaks and a view of the river across the street. Dianna loved it. This is when I began to discover that Dianna simply loved life and everything that came with it.

We settled into our little routine and had a great time playing house. The landlord dug us up a plot of land behind the apartment, and Dianna planted a garden. She had a bumper crop of corn, beans, and green peppers.

We soon had friends coming over. Our big entertainment was popping some popcorn and watching a movie on the TV we had received as a wedding present. The TV was a used Zenith with a 17–inch-round screen. We discovered that we could watch it for only 2-hour segments. The longer you had it on, the hotter the tubes got and the smaller the picture got. After about 2 hours, it was liking watch a movie through a keyhole. Most movies were about 2 hours, so by the end you and your guests were on the floor a few

JRAYMOND

71

inches from the screen, trying to see how the movie ended. My guess is that is why we received the TV as a gift. But hey, when you're young and in love, who needs more than 2 hours of TV anyway.

The landlords, Harold and Ruth Williams, were a great older couple, and they took very good care of Dianna and me. They let us use their phone when we needed to. They let us use their washer and dryer and even gave me a ride to work every day since they also worked at the base.

Each morning I climbed into the back seat of their 1960 Ford Falcon and off we went. It was a 15-mile drive, and Mrs. Williams nagged Mr. Williams the whole way to work. Mr. Williams would just drive along with his glasses on the end of his nose and sing or hum, completely oblivious to his wife's badgering. Then he'd light up a cigarette, and she would start up about his smoking. Mr. Williams would start coughing and roll down the window and spit while his wife would continue her rant.

Ole Mr. Williams would never say a word. One morning Ruth was in particularly good form and really laying into Harold. Just before we drove through the gate on the base, Mr. Williams turned to Mrs. Williams, looked her in the eye, and very solemnly asked "Ruth, how are your bowels?"

JRAYMOND

The Sleepwalker

Dianna didn't warn me before we got married that she was one of those crazy card-carrying sleepwalkers. Many strange nights have come and gone over the years. It started on the honeymoon.

It was our wedding night, and in the wee hours of the morning, Dianna shook me awake, "Jack, Jack, there is someone in the room and he's watching us!" "What? Where is he? I'll get him! Dianna, where is this guy? Dianna, honey!" I was in a cold sweat and ready to protect my new bride. I saw no one, nothing. I jumped out of bed, turned the lights on, and there was nothing. I checked under the bed, in the closet, nothing. I crawled back into bed to find Dianna sleeping like a baby. I laid there for quite awhile thinking this girl, my wife, is a bit strange.

This happened soon after we moved into our first place. Dianna woke me out of a sound sleep. She was out of bed and trying to pull me out by my leg, screaming "Jack, Jack, get out of bed! Hurry, before the bird gets you!" She was pointing to the gold eagle we had hanging on the wall over our bed. I just groaned and pleaded for her to leave me alone. I was tired and groggy and didn't want to play in her strange little world tonight. She said, "Okay, fine, let the bird crap on your head; see if I

Life Slightly Off Center

care!" With that she crawled back into bed and went to sleep. When I recounted what she did to her the next morning, she told me that I was crazy!

Then there was the time I woke up to find Dianna fully dressed and sitting on the dresser. She was mumbling something about the bed being electrified and that I'd better get out of it quick! I sat up in bed, turned the light on, and went hysterical laughing. There sat my lovely wife on top of the dresser with her hair in curlers and her bra over her sweater. I just wish I had had a camera, because that was a real Kodak moment!

One night I woke up to find Dianna was running all over the apartment, chasing a bird that only she could see. "Jack, Jack, help me catch this bird before he craps all over the new lamp shades!" she yelled. She had just bought new lamp shades, and we did have a parakeet, so I guess she just put the two together and went into her strange little world.

Another night I woke up, and Dianna was running all over the place. She had taken every picture we had in the apartment off the walls and stacked them up in a pile in the bedroom. I couldn't understand that one. I thought she liked my artwork!

One night I woke up to find Dianna sobbing her heart out. I said "Dianna, what is the matter?" She was shaking as she recounted the dream she had just had. "It was horrible. I dreamed there was a prowler in the house. I told you to go check on the baby while I ran into the kitchen for a knife. When you came out of the baby's room, I thought you were the prowler and I stabbed you over and over. There was blood everywhere," and then she starting sobbing again.

Now she had my attention and I was fully awake. I soothed her until she went back to sleep. The next day I was relaying the story to the guys in my office. One of them said he had read that some people actually act out their violent dreams. That was all I had to hear. Dianna was so active during the night that I could imagine her wandering around the house fully asleep with a butcher knife. I lay awake for several nights, waiting for the hacker to strike!

Years later, Dianna scared my sister Sally with one of these sleepwalking episodes. Sally lived with us for several months while we were living in Massachusetts. We all got along great except for one annoying habit that Sally had. Sally enjoyed smoking in her room. This scared Dianna, and she had asked Sally several times not to do it.

Sally ignored the request and continued smoking in her room. One night Dianna apparently was dreaming about Sally smoking, and she got up and wandered into Sally's room. She grabbed a sleeping Sally by throat and hissed "Don't ever, ever smoke up here again, do you understand me?" Sally, now fully awake and terrified, said Dianna had murder in her eyes. "Yes, yes, I promise you, I'll never do it again!" Dianna then quietly turned, left the room, and went back to bed. The next morning Sally was telling us what had happen. She said as soon as Dianna left her room, she jumped up and jammed a chair under the door knob. Sally did the "chair under the doorknob" thing from that night on, but she never did smoke in her room again.

One more sleepwalking story and I'll move on. Dianna had gone to bed early. The master bedroom was right off the family room. Our friends Bob, Jan, and I were watching TV. Suddenly Dianna came running out of the bedroom in her night-gown, yelling "Jack, Jack, where is Sheri? Did she come home yet? Oh my God, where could she be at this hour?!" All the time that she was yelling, she was running around the room. Bob and Jan were sitting there with their mouths open in disbe-lief. Then as quickly as Dianna had appeared, she disappeared, saying "goodnight y'all" over her shoulder. Bob looked at me with a puzzled expression on his face and asked "What the hell just happened?"

Dog Bite

My job on Hancock Field was working in the Protocol Office attached to the base commander. It was about 3 in the afternoon when the general's secre-tary buzzed me and asked me to run over to the general's house to deliver the mail. I had never done this before, but his driver was not around, so I got the job.

I knocked on the door and the general's 18-year-old daughter came to the door, clutching her bathrobe closed. She was accompanied by two yapping cocker span-iels. These dogs were going nuts and lunging at the storm door and me. I backed up. The girl assured me not to worry because the dogs didn't bite. She went to open the door, the wind caught it, and the door flew open, along with her robe, revealing that she was wearing nothing underneath it! Both the dogs jumped at me and one bit me in the leg, the other in the arm. I left in a hurry!

The whole scene was like a comedy sketch out of an R-rated movie, only none of us were laughing. Neither was the general or the general's secretary when I explained what had happened. I did leave out the part about seeing the general's daughter naked. I didn't feel that added a lot to the story, especially for the father. The general insisted I go to the base hospital and get the bite wounds checked out. I didn't want to, but he said go, so I went.

It was getting close to 5, and I didn't want to miss my ride home with the Williams. I got to the clinic and explained why I was there. I was then handed a long form to fill out before I could see the doctor. I said to the corpsman on duty, "Look, I really don't have time to fill this out. I have to catch my ride home. How about I come back in the morning?" He insisted that I fill it out right then. I got my name, rank, and serial number in organization right, but when it got to the question "location of bite," I wrote down Hancock Field.

The corpsman was looking over my shoulder and when he saw that, he grabbed the form, tore it in half, and said "Go home!"

Moving Blankets

It was Saturday, Dianna had to go to work at the base exchange, and I couldn't get the old Dodge started. Mr. Williams, our landlord, saw our predicament and told me to go ahead and use his old pickup truck parked in the barn. I pulled it out and just as Dianna went to climb up into the cab, she noticed that back was filled with moving blankets. She said, "Jack, maybe you better take the blankets out of the truck in case it rains." "It's not supposed to rain," I replied. "They'll be fine back there." So I took Dianna to work and then headed back to the house. Driving home, I flipped a cigarette out the window. A few more miles down the road, I stopped at red light and noticed big billows of smoke down the road. I thought to myself, *It looks like a big fire down that way...funny, I haven't heard any fire engines.* I continued on my way, going about 45 MPH when I looked in the rear-view mirror and see flames and black smoke billowing out of the back of the truck. Oh my God, the smoke I had seen blowing down the road was actually from the truck. I spotted a guy watering his lawn, pulled over near him, and asked if I could borrow his hose. I put the fire out, and after checking the damage, I found all of the moving blankets were destroyed. Oh boy, now what? I figured the cause of the fire had been my tossing the cigarette out the window. Damn, how was I going to explain this to Mr. Williams? He used those blankets when he did part-time work moving furniture.

I drove home and felt so bad—and so stupid. If only I would have thrown them in the barn like Dianna suggested, but no, not me—not Mr. Know-It-All. Now I'd have to buy new moving blankets with money we didn't have. Mr. Williams' moving jobs were few and far between so by the time I got home, I had devised this great plan.

I would just put the truck back into the barn, and Mr. Williams wouldn't be any the wiser until he needed the truck again. That might be quite awhile. Maybe we would have moved before he discovered that the blankets were missing from the back of his truck. It was totally the wrong thing to do, and looking back on it now, I am ashamed to admit it, but that is exactly what I did.

I never told Dianna what happened either because she would have insisted I tell him and offer to buy new blankets. So if there are any Williams related to the late Mr. Harold Williams of Phoenix, New York, send me a bill. I will gladly pay it with interest and finally be relieved of the guilt I have carried all these years.

Life Slightly Off Center

Snowplow

Our first year of marriage was very lean, money-wise. We usually ran out of money before we ran out of days of the month. But being broke was second nature to us, and it just rolled off our backs. We always had enough to eat, pay the bills, and once in a while enough extra to go out for the evening. We were happy, and finding an extra dime in the couch cushions was a bonus. It meant I could buy a cup of coffee at work.

Life was simple. Life was good.

Dianna could perform magic in the kitchen. She was able to make something out of nothing. There was this cake she made that we called the day-before-payday cake. It was made without eggs or milk. I don't know the recipe, but it satisfied my craving for chocolate and tasted great!

Dianna would take a can of Spam and make a Sunday dinner with it. She would take a knife and carve diamond shapes on top of the Spam, add cloves, top it off with a few slices of pineapple, bake it in the oven at 350 degrees for awhile, and presto! You have a poor man's ham dinner! It was fantastic!

It was about three weeks before our first Christmas, and we had spent whatever extra money we had on gifts for our families. We were as broke as we had ever been. This is when our used refrigerator decided to die. We called a guy to come look at it. He said it would cost more to fix than it was worth. I swallowed my pride and made a call to my dad. We could do without a lot, but we needed a refrigerator. I explained the situation to my dad, and asked if he could give me a temporary loan. I promised to pay it back as soon as I could. Dad said that yes, he did have the money, but felt if we had a few trials and tribulations in our lives, our marriage would be that much stronger. So he said no to my plea for a loan. Actually, as I look back on it, I'm sure my dad just didn't have the money to give me and that was his way of hanging onto his pride.

When I got off the phone, which was our landlord's phone, Dianna asked if I got the money. I explained what Dad had told me and she said, "You've got to be kidding. What are we going to do?" Well, luckily we lived in the snowbelt of upstate New York, and it wasn't long before Dianna devised a system that would last us till spring.

She put the frozen food out in the snow, milk and eggs on the enclosed porch, and fresh fruits and vegetables inside on the window sills.

It worked great. The food buried in the snow was marked with labels on sticks. All was going along great, until the night of a big snowstorm. Dianna was standing at the window and all of a sudden started screaming, "Oh my God, here comes the snowplow up the driveway!" The plow proceeded to bury all our frozen foods with tons of snow. We didn't find most of it until spring thaw!

All that winter, we put any extra money we had into the refrigerator fund and by spring we had enough to go to Sears and buy a brand-new fridge. It was such a thrill, like buying a brand new car. We spent hours in the store comparing brands and options. This was our first big buy, and we enjoyed every minute of it.

Maybe Dad was right. Maybe this was a good building block for our marriage.

Life Slightly Off Center

Bread

On our first Christmas, I surprised Dianna with a rocking chair I had refinished. In order to work on it without her knowing, I would call her from the office, telling her that I wouldn't be home until later because I had to work late.

I would then go over to a friend's house where I had the chair stashed in the basement. I would work on it for an hour or so and then head home. One particular evening, my friend's mother was preparing fancy little sandwiches for a party. She was using a round cookie cutter to cut the center out of each piece of bread. Dianna had asked me to pick up some bread on my way home, and you can guess the loaf I brought home.

The next morning, I was in the bathroom shaving when I heard Dianna scream. "What happened?" I yelled. She replied, "Look at this loaf of bread you brought home. There is a hole cut through the center of it." After careful examination, we decided that there must have been a mouse in it. Dianna couldn't figure out how the mouse could have eaten through an entire loaf of bread without disturbing the crust at either end. She insisted I take it back to the store and get my money back. "Don't get any more bread, just get the money."

I let her in on the joke, and we both had a good laugh!

Bad Knee

Dianna and I were married maybe 7 months or so when suddenly one morning I woke up and couldn't bend my left knee. I had always had a trick knee, but that was all. I went directly to the base hospital to get it checked out. The X-rays revealed that a bone chip had lodged in my knee joint. I was taken to the clinic and put in traction to see if that would help. I laid there for a week and it didn't help.

New Year's Day found me still in the clinic while a raging blizzard howled outside. I was shocked when Dianna showed up for visiting hours. "What are you doing? Are you crazy going out in this blizzard?" I couldn't believe Old Blue made it through this snow. She said, "I had to get the black-eyed peas to you." Dianna was brought up to believe that unless you ate black-eyed peas on New Year's Day, you would have bad luck all year. So, God bless her, she braved the storm to bring me my good luck for the year.

The beds in the clinic were arranged in a long row of about four or five deep. Dianna came in and accidentally kicked over my full urinal, which was sitting next to my bed. As the yellow stream ran under the other beds, we saw visitors jump up and out of the way of it. I thought it was hilarious, but Dianna was totally embarrassed, and the nurse with the mop was not amused.

After a week of being in traction and no progress, I was told I would have to meet a medical board. The doctors were convinced that I had chipped the bone in my knee before I had come into the service and that therefore they were not responsible to repair it. I asked how much the surgery would cost on the outside. Their quote was in the neighborhood of $10,000. The board decided I would be given a medical discharge immediately. So there we were. I needed surgery and Dianna was pregnant, and they were throwing me out of the Air Force...Happy New Year!

I went back to the ward totally distraught. What now? It seemed like our whole world was falling apart. This scenario had no place in "And they lived happily ever after." I was sitting on the bed with a pad and pencil and was going to write down our options. The only problem was that we had no options. Rather than let a blank sheet of paper go to waste, I began to doodle. That's me, Jack the doodler. My whole world is falling apart, and I'm sitting here doodling. I drew a cartoon of me in my

Life Slightly Off Center

Air Force uniform holding our bird cage, my pregnant wife in rags, holding our cat and dog, and we are walking through a raging snowstorm. The caption underneath the cartoon was THE AIR FORCE TAKES CARE OF ITS OWN! I managed to run off a bunch of copies and circulated them around the hospital. Believe me, they caused quite a stir! I was soon approached by a member of the medical board and asked what they would need to do to keep me quiet.

I requested to be put on limited duty until my wife had the baby so the government would take care of that expense, and then I would go quietly. I could perform my duties on crutches and would do so for the next five months. The board met again, and they agreed to my request. Ahhhh, the power of the pen!

I went back to the Protocol Office on crutches. I had been out of the office for several weeks, and the colonel I worked for wanted to know what was going on with me. I told him the whole story and that I would be in the office for the next five months. He asked if I wanted the operation, and I said, yes, of course. He went to the base commander, who was a one-star general, to discuss my problem. Apparently, several phone calls were made, and like magic I had a doctor calling me asking me when I would like to schedule the surgery, compliments of the Air Force. This was my first lesson on, it is *who you know* in this world and not *who you are*.

I was on a plane that week to Andrews AFB for the surgery. Poor Dianna was stuck at home, out in the country, in the middle of winter, all alone and pregnant. I was gone for about three weeks. I had to have a couple of weeks of physical therapy after the surgery. Finally the doctor said I could go home for a three-day leave. I thought I would surprise Dianna, so I didn't call her. There I was, on a Greyhound bus for hours and hours, in a cast from my ankle to my hip, going from Andrews AFB, Maryland, to Syracuse, New York. I got home to find Dianna gone.

Apparently, Dianna had caught a ride with our landlords, the Williams, who went to Long Island to visit their son. Dianna went to see her brother, who also lived on Long Island.

So there I am, alone in the apartment at midnight and feeling very sorry for myself. It was about at this time that I got the bright idea to get Ole Blue out of the garage and head up to Rochester to visit my folks. It was about a 60-mile drive. It was snowing like crazy and it was difficult driving with this giant cast on my leg. Somehow I made it, although it took forever because the roads were so bad. I went to Mom and Dad's house only to find it empty. Then I went to Billy's apartment—also empty. Everyone was somewhere that I wasn't! So I headed back to Phoenix and arrived home early on Saturday morning. I spent all day in our apartment alone.

Dianna arrived that night and felt so bad that she had missed me. We had our one evening together. We snuggled up in bed that night, and she felt my cast up against her leg and murmured "Boy, do I feel something long and hard!" I said "Girl, are you going to be disappointed!"

I caught the bus back to Andrews the next day and was gone for another couple of weeks. By the time I did get home, I was in great shape and ready to go back to work at full duty.

Thank God for Dianna and those black-eyed peas!! We have eaten black-eyed peas every New Year's Day since.

Pregnancy

We were married for three months when we found out that we were going to have a baby. We were totally thrilled. The first indication of Dianna's pregnancy was when she put the coffee on to perk, like she did every morning since we'd been married, the smell, which usually brought a smile to her face and a sigh, now made her sick. The smell of the coffee sent her running into the bathroom to hurl. We couldn't figure out what was wrong. Dianna went to the base clinic for some tests. It was about a week later that I got a call from the clinic telling me that my wife was pregnant and for Dianna to call for an appointment to see a doctor. WOW! This was big news...we're gonna have a baby. Yippeeee!!! Dianna was due to pick me up at the base that evening. I got in the car and said "How about you and I go out to dinner?" Dianna's response was, "Can we afford that, are you sure...if we can, yes, I would love, love to go out to dinner!"

We went to an Italian restaurant, and over the spaghetti, I took Dianna's hand and said "Big news, honey, we're going to have a baby!" Dianna was shocked and stammered "What? A baby, me? I'm pregnant? But shouldn't I be telling you?" I explained about the call I had gotten that afternoon. Dianna was thrilled. So there we are, barely enough money for the two of us, and we are about to be three! We were both giddy with excitement!

Dianna quit her job at the doctor's request because her legs were bothering her. Her job was a cashier in the Base Exchange and she stood all day. So now we were even poorer, but our attitude was: So be it, we're going have us a baby! Dianna never complained about having to drive the old '49 Dodge to her doctor's appointments. The car had holes in the floorboards and the heater didn't work. If it wouldn't start, which was most of the time, you had to take a screwdriver, a big one, and touch it to the battery and the celluloid, and that would usually get it going. Dianna would get bundled up, put a blanket over her legs, and be on her way.

One day in early spring, she was on her way to a doctor's visit when the Dodge just stopped smack dab on the railroad tracks. ("Smack dab" is Dianna's description of where the car stopped, which just goes to prove you can take the girl out of Mississippi, but you can't take the Mississippi out of the girl.) Now Dianna was terrified of trains. I guess the adrenalin must have kicked in because at eight months pregnant, she got out of that car and pushed it "smack dab" off those tracks!

I think that was the beginning of the end for Ole Blue. It eventually died and I don't remember what we did with it. I do remember going to Rochester to visit my family sometime in April because that is my birthday month. For my birthday, Dad gave me a 1954 Dodge 4-door. Well, actually it was a 3-door—one of the doors was missing. The car was salmon and white and had a matching interior. What this car had going for it were the whitewall tires and the working heater. Dad must have won it in a card game.

I said "Dad, this is great, but it's only got three doors." He said, "Don't worry about it. We'll go to the junkyard and get another door. No problem." Dad came home with the right door for that model car. The only problem was that the door was green. A green door on a salmon-colored car was not cool. In fact the whole salmon-and-white color combination was not cool. It was a good car, and we fondly named her Viola after my Aunt Viola.

We never got the green door painted. I told Dianna it added character to the car, and you could always find it in a crowded parking lot.

Dianna was totally exhausted the last few months of her pregnancy. One evening I was sitting on the couch watching TV, and Dianna was standing behind the couch with ironing board set up and ironing my uniforms. This was her least favorite thing to do. She was very quiet, and I wasn't paying much attention to her. It got to be about 10 in the evening and I said "Let's go to bed...Dianna, Dianna?" No answer. Keep in mind that this was a one-bedroom apartment, so how far could she be. I looked in all the rooms and couldn't find her. Where the hell could she be at this time of night? I searched the apartment again and kept calling "Dianna, Dianna." Then I heard a groan coming from the closet. I opened the door, and there on a pile of clean clothes laid Dianna fast asleep! Now that is what I would call tired. I woke her up and asked what she was doing sleeping in the closet? She said she was getting more clothes to iron and the pile of clothes on the floor looked so comfortable that she thought she would lie down in them for a minute or two.

In order to make some extra money to buy the baby essentials we needed, I started detailing cars for $10.00 each. I would take 6 to 8 hours working on each of these cars. When they left my place, they looked like new. One Saturday, a colonel from the Air Force base brought his Cadillac out for the full treatment. I told him to use my car to get back home and come back in about 6 hours and I should have his car ready to go. He warned me not to drive his car because it had a tricky battery and a lot of times would not start. I assured him I had no intention of driving his car, and I would see him later. He really looked like a clown driving off in that old salmon Dodge.

Well, I got his car all shined up and could not resist taking it out on the road. I yelled up to Dianna. "Hey, you wanna go for ride in this big fancy Cadillac?" She was really hesitant at first and asked if it was alright with the owner. I said "Sure, the guy even said to take it for a spin when you get it done, if you like." Well, it was a beautiful Sunday afternoon, Dianna finally climbed in, and off we went. We got way out in the country and the car just suddenly stopped.

Luckily, a couple of guys came along in a truck and stopped to help us. "This sure is one fine car you got there, boy. What year is it?" I was acting like a big shot and said, "Oh, I'm not sure. I pretty much trade 'em in when the ash trays get full." Well, they gave me a jump and we were on our way back home.

We got into the little town of Phoenix, and the damned thing stopped again. Another guy tried to give us a jump, but it didn't work this time. We tried and tried but nothing. So we started walking home. Dianna was due in two days, so she was pretty miserable taking this long walk and so worried about what the colonel was going to say about his missing car. As we approached our house, we saw the colonel standing in our driveway with his hands on his hips and not looking too happy.

I thought, *I've got to come up with something quick.* So I said to him, "I'm really sorry, but I had to take your car. I forgot that Dianna had to go to a baby shower today, and I just had to get her there since she was the guest of honor. That damn car of yours just stopped dead a few miles back, and we had to walk home and Dianna is due in two days!" Oh boy, did he feel bad. He was so sorry about the car and so sorry about Dianna that he gave me the $10.00 for the detailing and another $10.00 tip. Not a bad afternoon! Oh, by the way, Dianna had Sheri the next day!

I ran into the colonel on base several days later, and he was still concerned about my wife. I told him that the baby came a few days early and all was fine. He felt so bad about the early birth and blamed himself and the damn car. He then gave me yet another $10.00 and told me to buy something nice for Dianna. What a great guy!

Sheri's Birth

I came home from work as usual about 5:30 PM. It was Monday, May 27, 1963. Dianna was due any day now. As I walked into the kitchen, I noticed Dianna had only one place setting on the table. I asked "What's up, aren't you going to eat?" Dianna very calmly announced that she thought it was TIME and that she was going to get dressed. I stammered "TIME, you mean time, like this is it TIME?" She said, "I think so. You go ahead and eat dinner, and I'll get ready. I have to fix my hair."

I sat looking at the meat loaf and mashed potatoes with a lump in my throat and in a cold sweat. It's time and Dianna is fixing her hair, and she expects me just sit here and have dinner? I yelled to Dianna, "What can I do? I know, I'll call the doctor like we rehearsed!" I ran down to the landlord's house and banged on the door, yelling "It's time, it's time! I gotta use the phone." I tried to call the doctor, while Mrs. Williams tried to get me to relax. My first try was a wrong number. Instead of the doctor, I got an irate Italian guy who cussed me out in Italian for interrupting his dinner. I dialed again, this time more slowly. I managed to get my shaking fingers in all the right holes on the dial and successfully reached the doctor. I excitedly told the doctor who I was and that it was TIME! I asked "What do we do now?" He asked a bunch of questions that I couldn't answer and told me to please put my wife on the phone. I ran back up the stairs to get Dianna. After she hung up with the doctor, she turned to me and said "The doctor will meet us at the hospital. So I guess we had better get going."

There she was, bag packed, dressed in her best maternity outfit, hair fixed, makeup on—all ready to go have a baby. I was simply amazed at how calm she was. You would think this was her fifth child instead of her first. Me, I acted like it was our first!

We jumped into our trusty salmon Viola and off we went! It was about an hour drive to the hospital. The closer we got, the closer the pains got. I was really in a sweat, especially when Dianna, through clenched teeth, moaned, "You better hurry!"

Ahhh, there's the hospital. We made it! I parked the car, helped Dianna out, and grabbed the bag. I then started fishing through my pockets for a dime for the parking meter. Back then, a dime would buy you an hour on the meter. I wondered if an hour would be enough time—sure couldn't take more than an hour to have a baby. Dianna handed me a dime and said "Jack, come on, hurry up! It's TIME!"

Life Slightly Off Center

The hospital was at the bottom of steep incline. Once Dianna started down the hill toward the entrance, she couldn't stop and began trotting. All the upfront baby weight was forcing her into a trot. I grabbed hold of the back of her maternity blouse to slow her down. So there we were, trotting down a hill, Dianna first and me bringing up the rear.

Once we got inside, we were stopped by a nurse who asked a lot of questions, to which, of course, Dianna had all the answers. I kept saying, "Enough already. She's got to get into a bed; she is about to have our baby...it's TIME!" Apparently, you are not allowed to have a baby until all the questions are answered and all the forms are filled out. Finally, they put Dianna into a wheelchair, and she and the nurse stepped into the elevator. I waved goodbye and whispered, "Tell Johnny I said hello." As the doors began to close, the nurse forced them open and said "Sir, do you think we might take that bag?" "Oh yes, the bag; sorry about that. Here you go." I am not doing too well at this—we definitely should have had a few practice runs.

My remark about Johnny was in reference to what we had called the baby for the past seven months. I wanted a boy really badly. I used to take Dianna's pink and blue pregnancy pills and break them in half and insist she only take the blue half. It was a long running joke between us.

Well, all those pills, and all those months, and here I am in the Fathers Waiting Room. I'm chain-smoking cigarettes and pacing back and forth. This is what fathers did back then. You smoked, paced, and waited. There was no way you were allowed in the delivery room. It just was not done. You waited until the doctor or a nurse came to find you to tell you were a father, and then they would take you to see your baby through a window. I think I handled myself rather well during this stage of the birthing process.

Smoke, pace, smoke, pace, and finally two hours later the doctor came in to tell me I was the proud father of a baby girl! Mother and daughter were doing fine. He remarked about how fast Dianna had delivered and warned me that the next time she gets ready to have a baby to have her here on the hospital doorsteps a week ahead of time. He showed me where he had written WHOOSH! across the front of her records.

The doctor took me to see Dianna and the baby. Wow, there they were, my wife and brand new daughter. They were beautiful! This had to be the biggest thrill of my life! Dianna and I talked for awhile and decided that the name Johnny would not do and agreed on the name Sheri Diane. She was bald and had puffy eyes so we nick-named her Mr. McGoo. Our little girl, all pink and perfect, and I was thinking *Life Is Good!* We called my mom and dad and Dianna's mom with the good news, and everyone was thrilled. Dianna's mom assured us that she was on her way to help out.

The doctor said Dianna needed to get some rest and that I should get out of there. One last kiss for Momma and Baby, and I was on my way home. I walked out on cloud nine. I was so happy! We did it! We made a perfect baby! How about that?! Granted it wasn't a boy, but it was a perfect baby girl! I had heard that girls are closer to their fathers, so I was really glad we had a girl—thrilled that we had a daughter!

As I was driving home, I was singing and just in another world. I was so happy that I didn't see the red Volkswagen pull out from a side street, and CRUNCH, BANG! We'd become a crumpled mass of salmon and red. I jumped out of my car, and my mood instantly changed from one of being happy to being pissed off at this guy's stupidity for pulling out without looking both ways. My pissed-off mood was soon changed to humility when the guy explained that I was going the wrong way down a one-way street. So I was the stupid one, and this guy is pissed off at me for *my* stupidity. We were near Syracuse University, and the accident happened right in the middle of Sorority Row. I surveyed the damage—his car was destroyed, but thank God he and his girl who was in the car with him were fine. My car, the salmon bomb, had a major dent in the left front fender.

I had to call the police. So I knocked on the first door I came to and was greeted by a houseful of giggling college girls in shortie pajamas, having a pizza party. I asked to use their phone to report an accident. I told them about the accident and the new baby, and they were just thrilled for me. They gave me some pizza to eat while I waited for police to show up.

The police soon arrived, assessed the situation, and promptly wrote me a ticket for reckless driving. The officer informed me that I would have to appear in court the next morning and go before the judge. He said the usual punishment is a $30.00 fine and a couple of points on your license. Thirty dollars? You have got to be kidding! Thirty dollars is all I had in the world and that was exactly what it would cost to get my wife out of the hospital. I explained I was in the Air Force and we lived from payday to payday. (That may have been stretching it a bit. We actually lived from payday to halfway to the next payday.) Since the clinic on base was not equipped to deliver babies, we had to use the University Hospital and the Air Force picked up the bill, all except for the first $30.00. We had diligently saved the money so we'd have it when the time came.

Now what? Should I go to jail and not pay the fine—was that a choice? The officer was not buying my sob story and was not about to tear up the ticket. He simply said "I'll see you in court."

The next morning I went to court and was a nervous wreck. I wore my uniform to make a better appearance. I even considered carrying a Bible but thought better of that idea. I was sitting in the courtroom, and the judge was a very scary, no-nonsense kind of man. I can remember him to this day. He was pretty much bald,

Life Slightly Off Center

JRAYMOND

with a little red hair on the sides of his head, overweight, and very angry. The case before mine caused the judge to lose his temper. You could see his blood pressure rise because his face got redder and redder. He looked like he was about to pop! He threw the book at the poor guy. *Oh boy, I'm in trouble.*

Then it was my turn. An official of the court called out "Next case: John Raymond driving the wrong way down a one-way street, resulting in a collision with another vehicle." I went before the judge, with my knees shaking, my palms wet, and sweat dotting my forehead. He sat in his big chair towering over me, folded his hands, and asked in a very pompous tone "Well, Mr. Raymond, these are some pretty serious charges. Can you explain why you were driving down a one-way street the wrong way?" I stammered "Well, your honor, you see, um, well, um, I was not familiar with the university area, and, well, actually my wife had a baby last night, and I, um, was all excited and really not paying attention to my driving and um, um." He smiled, picked up his gavel, banged it down, and shouted "Thirty-dollar fine SUSPENDED!" He then leaned over his desk, shook my hand, and said "Congratulations, son. Now get out of here and go see your wife and baby." Wow, great, I did it, and I still had my thirty dollars to get Dianna and Sheri out of the hospital. YIPPEEEE!

When I arrived back home later that afternoon, I found Dianna's mother in the driveway. She explained that she had left her home in Buzzard's Bay, Massachusetts, right after she got our phone call the previous night telling her she was a grandmother. She drove for three hours and wound up back in Buzzard's Bay. Mom had apparently gone around one of those crazy traffic circles that are throughout Massachusetts, ended up going back the same way she had come, and didn't realize it until she was home again! She said, "I feel so stupid." "Stupid?" I said, "You don't know stupid!" I then explained stupid.

Between the two of us, we didn't do too well. On the other hand, Mother and Daughter came through this birthing thing with flying colors. I assured the new Granny that the next time, *we* were bound to do much better.

The Art of Buying Condoms

After the birth our first child, Dianna and I had a serious discussion on birth control. I was elected to take care of the problem. Buying condoms was not an easy thing to do and not being experienced in this field, it was especially hard for me. The small town of Phoenix, New York, had only one drugstore. I went off to make the big purchase and came back half an hour later empty-handed. I explained to Dianna that there was a woman behind the counter, and I was not about to ask her for a pack of condoms.

I went back three more times before I found a man behind the counter. I went up to the counter with a lump in my throat and nervously asked for a pack of pro... profa...prophylactics. He said "Excuse me, what it is you are looking for?" I again stammered *prophylactics,* and this time he got it and asked "What brand?" What brand? There are different brands? "Uh, what brands do you have?" I asked. He reeled off a dozen or so brand names, and I settled for the Trojans because that was the only name I had ever associated with rubbers. Do you want lubricated, nonlubricated, ribbed, nonribbed, he asked. This was getting as complicated as buying a used car, and now there were people waiting behind me.

In a cold sweat and with a red face, I blurted out nonlubricated and nonribbed. Whew, what an ordeal. He rang up the sale, dropped them in a bag, and handed it to me. I slunk out of there, knowing all eyes were on me. I felt like I had just committed a horrendous crime. As I drove home, I was thinking that there had to be a better way. Maybe I could send away for some by mail and have them delivered in a plain brown wrapper. Or I could become celibate—or maybe just have a dozen or so kids. Well, we'll worry about that later; but for now I was set.

Several years and three kids later, we were living in Omaha, Nebraska. Again, I was off to the store for condoms. I still wasn't any better about being cool about it. But I knew where they were kept near the checkout counter and that you could just help yourself.

The store was very busy with lines of people at the register. I didn't want anyone looking over my shoulder when I laid my big purchase on the counter, so I

Life Slightly Off Center

picked up some milk and bread. This way I could slip the pack of condoms between the milk and bread and no one behind me would be any the wiser. I breezed by the condom display and picked up a pack and stood in line.

My turn. I put down the milk and the bread and very slyly dropped the condoms in between. The two women standing behind me had no clue. I looked everywhere except at the counter or the girl ringing up my purchase. So far, so good. She bagged the milk and breadand then asked "Are these yours?" Did I detect a little disgust in her voice?

There on the counter all by themselves lay my pack of rubbers. Was the pack getting bigger and bigger? Was the word Trojan flashing on and off? I was dying and meekly said "Yes." She held up the pack for the whole world to see and yelled to the girl in the back of the store, "HEY MARGE, HOW MUCH FOR A PACK OF CONDOMS?"

I slunk out of the store and vowed to never again buy condoms. Celibacy had to be easier.

The art of being cool dealing with condoms does not exist in this family. We aren't even cool with selling them.

Dianna was working at the base exchange shortly after we were married. On her second day, a young guy came up to the cash register and asked for a pack of Thins. Dianna handed him a pack of "Thin" cigarettes. "No, no, that is not what I want." He winked at her and said, "You know, a pack of Thins." Thinking this guy was a little strange, Dianna handed him a pack of "Thin" razor blades. Now the guy is getting a little frustrated and made it clear that he wanted a pack of rubbers by the brand name "Thins" and lubricated! He even told Dianna that they were kept under the counter.

Dianna fumbled around under the counter and came up with the right pack of "Thins." I know that if it had been me in the same situation as that young man, I would have walked out with the pack of cigarettes!

One more story on condoms and we'll drop the subject—at least for now. Dianna's mom was working the night shift at the Trailways bus station down in Biloxi, Mississippi. This particular evening, all was quiet until a man came storming out of the men's room. He was demanding his quarter back, saying that he had lost it in the machine in the bathroom. Mom had no idea what he was yelling about and asked one of the other waitresses what machine the guy was talking about. The girl whispered that there was a condom vending machine in there.

At that, Dianna's mom got all flustered and stammered "Oh, I'm sorry, sir, we must be out of your size!" and she handed him a quarter.

93

CHAPTER 3

Rochester, New York

Going Home

After my stint in the Air Force was up and my four years were served, I decided to get out and go home to Rochester with my wife and daughter. It was a tough decision, but I felt I was doing the right thing. I thought it was so important to be near family now that I had a family of my own.

We found a small apartment down by Summerville Beach and I got a job at Kodak. Back then and for many years since then, Kodak was the place in Rochester to work. It was like the coal mines are to West Virginia. Generations worked at Kodak. The company paid the best and offered the best benefits. But I hated it. I didn't like the work or the crazy hours. You worked three shifts—days, afternoons, and nights. You changed shifts every week. The department I was in worked 6 days a week. It seemed like all I did was go to work.

I missed Dianna and Sheri and the simple life we had back in Phoenix. The reason for getting out of the service was to spend more time with family and friends. But everyone seemed to be on a different shift, and we just didn't see each other very often. Dianna also got a job a Kodak, and she loved it. She was a private secretary to some big shot who was going to take her with him on the new space program they were developing. Because Dianna worked days, we had to get a babysitter for Sheri.

This whole new life was just spinning out of control. With Dianna working days and me working three different shifts, we got to see each other for dinner one week out of three. I spent all my spare time looking for another job. My mother figured I was crazy. She just couldn't understand why Kodak wasn't good enough for me since it was good enough for my father, my brother, my uncles, and my cousins. "Jackie, what more could you want—it's good money and great benefits," she would ask. I tried to explain to Mom that I just did not want to spend the rest of my working life doing something I hated. I assured her that I would find something better. I went on some pretty crazy interviews, but the most bizarre one was applying for a job at a funeral home.

I arrived at this big old house on East Avenue. It was a rainy cold night and this guy who looked like Uncle Fester from *The Addams Family* invited me into the parlor. It was really strange. The thunder and lightning added to the experience. He was the funeral director, and we talked about the job and what was expected of me.

Life Slightly Off Center

I was to sell caskets and drive the hearse in funeral processions. He asked how I felt about working on Christmas Day because that was one of their busiest days (I kid you not). He then showed me where the caskets were on display and explained that you push the really expensive caskets to the grieving family. One of the big perks of the job was being able to drive the hearse back and forth to work. It was then that I realized there were worse jobs than the one I already had. I kept looking for something better.

It wasn't all bad while we were living in Rochester. We did have some good times with the family and friends. Here are a few stories to demonstrate the good times.

My Brother Billy

My sisters, Kathy and Sally, played this trick on our brother, Billy. They had just bought a label maker. It was a new model that had a small keyboard on which you typed the desired information, then you pushed a button and it printed out on a plastic strip. Before going into Bill's house for a visit, they typed BILL RAYMOND on the label maker. They found Bill in the kitchen, having a cup of coffee. They showed Bill the label maker and just raved about how neat it was. Sally explained that all you have to do is talk to the machine and it will print whatever you say—"Is that great or what!" Bill said "Wow, I never saw anything like that before, let me try it!" Sally told him to just say anything, like give the machine your name. Bill put the machine up to his mouth and in a booming voice said, "Bill Raymond" but nothing happened. Kathy said, "Billy, get closer to the machine and talker

louder and slower." So Bill said "B-I-L-L R-A-Y-M-O-N-D" louder and slower. Sally said, "Go ahead and push the button!" He did as instructed and presto out came a label with his name on it. He was absolutely amazed and said, "Boy, what will they think of next. This thing is great!" At about this time, Kathy and Sally dissolved into fits of laughter and told Bill it was all a setup. Bill felt like a real jerk.

Now after many years, we still give him a hard time about the amazing label maker. All we have to do is say "BILL RAYMOND" nice and slow, nice and loud, and we all break up. All except for Billy.

My Sister Sally

One evening Sally and Jim, Kathy and Ricky, and Dianna and I were at Bill and Reggie's house playing cards. All during the game Sally would excuse herself and go into the bathroom off the kitchen, which had a louvered door. You could hear her every move in there. It sounded like a racehorse taking a whiz. After about the 4th time, I said, "Sally, for crying out loud, why don't you use the bathroom upstairs?" She explained that she had a bladder infection and couldn't make it all the way upstairs. So for the whole evening, this went on. I was just so disgusted with the whole thing. I groaned every time she would head to the bathroom. "Billy, can you turn the radio up so we don't have to hear Trigger in there?" I asked. After hours of this torture—and it seemed like I was the only one bothered by this—they let me in on the big joke.

Sally had a jug of water in there and she would stand up on the toilet seat and pour the water into the bowl. They all had a great laugh! This just goes to prove the old saying is true: You don't have to drink and smoke to have a good time!

Sally Again

The evening before my sister Sally was to be married, she showed up at Mom's house in tears and confided to Mom that she didn't think she loved Jim and couldn't go through with the wedding. Mother being Mother said "You've got to be kidding. I paid sixty-six bucks for a wedding cake, so you will get married in the morning!"

Thirty years have come and gone since that night. Sally and Jim did indeed get married and have been living happily ever after. Ahhhhh, a mother's wisdom...they are always right!

My Sister Kathy

One evening my sister Kathy invited the whole family over to her house. She had been practicing on her new chord organ and was anxious to show off her new talent. There we sat— Mom, Dad, brothers, sisters, brothers-in-law, sisters-in-laws, and all the kids. As Kathy played her heart out, Dad gave us the signal to all get up and leave the room. So as Kathy played, we all left the room one by one. She went into her big finish and turned around expecting a big applause from her loving family only to find an empty room!

In the Raymond Clan, no one suffers from an inflated ego.

Kathy and Ricky

Kathy and Ricky were married for about eight years when Rick got the calling to become a Baptist minister. After a lot of soul searching and many discussions, they finally decided to take the big step. The big step involved selling their house, Rick quitting his great-paying job, and them moving the family to Missouri where he would attend the Baptist Bible College. After the decision was made, things happened very fast. Rick quit his job, and the house sold in a matter of weeks. All that was left to do was to pack up and hit the road. Rick bought travelers' checks for the big trip and handed them to Kathy for safekeeping.

The day of the big move arrived. Rick pulled up in front of the house in a huge rental truck. He and a bunch of family and friends spent the day loading it up. After the last item was loaded, Rick said to Kathy, "Ok, honey, we're all packed and ready to pull out; let me have those travelers' checks." Kathy paled and gasped "Oh my God, where is the hutch? The checks are in the center drawer!" Ricky got weak in the knees and groaned "Oh no, Kathy, please tell me you didn't put them in the hutch, please. The hutch was the first thing we loaded this morning!" After a frantic phone call to the bank, Rick got them to agree to replace the checks on the promise that he would return the ones he had when he reached his destination.

Life Slightly Off Center

By the time they got to the bank, Kathy was a nervous wreck. They were ushered into the bank officer's office, and Rick again explained what had happened. The bank official got a big laugh over the incident and said it sounded like an episode from *I Love Lucy*. Ricky still did not see the humor in any of this. He just wanted the checks and to be on his way. The banker explained that they would have to sign an agreement to return the packed checks. Ricky signed the document and then handed it to Kathy. She signed with a shaky hand, and in an attempt to replace the pen to its inkwell holder on the desk, she tipped it over, spilling ink all over the banker's desk. Now he wasn't laughing anymore even though this whole situation was getting more and more like a Lucy situation. After a futile attempt to clean up the ink, only making matters worse, Kathy could not get out of there fast enough. She tried to walk past Ricky to leave, tripped over his feet, and fell flat on the floor. She got up and headed for the door and pushed and then pushed again. Ricky came up behind her and pointed to the sign on the door that read PULL. Pull she did and their big adventure began.

You'll read more about Kathy in this book and wonder how she survived it all, but more important, you'll be amazed at how Ricky survived.

They were not in Missouri long, when it became pretty apparent that they couldn't make it unless Kathy got a job. Ricky was going to school full-time and working odd jobs part-time, but just couldn't make ends meet. Kathy looked and looked, but found nothing. She had no real experience since she had been a homemaker for as long as she and Rick had been married. One day she found herself in a pants factory, applying for a job. When asked if she had experience sewing, Kathy was desperate enough to answer, "Oh yes, I sew all the time" (What she really meant was "I sewed an apron once in home economics class."). Well, her little white lie worked, and she got the job. She was to report for work on Monday. Hooray! No more macaroni and cheese!

Monday morning arrived, and Kathy was up and ready to go. She put on her best dress with matching heels and had her hair all done up. She took one last check in the mirror. She liked what she saw and was out the door and on her way. Once Kathy got to work, she could feel a lot of strange stares coming from the regulars. These girls were assorted sizes. There were tall ones, short ones, fat girls, and skinny girls. They all dressed in jeans or shorts and T-shirts with their hair either in rollers or pulled back in a ponytail. A buzzer went off, the girls punched in, a door clanged open, and everyone went to their respective sewing machines. The boss showed Kathy to her industrial-size machine. Her job would be to sew the fly into the pants. Her official title was "fly hanger." The boss said, "Simply line the zipper up, hit the pedal with your foot, and zap—nothing to it." Then there was another loud bell, all the machines started up, and the girls began throwing pants at her.

Kathy thought, *I can do this; I've just got to relax. I know I can sew these zippers in place. OK, I hit the pedal, zing...oh my God, what happened? The zipper is attached to the pants cuff. I have to keep up, just throw pants into finished bin. I'll get better, next pair, zipper close to being in right position, try again, not good, needle through finger, OUCH!* Kathy turns to the girl behind her and says "Excuse me, but could you give me a tissue or something? I just cut my finger." The girl threw a dirty rag at her and barked "Don't get any blood on the pants!" Kathy somehow made it to noon. She had produced a bin full of pants with misplaced zippers.

Another loud bell signaled lunch. She sadly sat there at her machine, eating her sandwich, and being pretty much ignored by the other women. All the time she was wondering, *How did I wind up in this place?* A girl wandered over with a little bit of advice. "Honey, if you want to get ahead in this joint, you got to be nice to the boss." Kathy is one of the most naïve girls ever and so she thought that being nice to the boss was keeping him company at lunch. Kathy walked to the boss's office and asked if she could join him. After three or four times around the desk, Kathy finally realized what the girl meant by being NICE to the boss! Kathy was out the door, down the hall, up the stairs, and out to the parking lot in tears. She sat there all afternoon, waiting for Ricky to come and pick her up. That was the end of her Fly Hanging career.

Within days, she had another job at a day-care center. All the girls that worked there were student minister wives. These girls really knew their Bible, and most conversations revolved around the Bible. Kathy enjoyed the job but felt completely out of the loop since she had so little to add to these religious conversations. For my little sister to be happy, she had to be part of whatever group she was with. Kathy was determined to belong, to be a good and proper student's wife, and to really know her Bible. She studied the Bible weeknights and weekends and was really starting to get it. After a few weeks, Kathy went to work ready to show the other girls that she did indeed know her stuff. All was going well, and Kathy was holding her own in a conversation about the Old Testament. While they talked, they were preparing lunch for the kids. Kathy was lifting a big pot of boiling noodles off the stove, when some hot water splashed on her. She jumped back and said "Oh shit!" Then "Oops, sorry about that," but it was too late—the whole morning was blown with just one little word!

Kathy went from the preschool to a job at a very posh department store. She was assigned to the china department, which she really enjoyed. She was in her element. One day a customer picked out a silver tea set from a display. Kathy told her she would get her a boxed one from the stockroom. This particular set just happen to be on the top shelf. Kathy positioned the ladder, climbed up, and was reaching for the box when the ladder slid out from under her. She was able to grab the shelf and pull herself up. There she sat, waiting for someone to come and rescue her. The customer, after ten minutes, was getting very impatient and sent another clerk to go find Kathy and her tea set. The girl walked into the storeroom, yelling, "Kathy, Kathy, where are you?" To which Kathy replied, "I'm up here, you damn fool. Help me, please!"

The Headboard Story

Dianna came home one evening from a Tupperware party with a great story. After a few glasses of wine, a bunch of girls started telling stories that their husbands had made them promise never to repeat. In this particular instance, I will change the names to protect our really thin-skinned friends. We'll call these people Lori and Don.

One night Lori and Don were in bed. Don was in his usual state of horniness. Lori was in her usual state of ho-hum about this whole sex thing. Well, Don got his way with her and somewhere during the act started making sounds like a wounded bear. Lori was thinking, *Boy, ole Don is having a good time tonight!* Suddenly, he gave out a huge moan and startled Lori. She looked up and discovered Don's head was jammed between the rails of the headboard! This is all it took to send Lori into fits of laughter. The more Don moaned, the harder she laughed. After a lot of pushing, pulling, moaning, and laughing, they were finally able to get his head free. Talk about your mood breaker.

It was then that Don made Lori promise to never, and he meant never, tell anyone about this. Lori promised and swore never to tell another soul. But we all know that Lori is lousy about keeping secrets and now the whole world knows. Sorry, Bill—oh sorry, I meant to say Don.

The story that should have never been repeated spread fast, especially by me. This one was just too good not to be repeated. I told a bunch of friends just because it was just so dammed funny!

JACK RAYMOND

We were living in Massachusetts and figured it was safe to tell the Headboard Story since our friends in Rochester would surely never meet our friends from Massachusetts. Aha, but the plot thickens!

Dianna and I along with our friends Roger and Tina were driving to Rochester from Massachusetts for the weekend. The big event was a Hawaiian party at my sister Kathy's house. We arrived at the party, and the whole gang was there. We were taking Roger and Tina around and introducing them to our friends and family.

We got around to Don and Lori, and I said "Roger, Tina, meet Don and Lori." Roger reached out to shake hands with Don when suddenly those names rang a bell with him. He doubled over in a fit of laughter and said "Are you the guy with the headboard that we have heard so much about? Oh my God, now that's a funny story!"

Don, I mean Bill, I mean Don, was not amused and yelled "JACK!"

The Pad

A friend of mine had a painful cyst removed from the base of his spine. His doctor suggested that he wear a woman's sanitary pad for the next several weeks to take care of the drainage he would experience.

One morning I stopped at Don's house. Lori, Don's wife, and I were sitting in the kitchen having a cup of coffee. Don, having just gotten out of bed, came into the kitchen, stretched, yawned, and said that he had to change his pad and he would be right with us. Lori exclaimed "Oh, thank God, he's not pregnant!" We were still laughing when he joined us.

One day Don was sitting on a stool in a coffee shop. He was all hunched over and enjoying a big slice of apple pie and a cup of coffee. He felt like people were staring at him as they walked in or out of the shop. People would snicker as they went by. One guy even left in hysterics. Don could not figure out what the hell was going on until he got up to leave and discovered that his sweatshirt had ridden up his back, revealing his little sanitary belt across his back, which, of course, was holding his pad in place!

Back in the Air Force

Like I was saying before I started relating all these stories, working at Kodak was not for me. After I don't know how many job interviews and being totally frustrated, I stopped by the Air Force recruiter's office. No, there was nothing available in my career field, but he would call if something came up. About a month later, I got a call from the recruiter telling me about a position available in Florida.

This was my ticket out of Kodak, and I really wanted out. That very same day Dianna came home from work, all excited about a big promotion she had gotten. I was equally pumped up about a chance to go back into the Air Force and move to Florida.

We sat down and had a long discussion, and at the end of it, Dianna being Dianna forgot all about her great career at Kodak and asked "When do we leave?"

CHAPTER 4

Florida

Moving to Florida

Before leaving for the big move to Florida, Mom and Dad had a going-away party for us. It was great, and all our family and friends were there to bid us goodbye and good luck. It was gatherings like this that made me think that leaving everyone may have been a big mistake. But the papers were signed, the furniture was on its way south, so there was no turning back. We bought a new used car and named it New Blue. It was a 1963 Chevy Biscayne. Not too exciting a car, but one we figured could get us to Florida safely. It really killed me to turn in our 1957 Chevy. Now that was a beautiful car. Black, with all kinds of chrome, hard-top convertible, whitewall tires—it was a classic. It leaked oil like crazy, which indicated a crack in the block, so ole Gomer had to go.

We had the car packed and were ready to take off. We said our goodbyes and we were on our way. It was June 1964 and we were headed for our brand new life. We made it a two-day trip. When we got to Florida and could see the ocean and a beach, we pulled over. I grabbed Sheri, and we jumped into the ocean, clothes and all. It was a great feeling!

We checked into Orlando AFB and were told that there was no base housing available. This was not a surprise because life is never that simple. We stayed in guest housing as we looked for a place to live. We found a really nice little house with two bedrooms and nice screened-in porch. It was in a great neighborhood and fairly close to the Air Force base.

We rented the house and set up housekeeping. So far, life was good. I started working at my new job while Dianna stayed home with Sheri, who was now three years old.

Florida House

It was a great little house, with a beautiful yard, and it looked out over a small lake. The big drawback was that it did not have air-conditioning, and heat consisted of glass panels in the wall that radiated heat. These heaters were about as effective as heating a house with a toaster. Our first winter in Orlando was rather a cold one for that part of the country. We soon discovered that this house was not the best one for cold weather. We were freezing. Luckily, the place had a wood-burning fireplace, which we used whenever I could find firewood.

One particularly cold night, we had to drag our mattress out into the living room in front of the fire. We tacked blankets to all the doorways leading into the living room. We even tacked blankets over the front door. The little glass wall heaters were cranked up to max and probably got the room to 60 degrees. This was the evening that the landlady decided to pay us a visit to see how we were doing. She came in and sat down in the living room. We gave her a cup of coffee, and she lit up a cigarette. Looking around at the mattress on the floor and the blankets tacked up over the doors, she said, "My, oh, my, you sure have this place fixed up nice and cozy."

We made it through the cold snap and went almost immediately into hot weather. Dianna loved it. She was a Mississippi girl who was used to the unbearably hot, humid weather. I was miserable with the heat. I just moaned and groaned about it.

Our Dog Giggles

We were in Florida a month or so when we got a call from my sister Kathy. Her dog just had a litter of puppies, and she wanted to send us one. Six weeks later, we got a call from the Orlando Airport, telling us they had a puppy with our name on it and asking could we please come and pick her up.

The transportation fee was $16.00. Sixteen dollars back then was like a hundred dollars to us, and we didn't have it. Finally we broke our piggy bank and Sheri's piggy bank and came up with the money, and Giggles came into our lives. We gave her the name Giggles because we laughed when we saw this little shaggy mutt who looked like a little gray and white fur ball.

Our little fur ball Giggles grew into a big lumbering pain in the ass that shed hair, dug holes, and generally made a mess of the house and yard. Giggles was a handful, but when she came into heat, that is when all hell broke loose. It became our main goal in life to keep her from becoming pregnant. I believe that dogs have special network and once one of their own goes into heat, it becomes public canine knowledge. That is the reason every male dog within a five-mile radius suddenly showed up on our lawn. They hung around, patiently waiting for the "flowering female" to make her big appearance. Apparently, from the number of dogs that showed up, Giggles must have been the only female in Orlando accepting suitors.

We did whatever it took to get these horny dogs out of our yard. We hosed them, threw rocks, yelled, but they always came back. One dog in particular got our attention. He was a miniature terrier and if persistence were a factor in winning Giggles' heart, this dog would have won hands down. One day the terrier made his way into the yard only to be met by another suitor, a doberman, who had staked his claim to Giggles. The doberman attacked the poor little terrier and inflicted some major damage. I carried the wounded terrier to his home. His owner rushed him to the vet. Several days later, I heard a tap, tap, tap coming up the driveway. There was that little terrier coming for a visit with his left rear leg in a cast. A broken leg was the result of his confrontation with the doberman. Now that's what I call love, or maybe a good case of lust. I told Dianna I was going to invite this little trooper in and give him a step stool to help him reach his "objective"!

The terrier did the job, Giggles did get pregnant, and we all eagerly awaited the big event. The big day arrived, and Giggles was pacing, seemingly anxious and very

Life Slightly Off Center

nervous. She had all the signs of a dog ready to give birth. Dianna decided to take Giggles for a walk. Dianna, Sheri, and Giggles headed up the street to visit Dianna's girlfriend. Dianna had Sheri sit outside and keep an eye on Giggles while she went in and had a cup of coffee with her friend, Sally. The first puppy arrived while Giggles and Sheri waited, and two more arrived before Dianna could get Giggles home. When I got home from work that evening, I was greeted with the good news that mother and puppies, all nine of them, were doing fine!

Dianna thought it was a great learning experience for Sheri. As I tucked her into bed that night, I said "Well, kiddo, now you know where puppies come from." Sheri's reply: "Yeah, Dad, they come from Sally's driveway!"

JRAYMOND

Mom and Dad Come to Florida

Mom and Dad decided to come to Florida for a visit. The big news was that they were going to fly down. This was to be their maiden flight.

Back in the day, people used to get dressed up to fly. It was a big occasion. Mom was concerned about what outfit she should wear and asked Dad for some input. He said, "Whatever outfit you pick, make sure it's black. That way if the plane goes down, they won't have to change your clothes to bury you."

Mom was really worried about flying down and sure didn't need Dad's wise guy remarks. Dad was being pretty cool about the trip and acted like it was no big deal. Mom told us that when the plane took off, he squeezed her hand so tight that she thought he was going to break her fingers. Dad was scared, and Mom reassured him that it was wise that he wore his black suit! Well, they made it. Dad said how great it was. He couldn't believe how fast they got to Florida. He said "If we had driven, we would still be pulling out of the driveway!

Mom and Dad were with us for a week or so, and we had a great time with them. Their first morning, we were sitting out on the sun porch when Dianna came out with her hair in curlers, wearing a raggedy old house coat, and carrying a big pot of grits. She slapped the grits on everyone's plate while scratching her belly, and said, "Good morning, have some grits!" Mom looked at Dad, and Dad looked at me and said, "What the hell are grits and what has happened to Dianna?" We all had a good laugh.

While they were in Florida, I took my Dad on his first-ever deep-sea fishing trip. We got up very early in the morning and headed for Daytona Beach. We stopped for breakfast and had some bacon and eggs. Down South every breakfast comes with grits. The waitress put Dad's plate in front of him, and he said "What the hell is this? I didn't order mashed potatoes with my eggs!" To Dad, Florida was a different planet, one with too many grits.

We got to the boat and joined about 30 other guys for a great day of fishing. Everyone threw $5.00 into a pot. The guy catching the biggest fish would go home with the pot. Dad said to me, "I am going home with that $150.00. I just have this feeling that I am about to catch the biggest fish today." This was from a guy who had never fished before. Guess he figured he had beginner's luck working for him.

We got underway and it was pretty choppy. The sun was hot and poor Dad was not even getting a bite. It wasn't too long into the trip that guys started hauling in fish. I caught several big red snappers, which sort of pissed Dad off since he still was coming up with nothing. Then it hit—Dad's line went out, his reel was just singing. He put on the break and started reeling in. His pole was bent over the side of the boat. He wrestled with it for a good half hour. He was sweating like crazy, and I thought he was going to have a heart attack. I said, "Dad, let me take over." He refused my offer and said that he didn't need any help; this was the big one that was about to win the pot.

He struggled for another fifteen minutes when I noticed the guy directly opposite Dad on the other side of the boat was in a similar struggle with his pole, also bent over the boat. I thought that that guy may have the big one, or...then I realized Dad and this guy may have had their hooks crossed. That is exactly what it was—no fish, only a crossed hook. Dad was so disgusted that he refused to fish anymore and groaned all the way home about how much he hated fishing. The more he groaned, the more I chuckled to myself, thinking about our great Father and Son fishing trip.

One afternoon we took Mom and Dad out to the base. Dianna, Sheri, and Mom went off to the commissary and the Base Exchange while Dad and I went off to the

Club to have a beer while they were shopping. Dad always wore a hat. He wore what I think they called a fedora. It was a hat with a brim. Anyway we got into the club, sat at the bar, and ordered two beers. All of a sudden, all these bells and sirens start going off, and we didn't know what was going on. That was when the bartender came up to Dad and said, "Sir, whenever anyone sits at the bar with a hat on, he has to buy the whole bar a drink." Dad said, "What the hell are you talking about? I'm not about to buy everyone in this bar a drink. Are you kidding? Jackie, what kind of a place is this? Why I've never heard of such a thing. Hell, is my slip showing, too?!" So much for military tradition. We left in hurry.

At the end of the week, Mom and Dad left in their black outfits and made it home safe and sound, with lots of stories to tell about beautiful Florida. In fact, that was the beginning of their love affair with that great state, and the one they eventually moved to.

Sheri's Ducks

You can't live in Florida and not have a pool. We bought Sheri a little kiddie pool and put it out on the patio. The patio consisted of a cement slab outside the back door. That ole pool was used every day by Sheri, and on weekends Dianna and I would sit in it to cool off. Well, Easter came around, and like so many other parents, we thought, wouldn't it be great to buy Sheri some cute little ducklings. We did, in fact, buy six ducklings.

Sheri was thrilled until the cute little ducklings took over her little kiddie pool and used it as their favorite place to poop. So then began the daily task of cleaning out the pool and keeping the ducks out of the pool while Sheri was in it. Then the torrential rains common to Florida started. These rains came often and would wash the poor little ducklings down the driveway and into the sewers. My job was to go down into the sewer and retrieve the ducklings while Dianna hung onto my legs. This happened so many times that we thought it was time to find a new home for the cute, not-so-little ducklings.

There was a beautiful park down in the center of Orlando with a big lake and a

Life Slightly Off Center

fountain in the center. We had gone there often, and I convinced Sheri that this would be a great place for her ducks to go and live. She wasn't happy, but she agreed when I told her we would go down to visit them every Sunday and feed them. We made a big deal out of taking them to the park and letting them go into the lake. They paddled away, happy to have so much lake to splash around it. There were other ducks for them to play with, so Sheri left feeling good about their new home. Another bonus for not having ducks was that Sheri got her pool back!

Correspondence Course

My dream was to make a living as an illustrator. I saw an ad in a magazine where you take a drawing test, send it in, and then have your talent evaluated. I did it and soon was notified that I did have the talent to enroll in the Famous Artist School of Commercial Art. It was a correspondence course and the cost was $600. It may as well have been $6,000. There was no way we could afford it. The school did offer a payment plan of $25.00 a month for three years.

Dianna knew how badly I wanted to take this course, and she said just do it. I said that there is no way we can afford an extra $25 a month. We did not have enough money as it was to pay the bills. Dianna said, "Just do it, and we'll figure out how to pay for it." This was completely out of character for her. She was always really cautious about money and usually did without things before blowing any money. But she believed in me, and I'm glad to say I went for it. This course changed my life. I know that sounds pretty dramatic, but it is so true. You'll see how much as you read this book.

CHAPTER 5

Vietnam

Vietnam

After a year in Florida, I got the dreaded orders for Vietnam. That was the assignment no one wanted, but the one that we were all getting. I hated the thought of leaving Dianna and Sheri for a whole year, but this is part of the whole military package. So we went out and bought a brand new Volkswagen Beetle and headed back north to Rochester to say goodbye to the family. I took a 30-day leave and it was over in a flash.

Before I knew it, it was time to get on a plane to the war. The scene at the airport was really sad. My whole family was there, and everyone was crying. You'd think I was never coming home. My orders were for a place called Bien Hoa, Vietnam, and I was on my way.

I flew commercial to California. Then I took a bus to Travis AFB where I boarded a troop transport plane. After we got airborne, I began wandering up and down the aisle, asking if anyone was going to Bien Hoa. No one had ever heard of it. I figured I must be headed for a jungle outpost somewhere. I was getting very nervous. We landed in Hawaii to refuel, then we were on to Saigon, Vietnam, where most of the troops were unloaded. Then we were off to our specific destinations.

An Air Force airman boarded the plane and asked if there was a John Raymond aboard. I was really surprised to hear my name. I was sure he was going to tell me that I would be living in the jungle for the next year and he was there with a mosquito net for me. I said "I'm John Raymond." He shook my hand, introduced himself, and said "Come with me;" he cautioned me to run and keep low because of possible sniper fire. We got inside the airport, and he told me that they wanted me for an interview at the VNAF High Command. "Me? You want me for a job at the VNAF High Command?" He explained that my records indicated my protocol experience while I was stationed at Hancock Field. Wow, my little stint at the protocol office was about to pay off!

We jumped in a jeep and headed for the outskirts of Saigon. We drove through Saigon, which was a teeming mass of traffic. There were cars, trucks, jeeps, bicycles, buses, motorcycles, scooters, and rickshaws. The air was blue with exhaust and smelled of diesel fuel. It was bone hot and humid. There were soldiers, kids, women, men, goats, chickens, and dogs everywhere. It was so crowded and so noisy. People were shouting, horns were blowing, and this, I was told, wasn't even rush hour.

Lucky Break

We got to the Vietnamese High Command and I was ushered into an Air Force colonel's office and introduced to Colonel Downey, my soon-to-be new boss. He seemed wound a little tight, but was a pleasant enough guy.

He explained the mission. We were the liaison between the Vietnamese military and the United States military. It sounded pretty interesting and much better than my original assignment to Bien Hoa. The colonel interviewed me, and apparently he was happy with my answers and said I had the job. I was then taken to meet my new coworker Joe. He was an Army Spec 4, and we hit it off right away. He then took me into meet General Freund, the officer in charge of the whole liaison mission. He was a one-star Army general. He was a great guy and really made me feel at ease right away. He took me to meet General Vien, the Vietnamese four-star general who was in charge of the VNAF High Command. By the time I got out of there, my head was spinning. How in the world did I wind up with such a great job with all these high-ranking officers. It was mind-boggling. Who would have ever guessed that my limited experience with the protocol office at Hancock Field so many years ago would have a payoff like this one.

Things just kept getting better. Joe briefed me on all the details of job. Then he made a few phone calls to get me a place to live. I was to live in Hotel 77 in downtown Saigon. It was air-conditioned, with hot and cold running water and a maid to boot! Joe and I would share a driver and a jeep. The driver would pick me up at 7 AM at my hotel, then we'd travel to Joe's hotel where we would have breakfast in the chow hall. I guess it really wasn't a chow hall; it was more like a fancy hotel restaurant and the food was fantastic! After breakfast, the driver took us to our office at the VNAF High Command. The VNAF High Command was a beautiful park-like place. You would go from the loud, crazy streets of Saigon, turn into the compound and be in a different world.

Our hours were from 8 AM until 5 PM, with an hour or so for lunch. Jock, our Chinese driver, would pick us up for lunch. We'd go to the same hotel where we had had breakfast. After a great lunch, Jock would drive us to Tan Son Nhut Air Base to check our mail. Then to the office until 5 PM, back to the hotel for dinner, and finally back to my hotel.

What a sweet deal. It was totally incredible and when I wrote home about it, everyone was convinced that I had made the whole thing up just to make them feel better and not worry about me.

It didn't take long to get into the rhythm of things. Every day was pretty much the same. Each morning General Freund would yell from his office, "Joe, Jack, get in here and report to me now!" We'd run in, snap to attention, salute, and say, "Sir, reporting as ordered, Sir." He would then give us a big tray of fruit and hard-boiled eggs that General Vien's wife had sent to us. This was the routine every morning!

Friends

I made friends with several Vietnamese guards they had posted around the High Command building. One of them, Tran, invited me for lunch at his house. It was quite an honor for an American to be invited to a Vietnamese home. Tran picked me up at my hotel one Sunday afternoon. I jumped on the back of his scooter and off we went. It started pouring, but rain stopped nothing in that part of the world, so we just continued on our way. I had shampooed my hair the night before and apparently I hadn't rinsed out all the soap—I had bubbles coming out of my hair as we raced along. We got to his house and his whole family was there. Mom, dad, wife, kids, sisters, brothers, aunts, and uncles. All the men sat on the floor around a big table in the dining room, while the women waited on us. The women and kids ate whatever was sent back to the kitchen. They were all staring at me and giggling. There were kids scaling the cement wall around his house to get a look at the tall, skinny American. I felt like a rock star!

Tram had six kids, with another on the way. I asked Tram, "Why so many children?" He said that for each child, we received an extra bag of rice a month from the government. Boy, you can't argue with that logic!

All in all, it was a great experience and left me with new respect and good feelings for my new friends.

Mrs. Vien was always having fancy dinner parties at her home, and Joe and I were included on the guest list. Little did she know that back home we would be working the fancy parties. Mrs. Vien would call the office and invite us to what-

ever party she was having and ask, "Shall I send the Mercedes or the Chevrolet to pick you boys up?" We always opted for the Mercedes. Hey, if we're living the dream, might as well go first class. At these parties, each guest was assigned his own waiter who would take care of his every wish. Oh man, this was so much better than Bien Hoa!

Bien Hoa

That my new assignment was so much better than my original assignment would have been in Bien Hoa I know for a fact because after they assigned me to the VNAF High Command, I had to physically report to my original assignment in Bien Hoa and sign in. My new orders would be there, and the military personnel would process me in and then out, and send me back to Saigon.

I flew up to Bien Hoa, reported in, and was told I would have to spend the night and catch a flight back to Saigon first thing in the morning. I was assigned to a Quonset hut and a bunk. I turned in at about 10 PM.

Next to my bunk were a bunch of guys playing poker. As I laid there, I could hear a whistling noise go over the hut, ending in a big explosion. These guys didn't even flinch. I asked "Did you guys hear that? What's happening?" They said not to worry about it, it was just mortar fire. "Mortar fire—doesn't that bother you guys? I mean do any of them ever hit the target, like us?" I asked. These guys got to laughing and said "No, no, that is us firing out at the enemy. Go to sleep, you gringo!" I laid awake most of the night, listening to the mortar fire.

I was up at dawn the next morning and taking a shower in one of those gang showers in an adjoining Quonset hut. I was the only one there and was just soaping up when a Vietnamese woman walked in to do her laundry. She used the water from the showers to get her clothes wet and then she would beat them clean on the concrete shower floor. I instinctively covered myself with my hands. She looked up and smiled at me and said "no, no, is ok, me you, same, same!"

The Night Life

The next day I was back in Saigon and back into the routine. Joe and I became great friends, and I got to hanging around with him and his Army buddies. We went out drinking just about every night. We drank at the local bars and our beer of choice was Bom de Bom 33. It was called 33 because it was 33 percent embalming fluid, or so I was told. It was warm and tasted like crap. We drank it because that was what you drank when you were in Vietnam.

Curfew was at 2200 hours, and you were in big trouble if you were caught on the streets after curfew. It was always a race to see who got the cabs. The second choice was a motor scooter, and if you stayed too late at the bar, you would up getting a bicycle-powered rickshaw. They were the worst and so slow. One night I was forced to jump in one because that was all that was left. I yelled "Quick, Hotel 77. "The old guy was just pumping away and leaned over and said "I get you nice girl, very young, pretty girl!" I said "No, no, no girl, take me to hotel!" This guy was aiming to please and said "Maybe you like nice young boy!" "NO," I said, "TAKE ME HOME!"

I remember my first trip to a local bar. I went with Joe and his buddies and was totally unprepared for the night life in a Saigon bar. I walked in and was immediately approached by a bar girl asking if I would like to buy her Saigon Tea. I was a regular hayseed when it came to situations like this. So I bought her a Saigon Tea, and all of a sudden I have a girlfriend. She told me her sad story of how she wound up as a bar girl, and that she was supporting her brothers and sister because her mom and dad were killed by the Vietcong, and on and on. I was a sucker for a sad story. She said her young brothers and sister were home alone, and she was very worried about them. This, of course, is my interpretation of our conversation. Then a big tear rolled down her cheek. That was it for me. I said "Here's twenty bucks. Go home and be with your family." She was out of there in a flash and never looked back. My buddies asked what happened and I told them the whole sad story. They just laughed and explained that is the story all the bar girls tell. It is their way of making extra money! "Jack, you are a sucker. When a girl asks you to buy her a Saigon Tea, you say NO, and continue saying no all night." I soon got into the swing of things.

Life Slightly Off Center

Jack, the Do-Gooder

Going to the bar became a nightly event. I always passed a mother with two children, next to the bar. One child was a newborn that she kept in a cardboard box, and the other was a little girl of about 3 years old.

When any GI walked by, the mother would give the little girl a shove, and she would very shyly approach and say "GI, like to buy kiss for 5 piasters?" That is about five cents in our money. Most guys would just breeze by, ignoring her. Not ole Jack. Old bighearted Jack always stopped for a kiss and usually gave her 100 piasters. She was the cutest little kid. I wrote home about her, and Dianna sent me a doll to give to her at Christmas. I delivered the doll, and she was just so thrilled. As she opened the gift, her little fingers were trembling. She took the paper and folded it up real nice. She put the ribbon around her neck and when she got to the doll, you'd think it was a million bucks! She just squealed and gave me a free kiss that night. I watched as she took it to show her mother. Her mother grabbed the doll and put it under the stool she was squatting on. I was sort of perplexed by her reaction to the gift. I was told later that American dolls bring a big price on the black market. So there was another lesson learned.

The hotel where we had most of our meals was strictly for military personnel. There was always more than you could eat. I started collecting fruit and bread to take to the kids who hung around out in front of the hotel. After a while, a lot of the guys would bring whatever fruit and bread they didn't eat to me to give to the kids. This was a wonderful idea for awhile. I was happy to see all these hungry kids getting a little extra. The word got out, and it got to the point that I would be mobbed when I hit the street. It became really bad, and I had to stop.

My sister Kathy was a Girl Scout leader at home and wanted to do something nice for the kids in the local Vietnamese orphanage. She sent me a big box of goodies to take there. I asked around and was told that the orphanage got more than their share of contributions. It was suggested that I go to a nearby village and help out those needy kids. So I jumped in the Jeep, without Jock, and roamed the countryside, looking for this remote village to distribute Kathy's box of goodies.

Looking back on all the stupid things I did back then, it is a wonder I was not killed. I often forgot that there was a war going on and that you just did not wander around. I did find the village, and it was in really sad shape, so I pulled in. All these kids immediately surrounded the Jeep and were yelling and screaming for food. I tried to pass out what I had in an orderly fashion so they would all get something. I was then attacked by more kids, they were joined by their parents, and soon I had a mob scene on my hands. There were kids and adults all over that Jeep. They were pulling and grabbing and shouting "Me, me, GI, give me..." I had to get out of there quick. The goodies were gone, but they wanted more, and I had no more to give. I pulled away with kids still hanging on the hood. They eventually jumped off, and I sped away. They had even stolen a package I had in the back seat. It was a jacket that I was going to mail to a friend.

So, again, I learned. I was getting a real education on the Vietnamese culture.

Jack the Teacher

Then there was the time I volunteered to teach English to the Vietnamese. I would go to a compound that contained several Quonset huts where the classes would meet in the evening. I had nuns, soldiers, kids, farmers, mothers, and business people in my class. I would teach in English after the same class had been taught in Vietnamese. I don't know how effective that was, but the students seemed to enjoy it.

One night they wanted to know the favorite food in America. I told them hamburgers. I explained what it was, where it came from, and how it was prepared. I even drew a picture on the board. From the class, I would hear "Ahhhhhhhh," "Ohhhhhhhhh," and more "Ahhhhhhhs." I then asked them what was the favorite food in Vietnam? A woman raised her hand and said "Our favorite food is dog." This surprised me, and said "Dog! You really eat dog?" "Oh yes, dog very good, dog number one!" I said "How can you have dog, love dog, pet dog, and dog is part of your family, and then you eat it?" "Oh no, sir, we don't eat our dog, we eat neighbor's dog!"

I really enjoyed teaching this class and enjoyed getting to know the people. They treated me with such respect. It also got me away from being in a bar every night. Everything was going along great until the night I was teaching and the guy

Life Slightly Off Center

teaching in the hut next to mine was shot and killed. I never went back after that night. Call me a coward, but I was not taking any chances.

The people of Vietnam, for the most part, were good and kind people. They were doing the best they could under the circumstances. Most of them had known nothing but war their whole lives. Before we were there, they were occupied by France. The language had sort of a sing-song sound. Sort of like Valley Girls on steroids! There was no middle class—just the rich and the poor. While I was there, they were building the president's palace. It was huge and right across the street from a park. This is where the poor lived under the bleachers. I saw a lot of families living in shacks made out of flattened beer cans. All this was in the shadow of the new palace. I know we were over there fighting for democracy for South Vietnam. But I don't believe that the people cared much about democracy; they cared about being able to feed their families, to shelter their families.

After all the fighting, all the killing, I was in Vietnam to witness the first free election under the flag of democracy. Only one person ran for the office of president. It just drove the point home that free elections were not what concerned these people. Surviving was their main concern.

Six More Months

My job was pretty routine, but quite often General Freund would call me into his office and ask if I would like to go flying with him. That was always a great experience. We'd go off on a helicopter to some remote Vietnamese outpost where he would be scheduled for a meeting. We would go into a tent or building and be handed earphones so we could hear all that was said translated into English. I never knew my role in these meeting, so I would pull out a pad and pencil and write letters home. I am sure everyone figured I was the general's aide and was taking notes. Our helicopter trips would take us over war zones, or we would land on aircraft carriers. They were great experiences and made me feel guilty about having such a great job in the middle of a war.

After Joe and his buddies left Vietnam, I was pretty much of a loner. I was in my last six months and was tired of the bar scene; I pretty much just worked and hung out at my hotel. On Sundays I always flagged down a scooter and had him take me to the government swimming pool. Yeah, I know, there was a war going on all around me, and there I was going to the pool. Hey, what can I say, I was just one lucky bastard! One day, on the way to the pool, somehow my jock strap dropped out of the towel under my arm as I rode on the back of the scooter. I noticed it was missing and retraced my steps to see if I could find it. I found it alright, along with a bunch of kids who were completely puzzled. They were laughing at it and stretching it and trying to figure out what it was. I went up to claim it and tried to explain what it was, but they seemed to be even more puzzled when I walked away.

I often went to the marketplace to wander around. I always got my favorite bread there. It was what I thought was raisin bread, and I had been eating it for months before I found out from a Vietnamese friend that what I thought were raisins were actually bugs. "Bugs! Are you kidding me?" I guess with enough butter even bugs taste good.

The streets were always crowded. One of the most popular things were the street vendors. They reminded me of vendors back home who pushed carts around selling hot popcorn. In Saigon, the kids loved nothing more than the black gooey things the vendors sold. This stuff was better than popcorn, more popular than ice cream. Kids could not get enough of candied bats and ate them like popsicles.

Amazing Puppy

While wandering around on one of my trips to the marketplace, I found a guy selling puppies. One of the puppies caught my eye. It was a little brown mutt with perfect black dots all over its body. I mean, perfect dots, all the same size. It was amazing! I had to have this dog. This was like a Ripley's Believe or Not dog!

I paid 300 piasters (about $3.00 American) for the puppy. I had the dog named and making me rich by the time I got back to my hotel. I was stopped by the Vietnamese guard and told that dogs were not allowed in hotel. I explained that this was no ordinary dog—this dog was covered with perfect dots. There was probably not another dog like this in the entire world. The dog was worth a fortune! The

Life Slightly Off Center

guard just laughed and said the dots were ink. Ink? I didn't understand—why would anyone put ink on this dog? He explained that the vendors do this little trick to get dumb foreigners to buy their dogs. Well, by God, it worked!

My puppy was a fraud, and my fortune went up in smoke. The guard allowed me to keep the puppy overnight, but warned me that I would have to get rid of him in the morning.

Jock came by to pick me up as usual at 7 AM and we were off to breakfast. I had "Dot" with me. Jock made a fuss over the puppy and told me his kids loved puppy. So Jock became the new owner of Dot. A few days later, I asked Jock how the puppy was doing? Jock's reply, "Ahhhh, puppy delicious!"

A Miracle

One day Colonel Downey called me into his office and gave me $350 cash and asked if I would run down to a place in Saigon and pick up a motorcycle he had bought the day before. He figured it was small enough to throw in the back of the Jeep. Jock and I took off to look for the bike shop. The streets were teeming, and it was so hot. I said, "Jock, Let's stop for an ice cream." Ice cream in Vietnam was nothing more than frozen ice with some cream in it. Not great stuff, but it was cold. We spotted an ice cream vendor and Jock pulled over. I jumped out and bought the ice cream, joked with the vendor a little, and then we were on the road again. We went about 2 or 3 miles when I discovered the envelope with the money for the motorcycle was missing. Jock pulled over and we searched the Jeep. No envelope. Oh, boy, maybe it fell out when we stopped for the ice cream. Jock was well aware what was going on and although communication between the two of us was broken, we managed to understand one another. He knew it was a great deal of money. He also knew if it had fallen onto the street, we could forget it. That was probably a year's pay for the average person in Vietnam.

We turned around and found the same vendor. I went running up to him in a panic, asking if he had seen a brown envelope. He smiled and reached under his cart and handed me the brown envelope with the money still inside! I figured I had just witnessed a miracle! Jock couldn't believe it. I reached into the envelope and handed my new best friend a twenty dollar bill.

Guilt

There was a time when the guilt of being in a war and not doing anything significant really got to me. I kept thinking that if I had to be separated from my wife and daughter, I should at least be doing something worthwhile.

So I went to Colonel Downey and expressed my frustration and asked to be sent to a combat zone. I said I wanted to do my share in this war. He said "Jack, are you kidding me? You have without a doubt the best job in Vietnam, and you want a transfer? I can't believe it. I tell you what I'll do: Think about your decision over the weekend and come to me on Monday—if you still want to go, I will arrange it." I wrestled with it all weekend. Back then there was no communication back home other than letters, so I couldn't discuss my decision with Dianna. I just laid in bed tossing and turning. Do I go, do I stay? Do I leave a sure thing for something that might get me killed? On Monday morning, I walked into the colonel's office and told him I had decided to stay. He said "Good choice, Jack!"

Life Slightly Off Center

Off to See the General

The days and weeks went by, and I became a short timer. When you got down to a couple of months, you were known as a short timer, and you started marking the days off on a special short timer's calendar.

By this time General Freund had left the VNAF High Command and had been assigned a command in a combat zone. He wanted me and Joe's replacement, Bill, to come up and visit him. He wanted us to see what the real war was like. We planned on driving up the Bien Hoa Highway to visit him. Everything was all set—we'd leave on Wednesday and stay overnight. The week before we were to leave on our big trip, the headlines in the base newspaper read: "GIs Kidnapped off the Bien Hoa Highway." I told Bill, "Forget it. I am not taking the chance of being kidnapped. I am too short. I want to go home and this trip is not worth the chance."

General Freund called that week and asked if we were all set to come see him. Bill told him that he would make the trip alone because I had chickened out. The general said, "Let me talk to Jack." He called me a pussy. He said "How about if I

send a helicopter down to pick you guys up? Would that convince you to come?" I said "Sure, that would be great!" "Done! They will be there at 8 AM on Wednesday; well, maybe we better make it on Sunday. Is that good for you guys?"

Sunday came and the helicopter showed up as scheduled, and Bill and I were off to the front. General Freund met us as the helicopter landed with the base photographer and treated us like visiting VIPs. We had a great day. The high point of the day was watching the camp's mascot boa constrictor named Squeezie. This snake was about 10 feet long, and General Freund insisted that I put it around my neck while the photographer took pictures.

After lunch, we went out to observe the

camp's Sunday afternoon entertainment. The guys had built bleachers around a pit. In the pit, they placed a poor unsuspecting duck and Squeezie. We sat there for at least an hour while Squeezie suffocated and ate her lunch. The guys were making bets on how long it would take for the snake to complete the mission, and the guy with the closest time took home all the money. I guess when you don't have a football game to watch on a Sunday afternoon; you do what you have to do.

It was great to see General Freund. He turned out to be a good friend. Mom and Dad said they received a letter from him while I was in Vietnam, telling them what a great kid I was. I later heard that he was flying over a battle when a bullet came up through the floor of the helicopter, through his seat, and into his butt. I don't believe it was really serious, and I am sure it earned him a Purple Heart.

Short Timer!

Well, my short-time calendar indicated that I only had days to go before I would be getting on the big bird and heading home. I went down to the market to get a new suitcase for the trip. I bought what I thought was a genuine elephant-hide suitcase. It was a real beauty. I had visions of my stepping off the plane in Mississippi in my starched khakis and with my elephant-hide suitcase...won't my girls be thrilled to see me!

I had one thing to do before I left. I had promised Jock and the general's former driver that we would all go out for dinner. They had invited me many times and something always came up. We were running out of time so we set a date and nothing was going to keep us from going out. This was a big deal to these guys, and I was flattered that it meant a lot to them to buy me dinner. However, on that particular day, I had the flu. I dragged myself out of bed and met Jock and Charley, who were both Chinese, at what they called the best Chinese restaurant in all of Saigon. They were all smiles and welcomed me with open arms.

I was just getting sicker and sicker. We entered the restaurant, and I found the floor covered with chicken bones. It was perfectly acceptable for people to spit bones onto the floor. This didn't do anything to make me feel better. Jock explained that he would order what he thought I would like, and if I didn't like it, he would order me something else. First course: eel. This was a whole eel floating in a pot of boiling something or other. The eyes were looking up at me, the smell was overpowering, and I was ready to hurl as Jock took the eel out of the pot and starting cutting it up. "Jock, I can't eat that." He tried to get me to try it. "No, Jock, believe me, I cannot eat that." So Jock ordered me something that he was sure I would like. While Jock and Charley enjoyed their eel, the waiter brought me a plate of about 50 boiled pigeons' wings. These I could handle. I spit the bones on the floor with the best of them. It's funny—the women covered their mouths with fans while they were eating, then put the fans down as they spit bones or gristle on the floor.

The next course was pork wrapped around sugar cane. It was actually pretty good. I'm sure it would have been delicious if I would have felt better.

All in all, we had a good time. Leaving there, I felt bad. We all knew that we would never meet again. I was leaving two good friends behind in Vietnam. We hugged each other, we said our goodbyes, and I went back to my hotel and threw up.

Going Home!

One of the happiest days of my life was boarding the plane and heading for home. I had to change planes in Los Angeles and there was not a lot of time to spare. I was running through the LA airport to catch my next plane when my genuine elephant-hide suitcase burst open, spewing papers, pencils, underwear, socks, and souvenirs all over the floor. I scooped everything up and jammed them back into the suitcase; I got some masking tape from someone at the counter and taped the suitcase shut, checked it, and was on my way again. Next stop was Las Vegas. I had a brief layover there so I thought I'd call Dianna with my arrival time.

I called from a phone booth in the airport, and the phone just rang and rang. I was put out that my loving wife was not sitting next to the phone waiting for my call. I had, after all, been gone for a whole year! Ring, ring, ring, ring, ring... "Uh, hello," came a sleepy voice over the phone. "Hello, hello? Dianna, it's me, Jack. Are you OK? How come it took so long to answer the phone?" She seemed really confused. "Dianna, it's me, Jack, remember me?"

"Oh, I'm so sorry. I was so worried that I would miss your call that I dragged the phone from the living room and put it next to my bed. When it started ringing, I thought the phone was in the living room, where it always is, and I went running in there, still half asleep. There was no phone so I was on my hands and knees following the cord, which led to the back to the bedroom. I was so afraid you were going to hang up!" We got all the questions answered, and she and Sheri would meet my plane at the Biloxi airport.

Dianna and Sheri had spent the year I was gone in Biloxi with her mother. We arrived in Biloxi in a small 20-passenger plane. I walked down the steps, and Sheri spotted me. She came running across the tarmac and threw herself into my open arms. "Daddy, Daddy!" she squealed. I was shocked at how big she had gotten and how well she was talking. I was even more amazed that she remembered me. Dianna came running up behind her, arms outstretched, laughing and crying. It was like a scene from a movie. Home at last, and life was good!

CHAPTER 6

~~~~~~~

Massachusetts

Massachusetts

We stayed with Dianna's mom in Biloxi for a week after I got home from Vietnam. Our next assignment was Westover AFB, Massachusetts. So poor Dianna was once again being dragged out of the South she loved, back into Yankee Country, as she called it, by her damned Yankee husband.

Dianna had Giggles all dolled up at the groomers for our big trip. She was shampooed, cut, and fluffed and looked beautiful! We loaded up the Volkswagen bug, said our tearful goodbyes to Mom. We pointed the car north and we were on our way! As we drove along huge tuffs of Giggles' fur kept blowing around inside the car. Since my window was the only one open, the fur tufts would catch on my nose before flying out the window. After a few hundred miles of this, I said, "Dianna, can you please do something with that dog!" Dianna started digging through the luggage, and when I looked in the rear view mirror, there sat Giggles in my T-shirt and Dianna's kerchief around her head. I almost went off the road, laughing. It worked, no more irritating fur tufts flying around the car.

Giggles just sat up in the back seat, pretty as you please. People would pass us and spot the dog, get laughing, and beep their horn, or they'd go by and give us the thumbs up. We had a lot of fun with the whole situation. The funniest incident was going through a tollgate when the attendant spotted Giggles in the back seat and got laughing. He said "Oh my God, she looks just like my mother–in- law!"

JACK RAYMOND

Life Slightly Off Center

Chicago

Dianna wanted to go up through Kentucky to visit with her dad. I wanted to go up through Chicago to see my buddy Joe from Vietnam.

Ever since Joe had left, he and his mom had been writing to me, saying how important it was for us to stop in Chicago to see them. I said we would, and at this point I felt obligated. His mom was planning a very special dinner for us. Dianna was disappointed about not seeing her dad, but agreed to the Chicago route.

We arrived in Chicago about 12 noon, and the traffic was horrendous. I was driving and Dianna was reading the map while giving me directions. She was very, very nervous. At one point, I asked her to light me a cigarette. I looked over and she had two lit cigarettes hanging out of her mouth and she didn't even smoke!

The whole trip to Chicago was a complete bust. I called Joe at his office, and he acted like he didn't even know me. He met us at our hotel and took us to meet his mom. Nothing had been prepared for our Big Dinner. She acted like all the plans she had written me about over the past 6 months didn't exist. I was really puzzled. She insisted Dianna and I stay at her place and that Sheri stay at Aunt Sadie's apartment. I said, "No way. We'll just stay at a hotel."

We went out to dinner with Joe, and that was it. All this way to see my buddy and his family, and it was nothing. We left the next morning and never heard from them again. I really felt guilty about not going to see Dianna's dad. I promised her we would go see him after we got settled.

We finally arrived in Rochester and at home. It was great seeing the whole gang again. Mom and Dad threw a big Welcome Home Party for Dianna and me. We stayed a week and then headed to Springfield, Massachusetts.

Our New Home

When we arrived, I checked into Westover AFB and got my working assignment and the day I was to report to work. I would be working in personnel. Base Housing had nothing available at the time, so we had to find a place to live. We found a nice townhouse in a nice area that we could afford. Home was now 1215 Springfield Street, Springfield, Massachusetts. It didn't take long to get settled, and we were happy to be together again. We met a great group of people living there who had small kids, so Sheri was happy to have a bunch of kids to play with.

There were four apartment buildings surrounding a courtyard, and that is where everyone gathered on summer evenings and weekends. We'd get together, play touch football, have picnics, and generally were one big happy group.

Roger and Tina

Roger and Tina, who lived in the adjoining building, became our good friends. We all shared the same laundry room down in the basement of one of the buildings. Tina was pregnant and was really big and in the waddling-around stage of her pregnancy. Dianna often ran into Roger down in the basement when they did the wash.

Roger came up to me one day and said "Jack, you have got to keep your wife out of the basement when I am down there...she is driving me crazy. I haven't had sex in months. Dianna looks so great! Please talk to her." I told Dianna what he had said. While she was flattered and thought it was funny, she did stay clear of the basement when she knew ole horny Roger was around.

One night we were over at Roger and Tina's place watching a movie. It was an Alfred Hitchcock's movie called *The Birds,* about millions of birds attacking a whole town. It was a real nail-biter, a sit-on-the-edge-of-your-seat movie that Hitchcock was so famous for. During the commercials, I would run home and check on Sheri who was sleeping. On one of my trips back to our place, I got the bright idea to sprinkle birdseed on the outside windowsill of the dining room window. I figured it would draw all kinds of birds in the morning.

Well, we went to bed that night and Dianna was still shaking about the movie. It had really upset her. Dianna is not a fan of scary movies. The next morning she got up and went downstairs to make the coffee, and as she usually did, she pulled open the dining room curtains. Dianna was shocked to find dozens of birds on the windowsill and even more banging up against the window trying to get at the grass seed. Dianna let out a blood-curdling scream that brought me, Sheri, and Giggles running to see what was wrong. She was speechless and just kept pointing at the window and the birds. I got to laughing and told her what I had done. That was a big mistake, and I caught hell for it. Sometimes it is better not to take credit for a well-executed joke—just stand back and enjoy it!

I got a toboggan for our first Christmas in Massachusetts. Because of all the snow in that part of the world, that toboggan got a good workout.

I became the pied piper of the neighborhood. Every time we had a good snow on the weekends, I would knock on all our friends' doors to see if their kids wanted to go to the park tobogganing. I'd take off with a car full of kids and the toboggan tied to the top of our little red Volkswagen. After awhile, kids would come knocking on our door asking Dianna if "Mr. Raymond could come out and play?"

Man Eating Plant

We had a beautiful bamboo bird cage hanging in the dining room with a plant in it. The plant was growing like crazy and its shoots were hanging down between the bars of the cage. Sheri's friends were fascinated with this and wanted to know why we had to keep our plant in a cage. I told them it was a man-eating plant and not to go near it. I would then put my hand up near the plant and pretend it got me, then I'd start yelling "It got me, it got me, help!" and pull my hand away. I'd pinch myself so that it would leave a mark and show the kids. Their eyes were as big as saucers. These kids always made a wide berth around that plant and never took their eyes off of it when they walked through the dining room.

137

Having a Baby

Our mission back in those days was to have another baby. Sheri was almost five years old and was continuously asking us why she didn't have a sister. She would say "All my friends have a brother or a sister; why can't I have one?" One day she said "If I had a sister, I could get bunk beds like my friends!" She even suggested that Dianna go out and get a baby and I could stay home with her to babysit.

We had been trying everything. The doctor told Dianna that at certain times of the month when her temperature was just right, she was most likely to get pregnant. Dianna would call me at the office in the middle of the day, saying "Jack, come home now!" I would go racing home, do the deed, but nothing was happening. This exercise went on for months.

All our friends in the neighborhood knew we were trying. One day Dianna was vacuuming the living room after the Christmas holidays, when her girlfriend walked in to find Dianna banging the vacuum hose against the floor. Dianna said "I think I have a pine cone up my tube." The friend replied "No wonder you're having a hard time getting pregnant!" Everyone's a comedian.

Dianna finally found a doctor on base who took a special interest in her, and he promised her that she could have another baby. The first step was to go into the hospital and undergo a procedure where they shoot dye inside you and then x-ray to see if the problem can be identified.

The doctor found a lot of scar tissue and said that was the problem. He suggested we go home immediately and "do it"! The chances of a sperm reaching the egg were as good as they were going to get. Well, poor Dianna could hardly walk. It was a painful procedure, and she was all bent over, pale, and feeling very sick. The last thing she wanted to do was IT!

We got to the house, and her girlfriend Valarie saw how bad Dianna was and came running out to see if she could help. Valarie, being from England, thought that a cup of tea cured everything and was going to bring over a cup of tea for poor Dianna. I said, "No, not now, Val, maybe later." I helped Dianna up to the bedroom and into bed. During this very nonromantic, no candles, no music union, the bed collapsed! Like us, the bed was also worn out. Since we lived in the townhouse adjoining Valarie's, she had heard everything.

After I left for work, Val came over to be with Dianna and get her to drink a cup of her "cure-all" tea.

Valerie, whom I considered a good friend refused to talk to me. She avoided me at all cost. This went on for at least a week. I finally asked what was bothering her. Val said, "Jack, you are a pig! I heard you attack poor Dianna when you brought her home from the hospital! You men are all alike—PIGS! PIGS!" I explained to her why and what was going on. She was okay with me then, but I am sure she still figured men in general were pretty much PIGS!

It Worked!!!

Guess what, IT WORKED!!! Our first clue to its success was a few weeks later. Dianna put the coffee on to perk and got deathly sick from the smell. This was always a sure sign for Dianna. We were going to have a baby, and we were thrilled. Sheri was equally thrilled and asked if we could go shopping for bunk beds for her and her new sister. I explained that we didn't know if it was a boy or a girl yet. In fact we don't even know what color it would be. We could have a black baby, maybe a green baby, could even be a pink or yellow baby. So we'll just have to wait and see what we get. If we do have girl, then we would go out and get those bunk beds.

Dianna had a great pregnancy, and the months flew by. In January, John Keith Raymond came into our lives, and things would never be the same again. You'll see how true that statement is as you read on in this book.

When Dianna went into labor, we rushed to the hospital—or I guess "rush" isn't the word I'm looking for here. We actually hung around the house while Dianna finished watching a movie on TV. Again, Dianna was very calm about the whole thing. I hadn't learned anything from Sheri's birth and was in a panic.

We finally headed to the hospital. Once we arrived, I filled out the damned paperwork. Dianna was escorted to the labor room, and I was pointed to the father's waiting room. I had a good time there smoking cigarettes and shooting the breeze with the other soon-to-be new dads. I did spend some time in the labor room with Dianna, but of course, I was not allowed in the delivery room. That was the rule. I am a guy who hates rules, but to this one I say "thank God!"

Life Slightly Off Center

Our son, John, was born on January 21, 1969. He weighed in at a whopping 6 pounds 5 ounces. He looked just like Sheri when she was born. We did it again! Another healthy, beautiful baby! Boy, was that a happy day! We finally got to use the name JOHNNY! We had been saving that name for years.

Our kids were born long before ultra sound and it was always a surprise as to what you got. Mother and son were doing fine so I went racing home to give Sheri the big news. She came running out to the car when I pulled up in front of the house. She was just giddy with excitement. "Dad, Dad, did Mommy have the baby?" she squealed. "Great news, you are now the big sister of a little brother!" I told her. That just completely knocked the wind out of her sails, as I am sure that visions of bunk beds disappeared from her future. Then she asked all excitedly "Dad, what color is he?" "What color is he? Well, he's a little pink baby, of course," I said. Sheri just smiled and said that's good! I forgot that I had told her many months earlier that we wouldn't know if it was a boy or a girl or even what color it would be. I was surprised she remembered what I had said, but she did and was very much relieved when she knew she had a pink brother versus a green brother or a red brother. I mean how do you explain a green brother to your friends? So, Sheri was very happy!

Reenlistment Time!

To celebrate John's birth, we bought ourselves our first color TV. That was when color TV was brand new and we thought we had really made it. I mean, we were, as they say, in some pretty tall cotton. This was Dianna's way of saying you had come into some serious money.

Where did the money come from you might ask? OK, since you ask, the money came from out of the blue. It was time for me to reenlist in the Air Force or to get out and try civilian life once more. Dianna and I had many discussions about this and we never reached a conclusion.

I was up in the air about whether to stay in the Air Force or to get out. After the year in Vietnam and a couple of assignments that I was not crazy about, I was questioning my future with the Air Force. So now the question was: Do we make the commitment for another four years? When I left for work that morning, Dianna said "So what are you going to do?" I said "I still don't know." "So when you get home tonight, you'll have job for another four years or you may not have a job at all, right?" I said "Right" and gave her a kiss goodbye. I drove to work thinking that the responsible thing to do would be to reenlist. We had two kids by then; things were going along pretty well. I just couldn't get out and head back home. By the time I got to the base, I had made up my mind to stay in. I went to the reenlistment office and did the deed. It was not all that painful and even less painful when they handed me a big reenlistment bonus in cash. I asked them to break it down into one-, five-, and ten-dollar bills. I walked out of there with a stack of bills you would not believe! More money than I had ever seen. I couldn't wait to get home!

That evening I walked through the front door and was met by Dianna with John in her arms and Sheri by her side, and she anxiously asked what I had decided: "Are we good or should I start packing?" I took the wad of money and just threw it into the air and it came floating down to cheers, laughter, and a few tears. It was such a thrill to have all that money. We took a portion and blew it on the color TV and felt like millionaires!

Sheri Goes to School

Sheri started school during our time in Massachusetts. It was like; holy cow, where has the time gone?! School already! The morning she walked out the door to school was such a big deal to us. She was going to walk to the school with her friends. We were not ready to let her go. We followed her but did not let her see us. We hid behind trees and cars and thought we were doing pretty well. That is until we got almost up to the school, and Sheri turned around and waved goodbye to us!

Jack, the Nut Salesman

The Christmas before John was born, I got a job nights and weekends working at Sears. We needed the extra money for Christmas so it was just a temporary thing. My job was working in the candy department. I walked around the store in a red and white stripe jacket and straw hat hawking peanuts. I would shout "Get your red hot nuts right here at Sears! Be sure and get plenty of nuts for the big game this weekend!" I felt sort of like a jerk doing it, but hey, money is money. I got to be pretty good friends with Maggie, the woman who was the manager of the candy department and she was sorry to see me go after the Christmas holidays.

Well, time passed, and soon John was born. A few weeks after his birth, I had to go into Sears to buy a pair of galoshes or, as those of us from New York call them, a pair of rubbers.

The shoe department was right next to the candy counter. Maggie spotted me on my way to the shoe department and yelled out, "Hey Jack, hi...how's it going? Did Dianna have the baby?" I smiled and shouted back, "Yes, we had a baby boy, and we named him Johnny!"

"Oh great," she said. "Congratulations! What are you doing back here?"

"Oh, I just came by for some rubbers."

She just looked at me like that was more than she needed to know. I said "Oh boy, that came out wrong...I mean rubbers like for my feet!" I just went on and on trying to explain, but it was totally too late! I bid her goodbye and left the store without a pair of rubbers.

The Famous Artist Course

I mentioned earlier that I had enrolled in the Famous Artist Commercial Art Course while we were in Florida. It was a correspondence course. I worked on it while we were in Florida; I took it to Vietnam and worked on while I was there. Now we were in Massachusetts, and I had to finish it. If the course was not completed in three years, you had to start paying $25 for every lesson you mailed in late. I was down to my last two lessons and I didn't want to have to pay the late charges.

The lessons were quite involved and took some time to complete. On this particular Sunday, I had promised myself that I would finish the course. No matter how many hours it took, I would stay with it and get it done. I just needed some "alone time." Dianna arranged to take the kids to the lake with some friends and stay away the whole day. *Great, I would have the house all to myself.*

That particular Sunday was probably one of the hottest days of the year. It was a perfect day for the lake, but not so great for staying in a house without air conditioning. It must have been 90 degrees in that house, but no excuses, I was determined to get it done.

I set up a makeshift drawing table in the dining room, turned on the fan, stuck my feet into two buckets of cold water, and went to work. I did it—I got both lessons completed before Dianna got home. I put them in the mail the next day. What a great feeling, after three years, to have it all done.

Little did I know then, this course would play a major role in our lives.

The Planetarium

Sheri was about five years old when we took her to the planetarium. We thought it would be a good experience for her. By the time we got there, it was time for John's mid-morning feeding. Dianna opted to sit in the lobby while Sheri and I went inside. The theatre was packed. We finally found two seats in the middle. We got all settled in and were all set for this great experience.

The man giving the lecture walked to center stage, the lights were lowered, and there we were sitting under a huge body of sparkling stars. Sheri gasped in wonder. It was a very impressive sight. The speaker started talking, and I immediately detected a lisp in his voice. I don't know why, but this hit me so funny, and I was reduced to a fit of laughter. It was one of those bouts of laughter that you know is totally wrong, and the more wrong it felt, the harder I laughed. I was doing everything I could to control myself, but the speaker stopped several times because of me. Sheri was so embarrassed, and she kept saying "Dad, ssshhhhh, Dad, you've got to be quiet!" I was biting my lip, holding my hand over my mouth, and I just could not stop. Tears were running down my face. The people around us were also ssshhhhing me and looking at me in total disgust.

Several times I would get myself under control, and then the speaker would start talking and set me off again. I finally grabbed Sheri by the hand—or was it Sheri grabbing me by the hand—and we got out of there.

We joined Dianna, who was still feeding John. She asked, "What happened? How come you're out of there so quickly?" Sheri explained that her father was a complete idiot and had totally embarrassed her. Both Sheri and Dianna walked ahead of me just shaking their heads, while I brought up the rear pushing Johnny in the stroller. I was still chuckling as we left.

Sally

At one point during our stay in Massachusetts, my sister Sally came to live with us. Sally got to know all of the neighbors and enjoyed their company. One day Sally was outside hanging up the wash on our community clothesline. Out there with her was the neighbor from two doors down also hanging up her wash. Peggy was a great girl who happened to be married to the jerk of the neighborhood. Dave was a short guy with a Napoleon complex. He thought he was God's gift to the women and the biggest stud this side of the Mississippi. Sally came in the kitchen door, bent over with the giggles. I asked "What's so funny?" She replied that while Peggy was hanging clothes, she hung up Dave's jock strap, and through tears of laughter, she said, "It's an EXTRA SMALL!!"

Now that was funny! Word soon got around the neighborhood, and from that day on, ole Dave was known as Mr. Extra Small. He never knew this—it was just an inside joke among us all.

During Sally's stay, she was a great help to Dianna. Dianna was getting bigger by the day and her normal high energy was slowly disappearing. Sally's help was certainly welcome. It seemed to me that Sally was always doing the ironing.

JACK RAYMOND

One day I said to Dianna, "Look at that, Sally is ironing again. Let's pretend to get in a fight about her doing all the work around here and see what she does."

Dianna of course agreed because she loves a good joke, especially if they are not being played on her. We went into the living room where Sally was toiling over the ironing board. I said "Sally, you don't have to do all this ironing. Relax, you're here to visit. Dianna," I yelled, "Get in here!" Dianna came in and asked "What's going on?" I said "Why does Sally have to do all the ironing? You're just taking advantage of her good nature" and blah, blah, blah. We really got into a rip-roaring argument while poor Sally just started ironing faster and faster, saying "I love to iron, I love to iron. It's no problem, really, I love to iron!" Finally we let her in on the joke. She called us both jerks and then we all had a good laugh.

Shopping Day

Dianna's big day out came every two weeks when we got my paycheck. She and Valerie would go to the base commissary to do their grocery shopping and then head over to the Base Exchange to shop around. Val's kids were in school and Dianna always put Sheri in the base nursery. This gave them a whole morning without kids! After their shopping, they would go out to lunch. This routine went on for as long as we lived in Massachusetts. One day the girls got almost all the way home from their shopping trip when Dianna realized they had forgotten Sheri at the base nursery! Don't think I let her forget about that for a few weeks. On her shopping days from then on, I would leave a note: Please pick up shaving cream, blades, black shoe polish, and oh yeah, don't forget our daughter!

Sheri Playing Doctor

There was the time that Sheri and a few of her friends were caught playing "doctor" down in one of the basements. I learned they were pulling down their pants to show each other the goods. When we asked Sheri about it, she simply said, "I showed Scottie mine, and he showed me his. Jeffery didn't care and Krista didn't dare." And that was the end of the conversation.

Life Was About to Change

I was pretty unhappy with the work the Air Force was having me do. It was nothing but paperwork, and I found it bone-numbingly dull. I went to personnel to see about cross-training into a new field. My dream was to become an Air Force illustrator. This was a career field that most people don't even know exist. In order to cross-train into this field, I was told, I would have to submit my portfolio to the art department at SAC Headquarters at Offutt Air Force Base, in Omaha, Nebraska. Thanks to the correspondence course I had taken, I had a wide selection of samples of my artwork that made up a great portfolio.

I sent it off to SAC and kept my fingers crossed and prayed that I would pass their review. Word came back that not only did they like my stuff, but they wanted me there at SAC Headquarters as an illustrator! WOW!! I was ecstatic! Dianna and I were just goofy with happiness. Who would have ever dreamed that that correspondence course would lead to this. That course that we paid $25 a month for 3 years was about to change my whole life! We were going to Nebraska, and ole Jack was finally about to find his niche in life! HOT DAMN!!!!

I soon got orders to report to Offutt AFB. It was the summer of 1969. I called

Life Slightly Off Center

Mom and Dad to tell them the big news. Mom said "You're going where?" I said "Omaha, Nebraska." She asked "Where's Nebraska?"

Now you have got to remember, Mom never moved more than a block from the last placed she lived, so this was something she just couldn't understand.

"Mom, Nebraska is in the central United States." "Oh my God, you're not driving way out there, are you? Won't the Air Force fly you there, and ship your car?" "No, Mom, we'll drive, it won't be that far." I explained. "Jackie, you're going to drive that little Volkswagen with two kids, a dog, and a cat?" "We have to; I haven't the money to get a new car. We'll be fine, don't worry about us."

Little did Mom know that I had already traded our little VW bug for a big, beautiful, green Volkswagen bus. We had just paid off the bug and really needed a bigger car.

It was funny—our car payment went from $50 a month to $33 a month on the new car. It was such a great deal plus we had all that room! I didn't tell Mom about the new car because I didn't want her off the worry hook quite that easily. Mom loved to worry, and I didn't want to deprive her.

Sally returned to help us pack up. While she was there, I told her not to tell Mom and Dad about the new bus. Tell them things like Jack had to quit smoking because there is not enough room in the car for a pack of cigarettes. Sally flew back home after helping us get our stuff together for the movers. Every few days she would give Mom and Dad a few more jabs about us and that damn little Volkswagen. She said things like, "They have Johnny in a drawer in the back seat. Poor Sheri has to sit with her legs curled up because Giggles is on the floor in front of her! The cat box is on the floor in the front so Dianna has her legs up around her chin. They have that toboggan tied to the top of the car. I swear they look like a bunch of gypsies!"

Mother said "That is exactly what they are—government gypsies! I don't know how they can live like that. But, oh no, Jackie didn't want stay at Kodak. No, he had to go wandering the world and now he has to drag his poor family to Nebraska!"

Mom told me later that she and Dad would sit out on the porch swing trying to figure out a way to buy us a new car. There was no way they could afford one.

When we showed up a few weeks later and pulled into Mom and Dad's driveway in our brand-new shiny, big, green and white Volkswagen bus with a banner across the front reading "Nebraska or Bust," Mom actually jumped up in the air and clapped her hands together! Dad was waving his fist in the air, and we were all laughing while Mom was crying.

We stayed home for a few days and then we were on our way. As always, saying goodbye to all the great friends we had made in Massachusetts and then saying goodbye to our family was rough. It always was. You just never get used to that part of this life.

I once told my brother Bill how much I envied him staying in the same house in the same city all of his life. He said "That's funny; I envied you, always off to someplace new." I guess that would be the classic example of the grass always looking greener from the other side of street.

We had a great trip to Nebraska. Saw all kinds of new country and totally enjoyed all the room in our new bus. We'd stop about 4 in the afternoon at a motel with a pool. We'd all take a swim, have dinner, and then go to bed by 7 PM. Dianna, our drill sergeant, would have me up at 3 AM to load the still sleeping kids into the bus in their pajamas. They would get another five hours of sleep before we stopped for breakfast.

Dianna and I continued this pattern of travel long after the kids were grown and gone. One day we both thought, *what the hell are we doing? Three in the morning—this is crazy!* We now travel at a much saner pace.

We arrived safe and sound in Omaha on a hot, sunny summer day. We looked forward—with some apprehension—to our new life in this new place. Dianna, Sheri, Johnny, and I were ready for whatever Nebraska had to offer. The gypsies had arrived!

CHAPTER 7

Nebraska

Omaha, Nebraska

The first thing we did when we hit our destination was to go directly to Offutt Air Force Base and check in. Our next stop was the housing office, and of course there was no housing available. Even the guest housing was full. We put our name on a long list of people waiting for base housing.

I had a few days before I had to check in officially so we planned on using the time to find a place to live. This is always such a chore. We checked into a local motel and set up headquarters there. This was to be home away from home for a least a week. Then we started checking out the newspaper for homes to rent. We looked at many and finally settled for a cute little three-bedroom house with a two-car garage and a nice big yard. It was in the town of Bellevue, right across the bridge from Iowa and right outside the base. We had our furniture delivered and started the process of setting up our new home. We got Sheri registered in a local school. And so life began in Nebraska.

Jack Becomes an Illustrator!

I got my security badge to get into SAC Headquarters, and it was the nicest building on base. Our office was all windows and looked out over the whole base. I could not have been more impressed with this wonderful place to work. On my first day on the job, I met and liked everyone I was going to work with. Even the boss was a great guy! Some of these guys were to become good friends and others would become mentors to me.

This was the time in my life when I could not wait to wake up in the morning and go to work. I have felt like that pretty much ever since. I was finally doing just what I was meant to do, what I was best at. I had found my niche—I was an illustrator, and I was happy!

Hurricane Camille

We were not in Omaha too long when Hurricane Camille hit the Gulf Coast of Mississippi. Dianna's mother's house was pretty much destroyed. I think Camille hit on a Sunday. Dianna was scheduled to fly out the next day with the kids to go visit her mother but that trip was cancelled. Dianna had to go down alone and help her mom. The plan was for me to stay with the kids, and she and Giggles would take off in the VW bus, loaded down with supplies, and drive to Mississippi. She was taking Giggles for protection! That was like taking an unloaded gun for protection! But if Giggles didn't do her job, Dianna had a rolling pin as a backup and would use it if she had to!

Dianna took off, but not before she had filled the freezer with frozen dinners. Since I was going to be at home for a few weeks, I decided to paint the house. I had a deal with the landlord to paint in exchange for a month of free rent. Since we had no car, we did a lot of walking while Dianna was gone. Every morning I'd get the kids' breakfast and then I'd try to fix Sheri's hair just right, which was usually just wrong, and walk her up to school while pushing Johnny in his stroller. Then we'd walk home, and I would put the playpen out in the yard with Johnny in it while I painted the house.

It was fall and leaves kept falling into the playpen, which Johnny would eat and then proceeded to throw up. So between pooping, peeing, and throwing up, I spent many hours changing that kid! On particularly warm days, I would put John in the playpen in only a diaper; that way I didn't have to change his whole outfit every time he threw up. At about 2:30 PM we would walk up to the school and get Sheri. This routine continued for two weeks. Taking care of the kids while painting the house was exhausting! I'd let Sheri pick out the TV dinners we'd eat every evening. I'd bathe and put the kids to bed by 7, and I would be in bed by 7:30 PM.

I was never happier to see anyone in my life as I was to see Dianna pull up in that bus! She had even gone to the store on her way and got groceries and fixed us the most fantastic dinner! It seemed strange to eat off of a real china plate instead of a plastic tray divided into three sections. What was even stranger was that the food tasted great!

Dianna had some great stories for us about her trip. The best one I remember was the time her and her mom were out walking around the neighborhood. There

JRAYMOND

was total destruction everywhere they looked. They went by this old man sitting in his easy chair out in front of what used to be his house. It was all he had left. As they walked by, he was sitting there smoking a cigarette. On their way back, he was still sitting there, but now there was smoke coming out of the chair. He was yelling to his wife "Ma, Ma, the chair's on fire!"

Dianna's mom was telling Dianna that when the warning of the hurricane came, she took all her photographs and important papers and put them on her bed. She then headed for Hattiesburg to her brother's house for safety. She returned several days later. She was thrilled to see all the things she had laid on the bed were perfectly dry even though the waterline in her house was up to the ceiling. Apparently, the mattress had risen off the bed as the water flowed in and jammed up against the ceiling. When the water receded, the mattress was lowered back onto the bed. Amazing!

Dianna, her brother, Chuck, and some of his buddies were able to fix up the house so Dianna's mother could get back into it. The only thing that was in good shape was the outside walls. They had to replace everything, including the electric wiring, plumbing, new floors, drywall, and windows. They just about built a new house in two weeks.

Life Slightly Off Center

Our First House

We were in our new assignment maybe 6 months or so when a chance came up to buy our first house. Charley, a guy I worked with, had an assignment to Alaska and had to get rid of his house. He approached me to ask if I was interested. I assured him that there is nothing I would like better than to buy our own house, but there was no way we could afford it at this point in our lives. Charley said "Tell you what—you give me $500 and take over the payments and the house is yours!" I went home and excitedly told Dianna about it. She said "What color are his carpets?" "What do you mean what color are the carpets, who cares? This is a chance of a lifetime!"

Nope, she had to see if his carpets would go with our couch. I made arrangements with Charley to go look at his house, and we took a couch cushion along to make sure everything would go together. I couldn't believe this whole deal revolved around carpet color.

The carpeting was perfect! The house was perfect. It was a three-bedroom with a finished basement and a one- car garage and was in a great neighborhood. The school was right around the corner. Charley even threw in a new lawnmower and the patio furniture. What a deal!

A few weeks later, Charley and his wife and Dianna and I met at a lawyer's office in Omaha. I gave Charley the $500 we had agreed on; we signed the papers and split the lawyer's fee of $40. Then we all went out for a drink to celebrate! That was when life was simple. The house payment was $100 a month on a 30-year mortgage. How sweet is that for your first house? We were in heaven! So we moved once again with the help of some friends and stayed there until our next assignment.

It was great fun fixing up our own place. I loved having a yard of my own. The only disappointment was our Volkswagen bus would not fit in the garage, but hey, life is not perfect, right? We were now residents of LaVista, Nebraska.

One of the things we really liked was the chain-link fence around the backyard. We figured it would be great to be able to put Giggles, our dog, and Johnny, our son, out there to play and not have to worry about them. Johnny figured out how to climb the fence while we were still moving in! Giggles never figured it out—one out of two wasn't bad!

Diapers

One Saturday I was left to babysit the kids. Sheri was seven years old and Johnny about two years old. All was going well until we got to the part where daddy has to change son's diaper. Back then we used cloth diapers.

I often saw Dianna take a dirty diaper, put it in the toilet, holding it by the corner, and flush, and presto! the diaper is clean enough to put in the diaper pail. So there I was doing the flush trick with Sheri and Johnny looking on. Apparently, I did not have a good enough grip on the corner, because when I flushed the toilet, down went the diaper! If Dianna were home, she would have had a fit and insist we call a plumber. Me, on the other hand, was a little more laid back and figured if things got blocked up, we'll call a plumber then; if not, then all the better.

I warned Sheri not to say a word to her mother about the diaper going down the toilet. Sheri promised and crossed her heart; she would not tell on me.

A few days later, we were having dinner when Dianna asked, "Did you flush a diaper down the toilet?" "Why," I asked, "how did you know that? Sheri squealed on me, didn't she? Did the toilet back up? Sheri, I can't believe you squealed on your ole man, and after you promised!" Dianna said, "Hold it, Sheri didn't say a word. It was John. He was looking down the toilet today, and he kept saying, "Diaper go bye-bye! Diaper go bye-bye!"

I couldn't believe it—my son was just two years old, barely able to talk, and he squealed on his old man!

Life Slightly Off Center

Nuts

It was a cold night in Nebraska. We had just sat down to dinner, when Sheri, who was eight at the time, asked "Dad, what's nuts?" I said "It depends; use it in a sentence." She said "Kevin went down the hill on his sled, hit a tree, and hurt his nuts!" I was in shock; Dianna was on the floor doubled over in hysterics. I asked "Sheri, where did you hear that?" "Dad, we were out sledding today, Kevin hit a tree, and then he moaned 'Oh my nuts!' So what are nuts, Dad?" she asked.

By this time Dianna was out of control and was obviously not going to be any help at all. The best way to explain this, so my daughter would understand, was to pull down Johnny's diapers and show her. As I did this, I explained these are nuts, but the proper name is testicles. Armed with this new knowledge, Sheri piped up and said "So Kevin should have said 'oh my testicles!'"

With this, I left the table, stepping over Dianna, who by this time had completely lost it.

Another Baby!

I was at the office one day when I got a phone call from Dianna. She had been feeling kind of sick lately and had gone to the doctor. She said, "Guess what? We're going to have a baby!"

"That can't be," I said. "The doctor in Massachusetts said we were finished, that you couldn't get pregnant again!" "Well apparently he didn't know what he was talking about, because I am pregnant," she replied.

Yipppeeeeeeeeeeeeeee!!! I was thrilled. We were both thrilled. To have another baby was like icing on the cake! To have a baby without all the garbage of having to take temperatures and doing the "deed" on command was great!

Unbelievable!

Dianna's first appointment at the ObGyn Clinic on base was pretty exciting! They called out "Mrs. Raymond," and she and another girl stood up. Again, "Mrs. John Raymond," and they both continue to stand. Dianna talked to the girl with the same name and found out that they were both due at about the same time and that her husband was the same rank as me. When she told me this, I was all upset. I said "I sure hope they don't screw things up and give us their baby by mistake!" Dianna thought I was overreacting, as usual.

Then strange things started happening to me. I went to the dentist and he looked at the records and then looked into my mouth and said, "You don't have a cavity where it is indicated on the records." Sure enough he had the other John Raymond's records. The same mistake occurred when I went through my annual physical. I was getting worried.

The area we lived in had a little newsletter that was delivered once a month

Life Slightly Off Center

to the residents. I was reading it and said to Dianna, "I can't believe it, we've been here almost two years and they are just getting around to welcoming us to the community!"

It read:

> *A big welcome goes out to John and Dianna Raymond. They are originally from New York and have two children, a girl and a boy. John is in the Air Force and assigned to Headquarters SAC at Offutt AFB.*

The article continued by giving our address and few other facts. I said "They got everything right but our address." Dianna looked at the article and said "I bet this is the other John Raymond."

Curiosity got the best of me, and I just had to call him. I thought it would be great to meet. I got him on the phone and he was a real jerk. He was not interested in meeting me or my family. I asked, "Don't you think it is ironic that we have the same name, we're both from New York, and we both have two kids the same age and same sex. I mean that is unbelievable to me."

Talking to this John Raymond was like talking to a stump. He certainly was no credit to the name. We never did meet. But now I was really worried about the base hospital screwing up the babies when they came. I didn't want his baby, and I sure didn't want him raising ours!

Well, time passed and Dianna continued to grow. It was a wonderful pregnancy with no complications. She was actually glowing.

Sheri was back on the bunkbed kick and made me promise to get a set if this baby was girl; she just knew it was going to be pink!

Dianna was a member of the NCO Wives' Club on base. She went to all the meetings and totally enjoyed the companionship of the other wives. We attended an NCO Wives' Club-sponsored Hawaiian party. Dianna's job was to place leis around each person's neck as they entered the room. At the next meeting Dianna got up and reported that she had "laid 96 people" at the Hawaiian shindig. This report got a huge laugh from all the girls since Dianna happened to be seven months pregnant at the time!

Here is another incident that occurred during this pregnancy. We were at the Wives' Club Awards Banquet and enjoying the dinner when Dianna's name was announced as the winner of the award for the most sociable member of the club. This was met with a round of applause, which was followed by a huge round of laughter as Dianna waddled up to accept her award. She was now eight months pregnant! Some guy in the crowd yelled out "Now that's what I call being sociable!"

Mom and Dad's Visit

My mom and dad came for a visit. Dad really loved Nebraska and kept raving about how blue the sky was. One evening we got a babysitter and took Mom and Dad to the NCO Club on base for dinner. We were having a good time and enjoying a drink before dinner when Dad excused himself and went to the men's room. He came out with the front of his suit pants all wet.

I laughed and asked if he had an accident. He said "No, wise guy. I was washing my hands and the water splashed out of the sink and got all over the front of my pants. In an effort to dry them, I turned the hand dryer on and was jumping up at it trying to get them dry. Some guy walked in and saw what I was doing. He shook his head, looked at me in disgust, and muttered something about different strokes for different folks."

The Toy

Johnny was about two and a half years old and had developed the habit of walking around with his hand down the front of his pants. We didn't pay much attention to it. Figured it was just a phase that little boys go through. Now if he is still doing it when he turned 18, we'd worry. But at this young age, it seemed harmless enough.

My dad noticed John's preoccupation with his hand down his pants and said, "Jack, you've got to buy that kid some toys!" My reply to Dad was, "I think he's found one!"

Dianna aka Miss Fixit!

Dianna is the sane member of this family. She is the rock, our organizer, and the captain of the ship. Dianna is a very loving and giving person, and she can fix anything that has ever been broken in this house. She has repaired the dishwasher, the washing machine, the dryer, and the water heater, put in a garbage disposal, rewired lamps, and put a ten-speed bike together on Christmas Eve. Dianna has torn down walls and gutted a closet to make a study area for our son. She has built bookcases and I am sure she could build a house if she had to. In fact, if God ever needs another ark, I am sure he'll call on Dianna for help. She even knows what a cubit is!

One Christmas, Dianna's mother sent Dianna a circular saw and sent me a clock with two matching sconces. I was puzzled when I opened my gift and even more puzzled when I saw what Dianna had gotten. I said, "Your mom must have mixed up the name tags. I'm sure she meant the saw for me and the clock for you."

Dianna called her mom, and no, there was no mix-up. The saw was indeed for Dianna, the clock was for me. I guess she figured that I could at least tell time. Do you have any idea how humbling it was to be married to a woman who could fix anything, when I could fix nothing! I especially hated it when the neighborhood guys would come over to the house and ask to borrow my wife's saw!

Friends

Bob, my carpool buddy and fellow illustrator, and I were driving home from work in a raging Nebraska snowstorm. The snow was coming down like crazy. I was driving my faithful VW bus, and we were doing fine. We started up a fairly steep hill, got halfway up, and the back wheels started spinning. I hit the gas and the wheels only spun faster. Bob suggested we back down the hill and try it again

going faster. I nixed the idea and said, "Bob, what we need is some weight over the back wheels."

Now picture this: Bob was a really heavy guy; you might have described him as plump or maybe even fat. I said, "Bob, would you mind going in the back and sitting over the rear axle?" He did mind and was highly insulted that I would even ask, but he went to the back of the bus, while muttering something about feeling like a sandbag. Sandbag or not, it worked.

Up the hill we went and made it home safe and sound. I have always said, "It pays to have BIG FRIENDS!"

One evening we had Bob and his wife, Peggy, over to play cards. They were a great couple. Life for them was good, except for the fact that they were not able to have children. After several years of trying, they decided to adopt. The evening was going great—we played cards, chit-chatted, and had lot of laughs. This accompanied by good food and a few beers had us all feeling pretty good. Suddenly Johnny, our son, started screaming from his crib. I went running into his room to check on him. I found he had emptied his "poopy" diaper and had smeared it all over the wall, the crib, and himself. Oh yuck! What a mess and what a smell!

I called Bob and Peggy in to see what these cute little darlings were actually all about. They both stood there, staring in disbelief. Bob looked at his wife and asked, "Are we sure we really want one of these?"

They eventually adopted two beautiful kids and lived happily ever after...poop and all!

A Special Thanksgiving!

My sister Kathy, her husband Rick, and their kids Ricky and Rhonda came to spend the Thanksgiving holidays. They were living in Springfield, Missouri, while Rick was going to Baptist Bible College.

We were just finishing up our big turkey dinner when Kathy and Dianna said, "Don't anybody move, we're going to have dessert."

They came back to the table with two gooey dark chocolate pies complete with layers of whipped cream. They said to Ricky and me "Are you sure you want some of this?" We replied, "Sure, it looks delicious!"

With that, we both got a face full of chocolate pie! I couldn't believe they did that. We were shocked, and so were the kids! Moms don't hit Dads in the face with pies on Thanksgiving!

What a mess! There was pie on the walls, on the floor, on the kids—it was everywhere. Dianna and Kathy were bent over with fits of giggles. I asked Dianna whatever possessed her to do that. "Are you crazy?" I asked. "How long have you been planning this?" Dianna said, "It just happened. We went to get the pies, looked at each other, winked, and just did it!" It was the craziest thing Dianna has ever done. You sort of expect things like this with Kathy, but Dianna? No way!

I was scheduled to work at the club that night so I jumped in the shower and got dressed for work. Later I was at the club waiting on some customers when a big chunk of pie fell out of my hair. I felt around and found several more chunks in there! I hate it when that happens!

Dianna Becomes a Skaggs Girl!

It was Dianna's turn to get a part-time job to help pay for Christmas. It was November, and she got a job at a big department store named Skaggs. They were gearing up for the Christmas rush and welcomed Dianna aboard. Skaggs was like Walmart before there was Walmart. All the girls that worked there were fondly called Skaggs girls. Dianna swallowed her pride and donned the uniform, making her an official Skaggs Girl! One Saturday, she called me to tell me she had to work late, then abruptly said, "Oh, I gotta go," and hung up. Later that evening she related this story.

Her boss came over to her while she was on the phone with me and asked her to do him a favor. He pointed in the direction of the snack bar, where there was a really big woman, probably weighing about 300 pounds, standing there. The hem

on the back of her dress was caught in the waistband of her panty hose and she didn't have any underwear on. She was exposing her very, very large bare butt!

Dianna approached her and quietly said, "Excuse me, but it seems as though the hem of your dress is caught in your panty hose." The lady said "Oh, thank you" and very nonchalantly pulled her dress down and continued to wait at the counter for her order of hot dog and fries!

Just a Good Story

A friend of mind owned a bar in LaVista. I stopped by for a quick beer one time and he related this story to me.

He was having a Halloween party at his bar and was getting in the spirit of things. He tended the bar while dressed as a frog. His costume consisted of a pair of green tights and swim fins.

About 2:30 AM, all the customers were gone and Tom was closing the bar. The waiters and waitresses decided to go out for breakfast. Tom slipped out of his swim fins, threw a trench coat on over his green tights and joined the gang for breakfast. After they got to the restaurant, Tom excused himself and went to the men's room. As Tom stood at the urinal, this guy next to him asked, "So, who do you think will win the big game on Saturday? Would you like to make a small wager? I'll give you Nebraska and 5 points."

Tom said, "I don't even know you. Why would I make a bet with you"?

The guy looked Tom up and down, spotted the green tights and said, "What are you, some kind of a queer?" Tom, without answering, pulled up his tights and left.

JACK RAYMOND

Life Slightly Off Center

Kathy and the Kids

Dianna was getting pretty close to her due date when my sister Kathy and her two kids, Ricky and Rhonda, came to live with us. We picked them up at the bus station in Omaha and they looked like three lost immigrants searching for a home. They were all rumpled and tired. They had been on a bus for two days traveling from Springfield, Missouri.

Kathy's husband had graduated from the Springfield Baptist Bible College and was heading up to Montana where he said he had the calling. He was going up to big-sky country to find a place to live and get settled and then he would send for Kathy and the kids. Kathy and her kids were always welcome at our house, but little did we know it would be a three-month visit! Kathy and Dianna are like sisters, so they got along really well. Kathy enrolled the kids in the same school that Sheri attended. Sheri loved having her cousins with us, and Kathy would be there to help Dianna with the new baby.

One day, about two days from projected blast-off, Dianna was having pains in her lower back and stomach, which she thought might be the beginning of labor. Kathy was all excited and started timing her pains. This went on all morning and most of the afternoon. Dianna would report when her pains started and Kathy would note the time and duration of the pain on the notepad she had attached to a clipboard she was carrying around. Finally Dianna said, "Kathy, I think I am just having gas pain." Kathy threw down the clipboard and pencil in complete disgust and said "If you think I'm going to sit around all day timing your farts, you're crazy!"

Turns out that Steven, our little "Fart," was born that evening! I'll get back to his birth later.

Our Cat Dixie

Sheri and I were home alone one evening. Our cat, Dixie, being in her usual state of pregnancy, went into labor about 7 PM. She had established her birthing quarters under Sheri's bed. I pulled the box out from under the bed and suggested that Sheri sit down on the floor and watch Dixie have her kittens. I thought watching birth first-hand would be a great experience for a little girl.

I was busy in the kitchen when the first kitten was born. Sheri called out, "Dad, this is so gross; do I have to watch this?" I yelled "Sheri, it isn't gross, it's beautiful!" "But Dad, Dixie is eating her kitten!" "Oh Sheri, she's not eating her kitten; she is cleaning it up." "No, Dad, she's eating it!"

I went to check, and sure enough Dixie was eating her first-born kitten! By the time I got there, the kitten's head was gone. The kitten was apparently born dead or deformed. I've since learned that it is instinctive for the mother to eat such a kitten. At this point, Sheri went screaming from the room!

Well, so much for the beautiful experience of birth!

JACK RAYMOND

167

Dixie proved to be a very fertile cat and gave us a new litter of kittens about every six months. It seemed back in those days our mission in life was to find homes for kittens. Patsy, a little girlfriend of Sheri's, came by our house to pick out a kitten from the litter. She said that her mom said she could have a kitten, but couldn't bring it home until school was out for the summer. Since there were only a few more weeks of school, we said we would keep the kitten until she could take her home.

Every day after school Patsy would come over to play with her kitten. She was just living for the day when she could take her home. The big day finally arrived. It was Saturday and Patsy was coming for her kitten.

Dianna was having a garage sale, and things were more hectic than usual around the house. I was running down the basement steps with John in my arms when I heard an awful squeal. It was the kitten. I had stepped on it and had broken its back! Oh boy, did I feel terrible. Sheri was right there, saw what had happened, and just stared at me like I was a cold-blooded kitten killer! I told her how sorry I was and asked her to please call her friend Patsy and explain what happen. "Ask her if she would like to pick out another kitten. Tell her we still have two left."

I really felt bad when I overheard Sheri on the phone explaining to her friend. "Hello Patsy. Hi, this is Sheri. My dad just killed your kitten. Would you like to come and pick out another one; we have two left!" We never saw Patsy again!

Boys Town

Boys Town was a big attraction in the Omaha area. It was a home for orphaned boys and was founded by Father Edward J. Flanagan. One sunny Sunday afternoon we decided to take a trip to see this attraction. Dianna, our kids, Kathy, her kids, our dog Giggles, and I headed out to see Boys Town.

We never went far without Giggles. The kids ran off to play on the playground, while we strolled across an open field. Dianna had Giggles on a leash, when all of a sudden Giggles took off after a bee, pulling Dianna behind. Dianna tripped and was being dragged on her big pregnant belly across the field. I was running after them, yelling for Dianna to let go of the leash! Giggles must have dragged her a good 20 yards. If she had had a football, she would have made a first down! Dianna at this point was eight months pregnant and was teetering on her belly. Kathy was on the ground, laughing like a fool at the sight of us. When everything was said and done, Dianna was fine except for the grass stains on her maternity blouse!

Steven's Birth

Well, back to our son Steven's birth. The months had come and gone very quickly and pretty soon we were in the hospital having another baby. We were hoping for a girl and a set of bunkbeds, but it wasn't to be. Steven Walter Raymond came into our lives on October 5, 1971.

I had forgotten all about the other Mrs. Raymond who was due at about the same time as my Mrs. Raymond. I forgot, that is, until the night our son Steven was born. When Sheri was born, she was bald and had very fair skin. John was born with blond peach fuzz and also fair skin. The doctor took me into the nursery to meet my new son and I naturally went over to a beautiful fair-haired baby,

Life Slightly Off Center

saying "Oh boy, he looks just like John!"

The doctor tapped me on the shoulder and said "Mr. Raymond, that is not your son; this is your son here." I looked where he was pointing, and there was a baby with olive skin and black hair running all the way down his back. I said "There is no way that he is my son. Our kids are born with fair skin and blond hair!" That's when I thought, *Oh boy, they mixed up the babies just like I was afraid they would.* It took the doctor half an hour to convince me that this little guy was actually our son!

Many years later, our niece Rhonda was visiting us from college. We were sitting around the dinner table, talking and joking around, when Rhonda, who was sitting next to me, asked "Is Steven adopted or something? He seems so different from the rest of you?"

Yes, Steven is a little quieter than the rest of us, but he is a great kid and has always been a source of pride for Dianna and me. We wouldn't trade him for the world, even if it turned out he was the wrong baby!

Kathy's Long Visit

In order for Kathy to justify her long stay at our house, she was going to take care of the night feedings when the baby arrived. Dianna loved the idea and said it would really help her out. It was Steven's first night at home, and he woke up crying for his bottle at about 2 AM.

Dianna of course woke up and laid there in bed waiting for Kathy to get up and feed him. Kathy never did wake up. The next morning Kathy was all excited that her precious little nephew had slept through the night without so much as a whimper! What a wonderful baby!

Kathy just went on and on about how lucky we were to have a baby sleep through the night. Dianna finally stopped her and explained that Steven did in fact wake up and "Since, you, my dear sister-in-law, slept through it, I got up and gave him his bottle!" Kathy felt terrible and said it would not happen again. She would sleep on the couch in the living room, which was closer to the nursery. That night, like clockwork, Steven woke up at 2 AM crying for his bottle. Again, Kathy slept through the whole thing. Kathy really felt bad the next morning and yet again promised she would take over the night shift from that day forward.

That night Kathy curled up on an air mattress next to Steven's crib. There would be no way she would sleep through his feeding. The baby woke up screaming, and poor Dianna had to get up, step over the sound-asleep Kathy, and feed Steven. Kathy finally admitted defeat and said that she would do all the washing and cleaning. And we all lived happily ever after!

Life Slightly Off Center

A Good Neighbor

One of the neighbors in our LaVista neighborhood was a single mom of two young boys. One was John's age and the other a baby. Her mother lived with her. They were from Italy. Marisa spoke some English and her mom spoke none. We got friendly with them, and before I knew it, I became the man of their house. Every time something needed fixing, moved or painted, I was the guy they would call. I didn't mind; I was glad to help out.

One day Marisa called and asked if I could come down and take the air conditioner out of her window and put it down in the garage for the winter. I said "Sure, I'll be right over." She showed me the bedroom where the air conditioner was and then she left. I opened the window and the air conditioner fell out, dropping three stories and busting on impact! It was destroyed! I walked out of the bedroom and announced, "Well, the air conditioner is out of the window, anything else you need while I'm here?"

That little incident cost me a new air conditioner. That's what you get for being a good neighbor!

A Night Out

One of our favorite places to spend a Saturday night when we could get away and had a little extra money was the NCO Club on base. The food was great, and they usually had pretty good dance bands. We were at the club with some friends one night, enjoying a couple of drinks before the entertainment started. This evening's show was a comedian who turned out to be a very funny guy. He was a little raunchy, but still funny. He started telling a joke about a guy who was a masturbator. I don't remember the punch line right now, but we were all laughing—all except for Dianna. Dianna was the most naïve married lady on the planet and there were a lot of words back then she had never heard of. *Masturbator* was one of those words.

She said "Jack, I don't get it...what is a masturbator?" Now all ears at our table are tuned in, waiting to hear how I would explain this to my innocent wife.

I said "Well, let's see, you know how a guy who gets his first job on a fishing boat and is in training to bait fish hooks is called an apprentice baiter. After he is there for awhile and masters the skill, then he is called a masturbator." Dianna smiled and said "Oh, ok, but I still don't get the joke."

Our friends at the table were in hysterics at my explanation, and this confused Dianna even more. We talked when we got home.

Another Part-Time Job!

As I said, we really enjoyed going to the NCO Club, so when it became my turn to get a Christmas job, I decided to get a job as a waiter at the club.

I never did that type of work before, but thought it might be a fun place to work. My first night on the job, I was briefed by the bartender and other waiters to watch out for the women. Some would try very hard to pick you up! That sounded interesting. With tray in hand, I went to take my first order. It was a nice-looking girl who said she wanted a "slow screw." I could feel my face go flush, and I said "excuse me?" She repeated it again, "a slow screw," and then winked at me. I went back to the bartender and said "Boy, you weren't kidding. My first customer wants a slow screw; can you believe that?!" He just rolled his eyes, took a bottle of sloe gin, mixed it with orange juice, added a touch of cherry juice, and handed me my "slow screw."

One night they had me working the dining room. I went up to a table of about six guys and they ordered six beers. Now beers back in the day came in really tall bottles. I had to run up a flight of stairs and down a hall to get to the cocktail lounge where the bar was. I put in the order, paid for it, ran back down the hall and down the steps, while balancing six beer bottles on my tray. I got right up to the table and tripped, and the beers went flying all over these guys. One beer was spinning on the table while beer exploded out of its neck! What a mess, they were all wet, the table was a wreck. I was trying to dry them off with napkins and they said, "Hey, we're fine, just go and get us six more beers!" So back up the stairs, down the hall, and into the cocktail lounge. I pay out of pocket for six more beers and run back to the dining room. I get back and the table is empty. I thought, *I'll be damned, they left, and now I am stuck with six more opened beers!* Then I heard one of them say, "Just put them down!" They were all up against the wall and were not about to come near the table until all the beers were in place. I said "Okay, guess there's no tip here, right?" They all answered in unison "RIGHT!" They were the first customers of my shift.

I was assigned not only to the dining room, but also to the "pit" in the cocktail lounge. I went running down the stairs to the pit and waited on a guy and a girl. Scotch for him and a 7 and 7 for her. I went running up the stairs, put in my order, paid for it, ran down the steps into the dimly lit pit, and went flying across her legs, which she had stretch out into the walkway. The drinks went flying, the glasses broke, and she jumped up and cut her foot! I got that all cleaned up, found her a band aid, and apologized profusely. I then got them two more drinks—on me, of course.

So I was on the clock maybe half an hour by this time and was out probably 20 bucks and still hadn't made a single tip!

My boss had been observing me. He came up to me, put his arm around my shoulder, and suggested I take the rest of the night off. I did, because I couldn't afford to work any longer.

I guess my worst night at the club was New Year's Eve. This was my big chance to make a lot of money. The other waiters and waitresses were telling me stories about how much money they had made in the past. It was the big night! It was the night everyone got drunk and spent money like water. Oh boy, I couldn't wait. We were busier than hell and the tips were really stacking up on my tray. I was feeling really great when all of a sudden I looked and the money on my tray was gone! I had either lost it, or someone had grabbed it when I was running by. In either case, it was gone, and so was most of the evening. I worked that night from 7 PM until about 3 AM and walked out with a grand total of $15 in tips. I am sure that must have set some sort of record for tips made on New Year's Eve.

This was the end my career as a waiter. I did have some nights when I was not a complete goofball and made some good money. It was a great experience and gave me a whole new respect for waiters and waitresses.

The Stripper

Like I said before, the illustrators I worked with were a nice bunch of guys, and we had some great times together. One of them was named Dick. He and I got to be pretty good friends. We made plans to get together on a particular Saturday and go to a car show.

I went by his place to pick him up. He lived in downtown Omaha, in a crappy little apartment. He was married, with twins. I got there, and he asked me to sit down at the kitchen table and have a cup of coffee with him. I could see into the bedroom from where I was sitting. He called to his wife, "Hey, honey, honey, wake up, I want you to meet Jack!" She sat up in bed, exposing her naked breast, waved hello, and went back to sleep. I was shocked and I guess Dick knew it from the look on my face. He very nonchalantly said, "Oh, don't let that bother you. My wife is a professional stripper and her being naked is no big deal." He said it like he was telling me his wife was a schoolteacher. I mean, if your wife is a stripper, isn't that sort of a big deal? Okay, so my new buddy's wife was a stripper and I guess I'd just deal with that. Certainly if Dick was okay with it, I guess I could be okay with it. He later explained that he met her in a strip club; they fell in love, got married, and had twin girls.

Ahhh, another beautiful love story! But she soon goes back to being a stripper! Hey, if he's okay with her occupation, who am I to judge. Dick asked me not to say anything to the other guys at work about this. I agreed not to say anything. We went to the car show and had a great day. I invited Dick and his family to our house for dinner.

I checked with Dianna when I got home, and we set a date. I didn't tell her the girl we would be entertaining was a stripper. I figured she was better off not knowing.

They arrived on a Saturday evening a week later. Dick's wife was dressed in the sexiest outfit ever, and Dianna was sort of put off by it. I mean her boobs were practically jumping out of her top! Her outfit was a halter top with tight, tight pants hugging her hips. The makeup was over the top—she really looked like a stripper. I couldn't take my eyes off of her! In my mind, I kept hearing "next show at ten!" Dianna was giving me dirty looks all evening.

Their twins were beautiful kids about three years old. We were all sitting at the

Life Slightly Off Center

table having dinner and the twins were not eating. She would say things like "Eat your peas or I'll tear your arm off and beat you with the bloody stump!" Dianna just about choked on her baked potato with that one!

All and all, I would rate it as a pretty uncomfortable evening. When they left, Dianna was all over me. "Where in the hell did you find those people?" That's when I broke down and told Dianna the whole story.

"She's a stripper! You brought a stripper into my house; are you crazy, have you lost your mind? Don't you ever, ever...." "Okay, okay already, I won't invite them over again. But you've got to admit Dick is a pretty good guy and the kids seemed really nice." Dianna just went off in a huff and we never discussed our stripper again.

One more story about Dick's wife and we'll move on. (It just sort of fascinates me. To think I almost had a stripper for a friend!). It was a day at the office. There are ten of us at our drawing tables. We were all working on different projects and as always shot breeze while we worked. The subject got around to strippers. Now, no one other than me knew that Dick's wife was a stripper. This one guy started spouting off about strippers being the lowest form of life, they are nothing but sluts and no good, and on and on he went. I looked over at Dick and his face was beet red, and I really felt sorry for him. I told the guy doing all the talking to pipe down. Not all strippers are bad people, I argued. They just may be victims of circumstances. Maybe they need to make some good money to take care of their families.

"Jack, you're a bleeding heart! Grow up. A stripper is a stripper and there is no excuse for it!" On and on, he went—there was no stopping him. That night, on the ride home with the big mouth, I told him that Dick's wife is a stripper! He said "Oh yeah, and my wife is a hooker!" "Bob, I'm telling you the truth. His wife is a stripper." It took me all the way home to convince him, and by the time he dropped me off, he was feeling as low as pond scum (his words) about what he had said. The word stripper was never uttered in our shop again!

The Minister Comes Calling!

It seemed like every time we made a move, we would promise ourselves that we would start going to church. We usually started visiting churches in the area to see if we could find one we liked. We never did. Sunday to us was a day to sleep late and just hang around and do nothing. Here in Nebraska, we had visited one church in the area and had filled out a visitor's card.

The next week, there appeared a preacher at the door wanting to visit. Dianna wasn't home. Johnny was taking a nap, and Sheri was thrilled to have a visitor. I had the minister sit down and went to get him a glass of iced tea. As I handed him the tea, Sheri pulled open the coffee-table drawer to get him a coaster, and there in the drawer was my current issue of *Playboy*! Sheri gave him the coaster and went running off, leaving the drawer open. It was like the magazine had come to life and neon lights were flashing from its cover.

He looked, I looked, and we looked at each other; I smiled, he smiled, and I closed the drawer. After a few seconds of silence, we carried on with our conversation.

I felt like a real letch and never did go to his church again. And he never paid us another visit.

Run Away with Your Wife!

Raising three kids is a tough job. Dianna never complained and did a great job! I saw an ad in the paper for a "Run away with your wife weekend!" It was only $33, which included a night in the hotel, dinner, dancing, and breakfast the next morning. I said "Let's do it!"

We were just giddy with anticipation. A whole night with no kids! We hired a babysitter, gave her a list—well, maybe more than a list—it was actually several pages of instructions on the care and handling of our children. Steven was maybe eight months old and we were concerned about leaving him.

We took off for our big night and had a great dinner. Then we danced and had some drinks. All of our conversations were about the kids. This was because that was all we talked about anymore.

We went to bed that night happy, but very concerned about the kids. We had called the babysitter and she assured us all was fine. We went to sleep knowing we would not be awakened in the middle of the night by a hungry, crying baby. We would be able to sleep late because there wouldn't be kids jumping in our bed. Ahh-hhhhh, it was going to be so nice. So perfect! We would sleep late, have a casual breakfast, and then wander home.

At 5 AM, I woke up with Dianna staring at me. I said "What's the matter?" She said "Are you ready to go home?" "What? What happened to sleeping late; what happened to breakfast?" I asked. We were out of that hotel by 6 AM and home before the kids or the babysitter even woke up!

Guess you can take Mom and Dad out of the house, but you can't take the house...No, that doesn't make any sense. Oh well, you probably know what I mean.

More Trouble!

One night Dianna and I were, as they say, in the throes of passion when my knee locked, and I screamed in pain! She said "Oh my God, are you okay? I didn't mean to hurt you!" I said, "No, no, it's my knee!" "Your knee, how did your knee get involved in this?"

The next morning I could not bend my knee. I told Dianna I was going to the hospital on base to have it checked out. She warned me not to tell the doctor what I was doing when it locked. I assured her our secret was safe with me, and they probably wouldn't believe me anyway.

I got to the hospital and was laid out on an examining table. The doctor came in and started trying to flex my leg and asked how my knee had locked? "What exactly were you doing when this happened?" he asked. My face turned a crimson red, as I explained the circumstances. He said, "You've got to be kidding. I think I'd like to meet your wife!" X-rays revealed a piece of chipped bone about the size of a dime lodged in the knee joint. I would need surgery to remove it. He then laughed and said "I hope it was worth it!"

I was in the hospital for a week. My only visitor was Dianna. I was bummed that none of the guys from the office came by to see how I was doing. I guess my buddies just didn't care.

On my last full day in the hospital, all the guys showed up! It was great to see them. We laughed and had a great visit. I told them that I was so glad they had decided to come. As they were getting ready to leave, Bob said "We had to; the boss insisted that we come and see you!"

Talk about feeling like a chump? So if the boss hadn't ordered them to visit me, they probably wouldn't have come—that always makes a guy feel good!

We Hit the Trail

Sheri, like most seven-year-old girls, loved horses. Dianna and I took her on her first horseback ride. We got to the stables, and Sheri was beside herself with excitement with all these horses within petting reach. The guide suggested we put Sheri on a pony. He gave Dianna a rather old-looking horse with a sway back, and he gave me Big Red! I mean, this was a big horse and very spirited.

I am not a horseback-riding kind of guy, and this horse was just too much horse for me. The guide kept telling me to show the horse who's the boss. I did, and we discovered that Big Red was the boss! We had no sooner hit the trail when Big Red, the boss, thought the hell with this nonsense, reared up, spun around, and headed directly back to the barn! He ran into the barn and pinned my leg up against the stall wall. The guide had to come to my rescue.

Dianna said "I think I can handle Big Red; how about we trade horses?" So now I have the swayback, and Dianna has the horse with all the spirit. She immediately showed him who was boss. I showed my horse who the boss was, too, but my horse didn't care. His main objective was to make it eventually back to the barn.

Life Slightly Off Center

I guess there were about ten or twelve people on this trail ride. Sheri had a smile on her face that just would not quit. She was so happy! Both Sheri and Dianna were naturals on horseback.

Something must have spooked Sheri's pony because, all of a sudden, it broke into a full gallop! Dianna yelled "I'll get her," and pulled back on Big Red's reins—he reared up on his hind legs and spun around, and at a full gallop Dianna chased after Sheri and the runaway pony! She overtook the pony and still at a dead run leaned over and grabbed the pony's reins! Dianna got the pony under control and led it quietly back to the group. Everyone applauded. Sheri looked up at her mother with complete adulation. She must have been thinking *My mom is the greatest*! The whole scene was like something out of a Western movie and Dianna was Dale Evans!

Bill and Reggie Come for a Visit

Billy and Reggie came to visit us in Nebraska. They drove out with their four kids in their station wagon. It was a long two-day drive from Rochester, New York. Upon arrival, they rushed into the house all excited about seeing baby Steven for the first time! All attention was focused on Steven. Poor Johnny was sort of pushed aside so everyone could get a good look at the new baby.

Johnny, whom we had been trying to potty train forever without any good results, marched himself into the bathroom without anyone noticing, pulled his pants down, took his diaper off, climbed onto the toilet and did his thing, and yelled very loudly so everyone could hear him, "I POOPED!" Johnny just sat there beaming, as we all crowded into the bathroom. Dianna, Sheri, Uncle Bill, Aunt Reggie, Billy, Mark, Michelle, Chris, and I all applauded this magnificent feat! Ole Johnny was not about to let his baby brother get away with all the attention.

We had a wonderful visit with Billy, Reggie, and the kids. We did a lot of sightseeing and kept pretty busy every day. We had an aboveground pool in the backyard so the kids were always in that.

One night we decided to go out on the town. We hired a babysitter and went into Omaha for dinner. After dinner, we decided to stop into a joint for a drink. We walked in and there on the stage was a really heavy woman doing a strip. She was making all kinds of gyrations and then we heard a single clap. We were sort of laughing and wondering who the hell was clapping. We soon discovered that no one was clapping, it was the stripper's thighs slapping together!! At that we decided to leave and find another bar.

We found a nice place and sat down. Bill got a beer, the girls ordered gin and tonics, and I ordered a Brandy Alexander. After the waiter left, Bill, visibly upset, said "You should never order that kind of a drink—that is a woman's drink!" I said "You're nuts. I order them all the time!" He said, "Please do me a favor, and don't order one when you're with me; it's embarrassing!" By now Reggie and Dianna are just rolling their eyes. Since I am not one to let things go, I said to Bill, "I'll bet you five bucks that men order them all the time!" He took the bet, and we walked up to the bar and I asked the bartender if he would help settle an argument between my brother and me. "Sure," he said, "If I can, I'd be glad to help." "My brother tells me that a Brandy Alexander is strictly a woman's drink. Is that true?" I asked. The bartender chuckled and said "No, that is not true at all. We have men come in here all the time and order that drink." Then he added, "But they are all hairdressers!" That was my last Brandy Alexander!

We were about a week into the vacation when Bill developed a cyst at the base of his spine. He was in complete agony. We took him to emergency room, and the doctor fixed him up as best he could. He told Bill that he'd just have to live with it until it went away on its own. He gave Bill some pills and sent him on his way. The rest of the time he spent with us, we kidded him about being a pain in the ass!

Dianna and I felt so sorry for him as Reggie loaded him into the back of the station wagon for the long, long ride home. He couldn't even sit up at this point. Reggie told us later that every time she hit a bump, he would cry out in agony. At their first night in a motel, Bill couldn't take it anymore and pulled the dressing out of the cyst crater—the pain was instantly gone. He was fine for the rest of the trip! Reggie told us that even with the pain gone, Billy was still a pain in her ass!

Time to Move On!

We were at the end of our third year in Nebraska and loving every minute of it. We would have been content to stay for another three years, but the good ole Air Force had different plans for us.

I got orders to ALASKA! Alaska of all places! Who would have thought we'd ever get orders to go to the far north. Nobody goes to Alaska! Driving home that night, I was really worried about Dianna's reaction to these orders. She had once said many years ago that she would follow me anyplace in the world, but don't ever ask her to go to Alaska. "I just could not stand that place. It's so cold and so dark, I'd go crazy!" Well, her reaction was pretty much what I expected...she cried and cried and said "I don't know if I can go with you. Do you think you could go unaccompanied and let us stay here until you're done?" I said "No way! We'll all go, and it will be an adventure! It will be a great experience for the kids." "But Jack, I'm from Mississippi, and Mississippi girls just don't do Alaska. It is just not in our nature to survive in a place like that. Please don't make me go," she pleaded. It took a week or so and lots of pictures of that great land to convince Dianna that it might be an alright assignment.

We were due to leave in December, which to my way of thinking wasn't a great time to introduce your Southern wife to Alaska. But December it was, and I went over to the travel section in personnel to pick up our airline tickets. We were to drive to Seattle, Washington, and have the car shipped from there to Anchorage. We would catch a plane from Seattle. I looked at the tickets; they read Seattle to Guam and then to Alaska. I asked the guy issuing the tickets if there was some sort of mistake. He said "No, the tickets are correct."

"Correct, are you crazy?" I asked. "Do you expect me to get on a plane with three small kids and fly all the way to Guam en route to Alaska?" I asked. "I refuse to do that and I will not accept these tickets. This is the craziest thing I've ever heard." I said. He got a little put out, and said, "I am afraid you don't have any choice." I said, "Oh, I have a choice and I choose not to take these tickets! When you can issue me some tickets from Seattle to Alaska, call me!"

Now I am not the kind of guy who raises hell, but, come on, that was ridiculous. Two days later, I got a call from the travel section, telling me to come over and pick up my new tickets. These were from Seattle to Anchorage and then onto Fairbanks. Now, that made sense.

My sponsor from the base in Alaska called me to brief me on what to expect. His first question was "What kind of car do you drive?" I told him we had a VW bus and he said, "The first thing you have to do is to get a new car because Volkswagens don't do well up here." To prepare for our trek north, we had to trade in our beloved bus. Sheri and Johnny were just broken-hearted when we turned it in. We called the bus the Jolly Green Giant and had an emotional attachment to it. It was like leaving an old friend behind.

I went out and bought a brand new Chevy Malibu. It was a great-looking car, but not for a family of five with a sheepdog who were being shipped to Alaska. I don't know what I was thinking. The interior was black cloth that always had a very visible layer of white dog hair all over it along with children's footprints. We took a trip in the new car to North Dakota to visit some friends. The car seemed so small after driving the bus for so long. The kids were right on top of us, and Giggles sat in the back seat, on my side, and leaned her head over the front on my shoulder, panting all the way to North Dakota and back! I hated that car! It was going to be a very, very long ride to Seattle.

Life Slightly Off Center

Our next big project was selling our house. This also brought tears to Sheri and John's eyes. I remember John and me sitting out in front of the house with the FOR SALE sign staring us in the face. John was maybe three years old and just did not understand what was going on. He asked "Dad, why can't we just live in our house? Why do we have to go away?" I kept telling Sheri and him how much fun we were going to have in Alaska, but neither of them was buying it. They were in Dianna's camp and wanted no part of this great experience we were about to embark on.

The icing on the cake for John was when we gave his swing set to our neighbor Marisa for her boys. I got him calmed down only when I told him his buddy John (Marisa's son) was going to watch the swing set while we were gone, and when we got back, he would give it back to us. Then everything was okay.

We sold the house pretty quickly and after everything was said and done, we came out with a $6,000 profit. That was enough to pay off all our bills and still stick some in the bank for a nest egg! This was our first nest egg! What a great feeling to be heading north completely debt free and even with some money in the bank.

It was early December when the movers came to pack us up. We sent Sheri off to school and planned on leaving after she got home. We figured everything would be packed by then and on its way to storage. We were allowed to ship only a limited amount of household goods. Once the house was completely empty and the movers were gone, we went across the street to our friend's house for a cup of coffee and to wait for Sheri to come home from school.

We got talking and didn't notice the time. I looked across the street, and there was Sheri, sitting on the steps of that empty house, crying. I ran across the street and said "Sheri, what is the matter?" I figured she was crying because she had to say goodbye to her friends. But that wasn't the reason for her tears. Through her sobs, she said "When I got home and found the house empty, I thought you had left with-out me!"

Once again, we were leaving all the friends we had made in this great neighbor-hood. The neighbors had a going-away party for us and gave us a beautiful plaque that was engraved with Neighbors of the Year along with all their names. It was very touching.

This time not only did we have to leave friends, but we also had to leave our dog, Giggles, behind. We wanted to get settled in Alaska before she joined us. Our neighborhood friends had agreed to keep her for as long as it took us to get settled.

We pulled out at about three in the afternoon. We were a very sad bunch. It was one of those dreary, cold Nebraska days. Disappearing in the rearview mirror was our house, waving neighbors, Giggles, and the life we had known for the past three years.

Our Trip East Before We Headed North

We found out about our assignment to Alaska in June 1972. We had planned a trip back east that summer that would give us a chance to see everyone before we left for our next three-year tour. We didn't tell anyone about Alaska because we wanted to surprise them. I made up a banner before we left that read Alaska or Bust!

After two days on the road and a multitude of fast-food dinners, I suggested we stop at a nice hotel and get a really good dinner at a nice restaurant. Dianna said the kids were too young to go to a fancy restaurant.

After many miles and much discussion, I got my way and we checked into a nice motel with a pool and adjoining restaurant. We got all cleaned up and found ourselves in a very expensive, swanky restaurant, sitting at a table overlooking the pool. "Oh yeah, this is nice!" I said. Dianna was still skeptical about the whole thing. All was going well; we ordered dinner, and while waiting for the food to arrive, Steven, who was about six months old, started screaming. Nothing we did would quiet him down.

Dianna gave me one of those looks that said *you are an idiot* and I knew this would not work. She picked up the baby and left in a huff. Over her shoulder, she said "Have my dinner sent to the room!"

Hmmm, maybe Dianna was right, at least as far as Steven was concerned. John and Sheri were behaving beautifully. We got through dinner without a hitch. After dinner, Johnny announced that he had to go potty so I took him to the bathroom. John at this time was three years old and just newly potty trained. In the bathroom I got him all situated on the toilet. I told him when he got finished to come and find me. I would be right outside the door on the couch in the dining room. I was thumbing through a magazine when I heard silverware dropping on plates and people gasping. I looked up only to see John backing out of the bathroom door with his pants around his ankles. He bent over when he got to me and asked "HOW IS THIS, DAD?" At home I always checked his little butt to make sure he had wiped well before he pulled up his pants. I jumped up, grabbed him, and quickly took him back into the bathroom. I got him cleaned up and then had

Life Slightly Off Center

to walk back through the dining room, knowing every eye was on us.

By this time I needed a cup of coffee. I ordered ice cream for the kids and a cup of coffee. I sat back and lit a cigarette and relaxed. I can't explain how it happened, but somehow I caught the sheer curtains behind me on fire with my cigarette! It was nothing big—more of a melted hole than a fire. I was able to pat it out before anyone noticed. Needless to say, we left the restaurant quickly and went back to our room.

Dianna asked "So how did it go?" I said "Fine, just fine. The kids were great!" It was several days and a lot of miles later before I told her what had happen. I humbly admitted she was right, we were all too young to go fancy restaurant. We enjoyed fast food for the rest of the trip!

When we got a few miles from my folks' house, I pulled over and attached the Alaska or Bust banner to the front of the bus. Within blocks of the house, we stopped at a red light and a guy in another car leaned out his window and said "You're going the wrong way!

We finally pulled into Mom and Dad's driveway with our Alaska or Bust sign across the front of the bus! Mom just cried. I think she was getting a little weary of being the mother and grandmother to a tribe of wandering gypsies!

CHAPTER 8

Alaska

Journey to Alaska!

The trip to Seattle was for the most part miserable. We left in early December and hit snow all the way to the West Coast. Nobody should have to go to Alaska in December. That is the kind of place you go to in the summer and sort of ease into the winter and darkness. My memory of the trip is sort of fuzzy.

The one thing that stands out more than anything is how sick Steven was. He was vomiting and had diarrhea all the way. I remember how bad the car smelled. Since it was so cold, we couldn't open the windows for a little relief. Poor Dianna spent the whole trip changing diapers and cleaning Steven up. When we went into restaurants, we had our pick of tables—people would give us a wide berth because of the smell we brought in with us. We stopped at some friends' house in Great Falls, Montana, and Dianna spent the whole time we were there washing Steven's clothes.

One night we were going through a mountain pass in Idaho when we ran into a blizzard. The car was slipping all over the road. I pulled onto the shoulder and put chains on the tires, which helped get us to the bottom. Dianna was a nervous

wreck, and I was pretty shaky myself. We stopped at the first motel we came to. The place was awful, but it was dry and warm and out of the storm. By the time we reached Seattle, Steven was even sicker. I picked him up and could not get over how light he was. I took him to the emergency room, while Dianna stayed with the kids at the motel.

After a thorough examination, the doctor told me Steven was severely dehydrated. They were able to get fluids into him for the next several hours. The poor little guy still was not well when we boarded the plane to Alaska that evening. So far, this was not a fun trip, and the thought of getting off the plane into the dark and below-zero temperatures with a sick baby was not too thrilling either.

We landed at midnight on December 10, 1972, and life was about to take some drastic changes! We were met at the Fairbanks Airport by our sponsor, Bill Walsh. He was dressed in a big parka with a wolf fur-trimmed hood and white arctic survival boots. We walked out to his car, and it was freezing. He casually mentioned that it was 30 below! He drove us down the highway leading to the base. Everything was white on white. I just shivered looking out of the car window. It was like being on another planet. The sky was black. Then all of a sudden the sky lit up with the Northern Lights! The lights are almost impossible to describe. They were the colors of yellow, white, pink, and blue and danced across the sky! It was a fantastic show and cheered us all up. The aurora borealis was our welcome to Alaska!

After a 26-mile trip from the airport down the Richardson Highway, we pulled into the main gate of Eielson Air Force Base. The guard shack at the entrance looked like a log cabin. We drove through the gate and past a mile or so of barren snow-covered land and then we started seeing two-story concrete white buildings along the road. The white buildings surrounded by the white snow added to the starkness of this place we were to call home.

We checked into guest housing and were assigned two rooms with a bathroom in between. Exhausted, we all fell into bed and into a deep sleep. We would worry about living in this strange place in the morning.

The next day we decided to explore the base. We went all over by foot since we didn't have our car yet. Our first purchase was a sled to pull the kids around. The day was still dark and still very cold, but we managed to get around okay. We went to housing and put our name on the list. We were told we would be notified as soon as a house became available. Then we went onto Sheri's new school to get her registered. We ate our meals for the most part at the club, since there were no cooking facilities in our room.

Sheri Goes to School

Day three: Dianna got Sheri all bundled up for her first day of school. I took her by the hand, and we walked out into the cold, dark, and foggy morning. Up in Alaska, they have what is called ice fog. It is so cold that the air crystallizes and forms fog. Along the way, we ran into a lot of big black Alaskan ravens. These are black birds the size of small chickens. They look totally miserable. They stand on one foot with the other tucked up under its belly, and then they switch feet, trying to keep warm. Their beaks are covered in frost. I'm thinking, as we were walking along, *They have wings; why spend the winter in this place; why not fly south?* I just mention the cold, the fog, and the ravens to give you a feel for this very strange land we have suddenly found ourselves in. We got to school, and all the kids seemed happy and well adjusted to life in this frozen wasteland, so I felt better. Maybe I was just overreacting.

We met Sheri's teacher and she seemed very nice. I think I half expected to meet a woman in a red plaid shirt with her hair in braids. Sheri was quite happy with her new school. Before I left, I told her I would be back after school to pick her up. I said "Do not for any reason leave this school until I get here, understand?"

I was back to the school at 3 PM, and it was about 35 below zero and very dark. I went to where I was to meet Sheri, but she was not there. I went into the school, and the teacher said she had left with the other children. I looked again and again no Sheri. I began to panic. This weather was no place for a little girl to wander around in. After a very thorough search of the school and area, I ran back to guest housing, thinking maybe she decided to walk back to our room. No, she wasn't there, and now Dianna was in a panic, too! I ran back to the school, which was now dark and empty. I ran around to the back of the school and there on the steps, shivering and crying, sat our little girl. We hugged like we had never hugged before! We were both so happy to see each other. Sheri had walked out of the back door of the school instead of the front door and just sat there waiting for me. Thank God, she was alright!

The Long, Long Car Trip!

We were in Alaska a few weeks when I was notified that our car, which had been shipped from Seattle, had arrived in Anchorage. I had to fly from Fairbanks to Anchorage to pick it up. I hooked up with some other Air Force guys, who had also been notified about their cars. We flew down together, picked up our cars, and caravaned back to Eielson.

It was January; it was snowing and very cold. The temperature was about 20 below zero. The road before us was covered with black ice, and the farther north we traveled, the worse the weather was. Being January in Alaska meant that it was dark all day long. We started our 350-mile trek early in the morning. We were all nervous, being greenhorns to driving in this extreme weather. These were the days before cell phones, so once we started, there would be no communication between us.

I called Dianna before leaving to tell her I was on my way and should be there in about 8 hours. She of course cautioned me to drive carefully. This always strikes me as a strange thing for people to say: Why wouldn't you drive carefully? Well, about 12 hours later and after some hair-raising close calls, I arrived. Dianna was sick with worry and never happier to see me. She was in tears and asked what had taken so long? She said she had been half crazy all day!

During the long, long trip alone with no radio, no tape player, no CD player, and only my crazy imagination to keep me company, I came up with this story. God help me, this is the story I told to my poor wife!

The guys I was traveling with and I got into our respective cars and promised to keep each other in sight for the entire trip. This way, if one of us had trouble, we would have help. We left together and headed north to Fairbanks. It was snowing and cold and the highway was covered in black ice. None of us ever got above 40 mph the whole trip. We were on the road an hour when we came to a road block across the highway.

A guard came out of this little shack and told me that I was about to go around a mountain. The road was very, very narrow and barely as wide a car. He said "Once you start, do not stop; I repeat, do not stop!" The road conditions were very dangerous and he again cautioned me not to stop once I started. I asked "If the road is only one lane wide, what if I meet a car coming in the opposite direction?" He said "Don't worry about that. I already radioed the guard on the other side of the moun-

Life Slightly Off Center

tain and told him you were on your way and not to let any vehicles through from his side." Needing a little encouragement I asked "How do you handle the drive around?" He then told me that he had worked this stretch of highway for the past ten years and has never even met the guard on the other side because he's too afraid to go around!

So I start, slowly, slowly, carefully, picking up a little speed, okay, now I'm going 20 mph. Fast enough, nice and steady, curve up ahead. It is so dark and snowing...oh boy, car starting to fishtail!

"Oh my God," says Dianna. "Oh my God, I would have died...then what did you do?"

I tapped the brakes ever so gently, slowed down some, but oh shit, the left back tire went off the edge of the road! I couldn't go anywhere! I turned off the engine and opened the door to get out. There was nothing but blackness. To step out would be to step into nothingness! There was no road, only a deep bottomless ravine! Then I figured I could get out the passenger door. The door opened only slightly. It hit the side of the mountain! I was stuck! The snow was getting heavier, the wind was howling. (Here was where I made the sound of howling wind.)

"And, and...what, oh my God," Dianna says, through her tears. "Oh thank God, you're safe. Then what did you do, oh Jack!" (Now she's hugging me.)

This was when I started laughing and told her I was just kidding. "Kidding, kidding? You stupid jackass!" She hit me good and hard with a book she had in her hand. She now screamed "You stupid ass, how can you do that to me? Oh my God, I'll never forgive you for this one! You've gone too far with your kidding," and on and on she went and gave me a few more raps with the book. I did go too far, and I really felt bad. At times, I just can't help myself, especially when it was going so well. I loved the reaction I got, and I was now thinking this story deserved repeating!

Back in the day, we used to correspond with my mom and dad by tape recorder. It was too expensive to use the telephone, so the recorder was our best bet. The next day, I repeated my story on tape. The special sound effects of me blowing into the mike to simulate the wind were just so great! It sounded really eerie. The tape was in the mail the next day and on its way to my poor unsuspecting parents. A week or so later, I received a phone call from them telling me I was a bad, bad son. The story had scared the hell out of them both. My dad said that halfway through the tape, Mother squeezed his hand and said "Oh my God, I pray our Jackie makes it!" Dad said he just looked at her and said, "Why you damned fool, of course, he made it; he made this tape, didn't he!"

If the old saying "What goes around, comes around" is true, then I will have hell to pay one of these days!

Moose Creek

After we had our car, things starting falling into place. We got an apartment off base in North Pole. It was the Moose Creek Complex. We took the only one they had available, which was a two-bedroom basement apartment. It was like the apartment in the TV show, *Laverne & Shirley*. All we saw was people's feet walking by the windows. Dianna would say, "What did I ever do to deserve this?" A girl from Mississippi, winding up in North Pole, Alaska, living in the Moose Creek apartments, just wasn't right.

We got our stuff shipped up and had it delivered, and Dianna did what she always does: She made this place look like home! It was two days before Christmas when we had our stuff delivered and in that shipment were all the kids' Christmas presents that Dianna had wisely bought and shipped before we left Nebraska. I went out into the surrounding woods and chopped down a scrub pine tree, and we had a wonderful Christmas that year. Granted, it was a bit sparse, but who noticed?

We were all adjusting to Alaska and beginning to enjoy it. Sheri was happy with her new school and was making new friends. I was happy with my new job and liked the crew I was working with. Dianna was okay with everything. We were especially happy that Steven was doing well after being so sick. Johnny was happy and raising hell, so life was pretty much back to normal.

One day Dianna had a bit of an emergency. She found Steven sitting next to an empty jar of turpentine from a paint-by-number kit. She couldn't get hold of me, so she called a taxi and believe me, getting a taxi in North Pole, Alaska, is not an easy thing to do. She rushed Steven to the base hospital where she was met by our new friend Maryann.

It was Maryann's assignment to take care of Johnny while Dianna dealt with the hospital situation. She still could not get ahold of me. The doctors had no way of knowing whether or not Steven had ingested the turpentine, so just to be safe, they decided to pump his stomach. Dianna finally got hold of me and told me to go pick up Johnny at Maryann's house and then come and get her at the hospital. Steven was okay—not to worry.

I went by to get John and found he had taken a very expensive carved-ivory rose from Maryann's collection and was running around the house with it. She had been trying to get it from him for the past hour! Every time she would get near, he'd take off in another direction. John thought this was a very fun game, and he loved all the attention. She was a wreck by the time I showed up. I was able to talk John into giving me the rose figurine, which, by the way, Maryann said was worth a few thousand dollars! Our new best friend in Alaska was now our new best nonfriend in Alaska. She never ever volunteered to take care of our kids again! Actually, after that one incident, we never saw her much at all.

After a few months living at Moose Creek, we were notified that a house on base was available for us! We moved the next week to a three-bedroom duplex on North Street. Not huge, but much better than our two-bedroom basement apartment. Sheri actually had a room she could do her homework in rather than the closet she had been using at Moose Creek. We all settled in, and this was to be home for the next three years.

The Hondas

For Dianna's birthday that year, I bought her a three-wheel, all-terrain motorcycle. It was perfect for cruising around in the woods. Why, you ask, would you buy your wife something that was perfect to cruise around in the woods? Well, I saw an ad for two three-wheeled Hondas for sale in the newspaper for $700. Such a great deal! One for me and one for Dianna! She was not thrilled. I *was* thrilled, and we had some great adventures on those vehicles. For Mother's Day, since I like to give gifts with some sort of theme in mind, I got Dianna a helmet to wear when she rode her Honda. I even had her name printed across the back. How's that for a thoughtful husband?! Again, Dianna was not thrilled. She is one hard woman to please!

Here is one incident when we were out riding up in the mountains around the base on our Hondas. Dianna had Steven on her bike, sitting on the gas tank in front of her. He was probably about two. I had Johnny riding on mine. We were going along just fine and enjoying the beautiful landscape. Then we came across a moose and her babies on either side of the road. Now the one thing you never do is get between a cow moose and her babies. If you do, she will charge you and do major damage!

Dianna spotted them first and she screamed "Jack, a, a, mo...mo...mo...mooooooose!!!!!" We were headed right between them—the mother moose on one side of the road and her fawns on the other. Dianna jacked that Honda up faster than she had ever dared and went flying by the moose. I couldn't believe it. I guess it was her motherly instinct coming out. I went flying around the other side, and we made it! That was probably the last time Dianna ever rode her Honda. She wanted no part of it. Women!!

I taught Sheri how to ride the Honda, and she loved going out with me. One day we were riding around the lake on base. I had Steven, who was still a baby, on my bike. Sheri was behind me and doing great. Suddenly this kid came running up to me and screamed "Sir, sir, your daughter just drove into the lake!" I went flying back, and there was the Honda with the wheels up and no Sheri. Then she popped up spitting and crying! She swam to shore and was freezing. I put her on the back of my Honda, and we raced for home. Dianna took her and Steven into the house, while I went back to get the other bike. It was in the middle of the lake

Life Slightly Off Center

by the time I got back, wheels up. People were running from base housing to see what was going on. Someone had alerted everyone that a moose was crossing the lake! It wasn't a moose; it was my bike. I was able to get it out of the lake and home again. Dianna refused to ride her Honda ever again and would not permit Sheri to take it out.

So there it sat in the backyard. It eventually became a parts bike for mine. Every time I needed a part, I would simply take it off of her bike. Dianna's Honda soon looked like a skeleton on blocks.

Our next big purchase was a Chevy Blazer with four-wheel drive. Our little Chevy Malibu just was not made for the wilds of Alaska. And so began my collection of Alaskan toys!

Becoming One of the Boys

All the guys I worked with were big hunters and fishermen. I soon found out, if you don't hunt and fish, you are the odd man out. All conversations centered on these two subjects. I had never hunted and hadn't fished since I went deep-sea fishing in Florida. Dennis, a guy from the office, took me under his wing and planned to show me all the joys of hunting and fishing. He started out by helping me buy the right equipment to get the job done.

My first purchase was a high-powered rifle, with enough power to take down moose or caribou. Then I needed a pistol, just in case of what I didn't know, but I figured I'd better get one because Dennis said I needed one. If you get a pistol, you have to have a holster to carry it in. If you have a rifle, you have to have a bag to store it in.

Of course, I needed some really good fishing equipment. When you fish in Alaska, you need the best because the fish are the biggest. Top-of-the-line rod and reel, a net, and, of course, a fishing box are musts. By the time I left the Base Exchange, I was broke and wondering how I was going to explain all this stuff to Dianna. I guess I could justify it by telling her how much money we were going to save because I'd be bringing home the meat and fish from my fishing and hunting expeditions. Guess what? She didn't buy it!

Oh, I forgot, if you have a rifle, you have to have a gun rack for your vehicle, especially if you have a Blazer. I, as they say in Alaska, was all set for the big hunt!

The first order of business was to get the rifle sighted in. One Sunday Dianna, the kids, and I headed out to Birch Lake to do some target practice and a little fishing. The road to the lake was really rough. We were being followed by our friends Ben and Joni. They told us this story after we arrived at the lake. Ben said that, at one point, he looked over at Joni and asked "Do you have a bra on?" She replied "I did when we started!" That is a pretty good indication of just how rough road this road was.

On our way out, we spotted a lady hoeing in her garden with a black bear sitting behind her. I pulled over so the kids could get a good look at the "pet bear." It looked like an Alaskan postcard—a woman out in front of her log cabin, hoeing her garden with her pet black bear. Then the woman spotted the bear, screamed, threw the hoe in the air, and ran for her cabin with the bear in hot pursuit! Dianna yelled for me to get my gun! The gun was in the trunk, the bullets in the glove compartment, and the clip packed away with the picnic lunch. It is a good thing that the woman was quick and wasn't depending on me to come to the rescue. She made it to the cabin, in the door, and slammed it shut! Unfortunately, her little dog, a cocker spaniel, wasn't so lucky. The bear spotted it and went after him. The poor dog ran like crazy, the spit flying out his mouth when he ran past out car yelping and crying! The bear chased him for a bit, then lost interest, and wandered to the

Life Slightly Off Center

trailer next door where he rummaged through the garbage can and found himself a pizza. He sat down on his haunches, held the pizza with his front paws, and just ate away! Another Alaskan postcard!

We finally arrived at the lake. We ate our lunch, and then Dianna, Sheri, John, Steven, and I set out to find a good place to target practice. Steven was in the pack on Dianna's back. I, being the man, carried the gun, Dianna carried the baby. I set up some cans. Got the kids back a safe distance and began to shoot. First shot… miss…second shot miss…third shot…miss…fourth…miss…fifth…miss, miss, miss. I finally gave up and said the rifle was apparently defective. Dianna asked if she could try it. I said "Sure, but you'll just be wasting ammunition." So there she stood, rifle up in position, red flannel shirt, baby on her back. Yet another Alaskan postcard. First shot…bing! Can went flying. Second shot hit, third shot, bing! Another can went flying. Fourth, fifth, and sixth shots, all hits! I carried the baby back, Dianna carried the rifle. I sulked the rest of the afternoon with Dianna trying to convince me she was just lucky!

Moose Hunt!

September rolled around and along with it came moose hunting season. This is what Dennis along with 95 percent of all Alaskans had been waiting for. This was to be my introduction to big game hunting. Dennis and I headed out early one morning to bag a bull moose. We wound up on the edge of a pond that Dennis was familiar with. He posted me on the point and said for me to watch from there, while he circled around the pond. He was gone, it was very quiet, and I was very relaxed, feeling confident I wouldn't see a moose.

Then this moose just stepped out of the woods and stood within 10 feet of and stared at me. If you've never seen a moose before, you would be as astonished as I was at how big they are. We're talking the size of a Clydesdale horse without the Budweiser! Oh boy, where is Dennis? Do I shoot? No, I can't shoot. It's bull season and this is a cow. It is illegal to shoot a cow, even a big threatening cow!

I took one step back and she took one step forward. I took two steps back and

she took two steps forward. All the time we are staring into each other's eyes. My knees were shaking and I was thinking to myself, *Maybe I should have started my hunting career with smaller game, like maybe rabbits or squirrels.* My mind was racing. I remembered hearing that cow moose are very protective of their calves and will charge anyone that gets between them and their babies. *Oh boy, I sure hope she doesn't have a calf behind me!* It was so quiet and I was standing so still except for my knocking knees that a mouse runs across the toe of my boot!

We, my moose and I, had been at this stare-down for about half an hour now, and I figured it was time to do something. There was a small creek between us. I figured if I took two more steps backward, and she took two more steps forward, that will put her at the edge of the creek and she will probably stop there. Wrong...I went step, step, she went step, step and slosh, slosh, and she was now on my side of the creek! We were both still in constant eye contact. I finally cracked and yelled "DENNIS!!!! HELP!!!" At that the moose bolted into the woods. Dennis had been watching the whole time and was now doubled over, laughing hysterically!

Life Slightly Off Center

Happy Campers

It was our first summer in Alaska, and we were still considered newcomers. We were ready to experience everything Alaska had to offer. Our newfound Alaskan friends suggested we all go camping for the weekend up at Quartz Lake. Wanting desperately to fit in, we readily agreed. We had never camped in our lives so we had to go to the Base Exchange and get some camping equipment.

We started with a tent, then sleeping bags, camp stove, pots, cooking utensils, and a lantern. We spent about $500 in the space of an hour and left there ready to conquer the wilderness. Between the Blazer buy, the three-wheel Honda buys, my big gun purchase, and now this, our little nest egg from selling the house back in Nebraska was rapidly disappearing.

The weekend came and we all headed for the lake. It was a beautiful lake surrounded by pines. The water was cold and clear. Not a good swimming lake, but ideal for some serious fishing. We got our tent up with a little help from our experienced camper friends. They laughed when they spotted our brand new lantern: Why in the world would you guys buy a lantern, when it stays daylight all night here in the summer?

Good question; guess it comes from being novices to this sport. We all enjoyed a day around the camp fire. We managed to cook a meal on our new camp stove, and the kids were having a good time playing with the other kids in our group. It was a little cold during the day, and then that evening it started raining. It was felt good to crawl into our sleeping bags that night. The wind picked up and the rain got heavier. It was sort of pleasant hearing it pelting the roof of the tent. The pitter patter actually lulled us all to sleep. Sleeping outside was kind of fun until you rolled over onto a rock or the root of a tree!

Steven woke up crying a few times, scared by the now howling wind. It was actually a pretty fitful night. I woke up at one point to find Dianna holding up the center pole. I said "What are you doing?" She said the tent had already blown down twice while the kids and I slept through it. She was holding the pole to keep it from blowing down again. We got through the night and woke up to a downpour. You could actually feel streams of water running under the floor of the tent.

Dennis came by our tent and asked if I was ready to go fishing. He said "Fish

JACK RAYMOND

bite best when it is raining." Dianna told me to go ahead; they would be fine here. Well, we fished all day, and all day it rained.

We got a bunch of lake trout and took them back to camp to show our catch off to the wives. Believe me, they were not impressed. We all spent another miserable night in the tent, and that is when we decided that camping was not going to be our favorite Alaskan sport. We did try it several more times, and each time was worse than the time before.

We finally gave up and had a giant garage sale to sell all of our camping equipment. Not only did we not make money, but the guy who bought most everything we had also brought his measles-infested kids with him and our three kids wound up with the measles, too. The only thing left was the lantern. Seems like no one needed a camping lantern in the land of the midnight sun!

Life Slightly Off Center

Alaskan Weather

Time continued at a fast pace. The kids were growing up fast, and we had come to think of Alaska as home. In Alaska, you deal with about nine months of extreme cold, snow, and darkness. The summer brings huge mosquitoes, flies, gnats, and lots of rainy days.

To better understand our environment there, I will give you an idea of the weather systems in that part of the world. December 21st is the shortest day of the year. It gets light at about 11 AM and is dark again by 1 PM. When I say light, it is just a gray eerie light caused by the sun barely rising above the horizon. From that day forward, each day gains 6 or 7 minutes of daylight. These gains bring us to June 21st, which is the longest day of the year. This is caused by the fact that the sun never goes below the horizon. The light and dark seasons move into each other very gradually.

Summer in Alaska is very short, about two months. The highest the temperature got while we were there was 90 degrees. The record high in the Fairbanks area was 99 degrees. These temps are very rare. A normal summer day is usually around 70 degrees. It generally starts snowing in the hills around Fairbanks in September, and there is snow on the ground until Easter. The winter temps can go as low as 60 degrees below zero. A usual winter day is about 20 below.

I spent many mornings walking to work in the winter because my car would not start. I would walk about ten blocks. On an average 20-degree-below morning, my moustache would frost over, along with my eyebrows, and my eyelashes would freeze together. I would actually have to pull them apart several times as I walked along. The snow was very dry and it squeaked as you walked through it. More than once I wondered what in the hell was I doing there, as I walked along. There were many weekends in Alaska when it was just too cold to go outside. This meant we were stuck in the house. I can remember sitting around the breakfast table and all of us chanting "Another boring day on the island of PEGIE PEGIE!" On an especially cold day, say minus 60, we would do the old coffee trick. This entailed taking a cup of hot coffee and throwing it out the backdoor. It would turn to steam before it ever hit the ground!

The fun just never stopped! And they wonder why we stayed for seven years! When you describe Alaska to people, they find it hard to understand why we loved it. It was the great friends we made. In Alaska, very few people have family there, and your friends become your family. These are friends for life! Another thing you fall in love with is the beauty of Alaska. It just takes your breath away.

Our assignment was for 36 months. When it came time for us to decide if we were ready to leave, Dianna said maybe one more year, and then she would be ready to leave. I was all for that. The kids were doing great, so we stayed.

The Great White Hunter!

I was out washing the Blazer one day when a new neighbor walked over to say hello. We got to shooting the breeze. The conversation quickly turned to hunting and fishing. Since Mike was new to Alaska, he was anxious to get into the swing of things and was looking for someone to show him the ropes. I guess seeing me wash my four-wheel macho rig equipped with a gun rack, he figured I was one of those great white hunters he had heard about. Being the kind of guy I am, I let him believe it. I said "Oh yeah, sure, I hunt. Sure, whenever you get yourself a rifle, Mike, let me know and I'll take you out with me. While you're out shopping for a rifle, you had better get yourself a pistol, just in case."

Little did Mike know the only thing I had ever shot was a rabbit and that was at point-blank range. Two days later Mike was at my door with his brand new rifle and his new pistol, saying he was ready to try his luck. I swallowed hard and still being the kind of guy I am, we arranged to go hunting that Saturday.

We were on the road by 6 AM, heading for the hills in pursuit of caribou or moose—I wasn't quite sure which. It was a perfect case of the blind leading the blind. The only difference was that one guy didn't know the other guy was blind.

We drove to a place where I was told we might just spot caribou. We hunted for hours and didn't see anything. Being cold and hungry, we decided to pack it in and head home. Driving back, we crossed a small wooden bridge over a small creek.

Mike yelled "Jack, I think those are bear tracks! Let's stop and see if we can spot it," Mike said very excitedly. After all my big talk all day, what was I going to say? I'm afraid of bears? No, I was going to play this to the finish. I will continue to

Life Slightly Off Center

be the great white hunter for at least the rest of this day. I pulled down, around, and under the bridge. We got out, and after a closer inspection of the tracks, yes, by God, they *were* bear tracks. At Mike's insistence, I went first, since I was the experienced hunter. We walked about a mile and the tracks were getting fresher and fresher and I was getting paler and paler and Mike was just giddy with excitement. I suggested maybe we should turn back since it was starting to get dark. Mike, by this time, was so confident being in the company of such a seasoned hunter that he wanted to continue. Rather than let him know I was getting weak in the knees, we marched on. I heard a noise in the brush, reached up to take the safety off my rifle, and discovered my clip was missing. For all you nonhunters, your clip is the thing that holds the bullets that go bang, bang and scare off bears. I said "Mike, you better take the lead. "No, Jack, you go ahead, you're doing great." "No, Mike, you don't understand. I don't have my clip; I think I left it back in the truck, so you go ahead and take the lead." At this point, the overconfident Mike said, "Oh the hell with this bear; let's leave the poor son-of-a-bitch alone!" With that, Mike took off running back to the truck with me in close pursuit. That was the last time that Mike asked me to take him hunting.

The Southern Bell!

It was early spring and there it was, sitting on the "FOR SALE" lot on the base: the ski boat I had always wanted. Sure it was a little worn, and maybe a little old, but all it needed was some tender loving care. It needed me! I took Dianna by to see it and she thought I had gone off my rocker. "Jack, a water-ski boat in Alaska? Think about it: No one has a ski boat in Alaska," she said. Every argument I came up with failed to convince her of the good times we could have with this boat. It didn't help that it was snowing while we were looking at the boat. Her final words on the subject: "Jack, please do not, I repeat, do not buy this boat!" Well, me being who I am could not stop thinking about it and went ahead and bought it without her knowing. I just figured she would thank me someday.

I couldn't bring it home, so I took it to the base hobby shop and began working on it. I was always making up some lame excuse to get out of the house and go to the hobby shop. I even had my buddy Ben paint the name "Southern Bell" on the side of my now beautiful boat. The name on the boat was to soften the blow when my Southern Belle found out what I had done. I was ready to launch the boat and arranged for Dianna and the kids to meet me at a lake on the base. That is where Dianna would see it for the first time, bobbing in the water in all its glory. She arrived with a picnic lunch and the kids, and we sat at a table and were enjoying the day when she spotted the boat. She looked at it, looked at me, and simply said "You spell Bell with an 'e'" when referring to a Southern Belle. You jerk! I can't believe

Life Slightly Off Center

you bought that boat. What were you thinking?" I told her it would be great to have when her sister Betty and her husband Joe came up this summer. "I mean they are going to be so impressed and we'll have so much fun with it!" The kids were jumping with joy that we had a new boat and I was the greatest dad ever! Dianna finally gave up and was resigned to the fact that we were now boat owners.

Betty and Joe and their kids showed up in July. We planned on going to Birch Lake where we had rented a cabin for the week. Dianna, Betty, and the kids went ahead to the cabin while Joe and I went to the launch area at the far end of the lake to put the boat in the water. All went smoothly and we got the boat launched. I tied it to the dock and asked Joe how he liked the boat. Joe said "It looks great, but it seems to sit really low in the water." I explained that it was loaded down with supplies. But it continued to get lower in the water and that is when I discovered the plug in my pants pocket! My boat was sinking! We pulled it back out with the trailer and let it drain. I put the plug in and launched it again. I jumped in and rowed it out past the lily pads and went to start the engine...no keys..."Joe," I yelled, "I forgot the keys. I think they may be in the glove compartment?" They were, and I had to row back in so he could throw me the keys when I got close enough. I rowed back out, and now I was all set.

I was going to get this baby going, and we were going to have a great vacation! But now the engine wouldn't start. I checked everything and nothing worked. A guy came by in a little fishing boat and asked if I needed a tow. He towed me to our lakeside cabin. As I looked back, I saw Joe climbing in the Blazer, shaking his head. I guess he wasn't so impressed.

The boat remained tied up out in front of the cabin for the entire week, and I never did get it started. I was ribbed all week by Dianna about my great purchase. "Oh yeah, Jack just had to have that damned boat. I got to hand it to you, Jack, it sure does look pretty bobbing out there in the water!" she chided. Then she would ask Betty and Joe "if they were impressed with Jack's boat?"

I had the boat towed to the launch ramp at the end of our week. Brought it home and after some major repairs and more money, it was running like a dream.

Water Skiing

Dianna, the kids, and I took off to the lake for a picnic with our good friends, Bob and Jan. We were going to teach the kids how to water ski. Water skiing in Alaska is not a common thing. It is almost an oxymoron. The water never gets much warmer than 50 degrees, so even swimming is rare. Sheri, Bob, and Jan's son Roger were eager to try. We got Sheri in skis and were ready to take off when this woman came along the beach and asked if she could have a ride in the boat. I said, "Sure, come aboard." We took off and Sheri got up on the skis on her first try.

We were buzzing around the lake, and this woman was cheering for Sheri. I figured out by then that our passenger was just a little crazy—probably due to too many winters in Alaska. I'd slow the boat down so that Sheri would sink and then gun it and she would come back up and go skimming across the water. I couldn't trip her up. She was a natural on skis.

Every time I slowed the boat down, this woman would start slapping me on the arm and say, "Don't do that, you'll make her fall." We had a good round of skiing and brought Sheri in. The woman jumped out of the boat and ran up to a guy in a rowboat and asked if she could have a ride in his boat. Crazy!

The boating season was short, so we took full advantage of it enjoying our Southern Belle. My friends and I used it often to go fishing. All in all, while Dianna wouldn't agree, I would say it was a good investment!

Life Slightly Off Center

A Convertible?

I guess the craziest thing I ever bought in Alaska was a Volkswagen convertible. Now there are not a lot of ski boats in Alaska, but there are even fewer convertibles. Who knows what I was thinking other than I had to have it. Again, I bought it with Dianna protesting the whole time.

We did enjoy it for two months out of the year. At times in the summer it was almost too cold to have the top down. I loved the top down so I'd drive around with the kids on the floor out of the wind and the heat blasting. Tour buses would go by us and honk their horn, and the tourists would wave at the crazy people in the little yellow convertible! In the winter, we parked it in the front yard, where it was completely buried by the snow until spring. People would come by to take pictures of this oddity.

If you are keeping track, we now have a four-wheel-drive Blazer, a ski boat, two three-wheel Hondas, guns, fishing equipment, and a yellow VW convertible—and no nest egg! But we were having a great time!

Did I say we? Well, at least one of us was having a good time!

Moose Eye!

It was a daily routine for me and the guys I worked with to go to the chow hall for lunch. It was within walking distance of the office. We plowed through the snow to enjoy the great food. Each day of the week offered a different menu. Our favorite was Wednesdays when it was Mexican Day! I was eating my fried rice when I hit something solid with my fork. I cleared the rice away to discover an eyeball staring back at me! I jumped out of my chair and had a holy fit! I was ranting and raving about an eye in my rice! I was going to take it back to show the cook. We didn't have to eat this crap!

My buddies were all laughing and told me to calm down, that it was just a joke. The eye was merely a rubber ball. It looked so realistic with raised veins and such detail. I just had to take this eyeball home and play a trick on someone at some time. When I got home that evening, I noticed the guy next door had shot a moose and had it hanging on his front porch.

Sheri hated all wild game and refused to eat anything that was not bought at the commissary. She would even go through the trash to make sure there was a plastic meat wrapper in there, proof that it was store-bought, before she would eat the meat Dianna had prepared for dinner.

We were sitting around the dinner table when I said something about the moose hanging up on the neighbor's porch. Sheri said "Oh, that is so gross!" I said to Dianna, "I heard that the best parts of a moose are the eyes. Why don't you ask the neighbor if they would give us one to try?" "Oh Dad, stop, we don't need a moose eye; that is gross, gross, gross!" Sheri groaned. I then asked, "Sheri, could you run upstairs and get my wallet off the dresser?" "Sure Dad," she replied and up she went.

Dianna was serving dinner, and we all had meat loaf and mashed potatoes on our plates. I took the rubber eye out of my pocket, showed it to Dianna, winked, and put it into Sheri's potatoes, added more potatoes, and put gravy on top of it. Oh boy, this was gonna be good! Sheri came back, gave me my wallet, and then sat down to eat.

All was going along as usual. Sheri was telling us about her day at school as she ate and then it happened...she hit the eye, uncovered it, saw this eyeball staring back at her, and let out the most blood-curdling scream I have ever heard. She jumped up, and because she had been sitting up against the wall and was pinned in on either side by her brothers, she turned around and ran in place while she pounded on the wall. We got her calmed down, and we all had a good laugh. Sheri didn't think it was very funny. Looking back, it was a dirty trick and maybe one of the reasons that Sheri is a vegetarian today!

Staying in Alaska

Our year's extension was up way too fast, and I asked Dianna again if she was up for another year in Alaska. She said she could take another year, if it wasn't for the tiny little kitchen in our housing unit. This kitchen just drove her nuts. So I guess you think we had better move on then. She said "Unless you can get me a new kitchen, yes, let's get out of here." I went to base housing to see if we qualified for a bigger house. I had been promoted twice since we had been there, and the kids were getting older. These were factors that determined what type of housing a person is qualified for.

Hooray! We did qualify for a four-bedroom house because the kids were old enough to each have their own room. The new house was huge with a good-size kitchen and we could have it within four months. I went rushing home to Dianna to tell her the good news. "Surprise!" I yelled. "I got you a new kitchen and now we can stay another year here in Alaska! " We moved into our new house and stayed yet another year!

The new house had two bedrooms upstairs and two downstairs. Our plan was to put Sheri and John in the downstairs bedrooms and put Steven upstairs in the bedroom next to ours. Sheri was now about twelve, John seven, and Steven four years old. Steven and John had always been in the same room, and we were a little apprehensive about separating them. We figured Steven would be really unhappy not having his brother with him. After the first week of finding John in bed with Steven, we decided it was not a good idea to separate them. I would ask John, "Why are you in Steven's bed?" "Oh, Steven got scared and I came up to keep him company so he wouldn't be afraid!" he replied. Actually, John was the one who was afraid. I said to John "Since Steven is so afraid to sleep by himself, why don't we turn your room into a playroom and move your bed upstairs so you can be with Steven?" John thought that was a great idea!

Sheri loved being downstairs. She had her own bathroom and access to the front door without having to go by us for her early morning checkup. We had to make sure she was properly dressed. By properly, we were talking long underwear, stocking cap, scarf, heavy coat, and snow pants. She hated all this gear and especially the long underwear. If she could get out the door without the morning inspection, she was happy. She was especially happy not to have to pull a stocking cap over her Farrah Fawcett hairdo. Looking cool was more important than being warm.

One morning it was about 40 below and Sheri had made it out the door unchecked. I went out to start the car; it groaned and then died. Living in Alaska, you learn to make do; in this case, making do was walking to work. I hadn't gone far when a guy pulled up and offered me a ride. I jumped in and thanked him. As we drove along, I spotted Sheri up ahead of us. No hat, no ear muffs, no ski mask, but her hair sure looked great! She had her parka on, but no slacks—only very red legs extending from her very short skirt. She had her books in one hand and her trumpet in the other. She was the picture of coolness! The guy driving also spotted her and said to me, "Boy, oh boy, just look at that kid! What kind of parents do you think she has?" I said, "That's my daughter!" He swallowed hard and said, "Boy, she must be one tough kid!"

Life Slightly Off Center

LA Rams Obsession

John was football fanatic from a very early age. When I would put him to bed, his story of choice would be for me to read out of a book of football statistics. He would fall asleep with me reading about a player and all his stats.

His team was the Los Angeles Rams. In Alaska the football games came on about 7 AM because of the time difference. I would wake up Sunday mornings and find John sitting in the big overstuffed chair with his arm around a sleeping Steven staring at the TV test pattern waiting for the game to start. He would always say, "me and Steven are waiting for the game to start." John was about six years old and Steven was three years old at this time.

Getting him to go to Sunday school during football season was impossible. I convinced Dianna we were doing more harm than good by forcing him to church. He would go willingly in the off-season. I wrote a note to his Sunday School teacher, explaining why she wouldn't be seeing John for a few months.

John was such a character. He would dress up in his Rams gear if the Rams were playing. He had his helmet, shoulder pads, jersey, pants, socks, and even a rain slicker. He sat there in full gear. Every time the Rams screwed up or got scored on, an article of gear would go flying across the room! The Rams were traditionally a bad team and racked up plenty of losses. John, by the end of most Rams games, was sitting there in his underwear!

I've got to hand it to John—he never did give up on the Rams. The players on the Rams team were his heroes. In fact, any football player was a man to be looked up to. Me, being an illustrator, didn't score too many points with John.

An example of this happened one day while John and I were driving around in the Blazer. John was standing between the two front seats with his arm around my shoulder. I guess maybe he was about seven years old at the time. He was all excited about the Rams having open tryouts. "Dad, anyone can try out. Why don't you go down to California and just try?" I said "John, I can't try out for professional football. You have to have some experience. I have maybe one season in high school, and that's it." "But, Dad, you could at least try. Dad, it can't hurt to try. Come on, Dad, please?" I said "No, John, I am not going to try out for the Rams, and that's that." He looked at me, patted me on the shoulder, and said very seriously "Dad, you can't color the rest of your life!"

Both of our boys felt that being a pro athlete was the only profession in the world that was worth aspiring to. Having an illustrator for a father was not something you bragged to your friends about. I guess maybe it bothered me somewhat. You always want your kids to look up to you and admire your chosen career. One day I was sitting at my drawing table when Steven came up and was watching me draw. He said "Dad, that is really neat! I think I want to be an artist when I grow up." "You do? That's great!" I was feeling pretty good—finally, I was getting a little respect for my craft. Then Steven added "Yeah, I think I wanna be an artist, or maybe a butcher!"

Life Slightly Off Center

Jack, the Artist!

Being an artist in Alaska paid off pretty well for me. I got into a few money-making projects that help me rebuild that nest egg that I had so foolishly spent. The first thing I got into was wood-block prints. Ben, a friend, and I got into this and made a few bucks.

This is what we did: You take a piece of pine board about 10 inches by 18 inches by 1 inch and carve a drawing into it; then you ink it up, lay a piece of rice paper on the wet ink, and roll the back of the paper with hard roller. Presto! You have a wood-block print.

We specialized in Alaskan scenes, and they sold like crazy. My most popular one was an Eskimo blanket toss. We had them framed and hung them in our office at the graphic shop,

Ben and I became minor celebrities with our prints. We were big fish in a very small pond. A local Fairbanks frame shop would have us in their shop signing prints, and it was a big deal to have us there! We also had shows at the University of Alaska. We eventually started a mail-order business selling our wood-block prints.

T-Shirt Business

An Air Force officer walked into our graphics shop one day and asked if any of us knew how to silk-screen? He was responsible for getting shirts printed for the Winter Special Olympics. He had 300 sweatshirts in his car and would pay us $1,400 to print the Olympics logo on them. I said "Sure, we can silk-screen them." He dropped them off and said he'd be back in two weeks to pick them up. After he left, Ben asked "Jack, do you know how to silk-screen shirts?" I said "No, but how hard can it be? Come on, Ben, we can do it! I mean we're talking $1,400 here!"

We went to the base library and read up on silk screening. We rigged up some makeshift equipment, got the right kind of ink, and we were in business! Two weeks later, we were $1,400 richer! I said, "Boy, was that easy, let's invest the money into some good equipment and some shirts and start a business!" Ben agreed and we started BenRay Graphics. We were both illustrators and were able to come up with some great designs. Our most popular ones were: The Alaskan State Bird, which was a huge mosquito; the Alaskan Horny Critter, which was a dull sheep with huge horns; and another popular one was the Alaskan Hooker, which was a really sexy girl holding a fishing pole and wearing fishing boots. We sold shirts like crazy. Ben eventually left Alaska for a new assignment, so I bought him out and continued making and selling T-shirts. This little operation was to have a huge impact on our future.

One cold winter day I got a call from an Air Force Team doing cold weather testing on a small jet. The commander of the team, an Air Force colonel, asked if I could come to the hanger and paint an Alaskan mountain scene on the jet's tail.

I only had an hour to do it, since the plane was due to leave the hangar. As part of the test, once outside, the plane stays outside. I told him there is no way I could do anything that fast. He was disappointed and asked if I had any suggestions. I said that I had Alaskan designs that we print on shirts and I was sure that we could print one on the tail of his jet. I gave him the choices and he said "We gotta have the Alaskan Horny Critter."

I arrived at the hangar with my ink, screen, and squeegee. I crawled up onto the tail, someone held my ankles, and we got the job done. The Horny Critter was emblazoned on both sides of the tail, and everyone loved it! That evening I went to the barracks where the team was staying and sold Horny Critter T-shirts like crazy. That was me being the ultimate opportunist!

Life Slightly Off Center

Survival Training

We always had various teams visiting our base for training. Arctic Survival was a big one. Military personal would spend a week outside in the extreme cold of Alaska, learning the art of survival. A couple of the instructors would regularly pull this joke on their new trainees.

One of the lessons was the ability to recognizing different animal tracks and their droppings. For laughs, the instructor would set up a pile of what they called moose droppings. These were actually Tootsie Roll pieces shaped to look like a moose turd. The instructors, along with the students, would be walking through the woods and come across this set-up pile of moose turds. The instructor would point them out and say, "Here is an example of female moose droppings." The other instructor would then say "Oh no, these are definitely male moose droppings!"

The two instructors would then get into a heated discussion about who was right. One of them would take one and pop into his mouth, chew it up, and say "You're right; it is a female moose turd!"

Before we move on, I have one more story about moose turds. Most gift shops in Alaska sell moose-turd jewelry. These are actual moose droppings that are dried and coated with clear polyurethane. These are then made into earrings, necklaces, bracelets, and pins. I thought this was so cool and a perfect example of someone making lemonade out of lemons.

One year for Christmas we sent my Mom a moose-turd necklace and matching earrings. She loved them, but had no idea what they were made of, and we didn't tell her because she would never wear them. She told us that one day she was in church, sitting there with her hand up to her mouth, holding her beads, sorta chewing on them when they came apart in her mouth. She asked what were those things...they tasted awful!

I think we may have told her they were made of wood. The truth would have killed her or she would have killed us!

Educating the Children!

One evening the kids were all bathed and in their pajamas. We were all sitting around relaxing and watching Tuesday night TV. *Alice* came on, and in this particular episode Alice was dating a professional football player. As the show continued, the football player admitted to Alice that he was a homosexual. John came over to me and asked "Dad, what's a homosexual?"

Hmmmm, good question, John. I gave him one longer "Hmmmmmmm" while I thought of a good way to explain this to him. Keeping it simple, I said "John, a homosexual is simply a man who doesn't like girls." Satisfied with this answer, John went back over to the couch and curled up to watch the rest of the show. Dianna gave the kids a glass of milk and some cookies while they watched TV.

After the show, John came over to me with his glass of milk and announced "Dad, I am a homosexual." "WHAT! Why would you say something like that, John?" Being a little startled by my reaction to his statement, John stammered "Well, Dad, I love football just like the guy on *Alice,* and I hate girls, too!"

I said "John, a homosexual would marry another man!" John had just taken a big gulp of milk when what I had told him registered, and the milk came shooting out his mouth and streamed across the living room as John gasped, "Dad, that's silly!" I said "You're right, so let's drop it and have no more talk about homosexuals!"

The next show was *Police Woman* with Angie Dickinson. The show was about hookers. That is when Sheri came over to me and asked "Dad, what's a hooker?" I jumped up, turned the TV off, and shouted "That's enough TV for tonight! Everyone go read a book, please!"

JACK RAYMOND

217

John's Sex Education

I was sitting at my drawing table one day at work, all engrossed in a project. I looked up and there stood John. I asked "John, what are you doing here and how did you get here? Is your mom here?" "No, Dad, Mommy is not here. I rode my bike here and I have to talk with you," he replied. "OK, kid, so what's up?" I asked. John said "Dad, I gotta know about sex!" This shocked me since John was only eight years old!

"John, do you have to know right now, right here?" I asked. I suggested he wait until I got home and we could discuss it between just the two of us. He put his hands on his hips and said "I knew you wouldn't tell me," and then he went off in a huff.

When I got home that evening, John didn't mention it, so I didn't say anything. I had heard if they don't ask, don't push it. I took the coward's way out and just let it pass. I did go out the next day and buy a book titled *Explaining Sex to Children*.

JACK RAYMOND

It was very simple and had some good illustrations to help John understand. I wanted to be prepared for the next time the subject came up.

One day several months later, I was sitting at my drawing table at home when John came up to me and said "Dad, remember you were going to tell me about sex, but you never did? Can you tell me now?" I could feel my hands getting sweaty, and I knew this was it. This was the moment every parent dreads—the time for the BIG TALK!

I started fumbling through my files trying to find my *Explaining Sex* book. John asked what I was looking for. I explained to him that I had a book on the subject to help me explain to him. He looked at me funny and said "You need a book? What happened, did you forget?"

I gave up on finding the book and decided to go on my own. I said "John, I'll give it to you the best I know how. First let's talk about the parts of the body." John said "Oh, Dad, I know all that stuff. Let's skip that and get to the part where you lie down and laugh!" (This made me wonder if John had been listening outside our bedroom door.)

I got pretty graphic, drew some pictures to help him understand, and he seemed to get it. His reaction was a disgusted "UGH!" John said "You mean I have to do that to have a baby? Dad, I don't even like to kiss girls!"

I assured him that one day he would and would want to be as close as he could be to the girl he loved, and that was as close as anyone could be to another person. I said "Someday you will find the whole experience beautiful and wondrous!" After our talk, I asked John if he had any questions. He had just one. "Dad, where are these seeds you were talking about?" I explained where the seeds are, and he said "Wow, I didn't know that!" With that, he went running off. I breathed a sigh of relief and thought to myself that wasn't so bad, and I felt like I did a pretty good job. John returned two minutes later and said "Dad, guess how many kids I'm going to have?" I said "I had no idea, maybe five?" "No," he said. "I'm gonna have two kids!" I asked how he could be so sure of that. "Dad, I just checked, and I am going to have two kids, 'cause I got two seeds!"

Life Slightly Off Center

Crazy Friends!

One day I was standing in line at the post office on base mailing out tubes of wood block prints. I suddenly felt a sharp pain in my left leg and let out a yell and my packages went flying. I looked down, and there was our dear friend Nancy on her hands and knees biting my leg. I asked "What the hell are you doing? Are you crazy?" Nancy stood up and being very, very pregnant, pointed to her huge belly and said "That was for this! You, You!" and she just stormed away. This was part of an on-going game Nancy and her husband, Ray, played, called Let's Embarrass Jack. Nancy outdid herself this time. I was totally embarrassed and got some very strange looks from everyone in the post office. I didn't know whether to make a hasty exit or just suck it up and hold my place in line. I decided to stay. I finally got to the front of the line, had my packages weighed and stamped, and found I was 10 cents short on the postage. I was fishing through all my pockets, when the woman behind me tapped my on the shoulder, handed me a dime, and said "Here you go, mister...it was worth the show!"

Mom and Dad Come to Alaska!

My mom and dad were planning to visit us in Alaska. We hadn't seen them in almost four years and we were all excited. About a month before their expected arrival, Dianna started stocking upon dietetic canned foods. The kids noticed this strange food coming into the house and asked why Mom was buying it. I told them that Grandpa was a diabetic and had to have special food. Next question was "Dad, what's a diabetic?" I kiddingly said "Oh, that is someone that drools all the time." Now I have their attention, and they ask "Dad, does Grandpa drool?" I said "Oh yeah, his shirt always has a big wet spot on it; in fact, Grandma drools all the time, too!" "What? why, is Grandma a diabetic, too?" they asked. "Oh no, Grandma just drools so Grandpa doesn't feel like he is different," I answered.

I never thought anymore about this conversation until Mom and Dad came into the Fairbanks Airport. They spotted us and with outstretched arms came running over to us. Dad expected his long-lost grandchildren to run up to them with hugs and kisses. Instead the three of them are backed up against the wall recoiling away from their grandparents. Dad was astounded by their reaction and said "What the hell is wrong with your kids, Jackie?" "Hey, John, Sheri, Steven, come on and give your grandma and grandpa a big kiss and hugs" I said.

They still hesitated and whispered "Is Grandpa drooling?" Then it hit me. "Oh no, I was just kidding about drooling! Didn't I tell you I was just kidding? Oh, boy, I'm sorry; Grandma and Grandpa don't drool!"

"Drool, drool, what the hell are you talking about?" asked

JACK RAYMOND

Life Slightly Off Center

Dad. Poor Mother was completely confused. After everything was cleared up, the kids were all over their grandparents. On the way home, the kids were telling their Grandma and Grandpa about what I had said about him being a diabetic and how they were really dreading their visit. I felt really bad, and my parents thought I was sick.

Larry, a friend of mine and a real joker, warned me that he was going to play a trick on my parents when they arrived. I had no idea what he was up to. We pulled up to the Eielson base guard gate and there was Larry in his dress uniform acting like a gate guard. He stopped us, checked my military ID card, checked Dianna's dependent ID card, and then asked my parents for their passports. "Passport, I don't have a passport; aren't we still in the United States?" Dad asked. Larry insisted on seeing their papers. Dad pulled out his driver's license, his Kodak pass, and everything else with his name on it. Poor Mother was digging out her Sears and Penney's charge cards. Larry was very serious and said he would have to follow us to our quarters and search Mom and Dad's bags. Dad was just beside himself and said "Search our bags, what the hell is going on here?" Mother was almost in tears.

By the time we got to our house, Dianna had spilled the beans and told Mom and Dad that Larry was a friend, and he was just playing a joke on them. Mother said, "So, not only is my son sick, but his Alaskan friends are also sick. I wanna go home!"

We all had a good laugh. Larry came in, and we all sat around the table drinking coffee and catching up on the news from back home. Mom asked me to bring the bags in from the car. She needed Dad's medicine. Larry insisted on unloading the car. He said "You visit with your parents; I'll get the bags." After he was done, he yelled up that the bags were in the foyer. I went down the steps to the foyer to say goodbye to Larry. Larry winked at me and said "The small makeup bag is hidden in the hall closet. Tell your parents I'm a kleptomaniac. See you later!" Larry left and Mom came down to check on the bags. She said "Jackie, where is the small makeup bag? That is the bag with your father's medicine in it! I know it was in the car, I remember seeing it. Go check the car again," she pleaded. I did go out to the car, then came back in, and said "no bag." Mother is now getting panicky. I said "Mom, now don't get upset, I'm sure Larry took it." "Larry? Why would Larry take it," she asked. I explained that Larry was a recovering kleptomaniac and just couldn't help himself. He has been under a doctor's care and we thought he was better, but I guess he relapses every now and then. I'll call his house and ask his wife if the bag is there.

I pick up the phone and dial a bogus number and then pretend to talk to Sharon, Larry's wife. "Hi Sharon, this is Jack, I was wondering if you have a makeup bag there. We think Larry may have taken it from our car. It is my mom's and has my dad's meds in it. Oh, wait, I'll ask. Mom, what color is it?" "What color is it?" Mom said. "How many makeup bags do they have over there? It's blue." "OK, great, I'll be right over!" I hung up and told Mom that they did have it and I would go get it.

I let Dad in on the joke, and he loved it. Dad was the man who had taught me the art of joking so he enjoyed seeing his son in action!

Mom was now worried about poor Larry. She would say "He seems like such a nice guy. Is he a good family man? Does he have children? Is he good to his wife?" She would definitely pray for him.

Larry and Sharon came over for dinner one evening. To keep the "klepto" thing going, Larry slipped silverware into his pocket when he knew Mom was watching him. Mom kept her purse with her whenever Larry was around. After a week of this, Larry couldn't look Mother in the eye and finally said "Jack, I can't do this anymore. Your mom looks so sad when she looks at me. Please tell her it's only a joke!" I did tell her, and she hit me with her purse and gave Dad a few whacks for being in on it. She said "I am surrounded by sickos and now I really do want to go home!"

Before Mom and Dad arrived in Alaska, I had told the boys they were not to ask their grandparents for money to buy ice cream when the ice cream truck came through the neighborhood. Everyday about two in the afternoon, the truck would come by the house. John and Steven made sure they were near Grandpa. They would say "Grandpa, do you hear that?" (Refering to the ding, ding, ding coming from the truck.) Dad would say "No, I don't hear anything." Then the truck would get closer, and the ding, ding, ding would get louder. The boys would say, "Grandpa, do you hear it now?" "Nope, I don't hear anything." He, of course, knew exactly what was going on, but loved to see the kids squirm at little. As the truck passed by the house, Dad would say "Oh boy, I think I hear the ice cream man. Do you kids want some ice cream?" He would then hand them a buck, and they would be out the door in a flash and running after the truck.

One of the things we planned while my parents were in Alaska was a week at the lake. We rented a cabin at Birch Lake and figured it would be a great time for all of us. The day we were to go to the lake, Sheri had a softball game and couldn't miss it since she was the pitcher. I asked Dad if he could take Sheri to her game and then join us at the lake. That way we could have everything set up by the time they arrived. He agreed and he, Mom, and Sheri took off in the little yellow Volkswagen convertible. We hooked up the boat, loaded enough groceries for a week, and took off for the lake. We also had to take dishes and linen. It was a major undertaking, but we got it done and were all set by the time Mom, Dad, and Sheri arrived. I had to laugh as they pulled up...the top was down and Dad's hair was standing straight up; he looked like Einstein!

That night, after a good dinner, we were sitting around a campfire and were being attacked by the giant Alaskan mosquitoes! Dad said, "Being bit by Alaskan mosquitoes is like being hit by a bullet!" He finally gave up and went into the cabin to get some sleep. The beds were terrible. They were the rollaway type with that horrible bar running through the middle of your back. Dad got up the next morning with his Einstein hair and said what a bad night he had. He didn't get a wink of sleep and asked how long we have to stay. I told him we had the cabin for a whole week. He just groaned. He was just miserable, and asked if we decided to go home after one day, would they give you your money back? I lied and said they would, and so we packed up and headed back to the base and a comfortable bed. We were all so disappointed. We had looked forward to a week at the lake, but I guess that's life. Sure didn't want Dad to have a miserable week. Mom and Dad had saved and planned for this trip for so long and we didn't want anything to ruin it.

Dad was newly retired and loved to keep busy. I was running the shirt business out of my house. I would print them in the basement. Every morning Dad would have his coffee and then say, "OK, how many shirts have we got to do today?" After a few days, I was making up bogus orders just to keep him busy. When people would come over to pick up orders, he loved nothing better than to shoot the breeze with them. We would get through running shirts and then he would say "OK, time for a break!" And we'd go have a beer. By the time Dad and Mom left, I had a stock-pile of shirts that lasted for six months!

All in all, it was a great visit, and we were very sad to see Mom and Dad leave. It would be the last time we would see Dad: He died a year later. I'm so glad we didn't make him suffer through a week at the lake.

Sheri's Growing Up!

Our little girl was growing up just too fast. Sheri absolutely loved Alaska and loved life! She was into everything. As a young girl, she was a cheerleader for the football team. She decided she would rather be playing than cheering, so she did what she loved best—she became a jock.

Sheri was the center on the high school basketball team, the pitcher for the softball team, she played volleyball, loved skiing, and was even first trumpet in the school band. One thing about Sheri, if she decided she wanted to accomplish something, she accomplished it at 100 percent. She was always an honor student and pretty much just a great kid to have around the house.

I can remember the day when her growing up really hit us between the eyes. She asked if she could start dating. She was just fifteen and a half. We had previously told her she could start this dating stuff when she turned sweet sixteen. A big Christmas dance was coming up, and she just had to go. "Mom, Dad, everyone is going. Please let me go," she pleaded. So being the wishy-washy parents we were, we caved and said "OK." The next evening over dinner, Sheri announced that she had a date for the big dance! I said "Great. Who is this boy?" Sheri replied, "His name is Cedric Brown and he plays on the football team. Dad, I am sure you know him." Suddenly the kid's face pops into my mind. I ask "Sheri, isn't he black?" "Yes, he is, and he is really a nice boy," she said. Dianna just groaned and said "Oh my God!" I said "Sheri, you can't date a black kid!" Sheri jumped up from the table and put her hands on her hips and said "Dad, I can't believe it; you're prejudiced! After all these years of you preaching, all the lectures about equality, and you, you are the one who is prejudiced!"

Dianna tried to reason with her, telling her if she started dating black boys, none of the white boys would ever ask her out. She added that all the black girls on base would hate her. We gave her every reason we could think of, plus the fact that her grandmother in Mississippi would disown her! I said "What if you two actually fell in love and wound up getting married. Do you have any idea how hard your life would be?" "Sheri, believe me, I have seen mixed marriages and they are not easy." "But, Dad, I am not going to fall in love with Cedric, we're just friends!"

Nothing I said, nothing Dianna said would convince her that dating this guy would be a mistake. Finally I gave her my last argument. "Sheri, his parents are

Life Slightly Off Center

probably sitting around their dinner table right now having the same discussion. I'm sure they do not want their son dating a white girl." Sheri's reply: "Dad, I think you're wrong about that, since Cedric's mother is white!"

That was it, I gave up. "Sheri, you are not, repeat, not going out with Cedric Brown and that's that. I guess you're right, I am prejudiced. I just never knew I was until now," I admitted. "The bottom line is, unless you can find a decent white boy to go out with, you are not going to the dance, period!" With tears streaming down her cheeks, Sheri went running off to her room sobbing about all black boys not being decent and what was she going to tell Cedric? "He'll hate me!"

I know we handled it all wrong. In fact, we could probably write a book on How to Bring up Kids Wrong!

What did we know? This was way back in the 1970s and you just did not let your little girl date a black kid. I know it is probably hard for you to believe that we really are not prejudiced and do not think black boys were bad or not as good as our daughter. Dianna and I really did believe that Sheri would be hurt down the road, and our first concern was for our daughter. A few days later, the crisis over, Sheri announced that Cedric didn't hate her and she had a date with a "decent white boy!" I asked her what she had told Cedric about not being able to go with him. She said "I just told him you were prejudiced."

A week or so later, Dianna was talking with a friend. She asked who Sheri had gone to the Christmas Dance with. Dianna said "A kid named Toby Childs. He is a good-looking guy and is the quarterback for the school football team." With a strange look on her face, she said "You let your daughter go out with Toby Childs? Don't you know that he has already gotten two girls pregnant at the ripe old age of sixteen!"

So I guess that just goes to prove, you can never judge a boy by his color! A lesson well learned by us and one we have never forgotten.

Play Ball!

It was a beautiful summer Saturday and Dianna and I were in the bleachers watching John play Little League baseball. It was the bottom of the 3rd. Eric, the catcher for our team, walked up to the plate for his turn at bat. He was swinging the bat, warming up, when the umpire suddenly stopped the game and was in a discussion with Eric. Eric pointed to his left foot and we all sat there completely puzzled. Our puzzlement soon turned into gales of laughter when Eric starting working his "cup", which had apparently slipped into his sock, up the inside of his pants leg and finally after a lot of twisting and turning got it into position. With the cup in place, the umpire yelled "PLAY BALL!"

One more cup story worth telling: Our friend David told us about the day his son was playing in his first Little League baseball game. The umpire stopped the game and went over to one of the kids on the team. Because the player did not have a cup, he was taken out of the game. The umpire explained how seriously he could be hurt by not wearing a cup.

The kid went back to the bench with his head down and his lip quivering. David's son Randy, feeling sorry for his ousted teammate, reached down the front of his own pants, retrieved his cup, and offered it to the his fellow teammate. After the game, David commended his son for trying to help out, "but," he said, "Son, there are just some things we don't share."

Life Slightly Off Center

Skiing in Alaska

We did a lot of skiing in Alaska. There was a beautiful ski facility on base with a rustic old ski lodge. We spent many weekends there in front of a roaring fire, enjoying the best French fries we've ever tasted.

My first time on the hill was not good. As I stood there looking down, I was having second thoughts. Maybe I'll just hang out at the lodge. This hill is pretty steep. Maybe I should make my way over to the bunny hill. No, can't do that; John and Steven are over there. Having their dad on the bunny hill would completely embarrass them. It is bad enough I wasn't a pro football player.

Okay, so down I went, and I was flying! I had no idea how to stop. People are jumping out of my way. I thought, *How hard could it be?* Then I found out how hard it could be! I didn't stop at the bottom; instead I went through the weeds, narrowly missed some pines, and landed on my butt on the cross-country ski trail. I was lying there in a heap when a cross-country skier went by. He looked at me, looked at my skis, and said in disgust, "Those are the wrong kind of skis for this trail." After many falls, I got the hang of it and really enjoyed skiing!

Dianna had skied while she was a kid in Japan, so she took to it right off. The boys were not too happy on skis. They said it was too cold. Sheri, on the other hand, took to skiing like the wind. She loved it and was good at it. One Saturday they had a ski carnival and both Dianna and Sheri entered in the competition. I stayed home with the boys.

Dianna came home after a long day on the slopes with a trophy about 2 feet high. I was totally impressed that she had won every event she entered. She won the giant slalom, downhill as the fastest skier, and the ski jump! I said, "I can't believe you won all those events." She laughed and said "I won them all of them because I was the only one in my age group competing. I fell down the giant slalom, I fell off the ski jump, and I fell halfway down the fastest downhill event."

Then she told me about Sheri standing in line at the top of the hill, waiting to compete and having to go to the bathroom really bad, but not about to get out of the long line. It came her turn and she couldn't hold it any longer, so she skid and peed all the way down the hill!

The ski hill would shut down when the temps dipped to minus 20 degrees. We were there on a Saturday afternoon, and the manager was getting ready to shut it down because of the dipping temperatures. All of a sudden two teenage boys went flying down the hill streaking! Both of them were buck naked! I had to hand it to them, streaking at 20 below took a lot of balls!

There was one evening that is probably one of the most pleasant memories of my life. While it was happening, I thought to myself, *I will remember this time for the rest of my life*. It wasn't even a big deal; I just felt so happy and so content. We were at the ski lodge with the kids and a bunch of friends. We were night skiing and it was about 20 above zero—actually balmy for this part of the world. The snow was coming down in flakes the size of quarters—big, white fluffy snowflakes. I remember us all laughing and just having such a great time. Like I said, it wasn't any big deal. I often recall this memory if I find myself a little depressed, and I automatically feel better.

Are Comic Books Real?

One Saturday evening I was getting dressed to go out. John, who was then maybe five, was lying on our bed reading one of his monster comic books. During those days, John always had a comic book in his hands. At one point John looked up at me and asked "Dad, are comic books real?" I said, "John, of course they're real. We're in a family comic book right now. Everything we say appears in a bubble above our heads and people read about our family!" He said, "Aw, come on Dad, you're kidding." This was our kids' reaction to just about everything I ever said. I once told them to put on their raincoats for school because it was raining. Their reaction: "You're kidding. Mom, is it really raining?"

I said "No, I'm not kidding. Go ask your mother." Dianna was in the adjoining bathroom doing her makeup and listening to our conversation. She walked into the bedroom. Keep in mind the kids really trusted Dianna since she wasn't one to fool around too much. Her word was always gospel around our house.

John said "Mom, Dad said comic books are real, and we're living in a family comic book right now. Mom, is that true?" Dianna put her hand on her hip, started waving her finger at me, saying "Jack, how could you? You know the kids are not

supposed to be told that until they are fifteen years old. John is just too young to know!" With that, she left the room in a huff!

John was now wide-eyed and full of questions, the big one being "Dad, can someone get into a monster book?" I said "Sure, John, all I have to do is to call Comic Book Headquarters and tell them." He hesitantly said, "Dad, I think I want to go into a monster comic book." I asked, "Are you sure, John?" His reply "Yup, I'm sure!" So I picked up the phone, dialed a bogus number, and said "Hello, is this comic book headquarters? Well, this is Mr. Raymond, and my son John would like a transfer to a monster comic book. Oh, let me ask..." I held my hand over the mouth piece and asked John which book he wanted to be in? He told me the name of his favorite monster book and I relayed his request. "Ok, no problem. Ok, thank you, goodbye," I said. Ole John is just beside himself with excitement. I've never seen John with his mouth and eyes open so wide. "What did they say, Dad?" he asked, while jumping up and down on the bed! "The people at Comic Book Head-quarters said there would be no problem. They will erase you from this family book tonight and redraw you into the monster book." I said we better go downstairs and say goodbye to Mom, Sheri, and Steven. John went flying down the steps with his big announcement!

Dianna had gone downstairs earlier to alert Sheri and Steven that we were playing a joke on John and to go along with "whatever craziness your Dad is up to." Sheri, being a veteran of my jokes, fell right into place. Steven was too young to understand, so we were not worried about him giving away the joke.

John told everyone what was going on and that he was going get erased so he wanted to say goodbye. Dianna said "Oh no, John, please don't go!" We all gave John a big kiss and hug and wished him luck. I told him to go over and sit on the desk because they would probably start erasing pretty soon. He went over, climbed onto the desk, and just sat there waiting.

I said "Oh no, there go John's feet!" Dianna ran over and gave him another kiss and hug and told him how much we were going to miss him! I exclaimed "Oh boy, there go John's legs; there goes his belly!" Meanwhile John was looking down at his feet and legs, saying "Dad, they are still there." I said "Sure, you can always see them, but we can't because you're being erased!"

Then puff and John was gone! We all ignored him. John kept saying "I'm still here, I'm still here. Can anyone see me?" He pulled on Sheri's shirt and said "Sheri, I'm still here, I am really here! Can't you see me?" Sheri, being the trooper she was, just ignored him. I was sitting on the coffee table tying my shoes when the shoelace broke, and I said "Oh, damn, I broke my shoelace!" John went running into the kitchen, went to the drawer we kept shoelaces in, grabbed one, came running back, and dangled it in front of my face. I said, "Wow, look at that! A shoelace floating in midair—what a great trick!" As I laced up my shoe, I was watching something on TV. John stood directly in front of me, and we were nose to nose. I continued to stare like I was still watching the television.

It was about this time that the doorbell rang and Dianna went to answer it. It was our babysitter Laura. Laura was used to this other-than-normal household, and when Dianna said her to pretend that John was not here, she went right along with it. No questions asked. Laura walked into the living room and said "Hi Mr. Raymond, hi Steven, hi Sheri. Where is John tonight?"

Now John was getting panicky. He kept saying "I'm here! I haven't gone any-place! I'm still here!" We all continued to ignore him until he started crying that he wanted to come home. I said "Boy, I sure do miss John. This ole house just isn't the same without him." Everyone agreed that they wished John would come home. I said, "Let's try something. Let's all hold hands and wish for John to come home!"

We did this, and suddenly there were John's feet, then his legs, arms, his belly, and his face and John was home again! Everyone clapped and cheered! John came running to me, and we hugged, and through his tears, he said that he never wanted to be erased again!

This ranks as the worst trick I ever played on my kids. I have always felt bad about doing it and would never do it again. In fact, I called my mom a few days after this incident and told her about it. She got really upset and said she would be on the next plane to Alaska! She was coming to get my kids and said I shouldn't have children!

Life Slightly Off Center

Many years later, I was telling this story at John's 37th birthday party. I was surrounded by John's friends and family. I heard one of his buddies say "Talk about your Father of the Year!" I looked over at John, and he had tears in his eyes. I asked him later about the tears. John said "Dad, I cry every time I hear that story."

Mom was right...I shouldn't have been allowed to raise children. I should have settled for raising dogs.

Salmon Fishing

This was a big weekend. Ben and I were going to King Salmon for some really serious fishing. King Salmon is located below Anchorage and is where the salmon come in from the ocean to work their way up the rivers and creeks to get to the place they were hatched; that is where they will spawn. It is pretty amazing to think a fish could find its way back to its origin. We drove down to Anchorage and had to spend the night there before catching a small plane to fly into King Salmon.

We got into Anchorage really late and didn't want to check into a hotel for such a short period of time. We decided to wander around town until it was time to catch our flight. During this time in Alaska, the oil pipeline was being put in. The pipeline produced thousands of jobs and along with the workers came the hookers. There was a hooker on every corner. They kept coming up to Ben and me, asking if we wanted a date. At first it was sorta fun, but after awhile, it got to be irritating. Ben said, "Man, these broads are really beginning to bug me. Let's go find some place to get away from them." Another girl came up to us at about the time Ben was complaining. She asked if we wanted a date. I said, "No, I've got one," and at that I grabbed Ben's hand and we strolled along hand in hand for awhile. None of the girls bothered us again!

We got to King Salmon, which was a military fishing camp. We were issued a small motorboat and hit the high seas. It was great! The salmon were running, and we were about to experience every fisherman's dream. We were not out in the boat twenty minutes when Ben hooked a huge salmon! This fish fought like crazy! The pole was bent over and under the boat.

"Jack, get the net ready! I can't lose this one!" Ben said through gritted teeth. He wrestled with this monster for another half hour. Finally he had it up next the boat, close enough for me to net it. I scooped the net under the fish and completely missed it. The fish got a second wind and took off. Again Ben got it up near the boat—again I went for it with the net and again I missed. Ben screamed, "Jack, what the hell are you doing? If you make me lose this fish, I will never talk to you again!" I finally managed to get the fish in the net on the fourth or fifth try. After it was safely in the boat, I took a good look at the net and found the pole was loose. Every time I'd go to net the fish, the net would just spin around. At any rate, I got it into the boat—thank God—and continued to pull them in as Ben caught them. I had no luck at all. When we landed the boat up on the shore, the score was Ben: 6 big ones! Jack: 0.

I later decided to fish from the beach, hoping my luck would change. I cast out and recast and then cast out again. Guys all around me were catching salmon like crazy. I was catching nothing! Then it happened. I hooked into one of those monsters and brought it in without a fight. After I took a good look at it, I discovered it was not a monster and had a big seal bite out of its underside. This was not the King Salmon fish that I had in my mind mounted and hung over the fireplace! I must have set some kind of record by leaving the greatest fishing spot in the world with not even one fish to brag about.

Ahhhhh Alaska!

Ben, a bunch of guys from the base, and I went to Paxton Lake for our annual fishing trip in August. This was the spot where we caught huge lake trout. We'd always go home with a great catch. These were the best of times, and I have pictures to prove it!

One morning Ben and I crawled out of our tent, and we're just standing there soaking in all the beauty around us. It was a beautiful sunrise that reflected off the lake. We were surrounded by beautiful snow-capped mountains. Just when you think things couldn't be any more perfect than this spot, three majestic bald eagles

Life Slightly Off Center

flew overhead. I didn't know if Ben was going to faint or salute! Alaska was like no place in the world and to experience it was a real gift.

I get all goofy just thinking about those great days.

Ahhhhh Dianna!

Dianna was such a trooper and never complained about me being gone so much. There was a time when I really took advantage of the situation and probably should have been shot. In fact, if Dianna had shot and killed me, she most likely would have gotten off scot-free! They would have ruled it justifiable homicide.

My buddy Dennis and I went hunting for moose eleven weekends in a row! We would head out on Friday morning on our three-wheel Hondas to where we had a tent set up and wouldn't come back until Sunday afternoon. It was cold and miserable and we never even saw moose, but we had a great time!

Years later I was telling a friend of mine about this eleven-week hunting marathon. He just shook his head and asked "How do you stay married?"

I did take Dianna rabbit hunting with me one morning, so I wasn't all bad. In Alaska they have snowshoe rabbits that are white in the winter and brown in the summer. Dianna spotted one, took aim, and bang! She got it! She only wounded it. A wounded rabbit sounds like a baby crying; it is a terrible noise. Dianna is yelling "Jack, do something. Make it stop crying like that!" I went up and finished the job with my pistol. (I guess this may have been the "just in case" reason for buying the pistol in the first place.) We took our prize home. The boys and I went into basement to clean it. The three of us were all making gagging sounds because it sickened us so much. The family of great white hunters!

Dianna took the rabbit and threw it into a pot of boiling water. When Sheri got home from school and asked what was for dinner, we all answered in unison "Thumper Stew!" And we wonder why Sheri is such a dedicated vegetarian today!

I Finally Made It!

After our beloved dog Giggles died, we had decided no more dogs for awhile, but the house just didn't seem normal without dog hair all over the furniture and our clothes. We, or I should say I, just needed a dog around the house. So I went out and bought a beautiful springer spaniel pup. It was a pure-bred dog with a docked tail!

I was talking with Ben one time and he and I had grown up pretty much the same. Not poor, but not having a lot. I asked him what would make you feel like you've really made it in the world. For him it was a drawer full of T-shirts and underwear, which he had. For me, it was a pure-bred dog with a docked tail. So I guess we both had made it!

Lady

Springer spaniels are crazy puppies, very high spirited, but once they get past the puppy stage, you couldn't ask for a better, more loyal dog. We named ours Lady. We were to find out later that she wasn't much of a lady. She got out while she was in heat and got herself pregnant! She had ten puppies and, like our first dog, Mike, went into the dreaded milk fever. I had to rush her to the vet in town. She was almost dead by the time I got there. The doctor said it was indeed milk fever and that she had to have a straight shot of calcium. He said it would either kill her or cure her. It was amazing! We walked out of the vet's office and Lady was wagging her tail! Her puppies were maybe three weeks old at this point. The doctors said do not let her near the pups to nurse. We had to bind her up and bottle-feed the pups.

It was a three-week nightmare. Lady would be upstairs howling to get to her pups because of the pain she was feeling with her swollen milkers. The pups were crying to be fed and to be with their mother.

I took the pups to the vet on base to get their tails docked. As he was chopping them off, he'd throw them in a wastebasket. I asked what he did with the tails, and he said they just threw them out. I asked if I could have them. I told him I could make key chains with them and give one to each person who took a pup. He rolled his eyes and said help yourself. But I decided against it; I figured I would probably get them all mixed up, and the people who took the pups would probably wind up with the wrong tail key chain. Thankfully we found homes for all the puppies and swore we were never going to go through that again.

A year or two passed, and we ran into a dentist on base who had a beautiful male springer spaniel. He and I thought it would be a great idea to breed our dogs. We did and again we were having puppies.

Lady went into labor, and the first pup got stuck just as it was coming out. It was halfway out of the birth canal. It was turning blue and yelping. I said, "Dianna, quick get the vet on the phone." She did, and repeated what the doctor was saying over the phone. I was to take the puppy and push him back into the birth canal and turn him. Ugh, put my fingers in there? "Dianna, maybe you better do it; my fingers are just too big!" So she gave me the phone, and I gave the directions from the vet. This was a much better arrangement. The puppy finally came out and it was huge. It was the biggest one of the litter. I went upstairs to enlist Sheri's help. I told her we might need some long skinny fingers to help birth the puppies. Sheri sat there, running in place, and said, "I can't do it, I can't!" She got up and went running for the door, yelling "I'm going to Lisa's house call me when it's over!" The final count was nine beautiful puppies. She had ten, but the last one was born dead.

A girl came by when the pups were still really small and said she wanted to buy one. I told her they would not be ready to leave their mother for another three weeks. That was okay; she went down, picked one out, a female, and named her Peaches. She would come by every few days to visit her pup. I never saw anyone so crazy about a dog before. She was just living for the day when Peaches could go home with her. One summer day, a few months later, we met this girl, her husband, and Peaches down in Fairbanks. They were sitting on the curb with three ice cream cones, one for each of them. They were saying how much they loved the dog and that Peaches went wherever they went.

Her husband was a bush pilot, and they never took off without the dog in tow. It was probably a year later that we read in the paper that their plane had crashed and the three of them had been killed. We talked with her sister, and she was saying it was a good thing the dog was with them because no one else would have put up with that crazy dog!

We interviewed everyone who wanted a pup. It was our mission to make sure each one of them got a great home. We had only one left: the biggest one of the litter whom we called John Boy. A guy came by and said he was looking for a hunting dog. He was telling us how he trained them. He would take a ball, wrap barbed wire around it, and have the dog fetch it; when the dog clamped down on the ball, it would cut his gums and this is how they taught dogs to have a soft mouth for retrieving small game and ducks. That is all Dianna had to hear. No, sorry this dog was not for sale. There was not going to be a ball with barbed wire around it in John Boy's future.

And that was how we would up with two springer spaniels. Mother and son were a great pair. We used to hook them up to a sled and they would pull the kids around.

A buddy of mine called asking to buy a puppy. I said he was too late; they've all been sold. You mean you sold all ten already? I said we had nine pups; the last one was born dead. He said, "Actually that is the one I am interested in. We figured it would be great for our son to pull around the yard on a leash. We wouldn't have to worry about house-training it; it wouldn't need to be fed—that is the perfect dog for us!" That was Ray, one of our sicker friends!

Here is one last story about Lady. I came home from work one evening and was greeted by Lady in a getup you wouldn't believe. Dianna explained the outfit was to protect the carpeting since Lady was in heat and bleeding. Dianna had put on Lady an old pair of her silk panties with a hole cut out for Lady's tail and a Kotex pad pinned inside. To hold the panties up, she had a pair of my suspenders running from the waist to the dog's collar. I had to laugh—she looked so silly! I said, "I sure hope no one comes over to visit because they will think we are either crazy or very kinky!"

JACK RAYMOND

Life Slightly Off Center

Picnic Weather!

One day in late winter, it warmed up to 20 degrees above zero. In Alaska that was cooking-out-on-the-grill weather. It was common to see people out in short-sleeve T-shirts flipping burgers. After several weeks of 60 below, 20 above felt like a summer day!

I decided to take the kids on a picnic. I hooked up the survival sled to the three-wheel Honda, put John and Steven in the sled and Sheri behind me on the Honda. Off we went with our stash of hotdogs and cold drinks. We went out on the back road on the base and found a perfect spot. I built a fire, we roasted the hot dogs, and we had a great time. The few hours of sunshine we had that day was so enjoyable. We laid in the brush and look up at the sun. It felt so good on your face. It was starting to get a little dark, so we decided it was time to head for home.

I started the Honda and then went back to pack up the sled. John took the opportunity while my back was turned, to crawl onto the Honda and hit the gas. He went flying and had no idea how to control it. He knew where the gas was, and he knew that the more you pushed the lever forward, the faster you would go. He had it wide open and was heading for a bridge that was all rotted out. I could just see him hitting one of those huge holes in the bridge with the front tire and being thrown into the frozen creek below.

I was running as fast as I could and yelling, "John, John, STOP!!" He looked over his shoulder and just laughed. He thought this was a great game. All the time he was getting closer to the bridge. I ran all out, took a mighty leap, and luckily grabbed onto the chrome ring that was around the seat. I was then being dragged, and it took everything I had to crawl up on the bike and finally switch off the start button.

We rolled to a stop about a foot from a gaping hole. John was still laughing—until I put him over my knee and spanked his bare butt!

The Sorority

Dianna's big social outlet was being a member of the Beta Sigma Phi sorority. She and a bunch of girls got together for a meeting every couple of weeks. They were always going on trips, having luncheons and dances, and generally getting back at their husbands for all of their hunting and fishing trips. It was a great group, and both Dianna and I enjoyed socializing with them.

They had several formal dances every year. The girls would show up all dolled up in their fancy dresses and as they twirled around the dance floor, you could see their long underwear! In Alaska you never left home without your long underwear!

One year at the Sweetheart Ball, Dianna was crowned queen of the ball. We still have pictures of us posing, with Dianna in a beautiful dress and her crown and looking fantastic and me the geek standing next to her. All of our kids have enlargements of this picture framed and proudly displayed in their homes or offices. I was dressed in a navy blazer and red plaid pants that Dianna had made for me as a Christmas gift. To top this outfit off, I had horn-rimmed glasses and a cheesy mustache.

As good as Dianna looked, I looked that bad. I hate that picture, and the kids know it and they love it. Dianna being Dianna thinks I look great!

Miss Naive

Dianna still holds the title as the most naive woman ever! Here a few examples of how she has maintained this title.

She was working part-time evenings at the NCO Club on base. Part of her job consisted of taking phone calls and paging patrons. One night she got a call for a Sergeant Jack Off. Dianna thought nothing of this and picked up the intercom and paged, "Sergeant Jack Off, you have a phone call. Sergeant Off, Ser-

ATTENTION IN THE CLUB

JRAYMOND

geant Jack Off, you have a phone call in the office."

After several more Jack Off pages, causing a total laugh riot in the club, the manager came running up to Dianna, screaming "He's not here—hang up!" Poor innocent Dianna couldn't figure out why the manager was so upset. She just didn't get it until she got home and I explained it to her.

Another time we were at a party. Everyone was milling around with the usual chitchat going on. Dianna wandered into the kitchen and spotted a note posted on the refrigerator. It was a list of supplies for tonight's party. It read: beer, soda, chips, dip, paper plates, paper cups, ice, and a dildo. When she came to the last item on the list, she was puzzled and yelled across the room to me "Jack, what is a dildo?"

Idle chitchat stopped, the room went silent, and all eyes were on Dianna. One girl came up to her, grabbed her by the arm, and led her into another room to explain the mystery word. Dianna emerged from the room totally red-faced and ready to go home. That's my girl!

Saying Goodbye

If there is one thing you learn to do well in the military, it is how to say goodbye to friends. This is something that is repeated over and over again. Sometimes it is easier than other times. Saying goodbye to Kathy and Mike turned out to be easier than we had expected.

Mike and Kathy were being reassigned to the lower 48. They had been in Alaska for 36 months and thought that was enough time in this icebox!

Alaska is a funny place. People either hate it or they love it. There is no in-between. When describing Alaska, people never say "Oh, it was alright." When they describe Alaska, they will say, "Oh, it was so beautiful, the mountains, the wildlife, the midnight sun, the Northern Lights—everything about it was fantastic!" Or they will say "It was dark, cold, boring, and desolate—everything about it was awful!" Kathy and Mike's description would be the latter.

They were leaving on the midnight flight from the Fairbank Airport. Since we were taking them to the airport, Dianna invited them for a final dinner together. We were having a great time; well, most of us were. Mike was the exception. He was always uptight about something. This evening he was uptight about getting to the airport on time. We finished dinner and were preparing to leave; Mike and I were in the car with the kids, waiting for Kathy and Dianna. They were walking out the front door where our dog Lady was tied to the porch. When Lady spotted the girls, she proceeded to jump all over them, and Kathy wound up all tangled up in the rope and fell to the ground. Kathy and Dianna were laughing like fools. They both had a case of the giggles. It was a funny scene, but not one that rated a case of the giggles! Kathy and Dianna went back into the house. Mike was really getting upset. They finally came out and were still giggling. I asked what was so funny. Seems as though Kathy was laughing so hard when she fell that she had peed in her pants and that's what all the giggling was about. They had gone back into the house so Kathy could change. Dianna had given her a spare pair of her panties. Mike did not see the humor in this at all.

We headed to the airport, and it was going to be close. We said our goodbyes quickly and watched as Mike, Kathy, and the kids went through the security check. Oops, there seems to be a problem. The security person is pulling Kathy aside and checking her carry-on bag. Something had set off the alarm. Kathy's face was now a crimson shade of red, and she was totally embarrassed. Dianna said "Oh no, I can't believe this. Oh my God! I wrapped her wet panties in a piece of tinfoil and that is what set off the alarm!" Poor Kathy had to unwrap the tinfoil to show the guard her wet panties!

The moral of this story is: If you pee in your pants just before you are due to get on an airplane, do not wrap them in tinfoil. I repeat, do not wrap them in tinfoil—just throw them away!

Life Slightly Off Center

O. J. Simpson's Autograph

I was going to fly from Alaska to Rochester, New York. Our accountant suggested we buy a house in the lower 48 to offset some of the taxes we were paying. The plan was to buy a house and then have my sister and her family rent it. I called my brother Bill to tell him I was coming home. He said "Great; maybe I can get some tickets to a Buffalo Bills game!" That sounded good to me and even better to John. John was about seven and still crazy about football and everything related to football. O.J. Simpson was the running back for the Buffalo Bills and a huge star back in the day. O.J. was one of John's heroes and he begged me to get his autograph.

Bill picked me up at the Rochester Airport. He said he couldn't get tickets for the football game. It was all sold out. This was a real disappointment, mainly because I was determined to get John his autograph. As we walked through the airport, I noticed a lot of posters advertising Hertz Rent-a-Car.

The thing that caught my attention about these posters was that they pictured O.J. Simpson jumping over a suitcase with his signature splashed across the bottom. So I got the great idea to go to a sporting goods store, get a good football, come back to the airport and copy O.J. signature, and give that to John. John would be thrilled, and I would be the best dad ever!

A week later I was back in Alaska and presented the football to John with the coveted signature. He went goofy over it, and it became one of his most treasured possessions. The ball had center position on his dresser and was the first thing John would show off to his friends who came over to the house.

Life went on and John grew up and went off to college. O.J. Simpson grew older and was no longer a hero; instead he became a suspect in his wife's murder. I will never forget the Saturday that John came home from school all excited. He asked "Hey, Dad, do you know where my O.J. Simpson football is? I'm going to search this house from the attic to the basement; I've got to find it!" I said "John, slow down; what are you talking about?"

John explained that he had read in the local newspaper at school that some guy was willing to pay $10,000 for any authentic O.J. Simpson signature! "Can you believe it, Dad, my ball is worth a fortune, and I'm going to be rich!" he shouted, as he ran upstairs to start his search.

I yelled for John to come down so we could have a talk. He came into the kitchen and said "You want to talk, Dad? I've got to get busy. Can we talk later? Do you want to help me look for the ball? Come on, Dad, what's up?"

It was then that I started banging my head on the island in the kitchen. I stammered "John, I've got something to tell you that maybe someday you will think is funny. It won't be funny right now, and I never thought I would have to tell you. Maybe you had better sit down." John looked at me really puzzled and asked "OK, what is it? It can't be that bad, can it?"

"Well, John," I said, "I don't think that football is worth all that much, mainly because the signature is not really authentic." Then I admitted to him what I had done so many years ago. He was crushed and so disappointed that he was not going to be rich and even more disappointed in his father. After the initial shock, he asked how many other things I had lied to him about?

Talk about something coming back to bite you in the butt! O.J., if you are reading this, maybe you could send me your autograph and help me gain a few points with my son.

Football for the Boys!

Johnny joined a Little League football team on the base. He was in his glory! Steven was also a huge football fan but was too young to play. He was made the mascot for the team. As the mascot, he got wear a full uniform with pads, cleats, and helmet. He was one happy kid; of course, just being with John made Steven happy.

At practice the coach would have the kids do laps around the field. He would have Steven take off last, and he would warn the players that if Steven passed anyone, he would have to run another lap. Steven told us that he ran really slowly so he wouldn't pass anyone. He didn't want to be responsible for anyone having to take an extra lap. Even at five, Steve was a good, caring kid!

Friends would tell us they would go to the practice field just to watch Steven attempt to do jumping jacks. He was so uncoordinated at that age that he just could not manage to get his legs and arms going in the same direction. He was so funny!

At the games, Steven stuck pretty close to the coach, who wandered up and down the sidelines. One day we were sitting in the bleachers when we noticed the coach had accidently sent Steven into the game. Ole Steven went charging onto the field and must have been thinking *This is my big chance*!

Dianna screamed, "Noooooooo, not my baby!" She went running out onto the field in the middle of a play, dragged Steven to the sidelines by his shoulder pads, and gave the coach hell!

Roger

Roger, my buddy's sixteen-year-old son, was helping me one evening. We were running a bunch of T-shirts in the basement of our house. We were in the process of cleaning screens, when Roger got a big blob of red ink on his good pants. I told him to give me the pants, and I would try to get the ink out with some turpentine. I suggested he go hang out in the kids' toy room until I finished cleaning his pants.

In the meantime Dianna was upstairs having a sorority meeting. The meeting broke up, and Dianna was giving the girls a tour of the house. I was out in the garage working on Roger's pants.

Dianna told me later that she and the girls walked into the toy room and found

JACK RAYMOND

Roger on all fours in his "tightie-whities" playing with one of the kids' trucks. Poor Roger was totally embarrassed. Dianna just shut the door and continued the tour with no further explanation of the goofy teenager in his underwear playing with a truck in our playroom!

Steven Skipping

Steven was in kindergarten, and we were sitting in his classroom attending our first parent-teacher conference on his behalf. The teacher, Mrs. Robinson, was saying what a pleasure it was having Steven in her class and that he was well behaved and very eager to learn.

Then she laid it on us. There were a few problems that should be addressed now. Steven has trouble with his L sounds. She suggested we work on his la, la, la's at home. We agreed to do that, and then I asked, "What was the other problem?" She very seriously told us that Steven was having a hard time with skipping. "What? You're telling me that my son cannot skip! I cannot believe this; Steven comes from a long line of good skippers. I am just glad his grandfather is not here to hear this!" I was kidding, but apparently Mrs. Robinson was taking me seriously and tried to calm me down. Dianna told her not to pay any attention to me and that I was just giving her a hard time.

After that meeting, it was not unusual to see Steven and me skipping around the court at home saying our la, la, la's! I am proud to tell you that my son is now an accomplished skipper and he has his la, la, la's down pat!

Doing My Share!

One evening I was home taking care of the kids while Dianna was out with friends at a sorority meeting. I noticed the wall at the top of the stairs was all dirty with kids' hand prints. I decided to clean it up. I dug through Dianna's vast array of cleaning supplies and came up with a spray cleaner.

I coated the wall with a good layer of spray and began scrubbing it. The wallboard started coming off in chunks! The more I scrubbed, the bigger the chunks

Life Slightly Off Center

were! I thought *What the hell?* I looked at the can and was shocked to discover I was using Oven Off!

The kids couldn't wait for their mother to get home so they could point out Daddy's big screwup and tell her I had done a lot of cussing!

The End of My Hunting Career

One day I was up in our bedroom and noticed my pistol up on the top shelf in the closet. I always put it out of the reach of the kids and made sure it was unloaded. I took it out of the holster and was just fiddling with it when I accidently pulled the trigger. The gun went off and scared the hell out of me!

The bullet went through the wall of the closet, into the boys' room on the other side, and into John's mattress. Thank God, the boys were not in there. They spent most of their time in that room playing, but this day they were out with Dianna. It scared me so much just thinking about what could have happened that I vowed to never handle a gun again! Some people are not meant to have guns, and I figured I was one of them. The next day I sold my rifle and pistol to a friend. Even threw in my gun rack and thus ended the career of the Great White Hunter in the wilds of Alaska.

Not that it was much of a career, since the only thing I had ever shot was a rabbit.

The Vasectomy

Dianna and I were having a serious conversation about having more children versus not having any more. My vote was to have at least three more and hers was to stop while we were ahead. Dianna, being the logical one, reminded me that we had a long road ahead of us and that it was our responsible to get these kids educated. I finally conceded and said I would go see the doctor about a—Gulp!—vasectomy.

The doctor explained the procedure and said he wouldn't go any further until my wife was with me so he was sure she understood and was in complete agreement with me to have it done. Dianna was giddy with agreement; me, I was really hesitant. It just seemed so final. My big mistake was talking to guys who had the operation. They all had a horror story for me.

Dianna scheduled the appointment to get me "fixed" four times, and I called and broke the appointment four times! Dianna made the fifth appointment and promised the doctor we would be there. Of course, all the guys I worked with knew what was going on and kidded me about it on a daily basis. One of them even made up a card. The front of the card said Good Luck on the Operation and the inside had a graphic drawing of the site of the surgery, and it was really well done. He then passed it all over the building getting everyone to sign it! Some things are not for everyone to know, like a guy's vasectomy!

The day arrived and Dianna actually took me by the hand to the Wainwright Army Hospital and delivered me to the waiting doctor and his scalpel. I was ushered into what was the operating room, which also doubled as the linen supply room. I was told to strip down, and the doctor had me lie down on the table and spread my legs. He gave me shot to numb me up and then proceeded. Just about this time, another doctor walked in and struck up a conversation with my doctor, while observing the surgery. The doctor was followed by a corpsman, who joined the two doctors, and they all got into a discussion on moose hunting. Also, during the operation, other people kept coming in and out getting supplies. Now I am not an overly shy guy, but come on, this delicate surgery deserves some privacy! I was totally embarrassed and couldn't get out of there quick enough. Dianna was waiting outside the room and had a big smile on her face when the doctor reported I was officially fixed!

Life Slightly Off Center

Promotion and Headaches

We were in Alaska about six years when I got promoted for the second time. With the promotion came more responsibility. I was totally happy spending my days at my drawing table in the graphics shop. I now was the Detachment Commander and had to split my time between the graphics shop and the photo shop. The photo shop was across base; I would spend my afternoons there. I had six guys in the graphics shop and about ten guys in the photo shop.

The guys in the photo shop were a really tight group. They had just completely renovated their shop and it looked great. My coming in there was like the enemy taking over. I tried to get the man in charge to share his office with me and show me the ropes. He wanted no part of that, and we spent the rest of our time together on bad terms. There was nothing I could say or do to get on the good side of the dethroned boss.

I knew nothing about photography and felt like a fish out of water. The paperwork that came with this job was staggering. I hate paperwork and would go through it as fast as I could. I had a clerk I nicknamed Radar, and everyday he would bring me a pile of papers for my review and signature. I was very diligent about reading everything. Most of it I didn't understand, so after a few weeks, I signed pretty much whatever Radar put in front of me. I would just lift the corner of the paper and simply sign my name.

Radar was a very serious guy, and there was no joking around with him. He at one point said, "I can't understand how you can go through all this paperwork so fast. Do you even read it?" "Of course, I read it; do you think I would sign my name to something I didn't review?!" Well one day, ole Radar brought in the usual pile of paperwork for my signature. When I was done signing all of it, I called him to come and get it. He picked it up, stood there by my desk going through it, and said, "Ah haaaaa! Just as I suspected, you don't read this stuff!" At that he showed me one of the documents I had just signed. It was a supply order and it read as follows:

2 white horses for the officers
8 brown horses for the enlisted men
20 bales of hay

20 bales of straw
10 Western-style saddles

And on and on it went....boy, was I embarrassed. But it did teach me a good lesson, and I never sign anything until I read it. Thanks, Radar!

Moving On!

I had been assigned to the Alaskan Air Command for seven years. That is an extremely long time for any one assignment to last. I was alerted to expect a new assignment when my current extension was up.

We all loved Alaska and hoped to remain until I reached my retirement date. We planned to make Alaska our permanent home. We had picked out a piece of land and were ready to get hold of a builder to build us a house in North Pole, Alaska. But the Air Force had different plans for me, and I got orders in January to work in the Pentagon with a reporting date of June 15th. The thought of working at the Pentagon was exciting, but I still didn't want to go.

I went home that Friday evening to break the bad news to the family. I told Dianna first and she was really broken up. She suggested I not tell the kids until Sunday. She figured why ruin the whole weekend. Sheri, now sixteen and going into the 11th grade next year, would be affected the most from this move. She had been in the school system for seven years and was just so happy. She had tons of friends and a steady boyfriend; she was on the basketball team, on the softball team, in the band, and was head of the newspaper staff. Telling Sheri was going to be rough.

On Sunday, we took the kids ice skating and were having a good time. We took a break and went into the lodge for a coke and some fries. The perfect time for the BIG ANNOUNCEMENT! I said "Hey guys, I got some great news for you!" That is me trying to put a positive spin on this bombshell they were about to hear. "I've been selected to work at the Pentagon in Washington DC. Isn't that great! We'll get to move to Washington DC. and see all those great monuments and all that history; it is going to be so great!"

Steven was too young to care one way or the other. John asked, "You mean we have to leave Alaska?" I said "Yes, but we'll have a really great time!" He slammed his fist on the table and said "It is not fair; they can't make us leave here! This is our home and I am going to write the president!"

Sheri's eyes welled up with tears and said "I'm not going...I'll stay with Lisa and finish school here. Dad, how can you do this to me? All my friends are here!" I said, "Sheri, you are not going to stay here. You will go with us because we are a family, and I have no intention of dropping off our kids as we travel from base to base." "But, Dad, why?" she asked. I answered, "Because that's my job and we have to go where the Air Force sends us." "Can't you just quit your job, just quit going to work!" she cried. "Sheri, I can't do that. I would be considered AWOL, and I would be put in prison." Through her tears and a quivering lip, Sheri asked "For how long?"

Leaving Alaska

It was June 5, 1979. What a sorry sight we made that night at the Fairbanks Airport. We were heading back to the lower 48. Our time in Alaska was finished, and it hurt to leave our dear friends and this place we loved so much. After seven years, Alaska had become our home. After a lot of hugs and kisses from our friends who had come to see us off, we boarded the plane in tears.

Life Slightly Off Center

CHAPTER 9

Hello Virginia

Off to the Lower 48

We flew to Seattle where we picked up our VW convertible. Dianna and the boys changed planes in Seattle and flew on to Montana to visit with Kathy and her family. Sheri and I picked up the car and planned to drive to Montana to hook up with Dianna, the boys, and our dog Lady.

This was our first time in the States in many years and did not realize how serious the gas shortage was that summer of '79. The girl who delivered the car to the airport apologized that the car only had a quarter of a tank of gas, but that was all she was able to get. She couldn't even tell me where to go to get more. All the gas stations were rationing gas, and since it was Sunday, I might not even find one open. Sheri and I headed out in search of gas. I knew we were not going far on the little bit of gas that we had. After about an hour of driving, Sheri spotted a station open and we pulled in. The attendant, a pimple-faced teenager, informed us that they were not open until noon. It was about 10 AM so we decided to go have breakfast and come back later. We pulled up to the pumps about 20 minutes to twelve. The pimple-faced kid came out and said he wasn't opening until noon and that I couldn't park in front of the pumps. Okay, this is the game and this kid has all the cards and he knew it. I said "Oh come on, give me a break—we've got a lot of driving ahead of us. Can you just fill us up so we can hit the road?" Again he said, "I said, we are not open until noon and we may or may not sell any gas today." I thought, *You little piss pot*. The first person we run into in the lower 48 after all those years in Alaska is some punk with an attitude. Sheri could tell I was getting ready to blast this kid with a few expletives. She quietly said "Dad, we need the gas." Enough said, so I pulled over to a parking spot along side the garage. We went in and were sitting in the waiting room where we met a lady who was having her oil changed. She said the best way to get gas was to have your oil changed and then they would fill you up. I explained that we had just gotten an oil change and I wasn't about to get another one. She said she got her oil changed about once a week! The pimple-faced kid walked into the waiting room and says, "You can't wait in here; this is for customers only." Now I was getting really pissed off, and said "We are trying real hard to be a customer. Why don't you fill our car up and that will make us official customers, and we'll be on our way!" By then, it was 5 minutes till noon and I pulled up in front of the pumps. He came out, looked at his watch, and said "I said noon." This was

Life Slightly Off Center

one kid who would never know how close he came to getting beaten to a pulp. I am not a violent type of guy, but this kid was pushing all my buttons. I think he got a sense of that and so he started pumping the gas.

We now have a full tank of gas, the top is down, and we are finally on our way! We're driving along and I notice a lake off in the distance. As we approached it, I saw a bunch of naked people on the beach. It was a nude beach! I yelled for Sheri to shut her eyes! *I'll be damned,* I thought, *we've been in the States only a few hours now and we had to deal with a rude, arrogant pimple-faced teenager and now a beach full of naked people. I wanna go back to Alaska already!* This was a phrase that would be repeated many, many times in the coming year by all of us.

That night we stayed at a motel. Sheri put a picture of her boyfriend, Matt, on her bedside table, and I could hear her crying as she fell off to sleep. I thought to myself, *This move is going to be a hard one.* The rest of the trip to Montana was pretty uneventful. The big thing driving across the country was finding gas—it was the main focus of every day.

When we finally got to Kathy's house, we were shocked to find Mother there! She had flown from New York to surprise us. It was a great reunion! Mom traveled a lot since Dad's death the year before. She just didn't like staying home alone. We spent several days in Montana, and then we took off again. This time I had Johnny and Lady as passengers. Sheri had decided to spend the summer with Aunt Kathy and the family. She would fly back east in a month or so. Dianna, Mom, and Steven all flew to Rochester together.

John and I had a great trip across the country. Got to see a lot of beautiful sights and had the top down the whole way! We got into great conversations with people who were surprised to see a rag top with Alaskan license plates. Lady traveled in the back lying on the folded-down top. I am sure we were quite a sight!

We met up with Dianna and Steven at Mom's. We spent a few days there and then Dianna and I headed for Virginia to find a house. We arrived on Interstate 95 at 5 PM on a Friday near Washington, DC.

We had never seen so much traffic in our lives! And to top it off, it was June and 95 degrees and we had the top down on the VW with no air. What a culture shock! We both decided right then that we were going to hate this place! We had just come from a place where three cars at a stop sign constituted a traffic jam! It was so hot and sticky, and after all those years in Alaska, I am sure our blood was probably as thick as motor oil. We headed south on 95 to hook up with some friends we had met in Alaska and were now assigned to the Pentagon. We were looking for a place called Dale City.

Dale City

We found Bonnie and Dan and they graciously invited us to stay with them while we looked for a house in the area. I was really looking forward to buying a house. We had saved while in Alaska and had a bundle of money in the bank. In the area surrounding DC, $20,000 was not considered a bundle of money, not even a good chunk of money. When I mentioned to the real estate agent that we were prepared to put our $20,000 down so he could show us his best stuff, he just chuckled and rolled his eyes.

Finding a house was a nightmare! The ones we really liked we couldn't afford; the ones we could afford we didn't like. After two weeks of looking—and I am sure getting on Bonnie and Dan's nerves—we were desperate. One night Dianna and I were walking around the neighborhood in Dale City and talking about what we should do. She said, "I'm going back to Rochester to be with the kids; you can stay here and get a room in the barracks." I said, "No way." At that moment, we passed a house that was for sale and I said, "Let's buy this one!" We did buy that very house the next day! We were never crazy about it, but it was big enough for us all and had a nice backyard. The trouble with Dale City was the houses were on top of each other and they all looked the same. I had visions of spending our "bundle of money" on a house out in the country with a couple of acres. Boy, what a dreamer! Reality bites!

Life Slightly Off Center

Introducing the Kids to Virginia

We went home and got the kids and all drove back to Virginia and to our new home. Sheri arrived from Montana soon after we moved in. The kids hated the traffic, hated the heat, hated the new house, hated that they had no friends, and the icing on the cake—the biggest hate of all—was that this area had year-round school and the kids had to go into school immediately.

Keep in mind, they had just gotten out of school in late June and here it was the middle of July and they had to go back. I'm sure that if they had the money, they would have caught the next Greyhound Bus back to Alaska! Given the choice, Dianna and I would have gone with them!

They were all moping around one day, complaining that there was nothing to do and it was so hot, and blah, blah, blah. I was putting a new floor in the dining room and had just gotten all the plywood nailed down for the sub-floor. I said "Why don't you guys go and get your markers and draw on the plywood before I put the tile down? I've got to run to Hechinger's for more supplies, so you guys can draw on the floor until I get back." They were all keen to do that. When I walked back into the house, I was shocked to see what the kids had done. There on the plywood in huge colorful letters was written:

VIRGINIA SUCKS! WE HATE IT HERE! WE WANNA GO HOME!
WE LOVE ALASKA! ALASKA IS THE BEST! ALASKA IS HOME!

They filled the floor with all kinds of remarks about their new home. I think it did the kids good to get that out of their system because they were pretty much okay from then on.

Adjusting to Life in Virginia

We got the kids settled in school. The boys were able to walk to their grade school, and both of them liked it and were making friends. Things seem to be coming together for them. Sheri had to take a bus to her new school. She went from her school in Alaska of 350 kids to the new school with a graduating class of 1,100 kids. Sheri was just overwhelmed. She tried out for basketball and didn't make it, tried out for the softball team and didn't make that either. She was so depressed. She finally tried out and made the volleyball team.

One evening we were hanging out at the house when the phone rang. I answered, and it was a boy asking for Sheri. She chitchatted with this boy for a bit and then I heard her say, "Oh, thanks, but I'm busy tomorrow night" and hung up. I asked who she had been talking to; she said it was a really cute guy from her school and he wanted her to go out the next night.

I said "Why didn't you say yes? You don't like this kid?" "Oh, he's seems like a nice guy, but why didn't he call me last week to go out this week? Did someone else cancel on him, and now he needs a last-minute date?" I was so proud of Sheri at that moment. I mean she would have loved to go out with some kids. She was still the new kid at school and was not used to being stuck at home all the time. So, she had her big chance but she wasn't about to settle as this guy's second choice. To make her feel better we popped a big batch of popcorn and spent the evening looking at slides of the good ole days in Alaska. We did that all most every Saturday night for the first six months we were in Virginia.

Eventually we got involved in our new life in Virginia and found that things were not so bad. The kids made friends and we made friends, and that made all the difference in the world. All the kids were involved in sports, so we spent most weekends running from one field to the next. In the beginning we had only one pair of cleats. We would go to John's baseball game and as soon as that was over, we would take off for wherever Steven's game was with the cleats for him to use. We eventually came into some money and got a pair for each of the kids.

Life Slightly Off Center

The Jockstrap!

In the fall John got into Little League football. We went to sign him up and came home with a list of things he would need before his first practice. Things like a mouth guard, rubber-spiked cleats, and a jockstrap. John and I went up to K-Mart to get his stuff and while we were looking around he whispered to me "Dad, don't forget I have to get a jockstrap." I guess this is comparable to a girl getting her first bra! I don't remember all the details of our shopping trip that day, only that John and I did a lot of whispering and when I put "it" on the counter, John walked away red-faced, pretending that he didn't know me or had anything to do with that jockstrap.

John didn't want anyone to see it. I know he hid it, and it didn't see daylight again until his first practice. We happened to be closing on the house the day of his practice. Dianna had made arrangements for a teammate's mom to pick up John and take him to practice. In the meantime, we were sitting around a conference table at the lawyer's office signing papers. There were two attorneys, the couple we were buying the house from, and two real-estate agents. The secretary came into the room with the phone and told me I had a phone call. It was John saying he was all suited up for practice and was ready to go except for the j-j-jockstrap. (The word *jockstrap* was said in a whisper). You could never be too careful when talking about a jock-

strap—who knows who could be listening. "Dad, do I have to wear it?" asked John "John, yes, you have got to put it on," I answered. "Just go ahead and take off your pants and put it on. No, you can't wear it over your pants; it has got to go under them," I explained. "Well, son, I guess you'll have to take your cleats off to get your pants off to put your jock on. Sure, go ahead and put it over your underwear," I said. I continued with more directions on the proper placement of a jock in what I thought was a fairly quiet voice. I hung the phone up and turned around to face everyone sitting at the table, and they were all laughing like fools. I mean they had tears in their eyes. It was hard to get back to the serious business of the closing.

Kids Grow Up Too Fast!

I guess it took us all about a year to get into the swing of things. It was then that we found ourselves on a dead run every weekend. There was always a game to go to. One morning I was out raking the front yard; Dianna was heading for the car and said to me "Come on, let's go! John has a game, and we're going to be late!" I don't know, I guess I just wanted to dink around the yard some more, and I sure didn't want to go to yet another game. I thought to myself, as I tossed the rake, "Boy, I will be so glad when these kids grow up!" The second I thought that, I regretted it and have regretted it ever since. Because my kids did grow up, and believe me, they grew up too fast, and all of a sudden they were gone!

Not too long ago I was at a soccer game of a friend's daughter. I was sitting on the sidelines with one of the fathers, and he was saying how sick he was of going to games and being so much on the run all the time. I related my story to him, and he looked at me and said "Thank you for that." I have met up with him several times since, and he has told me that whenever he gets that old feeling of being fed up with kids and games, he thinks about what I had said and it puts everything into perspective for him.

On one of his visits, my brother Billy said to me after a full day of going to all the kids' different games, "So what do you want to do now that we have seen every baseball field in northern Virginia?" That sort of summed up our weekends back in the day.

Friends

During our time in Alaska, we made some really great friends. One couple, Jake and Anna, became one of our favorites. Whenever we had a party or any kind of get-together, they were always at the top of the list. They had a couple that they ran around with whom Dianna and I didn't particularly like. I had told Dianna that we didn't want to come between Jake and Anna's relationship with Dick and Patty. So, with that in mind, we never invited one couple without the other. We spent seven years in Alaska totally enjoying Jake and Anna and totally putting up with Dick and Patty.

We left Alaska and a year later Jake and Anna followed. They came to visit us in Virginia. One evening we were sitting around the kitchen table having coffee and reminiscing about the good ole days in Alaska. I asked "So how are your good friends Dick and Patty doing? Are they still in Alaska?" Anna gave me a puzzled look and said "What do you mean, our good friends? We thought they were your good friends. We personally couldn't stand them, especially that Dick—what a jerk! We figured you guys were great friends since they were invited to every party or get-together you had. That is why we invited them to everything we had, because of you two. We didn't want to come between your friendship." I said "Well, I'll be damned! So for seven years we put with those people, and none of us liked them!" We all had a good laugh over that discovery. We remain great friends with Jake and Anna but have never heard from Dick and Patty again.

Funny Stories

These are a few random funny stories that took place while we were living in Dale City, Virginia.

A Lesson in Cussing!

I guess this story was when Sheri was about sixteen years old and John was about eleven years old. We were sitting around the rec room watching TV when the television suddenly lost its signal and went blank. Sheri said "Dang it." John immediately piped up, saying "Dad, did you hear what Sheri just said?" I said "No, John, what did she say?" John's reply: "I'm not going to say it, but it starts with a D!" Sheri volunteered that she had said "Dang it." John said, "I can't believe it; she just said it again!" I said, "John, 'dang it' is not swearing; it's alright to use the phrase 'dang it.'" He looked at me with a puzzled look on his face and said "Dad, do you mean I can say 'dang it' if I want to?" I said, "Sure, John, feel free to say it if you want to!"

A few seconds passed and John hesitantly asked "How about SHIT?"

Garage Sale

Dianna loves going to and having garage sales. One Saturday she was in rare form and was selling everything that wasn't nailed down. Two of the things that sold were some of John's prized comic books and some artwork of mine.

John went crazy when he found that some of his comic books were gone. He spent the rest of the afternoon going around the neighborhood buying back all the comic books he could find. Dianna felt really bad about this and admitted that she had also sold a pastel drawing I had done of a Playboy centerfold. It was really good and I was pissed, and even more angry when I found out she sold it for a quarter!

We were eating dinner when the door bell rang. I found a kid about twelve years old standing on the doorstep with my centerfold drawing in hand. He said his mother wouldn't let him keep it, and he wanted his quarter back!

Kiss, Kiss, Kiss!

This story took place while Sheri was home from college for a few months and working on an internship at a local TV station.

Over the years Dianna and I had gotten into the habit of kissing each other goodbye in the morning three times. Just three short smacks—never two, never four, always three. This little ritual is repeated in the evening when I get home from the office. Kiss, kiss, kiss. We never gave it a second thought until Sheri said "Mom, Dad, that kiss, kiss, kiss thing every morning and every evening is driving me crazy. It is so boring!"

The next morning after our kiss, kiss, kiss and Sheri's snide comment of B-O-R-I-N-G, I whispered "Dianna, wear something I can rip off your back tonight and then beat me with the frying pan! I winked and said "Trust me." She gave me a knowing smile.

When I got home, the kids were sitting at the table waiting for dinner. Dianna was busy at the stove. I said "Hi gang" and proceeded over to Dianna. I heard Sheri say "Oh boy, here we go again: kiss, kiss, kiss." I grabbed Dianna and laid a passionate kiss all over her face, neck, and shoulders. I was running my hands all over her back, and then I tore her shirt off! There Dianna stood in her bra! Dianna screamed "What is wrong with you, you animal, and in front of the children!" She then began beating me with a frying pan! The kids were just dumb-founded and sat there wide eyed with their mouths open—we even got a gasp out of Sheri!

We soon returned to the routine of kiss, kiss, kiss. Sheri never complained again!

Family Day

Here's a story that took place in Washington, DC. It was a chilly Sunday afternoon. Dianna, the kids, and I were having ourselves a family day. It was a very rare thing for the five of us to be off by ourselves, but there we were, having a great time! We had just finished ice skating at the park and were heading to the Hard Rock Café for lunch.

Life Slightly Off Center

I was walking with the boys on either side of me, while Dianna and Sheri brought up the rear. This is when John said "Dad, since we're enjoying this nice family day, it is probably a good time for me to thank you for this huge nose I inherited from you!" Steven piped up at this point and said "Oh yeah, since we're thanking you for things, I want to say thank you, Dad, for these giant Dumbo ears I inherited from the Raymond side of the family!" This is where John jumps in with "THANK GOD WE SPLIT DAD'S ADAM'S APPLE BETWEEN THE TWO OF US!"

Pink Socks!

Steven was in middle school. He was in his bedroom getting dressed for the big end-of-year dance. He came out and looked like a junior Don Johnson. For those of you who don't know Don Johnson, he was a big TV star back in the '80s. He was best known for starring in *Miami Vice*. Steven was dressed in a white suit, pink tie, pink socks, and white shoes and topped it all off with a white brimmed hat. For that time in history, he looked cool!

I drove him and his buddy, who was also dateless, to the dance. I went back to pick them up after the dance and drove them to a restaurant where a bunch of kids were hooking up. Both Steven and Chad got into the car, but now they had dates and seemed very happy. I dropped them all off and told them I would be back at midnight to pick them all up. I was out in front of the restaurant waiting for them when Chad came out arm in arm with his date while Steven came out alone. I asked Steven where the girl was that he had gone in with. He said "Oh, she found someone else and dropped me." She had apparently, according to Chad, said to Steven "How serious can a girl get with a guy who wears pink socks!"

It's a Boy, Girl, Boy·······!

Our friend Joel called and asked us to babysit his dog while he and his family attended a wedding in South Carolina. It would be just a three-day weekend. We, of course, said sure. Joel dropped the dog off on their way out of town. It was then that he informed us that Mitzie, his Yorkshire terrier, was pregnant! But he assured us that Mitzie was not due for several weeks, so there was nothing to worry about. I said "No problem, have a good time. We'll see you on Tuesday."

That evening I took the kids to a high school football game while Dianna stayed home with Mitzie. Well, apparently ole Mitzie was not told that she wasn't due for two weeks because she had eight puppies that night. Mother and puppies were all doing fine. Joel called several times on Saturday concerned about his dog, and each time he called we assured him Mitzie was doing fine. We had decided not to tell him about the arrival of the puppies because it would mess up his whole weekend, and Joel being Joel would probably jump in the car and return immediately. Better that he and the family have a good weekend.

Joel called several times on Sunday and again on Monday. Each time he called, the report was always the same: Mitzie is fine.

We expected Joel and his family on Tuesday afternoon. I made a banner that stretched across the whole front of the house to greet them when they pulled into

Life Slightly Off Center

the driveway. It read: IT'S A BOY, IT'S A GIRL, IT'S A GIRL, IT'S A BOY, A GIRL, A BOY, A BOY, AND ANOTHER BOY!!! The family was just floored. They were so surprised, speechless until reality sunk in, and then they couldn't thank us enough. Joel had bred Mitzie with another Yorkie, and the pups would be worth quite a bit of money. Joel told us to pick one out and it would be ours. He said that was the least he could do for all our trouble. We declined the offer and sent them on their way with the new family.

The Pentagon

Working at the Pentagon was a whole new ball game for me. This was like being in the big leagues. The commute to work was rough. We would board a bus at the end of the street, then hit I-95, and be stuck in traffic for two hours. It was such a grind. I worked in the National Military Command Center under the Joints Chiefs of Staff. It was a high-pressure place to come to each day. This was especially true after my seven years in laidback Alaska.

Every Tuesday morning we had to brief the Secretary of Defense. Talk about pressure! The briefing would take place in a briefing room with six projection screens, with most of them going at the same time. We worked in the back, flipping the slides and running the movie projector to go along with whoever was doing the briefing at the time. We were supplied a script and a stack of slides and movies and had to make sure we were on the same page as the briefer. It was intense. Everything we did during the week pretty much led up to this briefing. I remember one day I was at my drawing table when a four-star general came to me and wanted to make several changes to a slide; I had less than 5 minutes to get it done. The slide had five layers of film to it, and I started to take it apart to make the changes. The general stopped me and asked what I thought I was doing? I said "Sir, I have to take it apart to get to the part of the slide you want changes made." He said for me not to take it apart and to figure out some other way to make the changes. Now I have 4 minutes to get it done! By now, my hands were shaking, and he was leaning over my shoulder, telling me to hurry up, saying that he had to brief the Secretary of Defense in 3 minutes! I finally said, "Sir, there is no way I can make these changes that fast." He grabbed the slide and walked out in a huff, warning me that this was not the end of this! Guess what, it wasn't. I caught holy hell from my boss. The lesson learned is, you don't tell a four-star general you can't!

The Demonstration

I was the office manager, among other things, and was responsible for ordering supplies for our graphics shop. One day I got a call from a girl representing the 3M Company and she was anxious to demonstrate the newest thing in Diazo film. We agreed on a date and I set about getting things ready for the demonstration.

There were eleven of us in our office, and I invited a few other graphic shops to participate. Because this was a pretty rowdy group, I warned them all before the briefing to pay attention and not to give this girl a hard time. They all promised to behave.

The day arrived, the girl arrived and all the illustrators arrived. Everyone took a seat and then the girl asked me if I could help her with the demonstration. Things were going smoothly for roughly the first two minutes, and then the guys started snickering. One guy couldn't contain himself and left the room in complete hysterics. He composed himself and returned only to be followed by someone else stumbling out of the room bursting with laughter. I'm thinking these guys are jerks! You get a pretty girl in the room and they have no idea how to behave.

In the meantime I was doing my best to salvage the demonstration. The poor girl was completely embarrassed and wrapped things up and left in a hurry! That is when I lost it and let this group of jerks have it.

"What is wrong with you jackasses? I can't believe you couldn't behave for an hour...what the hell did you find so funny?" Well, to my embarrassment I learned what was so funny and it was ME!

My fly was wide open the whole time! There I was up in front of the whole

Life Slightly Off Center

group, one foot on a chair, the other resting on the floor causing my fly to gape open! No wonder the girl left in such a hurry. The next morning I came into work and found a new nameplate on my desk "JACK the ZIPPER."

Finger Sandwiches

One of the things I enjoyed the most about working at the Pentagon was eating lunch outside in the Center Court on nice days. A lot of days I would meet up with Joel, a friend I had met in Alaska, and we would have lunch together. It was nice to get away from all that pressure for an hour. One day Joel invited Dianna and me to his wife's birthday party. He had rented a big tour boat and was having a whole gang of friends take a cruise up the Potomac River to celebrate. I said we'd love to come and I asked what we could bring. Joel suggested we bring finger sandwiches.

I had to laugh. In our crowd, no one brought finger sandwiches to a party.

That sounded like something a women's bridge club would have. I told Dianna and she laughed, too, and said, "If Joel wants finger sandwiches, we'll give him finger sandwiches!"

She went out and bought a cookie cutter in the shape of a hand. Dianna cut out the centers of the bread and spread the egg and tuna salads on the hand shape. She then folded down the first, third, fourth, and thumb down leaving "the finger" upright...thus making the perfect finger sandwich. We arrived at the party and our finger sandwiches were the hit of the party!

End of an Era

My assignment at the Pentagon was for eighteen months. My time in the Air Force was coming to an end after twenty years. Our original plan was to go back to Alaska and settle there. The kids were not too keen on going back since all their friends were now in Virginia. We decided to send out resumes and wherever the best job offer was would be where we would move to. We were pretty flexible at this time and ready for the next phase of our lives. The Air Force had been so good to me and the family, and I had no regrets about having stayed for twenty years. I

Life Slightly Off Center

could have stayed another ten years, but figured it was time to move on.

We got the kids all scrubbed up, I put on my dress blues, Dianna put on her best dress, and we headed to the Pentagon for my retirement ceremony. It was quick, painless, and very nice. A great ending to twenty great years! After the ceremony, we were all standing out on the steps of the Pentagon when my ole Air Force buddy Ray, also in his dress blues, came over to me and gave me a big sloppy kiss right on the mouth! This was Ray's way of being funny!

CHAPTER 10

NTW

National Tire Wholesale

Following my stint in the Air Force, my first civilian job was at National Tire Wholesale (NTW). I was scheduled to go to work for NTW in their advertising department. The corporate headquarters was located in Springfield, Virginia. I had interviewed for the job several months before I got out of the Air Force, and my new boss, Harry Viener, said that he would hold the job open until I retired.

On July 1, 1981, I entered the hallowed halls of NTW and thus began a whole new life in the civilian world. I soon found out that this was a crazy bunch of people, or at least it seemed that way after so many years of working with the military. While in the Air Force, we were directed to the base theater once a month for Commander's Call. At NTW, we were directed to the multipurpose room once a week for cocktails!

When I asked about taking a physical before starting the job at NTW, Harry said, "Bend over and touch your toes." I did, and he said, "You're fine!" I was there a week and had to go on a few days' vacation for some personal stuff. When I got back to work, I asked Harry whom to report the vacation days I used to. He said, "Don't worry about it; nobody cares." So this was my introduction to civilian life, and it was pretty unsettling to me.

Black Wednesday

I was there maybe a week when they had what was called "Black Wednesday." This was the day NTW was having major layoffs. The company lawyer came up to me, put his hand on my shoulder, and smugly asked, "So, Jack, how long have you been here now, maybe a week? How long do you think you're going to last?" He was laid off the next day...I lasted another 14 years!

Harry

Harry Viener, my boss and my friend, was a piece of work. He was one of the funniest guys I had ever met. He made going to work every day a pleasure. We had some great times together! One day he said, "Jack, let's go do a survey to see how many people are still using snow tires." It was January and cold. We went to a nearby mall parking lot and began going row by row checking car for snow tires. We lasted maybe half an hour and then Harry suggested we go to an afternoon movie. I said "You're the boss!" So off we went.

We were sitting there when who walks in with his family but Tom, the owner of NTW. They sat right down in the seats directly in front of Harry and me. We couldn't have gotten any lower in our seats. We didn't say a word during the whole movie and left before it was over. We smugly thought we had gotten away with it until Tom asked us the next day if we had enjoyed the movie!

Do I Stay or Do I Go?

I guess I was at NTW maybe two or three months and I did not have a sense of really being needed. I felt no real job security. One day I got a phone call from a government contractor wanting me to come to work for them. They had offered me a job while I was still in the Air Force, but I turned it down to go with NTW. I went to the interview, and it looked like a great job, with lots of job security. The people were mostly retired military. My kind of people! There were no daiquiris at four in the afternoon as part of the package. I identified with these people. They were all pretty serious and hard-working and we spoke the same language. The guy interviewing me gave me a week to make up my mind. They were very anxious to fill the position. I would be the director of a new department, responsible for getting all the necessary equipment and hiring the people I would need. I went home not knowing what to do. I felt guilty leaving Harry after he had held the job for me for so long. Dianna and I had a long conversation about the pros and cons of each position.

After a few days, I admitted to Harry that I was thinking about leaving. He was so hurt and so upset. He wasn't mad; he just wanted me to stay. He said "Jack, one of these days we'll be as big as Goodyear Tire, and you and I will be right at the top. You are getting in on the ground floor. You and I are going places. Just be patient, because it is going to happen!" Soon Harry had his friends and some of our coworkers calling me and pleading with me not to leave. I went home every night that week and wrestled with this decision.

One evening while Dianna and I discussed whether I should leave or not, I came up with this idea. I said "How do you think Harry would feel if I asked for a six-month leave of absence to take the new job just to see if I liked it. If not, I could go back to NTW?" Dianna thought it was a horrible idea. She asked "How could you possibly ask Harry to agree with that, after all the months he had held the job open for you!" She was right, and so I didn't ask.

Friday came, the day of the big decision. I had an appointment to meet with my prospective employer to give him my decision. Harry knew where I was going, and as I was leaving the office, he shook my hand and said "Do whatever you feel is best for you, no hard feelings." What a great guy! I guess I knew then what I was going to do. I went out and bought the guy I was meeting a bottle of good scotch and told him thanks a million for the opportunity, but that I was going to stay with NTW. He was as surprised as I was with my decision. I went back to the office, and as I walked in, Harry looked up and said, "So?" I reached out and shook his hand and said "Guess we're still partners, partner!" He told me that he had been sitting there all afternoon rehearsing what he was going to say if I did take the job. He was going to suggest I take a six-month leave of absence and try out the new job; if I didn't like it, I could come back to NTW!

This new civilian life of mine was just a little crazy, but I was starting to get the hang of it.

NTW Moves

The NTW corporate headquarters moved to Woodbridge, Virginia, about a year after I started. The new place was fantastic, all glass and ultramodern. Harry and I had a corner office with windows from floor to ceiling on two sides. The place had a hot tub, racquetball court, and showers.

We were living the high life! The parties there were spectacular! No expense was spared. When Tom threw a party, Tom threw a party. The grand opening of the new building was one hell of a celebration! There was food, drink, rides in the NTW hot-air balloon, and pony rides for the kids. Juice Newton, a big name in country music, was the entertainment. The opening was a huge success.

Life at NTW

As the years unfolded, life at NTW was interesting to say the least. Harry lasted a year in the new building, and then one day out of the blue announced to me that he was leaving. He and Tom had had another run-in, and Harry was out. So there I was minus Harry. I sure hated to see him go. Along with Harry went some really crazy times.

His replacement was Loren. He was a guy with not much experience in advertising, but he surrounded himself with good people and got the job done. We moved from our corner office to a windowless office on the ground floor and began assembling a staff. We eventually had four graphic artists, a typesetter, and a secretary for Loren. My title was creative director and my tasks were to design newspaper ads, billboards, story boards for TV commercials, and sports posters. We were also responsible for radio commercials and buying time on both TV and radio. I totally enjoyed my work at NTW and the people throughout the company were a great bunch.

We, in advertising, had an especially good time and spent most our days laughing! We got the job done, but had a great time doing it! Our office was crazy. We eventually had to make room for the hot-air-balloon pilot, the race-car driver, the model for the race car, a special events girl, and her assistant. Loren even had me hire an assistant for myself. He said to hire a little Jack.

"Little Jack" turned out to be a guy named Manuel. Loren didn't care for my choice, but I talked him into giving Manuel a chance. After Manuel's first week in the office, he asked me where we hid our cameras? I said "Cameras, what are you talking about?" He said "I feel like I'm in a situation comedy—this place is crazy!" It must have seemed that way to a newcomer, but to us it was a normal way of life. We had such great times, that ole gang of mine.

One day I had to leave early to run some errands and asked where everyone was planning to go to lunch. They said "the Japanese restaurant." I said "Great, I'll meet you there about noon." I got to the restaurant a little early and told the waiter I was expecting 10 to 12 people. He took great pains arranging furniture to set up for a party of 12. It got to be about 12:30 and no one showed up. I called Manuel and asked "Where the hell are you guys? I am waiting for you at Ming Lings. When are you all going to get here?" His reply "Oh, um, we are at the other Japanese restaurant and we have all ordered and are actually almost finished with our lunch. Are you coming over?" I was totally embarrassed having to tell the waiter that it turned out I would need a table for only one. He wasn't too happy either, as he moved all the tables back into their normal configuration. I'm sure he spit in my food, and who could blame him! I can't remember, but I hope I gave him a good tip!

Spray Glue

Before the advent of computers in the NTW Advertising Department, we did a lot of cutting and pasting. One day I was using spray glue to affix something to a board. The nozzle was clogged, so I took a knife and stuck the point in the nozzle to get it unclogged. It worked, and I got spray glue in both eyes! I panicked and jumped in the car and drove to the hospital's emergency room. Every time I

blinked, my eyelashes would stick together. Driving while holding one eye open is not easy, but it is doable!

I rushed into the emergency room only to be greeted by some pimple-faced kid sitting behind a computer. He casually asked my name, reason for visit, address, phone, insurance, and on and on. Finally, I said "Look, buddy, I may be going blind here while you are asking me all these damned questions. May I please see a doctor, now!" The pimple-faced kid, unfazed by the urgency in my voice, simply replied "The doctor is not available. Please have a seat." I said "Listen, I'll be in the men's room flushing out my eyes; call me as soon as the doctor is available, please!"

I was in the men's room about 5 minutes when I heard over the intercom "John Raymond, the doctor will see you now." I went to grab some paper toweling to dry my face and there was none. So I did the next best thing and grabbed some toilet paper to dab my eyes. Big mistake! The toilet paper stuck to my eyelids, and when I pulled it away, it just shredded. I went running out of the men's room with shreds of toilet paper hanging from my eyes and into the inner office to see the doctor. He took one look at me and said "What in the hell happened to you?" After he calmed down, but between fits and gales of laughter, he said "I thought you may have survived an explosion in a toilet paper factory!"

Life Slightly Off Center

Mommy!

Still more stories from the halls of NTW... One day a girl I worked with in Advertising related this story. Her husband was taking a shower, and their three-year-old daughter wandered into the bathroom and pulled the shower curtain back, getting a good look at her naked dad. Startled, he yelled "Amanda, get out of here, now!" Amanda went running to the kitchen, yelling, "Mommy, Mommy, Daddy has a TAIL!"

Tie Over the Shoulder

Mark, a coworker, and I were having lunch in the multipurpose room. I reminded Mark that we had a 1:00 PM meeting up in the 3rd floor conference room. Mark had to make a pit stop in the men's room and would be right with me. When he came out, his tie was over his left shoulder. I asked "Mark, what's with the tie? Is it windy in there?" Mark explained that he always puts his tie over his shoulder when using the urinal so he doesn't splash on it. I went completely hysterical. Mark couldn't understand what was so funny. I said I didn't know either—it just hit me funny. Then he got all zoned out about my reaction and asked if I thought he was weird with the tie thing. I assured him that I didn't think he was weird and "Let's get going." He said "Do not tell anyone about my tie thing, I mean no one! Do you understand, Jack? I mean no one is to know that I am some kind of weirdo who puts his tie over his shoulder when taking a pee!" "Okay, okay, Mark, let's go, we're going to be late." He had to stop by his desk to get some paperwork so I just went ahead. I walked into the conference room and there sat twenty of our regional managers. I knew them all very well, and they were a great bunch of guys. I told them I would explain later, but for now "just take your ties and put them over your left shoulder." They looked a bit puzzled, but did as I asked. Mark walked into the meeting, saw all the ties over the shoulders, turned to me, and said "JACK, YOU ARE A JERK!" We all had a good laugh after I told everyone what was going on; even red-faced Mark had to laugh!

Lunch

One day, while working at NTW, I headed over to the mall to grab a quick lunch. After I finished eating, I took my tray over to the trash can and emptied everything into it. Now when I say everything, included in that everything was my keys! This trash can was full and now I had to go through it. What a mess! The deeper I dove into the can, the worse it got. I never realized how nasty these things can be. Just about the time I was deeply involved in the search, a guy from the office came over to me, tapped me on the shoulder, and said, "Jack, I'll be glad to buy you lunch!"

Big Meeting

Every couple of months the regional managers from all over the country would come to the corporate headquarters to be briefed on what was coming up. Our part of this briefing was to let them know the type of advertising we were planning and what their budget was for the coming quarter. Loren would brief on the budget and I would brief on the advertising. As we walked into the conference room, Loren whispered in my ear "Jack, I want you to conduct the whole briefing, including the budget. I'll help you if you get stuck." Stuck, are you kidding? I knew nothing about the budget but okay, if this is what the boss wanted, I'd give it a try. After getting through what I knew, I started talking about the budget. I stammered a lot, while Loren whispered facts and figures to me. It was crazy. I was embarrassed, and I was getting some pretty strange looks from the people around the conference table. I finally said "Okay, enough!" I turned, looked at Loren, and said, "How about I sit on your lap, you put your hand up the back of my shirt, I'll move my lips, and you can do the talking." I got a big laugh from everyone—well almost everyone. A red-faced Loren glared at me and took over the meeting.

Loren was pissed to say the least and told me never to pull a trick like that again. I said "Don't you ever do what you did. If you want me to discuss budgets, give me a heads-up. I need more than a second's notice to brief on something I know nothing about. What the hell were you thinking?"

We both got over it, but I was never asked to talk about the budgets again.

The Tie Event

One day I was working with the laminator at the office. Suddenly, my tie got caught up in the rollers. I was going in fast and was not able to reach the off switch! A coworker came running to my aid when he heard my screams for help! I was just about up to the knot in the tie when he grabbed a pair of scissors and cut the tie and I was free! I owe this guy my life—well, maybe that's a little dramatic, but I do owe him, and I can't even remember his name.

My obituary flashed through my mind during this emergency.

Jack Raymond strangled to death by rogue laminating machine!
Jack was a great guy and is survived by his loving wife and three children.

Sheri called me a few minutes after this incident and went into hysterics when I related the story to her. I mailed her the laminated tie, and she had it on her refrigerator for years. She loved telling the story to anyone who asked why she had a laminated tie on her refrigerator.

Life Slightly Off Center

The Olympics

It was the winter of 1984, and Dianna and I were on a plane heading to Sarajevo, Yugoslavia, for the Winter Olympics. NTW had earned the trip by buying so much advertising time on the local radio stations. The package included airfare and admission to a ton of events, including the opening and closing ceremonies. I was shocked when they gave the trip to me, two weeks before we would have to leave. I excitedly called Dianna at school and asked how she would like to go to Yugoslavia for a two-week vacation? Dianna's response to this question was "Jack, if I had a list of 100 places I would like to go, Yugoslavia would be number 500 on the list!" When I explained it was for the Winter Olympics, she was totally blown away. This would be the trip of a lifetime.

We really had to scramble to get our passports and make all the necessary arrangements for the kids to stay with friends. We of course were in our usual state of being broke and had maybe two hundred dollars in cash and no credit cards. We didn't know how we were going to survive for two weeks in a foreign country with so little money, but just couldn't turn the opportunity down. A trip like this didn't come along very often.

We left on a Sunday. The Friday before, Dianna and I were playing in a soccer game on our co-ed soccer team. We played every Friday night. Our team consisted of a bunch of friends and we called ourselves the Fun Bunch. We were easily the worst team in the league and had only won one game in three years and that was because the other team didn't show up. At any rate Dianna got a line drive right in the face that night, and it knocked her cold. She wound up with two black eyes and a swollen nose. By the time Sunday rolled around and we were boarding our plane, Dianna looked like she had lost a major boxing match. Both eyes were deep purple with green highlights and her nose was spread across her face. She looked like the actor Karl Malden, who was known for his huge nose.

We flew out of Washington National Airport. Our first stop was Amsterdam. We had a layover and while there, we struck up a friendship with a young man from Connecticut also heading to the Winter Games. He became our constant companion for the next two weeks. His name was Bob, and to this day, we still exchange Christmas cards every year.

As we were landing in Sarajevo, I looked out of the window and thought, *what an awful-looking place.* It was gray and muddy and most of the buildings and houses were rundown. It was a real disappointment.

We checked into our hotel, which was actually a college dormitory with really short twin beds. It was cold and bare and another disappointment. But we put our bags down and rushed off to a hockey game across town. The air in downtown Sarajevo was blue with diesel-fuel fumes. Dianna got violently sick from this smell and right away developed a headache and an upset stomach. By the time we reached the hockey arena, she was ready to hurl the bad airline food she had ingested over the past 20 hours. We were sitting right behind Brent Musburger, the famous sports commentator. Dianna couldn't hold it any longer and almost puked on him. He gave her a look that said *Aw, come on, lady, please don't do this.* We ran out of there and Dianna let it fly in the main lobby of the arena. What a mess! She could not have felt worse. She was tired, sick, and ready to take the first plane back to the States!

Along with our friend Bob, we met a great couple and they also became our constant companions. They were Walt and Ann from Boston. He was the editor of the *Boston Globe.* After we got the hang of being there, we had a great time. As I said, the city could not have looked any drearier—there was no snow and it was so cold. On our second day there, it began to snow flakes as big as quarters and it continued to snow for the next four days and nights. The snow transformed this dreary place into a winter wonderland. The timing could not have been more perfect. It was like God commanded *Snow,* and it snowed and snowed.

Our first official event was the Opening Ceremonies. We were bused to a beautiful stadium 2 hours ahead of the planned program. There were security guards everywhere you went. They looked meaner than hell, carried machine guns, and always had a growling German shepherd on the end of a leash. As we were walking through the entrance to the stadium, we were stopped by a guard. He checked our tote bag, pulled out our camera, and said "You take picture of ground, now." I guess he was checking to see if it was actually a camera or some kind of an exploding device. I said "No, I don't

Life Slightly Off Center

want picture of ground, I take picture of ceremony." Now he was getting upset and shouted "You take picture of ground!" Dianna was getting very nervous and yelled at me to please take a picture of the ground. Again, I said "No, do not want picture of ground!" I was just fooling with the guy, but soon found that these guys had no sense of humor and you didn't fool with them. I now have a great picture of the ground. Dianna gave me hell all the way to our seats! She was going on about me always being Mr. Funny Man, and that I could have gotten us both shot! She said "You don't fool around with men toting machine guns and man-eating dogs!"

So there we sat in the freezing cold, waiting for the big event. I told Dianna I would go and get some coffee or hot chocolate to warm us up. I found that there was no coffee, no hot chocolate, and no nothing! I couldn't believe it. You had this captive audience and there was nothing to eat or drink. I talked with one of the locals and he told me they were not allowed to make any money on the games. Even though these people had contributed 15 percent of their paychecks over the past four years to build all the venues needed to put on the Olympics. Is that crazy or what? This was their one and only chance to make some good money and they were not allowed. Socialism is not a good thing.

A few days later, I was hunting for Olympic T-shirts to bring home for the kids. I finally found a vendor on the street selling shirts. I said "Ah, finally, I find a smart Yugoslavian making some money." He said "No, sir, I am from another country and have special permit to sell shirts." The lack of motivation by the locals just boggled my mind.

Our days were filled with every kind of winter sport you could think of: hockey games, ski jumping, downhill skiing, figure skating, speed skating, bobsledding, and more. One day we were at a bobsledding event, and I went over to a vendor to buy some of this great-smelling sausage. I stood in a line for more than half an hour. When I finally got to the front of the line, I pulled out my wallet and at the same time lost my footing and went flying down the hill with my money and cards spilling out of my wallet. I climbed back up the hill, collected my money and cards, and had to go to the back of the line. I was determined to get my sausage, and nothing was going to stop me. Dianna in the meantime was freezing and pleading with me to hurry up. By the time I reached the front of the line again, I was told that they were sorry, but all the sausage was gone! For all my trouble, I walked away with a chocolate bar.

We were into our second week when I came down with the flu. I was just miserable. Like I said, the beds in our room must have been designed for really short people and were so uncomfortable. The room was cold with no TV, and I was ready to go home. We Americans are so spoiled.

I just reread this story and it sounds like we had a miserable time at the Olympics, but all in all, it was a great time—an experience we would talk about for years. However, after two weeks of being cold, broke, and eating the local food, I was very happy to step onto the plane home. Dianna couldn't get enough of it and was sad to leave.

The whole time we were there, communication with the locals was very difficult. I thought if you talked loudly and repeated everything at least twice, they would better understand you. An example of this is me ordering a coke. I would yell "Coca Cola, Coca Cola." On the way home we had a layover in New York's Kennedy Airport. I went to the snack bar to get a coke. The guy behind the counter said "Can I help you?" I yelled "Coca Cola, Coca Cola." The startled guy said "Okay, man, take it easy."

After we were home about a week, I got a call from Walt whom we had met and became friends with at the Olympics. He was explaining that he had traded in his car and all the undeveloped film from our trip was in the glove compartment and was now lost. He and his wife were flying to Florida the next week and had a layover in Washington: Could I meet him at the airport with my photos from the Olympics so could he pick out the ones he liked and I could get him copies. He figured since we were together most of the time in Yugoslavia taking pictures, everything we had would pretty much be the same photos he had taken. I told him I'd be glad to do that and set up a meeting. All our photos were actually slides, and I figured Walt couldn't really see what he wanted by holding a slide up to the light. So when we met up with Walt and his wife and went into the bar, I set up my slide projector and we had a show right there. Walt's wife was totally embarrassed, and Diana kept saying "I can't believe you are doing this." The people in the bar along with the bartender enjoyed the show. Walt picked out the ones he wanted, and everyone left happy.

The Greeting Card Business

U-CREW

"The Greeting Card People"

It was probably around 1993 when this story happened. I was at NTW and all was well with the family and the world. One day I got a call from some old college buddies of Sheri's husband, David. They had earned their masters degrees from the Darden Business School at University of Virginia.

Gregg and Tim had come up with this great idea and needed me to help out. They wanted to start a line of greeting cards geared strictly to college kids. They felt it was a great untapped market. They would come up with the ideas and my job would be the artwork. It sounded great to me and we set up a meeting. We got together at Mike's Restaurant in Springfield, Virginia. At this meeting we discussed the concept and came up with some good ideas for cards. These meetings happened about every three weeks. They would give me their ideas, and I would take them and draw up cards. We would then get back together with more ideas and more drawings. It was going along great, and we were getting to be good friends. We totally enjoyed our meetings. It was a boys' night out with beer and good food.

We named the company The U Crew. Over a period of six months and a lot of brain-storming sessions, we had thirty prototype cards done. Gregg and Tim, the marketing experts, felt it was time to get reactions to the cards from college kids. We planned on meeting at Georgetown's University Pub to introduce the cards to our target audience.

I was at work one day and talking on the phone with Tim about our trip to Georgetown. We got all the details finalized and I would meet him and Gregg there at eight the next evening. Manuel was working at NTW with me and just happened to overhear my side of the conversation. After I hung up, he asked what I was up to.

I explained about our fledgling card company and our plans for Georgetown. He asked if he could tag along with me. He thought it would be an interesting evening. I said, "Sure come along."

That night, as I laid in bed trying to get to sleep, a great prank took shape in my mind. As long as Manuel was coming along and neither of my partners knew him, this could really work. I would get Manuel to act as if he was one of the Georgetown students and he would give us a hard time about the cards.

The next day at work I ran the idea by Manuel, and he was ready and willing to play along. I made a copy of one of the cards and put that at the bottom of the pile of original cards. Sheri happened to call me during the day, and I told her what I was up to. She was just giddy about it, and said she and David would drop by accidentally to see my prank in action.

We arrived at the Georgetown Pub at the appointed time. Manuel and I went in separately, so that no one would connect us. When I got inside, I found Gregg and Tim already there sitting at a table. Manuel went to the bar for a beer. I joined Tim and Gregg for a short meeting. We decided I would go find a college kid at the bar, invite him over to our table for a beer, and get his opinion. Before we got started, I presented my partners with T-shirts with our company name on them. They were very pleased, and we agreed that we were now an official company. I had given one of the T-shirts to Manuel earlier and told him to put it on under his regular shirt. This was all part of the big prank. I pulled out the stack of our cards and set them on the table. Gregg pulled out his notebook and pen prepared to take notes. Operation College Kids Reaction was on!

I went to the bar and brought Manuel back to our table. Tim explained to him that we wanted his opinions about the cards we stacked in front of him and that we'd like him to go through each one and tell us what he liked or didn't like. Well ole Manuel, being Puerto Rican, laid on his thickest accent, and the games began. He was going through each card and making snide comments about each one. Comments like: "No good, stupid, not funny," and he kept asking why we only had white people depicted in the cartoons. Why not blacks? Why not Hispanics? Gregg was taking notes like crazy and having a hard time understand Manuel's broken English.

Tim whispered to me "Jack, you couldn't find a student who spoke English?" Both Gregg and Tim were getting pissed off with all of the negative comments. Finally Manuel got to the last card in the pile, the dummy card I had made up, said "This is bullshit," tore the card in half, and threw it in the air. Tim grabbed Manuel by his shirt collar, yanked him out of his chair, and pinned him up against the wall, yelling "What the hell do you think you are doing, you idiot?! That card was an original, and you just destroyed it!" Tim was waving his fist in Manuel's now terri-

Life Slightly Off Center

fied face. At this point, Manuel unbuttoned his shirt revealing his U-Crew T-shirt and said "No, idiot, we work for same company!" By this time Sheri who had come by was howling, Gregg and Tim were totally confused, and they looked at me for some sort of explanation. The joke could not have gone any more perfectly—it was fantastic! I just looked at my very confused partners and said "GOT YA!"

Both Tim and Gregg's parting words were "We don't know how, and we don't know when, but you're going to pay for this. We will get you, Jack, and that's a promise!"

Years later, this innocent little prank would come back to bite me in the butt. They did get me and got me good. You'll see how as you read on.

Turning 50

My 50th birthday was fast approaching, and Loren, my boss, asked how I would like to celebrate it? I told him I would like to downplay it, something with just the advertising gang, maybe a low-key lunch. Turning 50 was hard enough and the fewer people that knew it, the better. So it was agreed: a small gathering for lunch.

The morning of my birthday I found a memo on my desk about a mandatory fire briefing on the third floor at 11 AM. By the time I arrived at the briefing, all employees were already there. Tom Benedict was conducting the briefing using a flip chart and a black marker. As fire briefings go, this one was as boring as you would expect. Ole' Tom was just droning on and on. I noticed there was this really big guy whom I had never seen before working on a copy machine in the corner of the room. Now when I say big, I mean BIG! I would guess he'd have tipped the scales at 350 to 400 pounds! All of a sudden, the fat guy looked up from his work and said "Excuse me, sir, excuse me, but I have never been in this building before, and I am afraid I would never find my way out if I followed your instructions!" I thought, *if I was that big and didn't know anyone, I would keep my mouth shut and just try to blend in.* Tom was highly insulted by this guy's interruption and asked if he thought maybe he could do a better job! The fat guy said "I know I could!" With that response, Tom threw the marker at the fat guy and said "You're on!" Me, I'm thinking this is some ballsy guy!

The fat guy waddled up to the flip chart and drew a door and then a sign over the door that said EXIT. He then pointed to me and asked "What does the sign say?" I said "Who, me?" "Yeah, you! What does this sign say?" he asked again. I said "EXIT." He said "I can't hear you, what does it say?" Now I was getting a little pissed and shouted "EXIT!" At that point, the fat guy turned around, dropped his pants, and said "What does this say?" There across his naked butt was written "HAPPY 50TH BIRTHDAY, JACK!" I was stunned, speechless, and totally blown away. The whole gang was going wild. It was all a big set-up and I must admit a good one. Out came the birthday cake and a chorus of Happy Birthday.

I was talking with the fat guy while we all mingled around eating cake. He told me that he and his mom travel around in a van. Mom writes the messages across his butt, they do the party, Mom cleans off the message and writes a new one, and off they go to their next gig. "Business is great!" he said.

Afterward I was thinking that when most guys have a birthday at NTW, they get a sexy little stripper; me, I get the fat guy!

After our quiet lunch to celebrate my birthday, we came back to the office. I was hustled off to the multipurpose room where a belly dancer entertained me with her gyrations. Because I was 50 years old, there was a guy dressed up as doctor and a girl dressed as a nurse to check my vitals while the dancing was going on. My birthday cake was grey and black. As I was handing a piece of cake to one of my fellow employees, he said "All that's left to do now is to die!" This was a rough crowd!

Here is one more story about me turning 50. As you recall, turning 50 was really tough for me. I wanted to keep it quiet and maybe just sort of glide through it without a lot of people knowing I had actually reached this ripe old age while still looking so young. This was my thinking, and believe me, no one else thought this way. If the truth be known, I probably looked 55 when I was only 45. I think it was the gray hair working against me. For years, long before I was eligible for the senior discount, I was asked if I wanted it. No, I didn't want it and I especially did not want to be asked. I have a magic mirror in my bathroom and if I hold my head a certain way, by God, I am still really young! If I get the lighting just right, I am not only

Life Slightly Off Center

young, but good-looking to boot. Love that mirror!

So far, gliding through my 50th without a lot of hoopla was not working. We had the big celebration at work, a neighborhood party, and my buddy Chuck and his wife from New York took us out to a very fancy restaurant for yet one more celebration. After dinner, a huge cake was delivered to our table along with ten singing waiters. Okay, enough, it is official, I am now 50 years old and everyone knows it! I really appreciated everyone's good wishes and would have been hurt if my birthday had not been recognized. So, after a week of celebrating, I was ready to let it go.

Sheri called and wanted to take Dianna and me out to dinner to celebrate my birthday. I asked "Is it going to be a party? If yes, then no, I don't want to go." I told her my face was beginning to hurt from all the smiling I had done over the past week. She assured me that it would be just Dianna, me, Sheri, and her husband, David. Okay, great, it would be a nice quiet evening with just the four of us.

Saturday rolled around and we were on our way to meet Sheri and David for dinner at Generous George's in Old Town, Alexandria. I was really looking forward to seeing the kids and catching up on all the news. We met them at the door and followed the waitress to our table. Our table turned out to be a head table in the middle of a party room full of family and friends who screamed SURPRISE!! I was floored; I was so surprised and after the initial shock was really happy to see everyone.

During dinner they passed a mike around to all of the guests, and everyone had something to say. I was in a room full of comedians! The one thing I remember most was when they passed the mike to Karen. Karen was so shy, and this coming from her was a shocker. She said "I am from 'Rent a Friend,' so I don't really know Jack, but he seems like a nice enough guy." This brought down the house.

After dinner and all the speeches, everyone was mingling around chitchatting. This was when a waiter came up to me and said "Sir, you're going to have to watch your language because we are getting complaints from the other patrons about your profanity." I couldn't believe it; I was not a guy who swore. The worse I ever said was hell, damn, and an occasional shit, but that was it. I told the waiter I would watch it and was sorry.

About a half hour later, the manager came up to me with the same complaint. Again I was shocked that people were complaining about my language. He explained that it was a church group, and they did not appreciate my foul mouth. The manager said if I kept it up, I would be asked to leave. Wow, you have got to be kidding! I was going nuts trying to figure out what it was that I was saying to offend these people. Another half hour passed and the manager appeared, this time with two big waiters. The manager informed me that I would have to leave the restaurant, and the two waiters grabbed my arms and escorted me out of the building.

I was completely shocked, dumbfounded, and confused and could not figure out what was going on—I was being escorted out of Generous George's in complete humiliation. As they were taking me out, they happened to stop at a table where my old greeting card partners, Gregg and Tim, were sitting. They looked up at me with big smiles on their faces and said "GOT YA!"

CHAPTER 11

Clippership Drive

The Big Move

It was August of 1985 and the Raymonds were on the move. We were moving from Dale City, Virginia, to Stafford, Virginia. After seven years we were finally moving into our dream house. Guess I should maybe clarify that. It was *my* dream house. The house I had been searching for ever since the day we arrived in Virginia. We settled for the house in Dale City and were originally only going to be there for eighteen months or so and then head back to Alaska. That didn't work out, and eighteen months turned into seven years.

During our seven years in Dale City, we met a lot of great people and had a lot of good times. Most notable was the adult soccer team we played on every Friday night during the winter. These people became our best friends, and our team became known as the Fun Bunch. And boy did we have fun! We never won a game in the three years we played, but the parties after the games were fantastic! Oh, I almost forgot, we did win one game; that was a forfeit because the other team didn't show up.

The Fun Bunch was the gang helping us move to our new house. We all helped each other move so we spent a lot of weekends in U-Haul trucks. It was a typical hot and muggy Virginia summer day. I had rented two trucks, they were fully loaded, and we were ready to pull out. Then it hit me! Wait, we forgot the Japanese maple tree in the backyard. This tree was about a foot tall when we moved into the house. It was in sad shape, and I had been nursing it for all those years. When I finally found the right spot in the yard for it, the tree just took off! It turned out to be a beautiful tree, and I just couldn't leave it behind. I had dug it up, wrapped the root ball in burlap, and it was ready to go. It was to be planted in the front yard of our new home. The tree was probably about 10 feet tall. One guy said "You've got to be kidding! What the hell, are we taking the lawn, too!?"

Dianna and the kids were not too keen on moving. They were happy where we were and couldn't understand why I insisted on moving. For a while, Dianna would go with me to look for a new house, but after several years she gave up and said "If you find something you really like, come and get me, and we'll take a look." She wasn't into this random house hunting.

Finally I found it and it was perfect! Dianna loved the model and we arranged to have it built on a little piece of land in Aquia Harbour. Our house payments

Life Slightly Off Center

would go from $400 a month to $1,100 a month! This was a big and scary step, but we did it and never looked back.

We lived in this house on Clippership Drive for more than twenty years and this was really home to us. We saw our kids graduate from high school and college while we lived there. They married and had kids while we lived there. We all laughed, cried, and pretty much lived the life while there.

We met some of our dearest friends while living on Clippership Drive. There was Karen and Judd, the next door neighbors who became so important to us. Karen became Dianna's best buddy, and they spent almost every Saturday going to garage sales. We shared so much of life together—births, deaths, wedding, graduations, sickness, holidays, and lots of laughs.

Our neighbors on the other side were Pete and Mary Beth. Pete was the Marine with the beautiful wife! We had so many good times with these guys. Pete and I got to be good friends, and you'll enjoy reading about some of the adventures of Pete and Jack.

Brad and Linda lived across the street. Brad was also a Marine and flew the presidential helicopter out of Quantico. We had many good laughs together. Down the street lived Mike and Barbara. He too was a Marine and rose to the rank of a four-star general. Paul and Michelle also were a Marine family and two of the kindest and most generous people I have ever met. Jennifer and Jim were also great friends from the Harbour. We had such great times together. We love these guys!

We were pretty much surrounded by Marines since Quantico Marine Corps Base was not far from our subdivision. Our kids, the Marines, and the other friends we met while living in the Harbour were all great and especially good fodder for the following stories. They were characters, but really good people.

Shadow

Back in the day on Clippership Drive, we enjoyed lots of coffee, conversations, and laughs. Karen used to come over just about every evening after dinner and have coffee with us. We solved many of the world's problems over those cups of coffee.

One evening Karen called and asked if it would be okay if she and Judd came over for coffee and to discuss a family problem. We were all sitting around the kitchen table when they laid this on us. Benji, their youngest son, who was in his first year of college, had called with some big news. Ole Benji was sleeping with a black girl at school, and her name was Shadow! I was stunned, not by the fact that he had a black girlfriend, but by the fact that anyone who was black would name their daughter Shadow! It just struck me so funny, and they were so serious. I was really struggling to suppress laughter—I mean, come on, Shadow! I finally couldn't hold it in any more and went into fits of laughter; I actually fell on the floor doubled over with the tears flowing. Dianna was consoling Karen and Judd. All I could say was "Shadow? Are you kidding me?!" Finally, Karen and Judd started laughing and admitted that the new girlfriend was actually a new black lab puppy that Benji had bought and named Shadow.

Months later, my brother Bill was down visiting us. As we sat on the front porch, enjoying a beer, ole Shadow, who was now Karen's dog, wandered over. Bill was petting Shadow and asked what her name was. I told him and the story about the night Judd and Karen came over to tell us about Benji and Shadow. Bill went into hysterics. He loves a good laugh. Bill left that afternoon to head back to New York. He had been gone for an hour or so when I got a phone call from him. He said "You'll never guess where I am. I had to pull over to the side of the road because I got to thinking about Shadow and I started laughing so hard that I couldn't see to drive. Oh my God, that has got to be one of the funniest stories I've ever heard!" Bill was still laughing when we hung up.

Life Slightly Off Center

Ahhhh, the Joys of Owning a Boat

Judd, our good friend and neighbor, was a fellow boat owner. This was his first boat and he was excited about having it. The only problem was that Karen hated boats and was terrified to go out on one. She couldn't swim and was deathly afraid of deep water. Judd figured that if Dianna and I went out on the boat, he could convince Karen to go. He promised her that he would go nice and slow and she could keep her life preserver on the whole time. She finally agreed to go. We packed a picnic lunch, climbed aboard, and headed down the river. It was a hot, humid summer afternoon.

Judd was going so slow that there was no breeze at all. I asked him if he could speed up just a little. He responded "No, Karen is just beginning to relax and is actually enjoying herself." We were going slowly down the river, barely making a ripple, when a speedboat went speeding across our path creating a huge wake. The bow of our boat went up and then plunged down, sending the bow underwater. The boat popped back up, taking on a lot of water! Poor ole Karen was on her hands and knees screaming. I said "Oh boy, Judd, we have taken a lot of water!" Karen looked at me and said, "Jack, THAT AIN'T ALL WATER!"

That was the end of Karen's boating adventures. She never went near that boat

again. It wasn't too long after this incident that the boat sat sadly in Judd's drive-way with a FOR SALE sign on it.

My brother Billy had a similar situation. He had a boat and a wife who hated boats. The kids loved going out with him. One sunny Sunday afternoon, after much cajoling, Bill finally convinced his wife Reggie to go out. He was sure that once she tried it, she would be hooked. All aboard and off they go. Reggie always knew what to wear, no matter the occasion. So there she sat in her very chic boating outfit topped with a wide-brimmed straw hat. She was the picture of a veteran boater. Bill took it nice and slow. They got into the lake and buzzed around for awhile. Bill anchored and the kids swam off the boat, and then they all enjoyed a picnic lunch on the beach. After a relaxing few hours on the beach, it was time to pack up and head back. All in all, the day was perfect. Bill left the lake and headed into the Gen-esee River to dock the boat. Now this was a dirty, nasty river, but it was where people docked their boats. Billy pulled up to the dock and said "Okay, everyone out." Reggie was first. She put one foot on the dock while her other foot is still in the boat. The boat started drifting away from the dock, farther and farther, and there was poor Reggie straddling the dock and the boat. Her legs spread to the max and splash, she was in the filthy river! Down she went and up she came, spitting out river water and cursing Billy and his dammed boat. Her beautiful wide-brimmed straw hat was now floating down the river, never to be seen again!

Like for Karen, this was the end of Reggie's boating career.

Our Friend the General and His Wife

The first person we met when we moved to Aquia Harbour was Barbara Williams. She lived down the street in one of only a few houses in the new neigh-borhood. Barb's husband, Mike, was a Marine colonel and was stationed overseas for a year. Once he finally came home, we got to be pretty good friends. Mike and Barb are the parents of Matt, whom you will read about soon. Here are a few stories about our relationship.

It was Christmas Eve day, and Dianna had the day off from school. Our old, old dog Lady was in really bad shape, and she thought it would be a good time to take her to the vet to be put down. She had asked me to take Lady, but I just couldn't bring myself to do it. So she did it, and that night at dinner announced that Lady was gone. The kids were astounded that she would do anything like that on Christmas Eve of all days! From that day on, for the next year or so, after dinner, one of the kids would say "I'll scrape my leftovers into Lady's dish...oh, that's right, I forgot—we don't have a dog anymore, because Mom killed her on Christmas Eve!"

At any rate, that Christmas Eve we were having all the neighbors over for a party. Dianna and Barbara were sitting on the floor around the coffee table having a conversation. There was a mangy little mutt that was always hanging around Barb's house and she was always calling the animal shelter to come and get him. He was usually gone by the time they got there. She was telling Dianna that the mangy mutt was back that day, but she didn't have the heart to call the shelter to come and get him since it was Christmas Eve! Dianna just slid underneath the table!

Barb and Mike eventually moved to Washington, and we stayed in touch via Christmas cards. He continued to rise up through the ranks. Mike had just made his first star, and I called to invite him to a neighborhood Christmas Eve party. He answered the phone and I said "Can I please talk to General Williams." He said "This is Mike." I said "No, I want to talk with the General." We went back and forth with him telling me he was Mike and me insisting on talking with the General! He finally figured it out and said "Jack!" I invited him and Barb to the Christmas party, and he graciously accepted. I said "Hey, Mike, can you do me a favor and wear your uniform?" I told him all my friends would be really impressed that I actually knew a general! I was working at National Tire Wholesale at the time and he said "Okay, Jack, I'll make a deal with you: I'll wear my uniform if you'll wear a stack of tires!"

Now a two-star general, Mike sent us an invitation to Iwo Jima Memorial Park down in D.C. to see the Marine Corps Silent Drill Team. I had heard how impressive this team was and was anxious to go. On the day of the event, Dianna came by Varsity Graphics to pick me up. She was driving our daughter Sheri's two-seater convertible. She was all dressed up and looking very nice. I told her we couldn't take the convertible because I had to give Manuel a ride into the city, so we would have to go in the company truck. Dianna said "You have got to be kidding; we can't go in that truck!" The truck was in pretty sad shape and had Varsity Graphics Custom Printed T-Shirts plastered on both sides and the tailgate along with decals of different colored T-shirts. She said "We can't go in that thing. I refuse to be seen in that junk at such a dignified affair!" I assured her we would park the truck out of sight and would walk over to the park. We dropped off Manuel and headed to Iwo Jima

Memorial Park. We must have circled the park six times and just could not find a place to park. There were Marines stationed at the gate into Iwo Jima, and I pulled over to ask them where I might find parking. I showed them the invitation we had received from Mike. All they saw was the two-star flag imprinted in gold and red on the invitation and immediately swung open the gate, snapped to attention, and said "Right this way, sir!" Dianna said "Oh my God, no," and kept getting lower in her seat as we made our way up the winding path to the famed statue. At every curve in the path, a Marine was stationed and would salute as we drove by. We looked like *Sanford and Son* and Dianna was dying! She glared at me and said "I'm going to kill you!" I, being forever the optimist, I thought this was great advertising.

We were directed into a reserved parking spot; Dianna's door flew open and there stood a Marine in his dress blues with his arm extended, who said "Good evening, welcome to Iwo Jima!" Dianna took his arm, smiled at him, looked back at me with daggers in her eyes, and off we went. I walked behind Dianna and the Marine. Dianna was just gushing and said how impressive this whole thing was. He said, "Ma'am if you think this is impressive, you should come to the Barracks on Friday night." (The Barracks is Marine Corps Headquarters in downtown DC where the Drill Team performs under the lights on Friday nights during the summer.) I knew what he was talking about, but figured I'd give him a hard time. I tapped him on the shoulder and said, "Excuse me, but did I just hear you invite my wife to your barracks on Friday night?" "No, sir, you misunderstood me," he said. Dianna said "Oh, Jack, be quiet; that's the best offer I've had in years!" "No, Ma'am, you don't understand!" he pleaded. By now, this Marine had sweat dripping off his nose and was visibly shaken up. I wasn't about to let him off the hook quite yet. I asked "What is your name anyway? This just might come up in my conversation with General Williams this evening." "My name is Gunnery Sergeant Ramos, sir!" That's when I grabbed his arm and said "I just kidding with you; relax." That was a good lesson for me—you don't kid with Marines when they are on duty. He never cracked a smile, and after showing us to our seats, walked away. I am sure he must have been thinking *What a jerk!*

That next weekend I was relating this story to a neighbor. He was a Marine stationed at the Barracks. He asked "What did you say his name was?" I said, "Gunnery Sergeant Ramos." "You have got to be kidding—that guy works for me." I said "Well, when you see him again, tell him Jack Raymond says hello!"

Life Slightly Off Center

Neighbors

We totally enjoyed the neighbors on Clippership Drive, except for a couple of guys. One lived behind our house and the other lived next door. They were good buddies and kept a good supply of each other's beer in their refrigerators. I never saw either of them without a beer in his hand. They were forever after me to have a drink with them. I didn't want to get evolved in their little clique so I always had an excuse for not joining in. I was usually too busy—I had to cut the grass or rake the leaves, etc. One day they asked, and again I said no, so Dave says to Mike, "Jack thinks he is too good to drink with us." I sure didn't want them to have that impression of me, even though it was probably right. The next day, Sunday, I saw the boys up on Mike's deck enjoying a beer and shooting the breeze. I went over and said "Hey, how are you guys doing?" Mike said "Hey, Jack's here. I can't believe you came over to join us for a beer. Hey, this is great! What's your pleasure Jack? We have Coors and Bud Lite!"

I replied "I don't want a beer, just came over to see how you guys are doing. Everything okay?" "Sure, everything is great. Come on and have a beer with us." They just kept it up. I finally said "Look, guys, I've got a real drinking problem. I've been sober for three years now and am not about to start." I don't know where that came from. I actually had no problem with alcohol, but wanted to get them off my back about having a beer and it worked! Their response: "Oh, boy, sorry, Jack, we had no idea; how about a coke?" I said "No, I have to get going. I'm working on the front lawn and want to get it done. Good to talk with you guys!" As I walked away, I'm thinking, *Okay, everything is alright now. I'm not too good to drink with these guys. I'm now an okay guy with a problem!*

The next morning I was out in my driveway cutting wood with my chainsaw. My two new buddies came over to shoot the breeze. So we get to talking, and the conversation turns to Spanish-speaking people. Soon my "buddies" are really slamming Hispanics. These guys are real bigots. Little did they know that some of our dearest friends were Puerto Rican. I didn't like what I was hearing, so I said, "Before you guys say anything else, I had better tell you that I am Puerto Rican." They were stunned and couldn't understand how a guy with the last name of Raymond could be a Puerto Rican? I explained that because of people like them, my father changed our name from Raymondo to Raymond and found life to be a lot easier for us here in the United States. These guys just drifted away and never invited me for another beer; in fact, they never spoke to me again.

Later that evening at the dinner table, I told Dianna what had happened, and she got a big laugh over the whole thing. I said they are probably sitting around their dinner tables right now with their families, discussing the "drunken Puerto Rican who lives next door."

The Marines Have Landed!

It was Super Bowl Sunday and we were having a small party. The first guests to arrive were Ben and his new bride, Amanda. I had met Ben at the base gym at Quantico. He was a 2nd lieutenant going to Basic School. I guess he had been in the Marine Corps a couple of months. Ben was a great guy and a gung-ho Marine. We were sitting on the couch waiting for the game to start when Paul, a retired Marine colonel, arrived. Having never met Paul, Ben leaned over to me and asked who Paul was. I said "Oh, he's our gardener; a really nice guy—you'll like him."

Keep in mind that Marines are a very different breed of people. Respect between ranks is very, very important. I introduced Paul and Ben and told Paul that Ben was from Minnesota. They got into a conversation, and Paul asked Ben what he was doing in this part of the world. Ben went into a detailed description of Basic School, how the school worked, what was expected of the troops, and a brief history of the Marine Corps. He was talking in very basic terms so the "gardener" would understand. After about 5 minutes of this, Paul, obviously a bit miffed, said, "What the hell are you talking about? Don't you know you are talking to a retired Marine colonel with more than 30 years in the Corps? You're not talking to some green-horn, civilian; I was in Basic School before you were born!" At this point Ben sat up straight on the couch and said "Oh, excuse me, sir, I didn't know!" From then on, it was "Yes, sir" and "No, sir" when Ben addressed Paul. When Ben got the chance, he leaned over to me and whispered "Jack, you are such a jerk!"

Ben has since transferred to Iraq and then onto Guam. We still stay in touch via e-mail. All his e-mails to me are addressed to Jack the Jerk!

Life Slightly Off Center

Another Marine Story

On my way to work every day, I would stop by the gym at Quantico for my early morning workout. Like I have said, Marines are a different breed, and I soon discovered that my being an Air Force veteran did not earn me any points with these jarheads. So I didn't volunteer my history to every Marine at the gym. I got friendly with a few of the guys, and the question always came up "So, are you a retired Marine?" When I told them I was retired Air Force, this was usually met with a snicker and a "Well, nobody's perfect!"

One morning I was coming out of the showers shivering and warned a Marine friend of mine who was just getting ready to go into the showers that there was no hot water and that the water was freezing! His smart-ass reply was "Oh my God, are you kidding, Jack?! That would probably be justification to shut down an entire Air Force base!" I just walked away muttering something about jarheads being jerks!

J.RAYMOND

Brad, the Pilot

Brad, a Marine helicopter pilot, flew the presidential helicopter and was away from home a lot. It seemed like every time he was on assignment, some emergency would come up with his wife and kids. Since they were neighbors and good friends, we were always there to help out. The emergency usually involved his wife or one of the kids having to go to the emergency room for one thing or the other. The drill was that Dianna would take Linda to the emergency room while I stayed to babysit one or both of her kids. This was when Brad would choose to call. I'd answer the phone and Brad would say something like "Jack, why are you always at my house when I not home?" This became sort of a running joke with everyone but Brad, who did not see the humor in it.

I remember one day in particular. It was a Saturday morning, and Brad was coming home after a week's absence. He had been at Camp David with President Bush. I was out working in the front yard. As Brad pulled into the driveway, Linda, not seeing him, walked out the front door and came over and was talking with me. Brad had walked in the back door and, not finding Linda, came outside and spotted her across the street. He came charging over to us and yelled, "Again, you two are together! Just what is going on?" With that, he scooped her up in his arms, walked back across the street, and shouted over his shoulder, "Jack, I told the president about you, and he advised me to keep my eye on you!"

Then there was the day I was out spreading fertilizer on the front lawn. Brad came over and said "So it's that time of year?" I said "I guess it is about time for the spring application." He said "You know, Jack, I do whatever you do—you fertilize, I fertilize, you plant grass seed and I do the same—but it's not working. Your lawn looks great, and mine looks like crap. What's your secret?" "I don't know, Brad, I guess I just have a green thumb." Just about that time, Dianna yelled out the front door, "Jack, the Aquia Harbour Garden Club is on the phone and want to know if they can include our yard on their annual spring tour?" Brad looked at me in disgust and said "I'm going to sneak over to your yard at night and pee my initials in your grass. The Garden Club ought to enjoy that!"

I was a yard nut, and the place did look great. I was always out digging, planting, cutting, and raking. Karen said she would give people directions to her house and the comment she got most often was "Oh, you live next door to that house with

Life Slightly Off Center

the beautiful yard?" After awhile, she would give her directions like this: "You know that house on Clippership Drive with the beautiful yard? We live next door!" I was out in the yard one day, when Karen's husband, Judd, came up to me holding a flat of flowers and said to me "This is war!"

Pete the Marine

Pete and I became great friends, and we had some good times together! He was a funny guy, and so we were always ribbing each other. I used to give him a hard time about his height or the lack of it. I would say, "I'm surprised you got into the Marines, as short as you are!" He would call me his freakishly tall friend.

Pete to the Rescue!

Pete and I were on our way to the base gym for a hot game of racquetball. We were at a stop sign when suddenly a women driving in the opposite direction pulled over to the side of the road. She began screaming "Help me, help me, please someone help me!" Pete jumped out of my truck and ran over to the woman. He got halfway across the road when she slammed down on the gas pedal, burning rubber as she swerved away, leaving Pete in the dust. He climbed back into the truck, and I anxiously asked "What do you think we should do? Should we call 911? What'll we do, should I try to catch up with her?" Pete thought for a second, turned, looked at me, and calmly said "Let's go to the gym."

Pete and His Rat!

Pete and his daughter, Nina, took her pet rat to the vet. Pepper the rat had developed an infection in her eye. The vet examined Pepper and made the sad announcement to Pete and Nina that Pepper's eye had to be removed! The vet told Pete to go to the waiting room while he figured out the price for the surgery. Pete could then decide whether or not he wanted to proceed. The vet's assistant came out after a few minutes and said it would cost $400 for this surgery. Pete screamed, "Four hundred dollars for a five-dollar rat! Are you kidding me? Is this some sort of sick joke? Where do you hide your cameras; this has got to be *Candid Camera*!"

The assistant assured Pete that it was not a joke, that he was not on Candid Camera, and that Pepper would die without the operation." Nina's eyes filled with tears, and she pleaded with Pete to help poor Pepper. Pete felt so bad for his crying daughter, but there was no way he was going to pay that amount of money to save a $5.00 rat! The assistant told Pete she would go back and talk with the doctor and see if he could bring the price down. Pete said it was like buying a used car with the salesman negotiating with the manager for a better price. The assistant went back and forth and finally got the price down to $90.00 plus $135.00 for medication. Such a deal! Pete said his big mistake was taking Nina with him. He just couldn't bear her big tear-filled eyes and finally agreed to the price. The $5.00 rat was saved!

Life Slightly Off Center

The next day I called Pete from my office and asked, "What color are Pepper's eyes?" I told him I had run into a guy who sold animal prosthetics and said he could give him a good deal on a rat eye! Pete, who was completely disgusted with me, the vet, the rat, and especially himself, said "Jack, do you lie awake at night thinking of ways to torture me?"

Another Pete Story

It was a warm fall Saturday in September. Pete and I had rented an aerator for some yard work. We spent the whole day aerating, seeding, and fertilizing our lawns. We finished about 4 in the afternoon and were loading the machine onto my truck to take back to the rental center. This machine was very heavy, and we were really struggling to get it loaded. We got it loaded and I was pushing it toward the rear of the bed when Pete's hand got caught in one of the wheels! Pete screamed in pain! I didn't know what to do. Do I push it forward or pull it back? Pete yelled "FORWARD...PUSH IT FORWARD!" I did and his hand was freed. He had a nasty gash and was bleeding badly. I got him into the house and yelled for Dianna to get some ice for Pete's hand. Pete suddenly went pale and fell to the floor. I figured he was going into shock so I put his legs up on a kitchen chair. Pete whispered, "Jack, Jack," his voice very weak. He motioned for me to come closer so I could hear what he was trying to say. I kneeled on the floor and put my ear near his face and said "Pete, what is it?" I figured he thought he was dying and wanted me to tell his wife and the kids that he loved them! Instead, in his very weak voice, he asked, "Can you get me a coke?"

Footnote: After all the excitement, Dianna asked Pete if the coke had something to do with survival training he had learned in the Marine Corps? Pete replied "No, I was just really thirsty!"

A Man and His Chainsaw

One sunny afternoon I headed out the door with my trusty chainsaw to cut some logs into firewood. Dianna panicked every time she saw me with this piece of equipment. She warned me incessantly to be careful. This particular afternoon she was more anxious then usual and said "I'm going to take a nap. I just can't stand to watch you with that damn saw!" I proceeded to cut wood for about an hour. I got bored and decided to go work on my old Volvo. I was in the process of restoring this car and it needed some sanding before I got it painted. I was sanding the left front fender when I cut my hand on a jagged piece of metal. It was bleeding like crazy, and I went running upstairs into our bedroom and woke Dianna up to help me.

She went nuts at the sight of all the blood and figured I had cut my hand off with the chainsaw. "Oh my God, I knew this would happen! Oh, my God! Oh, my God! That damned saw!" she cried. I explained what had happen, and then she was okay. We had no bandages in the house, so Dianna, being the resourceful person she is, wrapped my hand in a sanitary napkin and sent me off to the emergency clinic at the base hospital.

The nurse took one look at my bandage and said, "Maybe we better change

Life Slightly Off Center

your dressing before you see the doctor." I said "Why bother, these things are great!" She ignored my comment and proceeded to put a respectable bandage on my wound. The nurse had me sit on a gurney and said the doctor would be right with me. The doctor spotted me from across the room, rushed over, grabbed my throat, and asked "What happened?" I said "Doc, I cut my hand." In the meantime he was feeling my Adam's apple and again asked what happen to my throat. I said "Nothing, I just have a big Adam's apple." After a few more comments about it being the biggest one he had ever seen, he concentrated on my hand and stitched it up. After a few more comments about my Adam's apple, we went our separate ways.

The Morning After

We were in Charleston, North Carolina, to attend the wedding of Noreen and Tony's son Chris. These were good friends of ours from the days we all played on the Fun Bunch soccer team. Most of the old gang was there for the wedding.

It was Friday night, and we all attended the rehearsal dinner and afterward we hit a few of the clubs in Charleston. Even though, it was late, we decided to hit one more club before heading to our motel. In this club, we ran into Chris, the groom, and a bunch of his friends celebrating Chris's last night of freedom. By the time we got there, ole Chris was feeling no pain. We closed the place down and were heading back to the motel. As we pulled out of the parking lot, we found Chris wandering in the middle of the street. He explained that all his friends had left and forgotten him. Our car was full. We had three guys in the front seat and four women in the back seat. Dianna was one of those women. We couldn't leave Chris, so we had him crawl into the back seat and lay across the laps of the four women. Chris was in really bad shape, and as we drove over this huge bridge, Chris started to moan and groan and made noises like he was ready to hurl. Dianna had Chris's head in her lap and, knowing what was about to happen, rolled down her window and struggled to get his head out of the window. Chris let loose and gobs of vomit came up, some of it going out the window, but most of it blowing back into the car all over Dianna. She literally had chunks of it in her hair. We couldn't get this drunken kid home fast enough. We pulled up to his house, carried him up the steps, and rang the bell. Noreen came to the door and said "Oh my God, what happened?" We explained what had happened and that her son had actually thrown up all over Dianna. That evening, back at the motel, Dianna was combing chunks of vomit out of her very expensive hairdo.

The next morning dawned sunny and warm. It was a perfect day for a wedding. Noreen told us that Chris stumbled down to the kitchen with a major hangover. His mother asked if he realized what had happened the previous night. Chris had no idea. The evening, especially the latter part of it, was a complete blank. Noreen told him that, among other things, he had thrown up all over Mrs. Raymond! At this, Chris buried his head in his hands and moaned "Oh, no, please tell me that didn't happen. Oh my God, throwing up on Mrs. Raymond is like throwing up on the Virgin Mary!"

At the wedding, Chris would not even look at Dianna. He was so embarrassed. During the reception, Chris finally worked up the nerve to approach Dianna and apologized profusely to her. All was forgiven, and a great time was had by all!

John, Our Official Car Wrecker

John was our official car wrecker. The first victim was a little Ford Fiesta we had bought for Sheri while she was in college. The car turned out to be a real lemon, and we decided to get rid of it. It was sitting in our driveway with a FOR SALE sign on it. One morning John asked if he could take the car into Springfield, saying "it would be great way of showing off the car. Just think how many people will see the car with the FOR SALE sign on it. Why I'd actually be doing you a favor by taking it. How many people do you think will see that the car is for sale just sitting in our driveway?"

Well, John had a good point. I said "Go ahead and take it, but be very careful. Springfield is a busy place." Later that day, I saw the Ford sitting in the driveway with all four wheels splayed out and on closer inspection one of the hub caps was missing. John was nowhere to be found. Finally he came home, and I asked what had happen to the car. He said, "Nothing; whaddaya mean...the car is fine, isn't it?" I said, "John, look at it—the wheels are all screwed up and there is a hub cap missing...what happened?" He admitted that he had driven it into a ditch and after a lot of tire spinning finally got it out. "It was sort of driving strangely on the way home, like real wobbly." Well, I cannot remember what the damage was, but it was major. It was major enough to take the selling price from $800 to $50. There sat the Fiesta with the FOR SALE sign on it, just like it had been before John drove it off to advertise it for me. The only difference was now it had splayed wheels and three hub caps and on the FOR SALE sign, we added CHEAP. It pays to advertise!

John's next victim was Dianna's little Honda station wagon. This one was not his fault. He was out delivering pizza when a girl ran a red light and broadsided him. We got a panic call from his buddy, saying, "John has been in a terrible accident and you gotta come now!" We went racing to the scene of the accident, which was right outside the gate of our subdivision, to find the Honda completely crushed and a fireman cutting the driver's door off with the "jaws of life"! John was still in the driver's seat with a white sheet covering him. My heart just raced. Dianna jumped out of the car while it was still moving and almost fainted. She was caught by a friend before she hit the ground. There is nothing more sobering or scarier than seeing your son in a crushed car with a sheet over his head. The rescue workers assured us that John was okay. They put the sheet over him to protect from flying glass while they cut the door off. John was rushed off to the hospital and, thank God, he was okay. Only a few bruises on his knees and a bit of a backlash. He walked out of the emergency room with only a neck brace. The Honda didn't fair quite so well—it was totaled. That was car number two.

Then there was my Volvo—the old clunker I had bought from a friend and had spent months sanding and pulling out dents. This would be victim number three. I had it painted, put on new whitewall tires, and it looked fantastic. The tires were 24 hours old and the paint job a week old when John said those six fateful words: "Dad, can I take the Volvo?" "What, where, why?" was my nervous response to his request. He wanted to borrow the car to take his girlfriend to Fredericksburg to take her SATs. "OK, John, you be really careful. You know I just had it painted and, and, well, just be really careful. Okay?" "I will be really, really careful." He said, rolling his eyes.

John took off in a cloud of dust, and the next time I saw him, he was explaining what had happened. He and his girl were coming back from the test and were traveling on a back-country road. His right tire went off the road, he overcorrected, and the car swerved to the left, went into the ditch, flipped over, and landed on its newly painted roof! He said gas was pouring out, and he and his girl were hanging upside down in their seat belts. The rescue workers pulled them out and away from the car, fearing a fire from all the gas. After hosing the car down, the cop said if there was anything he wanted to get out of the car, he better get it now because they were towing it away. At this point I asked if he had gotten the registration out of the glove compartment. How about the insurance card? "No, Dad, the only things I got out were my 7-11 Slurpie coupons."

"So, John, how bad is the car?" I asked. "Boy, I can't believe it, all you care about is your car, how about me, how about my girlfriend. Do you care how we are doing? No, Dad just cares about his dumb car!" He, of course, was right, and I felt really bad about being such a jerk, but it was such a nice car and it took so much work to get it looking so good...and the new tires and all the money and....ah, but I digress, the important thing was that no one got hurt and after all it was just a car, but such a great car...

The next day I got a call from the insurance company. Yes, sadly the car was totaled and was going to be towed to a junkyard in Richmond, about 60 miles from our house. If I wanted anything out of it, I could go to a service station where it had been towed, which was about 5 miles from the house. I went rushing over only to find the car had already been sent off to Richmond. I called the insurance company back to tell them that I didn't get a chance to get what I wanted out of the car. The agent said she was headed in that direction the next day and would stop by and get what I wanted. Just to give her a hard time I said "There was my wife's diamond dinner ring in the glove compartment." She asked the value on that. I replied "About $5,000. Oh, and there is her mink stole in the back seat. I guess that would be valued at about $3,000." The agent was getting nervous, so I let her off the hook and told her that I was just kidding. And the only thing I needed was the registration out of the glove compartment. She said "Oh, boy, did you have me scared!"

A few days later I was at my desk when the receptionist called and said there was a woman in the lobby wanting to see me. I went out to find the agent from the insurance company with a check for me along with my registration. I said "This is what I call service." She replied that she had to meet me, the guy who almost scared her to death with his little joke. She said I was the talk of the insurance office for the rest of the day.

John later told me that I really should thank him for wrecking all the cars he did, because every time he wrecked one, we got a better one. What can you say to that logic? I mean, where would we have been if it weren't for my boy John? There is no telling what kind of junk cars we would be driving today! All I can say is "Thank God for John!"

Life Slightly Off Center

The Party

It was late June and Bill and Reggie were visiting us for a long weekend. We were planning on going out to dinner and to the movies. John was home from college and frantically looking for a summer job. One possibility of employment was selling smoke alarm systems. He had had an interview that day, and they had given him a system and told him to demonstrate it to someone and to get their reaction. John wanted us to sit down at the kitchen table and let him demonstrate this fantastic new smoke alarm system. I told him we had reservations at a restaurant and to make it quick. So there we sat while John excitedly went through his rehearsed speech. I caught Bill rolling his eyes and asked John if he could speed things up a little. Halfway through the demonstration, he had to call the guy who had interviewed him that day to tell him how the demonstration was going. Again, I asked John to hurry it up. Part of the demonstration required John to put a piece of paper in a glass bowl and light it on fire. This was to show us just how sensitive the detector was.

In doing this, John actually caught the tablecloth on fire, which we quickly put out and guess what, the alarm system never went off. I asked John, bottom line, what is the cost of this thing. John proudly announced that it was only $600, but if we bought it today he could get it for us for only $450. I said "You've got to be kidding! Why anyone would want to buy this damn thing that obviously doesn't work for $600 when they could go to Lowes and buy a smoke detector for about twenty bucks?" I advised John to forget it and to keep looking for a summer job. So that was the end of that, and we rushed out the door to make our dinner reservations. I told John we would probably be home by midnight.

We missed our reservations and had to wait for a table. By the time we finished dinner, it was too late to make the movies. So we decided to head for home. We got home to find a full-blown party in progress.

John and all his friends were having a great time. There were kids on the deck, in the living room, a line waiting to use the bathroom, with the music blaring and the beer flowing. I was livid! John was shocked that we were home so early. I asked him what the hell was going on? He explained that it was his buddy Eric's birthday and his mom wouldn't let them have the party at his house so he invited everyone here. I said "Well, you can un-invite everyone and get them the hell out of this house."

I was so angry with him. He said "Dad, you are embarrassing me in front of my friends." This got me even angrier, and I told John to get rid of everyone now, and if this was embarrassing, he hadn't seen anything yet. John, being the diplomat he is, made one last attempt to save his party and said "Dad, if you think about it, you should really be thanking me for exposing you to real life parenting situations. You are going to never learn anything from Sheri or Steven because they're perfect." I said "John, enough! I want everyone gone NOW!"

Looking back over the years, I guess I *should* thank John for all the real-life parenting situations we found ourselves in. John was a great teacher. John is now a parent and his son Tucker is teaching him some real-life parenting situations. John once said to me if there was anything to this reincarnation; he wanted to come back as Tucker. To this I replied "John, you *were* Tucker!"

The College Kid!

John was packed and ready to head out to James Madison University to start his college career. Little did we know what a wild ride we were in for. Sheri had graduated from Radford University a few years before and that experience went without a hitch. Sheri was always on the Dean's List, made Student of the Year three years in a row, and always came home with a new award. This kid worked hard and it really paid off. Sheri was amazing! We sort of expected the same experience with John, but alas, it was not to be.

John's major in college was girls, beer, and the fraternity. He did all three very well. I think he was on campus maybe three months when he was asked to leave the dorm. He had constructed stalagmites out of beer cans and had them hanging from the ceiling, causing it to cave in! He had to move off campus, which, of course, increased the cost of sending him to school. I don't know most of the things the kid got into, and I'm better off not knowing. I do know he had a great time doing them.

One time John came home from college and proudly showed us the Golden Door Knob Award he had won. I said "Wow, John, that's great, what did you do to earn it?" He earned this prestigious award for swallowing the most live goldfish at a fraternity party! That's our boy!

I remember the time Dianna was packing John up to go back to college for his third year at James Madison. Dianna opened John's dresser drawer and found several packs of condoms! She yelled "Jack, come in here!" I found Dianna all upset and John in the corner of the room trying to look busy. Dianna cried, "Look what I found in your son's dresser! Can you believe it?" I said "Dianna, the boys are too old for us to be going through their drawers; it is time to just back off and let them be."

At about this time John piped in "Mom, it's not like I ever used them, but don't you think it better to be safe rather than sorry?" In her own defense Dianna said, "Jack, I wasn't going through his drawers; I was simply looking for the pillowcases I kept right here. John, where are those pillowcases?" John, trying to inject some humor into this embarrassing situation, said "That's what I used before I got the condoms!"

Poor Dianna gave up and walked out, while I collapsed in a fit of laughter. It was about this time that I first suggested to John that he drop out of college and become a standup comedian! John said "Most dads would advise their son to finish college and then try becoming a comic. Not my dad!" John did finish college.

Good Friends, Good Soup

Our good friends Jim and Jennifer invited Dianna and me to their home for a dinner party. Since my brother Bill and his wife, Reggie, were visiting us, they were also included in the invitation. Our good buddies Marybeth and Pete were also there. When we entered Jim and Jennifer's house, we were greeted with all these fantastic smells. We sat down at a beautiful dining-room table. Jen had pulled out all the stops and was using her good china, crystal, and linen napkins.

The first course was soup. Jennifer ladled it into everyone's bowl while explaining that this soup was her grandmother's secret recipe and she had been cooking it all day. All I heard was *ohhhhs* and *mmmms,* and this is so delicious. Reggie was asking for the recipe, and I was saying "Oh boy, Jen, this soup is great, the best I have ever tasted." About this time, Jennifer, Jim, Pete, and Marybeth broke into fits of laughter and in unison yelled, "APRIL FOOL'S!" The soup turned out to be nothing more than hot water with salt and pepper! It was a total setup and we fell for it big time. It was one of the best April Fool's jokes ever played on us. I can't tell you what we had for dinner that night, but I will never forget that soup!

315

What Is It?

We had just finished watching the very scary movie Cujo. The plot of the movie was about a St. Bernard going mad with rabies and practically tearing a car apart with a mother and child inside. I mean this was an edge-of-your-seat, heart-thumping, nail-biting movie. Dianna spent most of the movie in the hallway peeking around the corner. She was terrified!

It was late when the movie was over. I went outside to close the windows in my truck. It was a black night and I couldn't see my hand in front of my face. As I was walking back up the driveway and thinking about the movie, I heard a rustling sound. When I stopped, the sound would stop.

I started to walk, and the sound started up again. I really was getting scared. What was going on? Walk, rustling, stop, silence. Very scary. I started running and the sound kept up with me. Now I was panicked and ran up onto the porch and switched the light on. There is our trusty dog Lady dragging a potted fern. Somehow Lady had gotten the wire hanger tangled up in her collar and was pulling the plant around. I opened the screen door and yelled for Dianna to stay inside because there were man-eating ferns surrounding the house!

Our Dog Ski

After Steven went off to college, the house took on a quiet gloom. All of a sudden there were no kids and friends of kids running in and out. No more slamming screen doors, no more worrying about the kids coming home late, no more Friday night football games. I was suffering from the dreaded empty-nest syndrome. Dianna approached the empty nest much differently. To her, it meant no more huge piles of laundry, no more piles of ironing, and no more big meals to prepare. Dianna was totally enjoying this new phase of our lives.

I couldn't take it and told Dianna I needed a dog to help fill the void. So, off I went to the local dog shelter and came home with a mixed breed mutt. I named him Ski. He sure helped fill my empty nest because he was always there when I got home from work, with his tail wagging and totally glad to see me.

We let Ski have the run of the neighborhood while we were at work. Ski developed a daily routine. In the morning he would check out the neighbor's porch for shoes that were left there. He would bring home sneakers, shoes, slippers, and boots. He would only take one, leaving its mate on the porch. He hid his collection under my old '50 Chevy that was parked out in the garage. Eventually ole Ski had quite a collection. The neighbors caught on to Ski's little game and would come over to our house and ask if they could check under the Chevy for whatever shoe they were missing. Most of the time it was there!

Another part of his day was spent at local construction sites where he excelled in stealing the construction workers' lunches. Ski would take off at about noon, come home with a bag lunch, and enjoy it under a shade tree in the backyard. I remember one day he came home with a Super Big Gulp clenched in his jaws!

Ski just loved me and was always bringing me sticks. One afternoon Dianna, the neighbors, and I were standing in the front yard just shooting the breeze. Suddenly, Ski came up to me with another one of his sticks. The only difference was that this stick had a huge beehive attached to it! Angry bees were swarming all around Ski's head, while he was just oblivious and only wanted to please me with the gift of this stick. We took off in four different directions with Ski in hot pursuit of me! This is now a game and Ski was having a ball! I was running behind my neighbor Judd who turned around and yelled "Quit following me! He's your dog!" All ended well, except for a few bee stings on ole Ski's nose.

Life Slightly Off Center

Our Dog Molly!

Years ago we had a beautiful English springer spaniel named Molly. She was given to me for Christmas by Dianna and the kids. I had asked Santa for a dog, but never expected such a fine dog with a long line of pedigree. This fine dog turned into the dog from hell! Molly must have read the puppy manual from cover to cover before she came to live at our house. She did everything a puppy is expected to do. Molly peed and pooped only on carpeted areas of the house; chewed, whined, barked, tore, ripped, destroyed, dug, and ran in the opposite direction whenever she was called. One day we made the mistake of leaving her in the garage while we were off at work. We came home to find the contents of the garage completely destroyed! Nothing, and I mean nothing, had escaped the jaws of Molly.

I lost it and shouted "Why you, you son of a bitch!" Our next-door neighbor heard me and yelled back "Jack, I thought her name was Molly!" We finally gave up and put a fence around the backyard. We figured Molly would have some freedom and yet be contained. I cannot even venture a guess at how much this pedigree puppy had cost us up to that point. With the cost of fencing, all the things she had destroyed, not to mention the vet bills, I didn't even want to think about it. Every time I would complain about it, Dianna was right there to remind me that I was the one who wanted a dog. I told her "If I ever ask you to get me a horse, just shoot me!" At any rate, the fence went up and Molly had the run of the yard all day while we were at work. This gave her enough time to completely destroy the backyard. Not only did she dig holes, but she actually pulled up sod we had planted. Molly especially liked the expensive shrubs. They didn't have a chance with her. Soon the yard looked like a battlefield!

Well, life went on and Molly grew up and we all survived her growing up. She became my dog, my buddy, my constant companion. Molly went to the shop with me every day. Mornings, we would stop at McDonald's and each enjoyed a sausage and egg biscuit. On the rare occasions when Molly was not with me and I'd pull up to the McDonald's drive-thru window and order only one sausage and egg biscuit, the cashier would remark "Oh, nothing for Molly this morning?"

We would normally drive to work in my company pickup truck. Ole Molly loved sitting up there with me in the front seat. On occasion I would drive my Chrysler convertible to the shop. Molly liked sitting in the backseat and letting her ears flap in the wind. One evening we were heading home in the convertible. I had some boxes in the backseat alongside Molly. I didn't know it, but Molly had climbed up on top of the boxes and when I took a corner too sharply, she went flying out of the car. All I heard were her nails raking across the boxes trying desperately to hang on. We were on a divided highway when it happened, and I had to travel several miles before I could turn around to go and get her. She was sitting on the sidewalk, in a daze, and looking like "what the hell happened?"

Another time we were headed out of town and decided to take Molly. Dianna and I were in the front seat of the truck and Molly was back in the bed of the truck. We stopped to get a bite to eat at McDonald's. We got out of the truck and Dianna said "I thought you were going to bring Molly with us?" Molly had apparently fallen out. We went back to look for her and found her charging up a steep hill trying to catch up with us!

What a dog!

Molly's diet consisted of dry dog food and table scraps. My kids and grandson Cooper were always after me about the table scraps being bad for Molly. My way of thinking was that dry dog food must be about as tasty as compacted sawdust and a dog needed some people food to be really happy. Making Molly happy was now part of what I did.

The years flew by and before I knew it, Molly was 14 years old. The ole girl was slowing down and not feeling too good these days. This particular weekend Dianna and I were heading out of town to visit the kids and grandkids. We had arranged for our neighbor Benji to look after Molly. We no sooner got to our daughter's house when we got the call from Benji telling me that Molly had died. I went weak in the knees. Oh boy, my buddy was dead! I told Benji that I would head for home to take care of things. Benji said "No, Jack, we'll take care of everything. Pete and I are going to bury Molly for you." I was grateful for that and hung up with a broken heart.

The next day we all went off on a picnic. I was driving my truck and had my four-year-old grandson Cooper with me. He said "Pops, I'm really sorry about Molly." I said "Yeah, Coop, me, too; she was a great dog." Then Cooper started waving his little finger at me and said "You know, Pops, what you get when you feed a dog people food? I'll tell you what you get, you get a dead dog!" Great, my dog died, and the next day I was getting a lecture from my four-year-old grandson. It was a very humbling weekend.

When we got home, I found Molly's grave in the backyard underneath the maple tree. It had a stone and flowers on it. Benji came over and was telling me that he was doing the digging and Pete was doing the supervising. While Benji thought

Life Slightly Off Center

it was deep enough, Pete would say "Just keep digging, we don't want Molly coming back up." Benji said "By the time it was deep enough to please Pete, we could have buried a man six foot tall and standing!" Molly was a good dog and a good friend, and I still miss her even today.

Our Dog Katie

At the urging of my sister Kathy, I bought Dianna a bichon frises puppy for Christmas. I found a breeder on the Internet and called to find out if they had a female available. They did and the price was $750! I yelled, "Seven hundred and fifty dollars, you have got to be kidding! For that amount of money I could go and buy myself a horse!" The dog breeder very calmly said "Well sir, maybe you *should* go buy a horse."

I didn't buy a horse. I bought a puppy that was the size of a hamster! I would look at that little ball of fur and think $750! Then I looked at Dianna and saw how thrilled she was with this Christmas gift, and I knew it was worth every penny. I think I may have earned about ten good-husband points! So $750 turned out to be a bargain for that many coveted points!

It was love at first sight and Dianna named her new puppy Katie McGee. Katie was a real girlie-girl kind of dog. Dianna had her professionally groomed. Katie would be shampooed, get her puff-puff cut, be perfumed, and get bows behind her ears. Katie was the kind of dog I always swore I would never own. But after awhile I got used to her and her prissy look.

One day I was out walking Katie when a lady stopped me and went on and on about what an adorable puppy I had. She just loved the bows behind her ears. Now I am embarrassed. What could this lady be thinking? A big guy like me walking this little white ball of fur with bows in her hair. Trying to regain what was left of my masculinity, I said "This is actually my wife's dog." She looked at me, then looked at Katie, and said "Oh, yeah, sure she is." After this encounter, Katie and I cut our walk short and headed directly home.

Life Slightly Off Center

A Man and His Dog

Gary, a guy from the neighborhood, was built like the Titanic. He was tall, all muscle, and a cop. He would walk the family dog, which was a little white poodle-type dog named Precious. Every time he would walk by our house and I was out in the yard, I'd give him a hard time. I'd say, "Ahhh, a man and his dog—it's like a Norman Rockwell painting. What is the dog's name again?" Gary would groan and say "Come on, Jack, give me a break!" But there were no breaks in that neighborhood.

I found myself on the other end of the ridicule when I was out walking our new "foofoo" puppy Katie. She was dressed in her little red sweater and bows on her ears. I was startled when a cop car pulled up beside me with its lights flashing. It was Gary, and he was in hysterics! He leaned out the window and said, "Ahhh, a man and his dog—it's like a Norman Rockwell painting! What's her name?"

Ferret Fiasco

Steven was moving into an apartment that did not allow animals. Being great parents, we accepted the responsible of taking in his two smelly ferrets. This was to be a temporary situation until Steve could find a home for them. The temporary situation lasted about three years. I finally had had it and told Steven to do something with these critters. Dianna loved them, but was also ready to see them out of our laundry room. I suggested to Steven that he take them up to the local pet shop to see if they would buy them. He did and told the owner of the shop that they could not be sold separately because they had been together their whole lives. The owner agreed to buy them and sell them together.

I came home one day and told Dianna I had stopped by the pet shop and saw that there was only one ferret left. The clerk said the other one was already sold. Now Dianna was really attached to these animals and got very upset that they were not sold together. I said "I think the one that was left recognized me, because he came up to the glass and put his little paw up and I swear he had a tear in his eye!" At this Dianna went bonkers and started crying and carrying on about going to get the ferret and bringing it home! Then she really got upset when I told her I was only kidding. Both ferrets were still there together and seemed well and happy. Dianna just does not appreciate my humor at times. Again I got "You are such a jerk!"

I'm pretty sure that when Dianna buries me one day, my tombstone will read: *Here Lies Jack the Jerk, the husband I put up with for the past hundred years.*

The Cruise!

Several years ago, the kids chipped in and bought Dianna and me a cruise to celebrate our 40th wedding anniversary. The big day arrived and we were flying down to Florida to meet up with the ship. This was our first cruise, and we were both very excited. During the flight, I was reading the brochure about the cruise and that's when I discovered that it was a NONSMOKING cruise. John had booked us on a nonsmoking cruise. Boy, was I ticked.

I wasn't big smoker, more like a closet smoker. I did enjoy the ole tobacco every now and again. It was especially good with a cup of coffee or a cold beer or after a big meal. There were times when nothing tasted better than a cigarette. I tried to hide the fact that I indulged, but Dianna, the kids, and our friends knew. They just let me play my little game.

So here we were, heading for a week of sun, fun, relaxation, good food, and lots to drink and NO cigarettes! What a bummer! I was moaning the rest of the way to Florida. I said it would be like me booking John on a nonbeer cruise. Dianna had no sympathy; she said "Get over it and let's have a good time." That was easy for her to say, since she didn't smoke, not even a little.

As we approached the ship, we could see a huge no-smoking logo on the bow and another on the rear. The literature on the cruise explained that anyone caught smoking or with any smoking material on them or in their cabin would be fined $275 and be put off the ship at the next port. It would be up to that person to find his own way home at his own expense. These people were very serious and this put Dianna into her nervous mode. She just knew that I would try to sneak a smoke and that we'd be thrown off the ship somewhere in Bora Bora and never be heard from again! At the gangplank, we were met by a steward all dressed in white and holding a big plastic bag. He had everyone drop their cigarettes, pipes, cigars, lighters, or matches into the bag and assured us we could get them back at the next port.

We were two days into the cruise and having a great time. The food was excellent and the accommodations everything you could wish for. There was always something going on. Just lying by the pool was great. I almost forgot I wanted a cigarette! I was wandering around the ship and happened to run into a couple from Brooklyn and we struck up a conversation. The wife was saying how much she was enjoying the nonsmoking cruise. She was going on about the air being so clean, with no smell. Ahhh, isn't this just so wonderful! I said, "Lady, I could kill for a cigarette right now. I am about to chew off my arm!" She looked at me and said "Oh, you smoke? That's funny, you don't look like a smoker." I asked what smokers look like. She said "Oh, they are usually sort of brownish and yellowish and they smell!" Her husband had a good laugh when I told him my son had booked us on the cruise and that my wife was going crazy with worry thinking I'd get thrown off before it was all over. Since Dianna was not with us, I came up with a plan. I asked my new friend if he would like to help me play a joke on my wife. He said "Sure, what do you want me to do?" I said "If you see me around the ship and I am with my wife, just come up to me, introduce yourself as a crew member, and say that you found a pack of cigarettes in my cabin. Grab me by the arm and say you are escorting me to the brig." He agreed it would be a great joke and he would be looking for me.

Several days passed and I forgot all about our big plan. One evening we were sitting in the theater waiting for some big musical production to start, when this guy showed up in his tux and asked me if I am Mr. Raymond and if I was in cabin 230? I answer, yes. He said, "Mr. Raymond, please stand up," and he proceeded to pat me down and said very loudly that cigarettes were found in my cabin. All the while Dianna is totally embarrassed and moaning about me screwing up the whole vacation. We are attracting a lot of attention from our fellow shipmates. I was somewhat confused since I didn't recognize this guy all dressed up in a tux as my partner in crime until his wife yelled from the balcony "Hey, Jack, we got you on video!" We all had a good laugh. Well, all except Dianna who called me an idiot!

We got off the ship after several days out to sea. Dianna was going off to do what she does best, shopping. I was still dying for a cigarette and decided to walk the beach and maybe find a place to buy a pack of cigarettes. I'm walking along and this native comes up to me and says "Hey, mister, how would you like nice girl?" I said, "Only if she has a pack of Marlboros?" He looked at me, figured I was some kind of a weirdo, and walked away muttering about crazy Americans.

One other time we were in port and an announcement came over the loudspeaker that we would be pulling out of port in 45 minutes. This meant I had 45 minutes to run down to the dock, bum a cigarette from someone, have a smoke, and get back on

Life Slightly Off Center

ship. Perfect. I told Dianna my plan; she just looked at me in disgust and said "You and those damned cigarettes, you just keep pushing it!" I jumped on the elevator and was heading down when it suddenly stopped. I was stuck in the elevator for more than an hour. I banged on the door, yelling for help, until someone finally heard me and got someone from the crew to let me out. In the meantime, the ship had left port and Dianna was frantic looking for me, just knowing I had missed the ship because of those damned cigarettes! When we finally found each other, she was actually glad to see me!

We finished the trip without incident and had a great time to boot! Which just goes to prove one thing...you don't have to smoke and drink to have a good time! It helps, but it's not necessary!

Farewell...My Old '50 Chevy

1950 CHEVROLET

My old 1950 Chevy was sitting in the driveway, a sad picture of a once-classic car, suffering from too many years of neglect by me. When I bought it, it was in pristine condition and the envy of all who saw it. Everything about it was perfect. The paint, the chrome, the body, the interior, the engine...all perfect! In fact, the guy I bought it from almost made me feel like I was adopting it. I must keep it in a garage, change the oil once a month, and wax it at least every six months. Now, many years later, there it sat, an eyesore and a bone of contention between my wife and me. This classic was now known as Jack's piece of junk. Finally, Dianna, after years of bugging me about getting rid of it, said "Jack, the car has got to go—PLEASE!"

After much soul searching and a couple of letters from the homeowners' association, I finally admitted to myself that I would never have the time or money to bring it back to its original condition. So I put it up for sale. I advertised in a classic car magazine. Within days, there was a wrecker in my driveway, hooking up my ole friend and taking her away. It brought a tear to my eyes as the old Chevy disappeared around the corner. Dianna clapped her hands in glee!

Several days later, I got a phone call from some old codger inquiring about the car. I told him that I was sorry, but the car was already sold. He said with complete disgust in his voice, "How could you sell a 1950 Chevy? That is one of the finest cars ever built. I cannot understand how you could let a car like that go" I explained to him that my wife had given me an ultimatum—it was either her or the car. The old geezer's reply to this was "I would have told her to have a good trip!" After the old guy hung up, I got to thinking about all the great stories that were associated with that beautiful old car. Here are a few......

John and Steven and the Chevy

One morning at breakfast, John asked to drive my prize possession, my '50 classic Chevrolet to school. I had never let John or anyone else drive it. It was John and Steven's first day at their new school. John said "What an impression the Raymond brothers could make by pulling up in the Chevy. The kids will be so impressed; we'll be like instant hits at North Stafford High School! Come on, Dad, please let us take it, just this one time. I promise I'll be so careful."

His pleading paid off and I reluctantly agreed. I told him to be sure and use hand signals because the turn signals are broken. John vaguely remembered something about hand signals from driver's training, but needed a quick refresher course. We ran through the hand signals as Steven looked on. When John was learning to drive, I taught him in the family car, which had an automatic transmission. He also learned how to drive a stick shift in another car that we had. So he was okay with the stick shift and the clutch concept. As they pulled out of the driveway, waving and beeping, I just stood there with a lump in my throat, knowing I had made a big mistake. I was anxious all day at work and just couldn't wait to get home. I pulled up to the house. There sat my baby, my Chevy. After a quick check, everything seemed intact, and I was so relieved. I went into the house and ran into Steven. "Steven, how was the trip to school?" I asked. He said, "Great, Dad, the kids went crazy over the car!" "Great, and you made it alright, no dents, no dings in the parking lot?" I asked. "Did John remember to give the hand signals?" "Steven stammered a bit and said "well, Dad, not quite; I actually gave the hand signals. John said he was too busy driving and shifting and for me to do the hand signals out my window!"

Dianna and the Chevy!

Dianna worked at the local middle school in Woodbridge, Virginia. One day I picked her up in the old Chevy. One of the teachers noticed the car and asked Dianna the next day if she would be willing to drive the Chevy to school one day. He was teaching about the 1950s and said the car would be a great example of what the cars looked like back then.

Dianna asked if she could drive the Chevy to school for the kids to see. She promised nothing would happen to it. "In fact, I'll tell the kids not to even touch it." Again I hesitantly agreed. The next morning Dianna was off to school in my baby and again I had a lump in my throat.

Little did Dianna know, but I had removed the back bumper the week before and had taken it to a shop to have it rechromed. I hadn't told Dianna what I was up to. All she would see was dollars going out the window when there were so many other things we needed. So any money spent on the Chevy was just between me and my car.

That evening Dianna came home and reported that the kids at school loved the car! I went to the garage and made like I was checking over the car. I immediately came rushing back into the kitchen and yelled "The rear bumper is GONE!" Dianna panicked and went running out to the garage and saw that the bumper was indeed gone. She kept saying "OH MY GOD, OH MY GOD! Mr. Smith promised me he wouldn't let those little monsters touch your car! OH MY GOD, I AM SORRY, WHY

WOULD THEY EVEN WANT YOUR REAR BUMPER? OH MY GOD, I'LL GO BACK TO SCHOOL AND SEE IF I CAN FIND IT. OH MY GOD, AND I AM SO SORRY, JACK!" Then Dianna looked at me and asked what I was laughing about? I told her where the bumper was and that I was just joking with her. She didn't see the humor in my little joke at all and muttered something about me being such a jerk! I believe that was the last time Dianna ever drove the old Chevy.

Footnote: If I had a dime for every time I have been called a jerk, I'd be a very rich man today!

Matt and the Chevy!

One summer afternoon I was out in the driveway putting yet another coat of wax on the Chevy. Matt, our fourteen-year-old neighbor, stopped by to admire the car. His comments of "neat, cool, beautiful" and another "neat" and "cool" pretty much summed up our conversation. Matt asked if he could sit in the driver's seat. I said "Sure, go ahead." Matt slid in and was playing with the steering wheel and just pretty much enjoying himself. Then he asked if he could start it so he could hear the engine.

I said "Matt, I'll bet you five bucks that you can't start it." He took the bet and proceeded to turn the key and nothing happened. "Mr. Raymond, are you playing with me? Is the battery dead or something?" he asked. The old Chevy, like most cars of that generation, had a starter button. So you turn the key and then hit the starter button, which is located on the dashboard to the left of the steering wheel.

I said to Matt, who happened to be barefooted, to put his big toe on his right foot on the button on the glove compartment, turn the key to the ON position. Now take the big toe on your left foot and put it on the starter button. You have to picture this to see the humor. There was Matt sitting in the front seat spread-eagle; he hit the starter button and the ole Chevy came to life! A big smile spread across Matt's face, and he said, "This is soooo cool!" I got laughing like a fool! Matt asked "What was so funny, Mr. Raymond? Are you laughing at me?" I said "Matt, just think about it: Can you imagine a woman back in the '50s in a dress having to get spread-eagle to get her car started!" I explained that the button on the glove compartment had nothing to do with getting the car started. Matt sat there with a puzzled look on his face and asked "Mr. Raymond, does this mean I owe you $5.00?

While we are on the subject of Matt, another story comes to mind. His mother, Barbara, told us that Matt came home one day scratched, cut, and bleeding. She was all upset and said "Oh my God, Matt, are you okay? What happened?" With a smile on his face, he explained that he was riding his bike past our house and Sheri, home from college for the weekend, was out washing her car in her bikini! Matt said he ran his bike into the ditch and got his foot caught in spokes! Barbara, very concerned for her son, asked if anything was broken. With a goofy smile on his face, his only reply was "Sheri is so HOT!"

Roger and the Chevy!

You probably remember me mentioning Roger, our friend from Alaska. Roger called me one day while we were living in Dale City and asked if he could come and live with us for awhile. He explained that he had just graduated from high school and was not ready to go to college. He pretty much needed a place to chill out, while he figured out what to do with his life. Dianna and I were glad to have him as part of our family. Roger stayed for nine months or so.

One weekend Roger and I was heading to Carlisle, Pennsylvania, for one of the biggest car shows on the East Coast. We were driving up in my 1950 Chevy. We stopped for dinner about halfway at a restaurant and had settled into a booth. I guess I should tell you that Roger was a great-looking kid. He was Brad Pitt good looking and always got a lot of admiring looks from the girls. At any rate, we're sitting there, shooting the breeze, when the waiter came over with two drinks, compliments of a couple of girls sitting at the bar. Roger took his drink and smiled and tipped his glass toward the girls. I took mine and did the same and started to take a drink, when one of the girls shouted, "No, no, both of the drinks are for him!"

Now that is what I would call a humbling experience.

My 1975 Olds Convertible!

I was like a kid on Christmas morning! Up at 5 AM, dressed, and ready to go! What was all the excitement? Today was the day I was going to pick up my 1975 Olds! This was one beautiful car. A burgundy convertible with a white top, rolled and pleated leather upholstery, whitewall tires with wire wheels, and only 60,000 original miles on it! I mean we were talking a real beauty, a real classic! Being the car nut that I am, I was just beside myself with excitement!

I had asked Dianna the night before about getting up early and going to breakfast and then on to pick up the car. We stopped for breakfast and I could hardly sit still. I kept asking Dianna if she was finished. Finally she said, "Yes, Jack, I'm done." I said "Okay, let's get going!" We got into the truck and Dianna said she had to stop at Home Depot first. My response to this, in one word, was "NOOOOOOOOOO!!!!!" I said "We will not stop at Home Depot, we will not stop anyplace—we will go directly to the new car! Understand?" She muttered something about men and their toys.

We were traveling down I-95 and had to go about twenty miles. I was going quite a bit over the speed limit, and Dianna said "Jack, slow down, you are going to kill us!" I reluctantly slowed down some. Good ole Dianna, in an effort to calm me down, began telling me this joke she had heard at school. It went like this: These two girls were talking. The one girl said "Look at this beautiful diamond ring that my husband gave me when I had my first baby!" The girlfriend replies, "THAT'S NICE." The first woman said "You see this beautiful diamond bracelet? Well, my husband gave me this when we had our second baby." The girlfriend's reply was again "THAT'S NICE." The first woman pointed to the beautiful Cadillac parked in the driveway and said "My darling husband gave me that car when we had our third child." And again her girlfriend said "THAT'S NICE." The first girl then asked "Tell me, honey; what did your husband get you when you had your first baby?" The girlfriend's reply "Oh, he gave me a book on etiquette." "That's it?! He gave you a book?" "Yes, and I found it very helpful. Take for instance when someone is telling me things that I don't care about, I don't say 'I don't give a shit.' Now I simply smile and say "THAT'S NICE."

We finally pulled up to the house with the car. There it sat, just as beautiful as I remembered. I jumped out of the truck. I was going crazy over this car! "Dianna,

Life Slightly Off Center

look at this thing! How about that paint job; the color, could it be more perfect?!
Look at the top, it looks brand new, and take a look at the upholstery...white rolled
and pleated leather in perfect condition. Oh my God! Dianna, check out these wire
wheels, perfect, right!" I opened the hood and said, "Look at the condition of this
engine and it only has 60,000 original miles on it! I think I have died and gone to
'Oldsmobile Heaven!'" It was at this point that Dianna patted me on the head and
said "Honey, THAT'S NICE."

Introducing the Olds to the Family!

It was one of those perfect East Coast fall days, sunny and about 70
degrees. The leaves were in full color, in shades of yellow, red, and orange along
this beautiful stretch of country road. There were horse farms on either side of the
road with beautiful horses lazily grazing. It looked like a setting for a great car commercial and there it was, the star, my beautiful Olds. It had a fresh coat of wax, the
top was down, and I'm thinking, *Boy, it doesn't get any better than this!*

We were on our way to Charlottesville and my son John's house to celebrate our grandson Carson's birthday. The whole gang would be there, and it would be their first look at this beauty! This car that was an example of General Motors at its best! I got exactly the reception I was hoping for. Everyone went nuts over the car (and I might add here that I didn't get one "THAT'S NICE" from anyone). The grandkids were especially excited about the car. Our oldest grandson, Cooper, is a real car nut. He was about seven years old when he first laid eyes on this magnificent machine. He walked up to the car and began stroking it. He said "oh, Pops, wow, the color, the wheels, and it even has whitewall tires. Oh boy, Pops, it is just perfect!"

After the presents were opened and the candles were blown out, we found all the grandchildren sitting Indian style in the driveway, eating their cake and staring at the car. I later took the three oldest grandchildren for the ride that they had been begging for since we had arrived. The three of them were in the backseat and just talking up a storm. Suddenly the conversation became a whisper. The next thing I heard was Cooper asking me, "What will you do with this car when you die?" I said, "Oh gosh, Coop, I don't know. I guess maybe I'll leave it to my grandsons." This was exactly what they wanted to hear. Now the conversation got all excited again with plans for sharing the car and maybe they could rent a garage together and maybe each one would have the car for a week at a time. They had all the logistics figured out. Conversation in the backseat became a whisper again and all I could hear was "No, you ask him; no, you ask." Finally Cooper stepped up to the plate and asked, "POPS, HOW OLD ARE YOU ANYWAY?" My guess is they were trying to figure out how long they might have to wait to have this dream come true.

Best Christmas Gift Ever!

To my surprise and dismay, my beloved '75 Olds would not fit in our garage. It was just too long and the thought of having to leave it out in the elements killed me. It bothered me so much that I suggested to Dianna that we look for a new house with a bigger garage. She was astounded that I would even consider a new house just so my car could have a nice dry place to live. After being shot down on

Life Slightly Off Center

this idea, I started trying to figure out how we could extend the garage. This turned out to be another crazy and expensive idea.

It was getting toward Christmas and Dianna asked what I wanted. I said "All I want is for my car to fit in the garage." Dianna's response was for me to get serious. I said "I am serious; that is all I want for Christmas." She suggested maybe a new car cover, but I knew that wouldn't work. Nothing works better that a garage.

One Saturday, I drove the Olds to work. When I arrived home that evening, there was a big Christmas wreath hanging on the garage door. As I pulled up, Dianna opened the garage door and said "Pull that baby in here!" I was baffled and said "What? You know it won't fit." She insisted and so very cautiously, I eased my way into the garage. Slowly, slowly, I pulled in and was amazed, delighted, and giddy at the fact that that my prized possession actually fit, with an inch to spare. Wow!

I couldn't believe it. Dianna had spent the whole day taking down shelves and rearranging everything in the garage. She had even padded the wall in the rear of the garage so the front of the car would not scrape up against it. Now that is what I call a Christmas gift! I was so happy and was again totally blown away by Dianna and her ingenuity. As wives go, she is the BEST!

The Big Trophy

My brother, Bill, is also a car nut and has a beautiful 1970 Chevy Malibu in mint condition. Last year he and his car won BEST IN SHOW at the big car show at Charlotte Beach in Rochester, New York. This is exactly what he needed to give me a hard time. I had entered both my 1950 Chevy and my 1975 Olds convertible in several shows and always walked away empty-handed. Whenever we go up to visit Bill and his family, he always brings out the damned trophy just to make sure I had not forgotten that he won one!

One day I was telling my friend Pete about the trophy and how I wished I had one to show off to Bill. Pete said "You want a trophy, my friend? Well, by God, we're going to come up with a trophy that will knock your brother's socks off!"

Pete was at a garage sale one Saturday afternoon, and in the coroner of the garage was a box full of old beat-up trophies marked FREE! Pete called me to tell me about his find and to come over to help him build my trophy! "We'll show your brother what a BEST IN SHOW trophy should look like." We went through the box and took different parts from trophies and combined them with others and on and on until the damned thing stood 5 feet tall. To add to the glitz, I had a couple of plates engraved—one read "1975 OLDS BEST IN SHOW' and the other "JACK'S CAR IS BETTER THAN BILL'S CAR." We affixed them to the trophy and then stood back to admire our handwork. Pete said, "Now that's a trophy!"

I called Bill to tell him I had finally won a BEST IN SHOW and would bring the trophy with me the next time we came up for a visit. His reply, "Oh, Jack, you don't have to bring it with you; I'll see it the next time we are down your way."

I couldn't wait to show it to him, so we planned a trip to Rochester in early summer. I packed that 5-foot baby in the trunk and chuckled all the way to Rochester. Of course Dianna thought I was nuts. We got close to Rochester and called Bill to tell him we would be there in about an hour. He said "Meet us at Schaller's. We're all going down there for a burger." When we arrived, the whole gang was there and we were sitting around laughing and having a good ole time. I steered the conversation to what else but car shows, and that led to winning, which naturally lead to trophies. "Oh, I just happen to have my trophy in the car. I'll go and get it. Oh no, it's no trouble at all!" I said. "I am anxious to show it to someone who will appreciate it." As I walked back into the restaurant with this huge gaudy trophy, an old guy stopped me and asked, "What the hell did you have to do to win that?" When Bill spotted me and my trophy, his only comment was "Holy shit!" He was totally amazed at the trophy and said that this must have been one big car show to give out trophies like this one. Then he read the engraved plate that read "Jack's Car Is Better than Bill's Car!" He rolled his eyes and said "You jerk!" We all had a good laugh!

Footnote: This story is the perfect example that while men may grow older, they never grow up! If you doubt that, just ask our wives!

Life Slightly Off Center

Gone Fishing

I was visiting my son Steven in Richmond, Virginia. He had recently graduated from James Madison University and was in Richmond working as an intern for the Richmond Renegades, a pro hockey team. He was earning a mere stipend and working long hours, but he was living his dream of being associated with a pro sports team.

I never realized how broke the kid was until this visit. He asked "Hey Dad, you want to go fishing?" I said "Sure, I'd love to go!" This request was a pleasant surprise and I jumped at the chance to bond with my son. So there we were, fishing on the James River and pulling in some good-size fish. I said "Steven, I didn't realize you liked fishing. If I had known, I would have taken you when you were a kid. You never seemed that interested." He replied "Dad, I hate fishing and would much prefer being back at the apartment watching a football game on TV. I'm here fishing so I can eat." He explained that one of his roommates was a hunter and the other roommate was a local Campbell's Soup distributor. They lived on fish, venison, and soup washed down with water. On payday, they washed it down with a Bud Light!

Dianna at the Pharmacy

Dianna was sitting in the pharmacy at the base hospital, waiting for her prescription to be filled. She had been sick all week and had come into the hospital to get checked out. The doctor reassured her it was nothing more than a stomach virus and prescribed something to settle her tummy and stop the diarrhea.

After about a 15-minute wait, her name was called over the PA system—that is, almost her name. Dianna slid down in her seat as the PA blasted all over the waiting room! "DIARRHEA RAYMOND, DIARRHEA RAYMOND! Your prescription is ready for pickup."

And yet again..."DIARRHEA RAYMOND, DIARRHEA RAYMOND! Please pick up your prescription."

Dianna said she could just feel everyone looking around for the lady with the first name of DIARRHEA. There was no way she was going up there at that time to claim her medicine. She sat there for another 15 minutes and finally went up to the pickup window and told the corpsman behind the counter that she was Mrs. Raymond and that the first name was DIANNA!

Life Slightly Off Center

The Wedding

The big wedding was scheduled for Saturday. This would be a second wedding for both Sheri and Tom. They were totally crazy about each other and nothing was going to put a dampener on this big event. Not even Hurricane Isabel, which hit Virginia the Friday before the wedding. All the grand plans were scrapped and alternate plans were quickly made. The power was knocked out pretty much everywhere.

The fancy dinner party to be held on Friday evening wound up taking place in John's basement on foldout tables by candlelight. Saturday dawned hot and humid, and the lack of air conditioning was sorely felt by everyone. The temperature in the church was probably pushing 85 degrees. It was a beautiful service, and no one seemed to mind the temperature or the lack of the electric organ. Sheri and Tom were just beaming.

The reception was outside and was put on without any power. It went on without a hitch. It couldn't have been nicer. Sheri was so happy. She had finally found the right man! She once confided in me that the man she married would be the man who could "knock her socks off!"

During the reception I got up and toasted the new bride and groom and presented Tom, my brand new son-in-law, with a trophy. It was a sock mounted on a pedestal with a gold plate reading "Congratulations to the man who knocked my daughter's socks off!" Tom still has this trophy sitting on his dresser. And they have lived happily ever after!

CHAPTER 12

Varsity Graphics

Varsity Graphics

Life continued at a breakneck pace on Clippership Drive. Sheri had graduated from Radford University and had gotten married and was working and living in Alexandria, Virginia. The boys were in high school. John was a senior and Steven was in the tenth grade. Getting Sheri through college was financially tough, and the thought of both the boys in college at the same time was frightening. I was discussing this with Sheri one day, and she suggested I go back into the shirt business like I had done in Alaska to make some extra money. She said you could set up shop in the garage.

I nixed the idea, since I didn't have the extra money to buy the necessary equipment, and that was the end of it. For Christmas that year Sheri gave me a gift that was a box wrapped up with a squeegee on top. The engraved gold plate attached to the squeegee read "GO FOR IT!" I unwrapped the gift and I found a cigar box full of money! It turned out to be five hundred dollars! Sheri said now you can buy some equipment to start your shirt business. Wow! I was just blown away with this wonderful gift, even more blown away when I found out that this was Sheri's very first Christmas bonus. Such a nice girl!

This turned out to be the seed money for what would turn into Varsity Graphics. We outfitted the garage with a small shop, bought some inexpensive equipment, and PRESTO we were in business!

Time went on, and John went off to college. He went to James Madison University and he loved it! He especially loved the beer, the girls, the freedom, and the frat life! Steven followed John to James Madison University two years later. He also got into the beer, enjoyed the freedom and the girls, and became a member of the same fraternity as his big brother.

I, in the meantime, was cranking out the T-shirts and making the extra money it seemed we needed constantly for the boys' tuition. Between Dianna, the boys, and the shirt business proceeds, we got them through school.

Our Crazy House

Things got pretty crazy at times around our house. Here is an example of just how crazy it could get: Manuel, my Puerto Rican buddy, was there and we were planning on running shirts after we finished dinner. Roger and his wife, Naomi, were there with her mother who was visiting from Japan and did not speak any English. John's girlfriend Stacey showed up with her cousin and her cousin's newborn baby. Stacey had just picked them up from Reagan National Airport; they had just flown in from California. The cousin was sitting on the couch in the rec room nursing her baby. Everyone was talking at once, and poor Dianna was rushing around trying to get dinner on the table.

Just about then the phone rang. It was Dianna's brother, Kenny. Kenny had a friend in Turkey and was calling to see if his friend's daughter could come and live with us for six months while I taught her all about screen printing and the T-shirt business. I explained what Kenny wanted to Dianna and asked what she thought about this girl coming to live with us. Dianna, who by now was completely out of her mind, shot back at me through gritted teeth "Sure, why not? Tell her to bring the whole family!" The girl on the couch nursing her baby said at this point, "This is the craziest house I have ever been in!" I said "You think this place is crazy? You know what I think is crazy—I think it's crazy that there is a girl sitting in my house nursing a baby and I don't even know her name!"

Life Slightly Off Center

The Itch

I was still working full time at NTW and doing the shirt business at night and on weekends. The business kept getting bigger and bigger. The orders just never stopped coming in. This was about the time that I started thinking that maybe I should do this on a full-time basis. Dianna thought I had gone off my rocker and asked me not to even think about it. She just couldn't understand why I would leave a great job, doing something I loved, with people I enjoyed working with, and jump into something with no security. She was right—it *was* crazy to even think about it, but I couldn't help myself.

The years rolled by, the boys graduated and were off on their own, the house was almost paid for, and I'm thinking *This is my chance to do it!* I saw this as my window of opportunity to take Varsity Graphics to a full-time operation. The kids were all for it. Their chant was "Do it Dad, do it!" Dianna's chant was "Please don't do it; don't do it, please!" By this time I had been at NTW for fourteen years and it was a lot to give up. But I had this itch to be my own boss in my own business.

This itch had to be satisfied, and I could not stop thinking and planning. Dianna and I discussed it constantly. She said to me at one point "Jack, what if you fail, then what do we do?" My reply was, "What if someday when I'm eighty years old, I am grumbling about the fact that I should have tried!"

That got her. She gave me her blessing and said go for it! I told the kids and they were ecstatic, assuring me that they were behind me and had no doubt that I would succeed.

The Big Decision

Soon after the decision was made, I typed up a letter of resignation and was on my way to work to turn it in. I was on cloud nine; I was so happy at the thought of actually doing this. I stopped at McDonald's for breakfast and who did I run into but an old friend from my days in the Air Force. I knew he had started his own business and was anxious to ask how he was doing. It was like kismet running into him after all these years. I was telling him all my plans and was anxious to hear how his business was going. He said "Not good. In fact, it went down the toilet! I lost my boat and may even lose my house."

After leaving him and hearing his sad story, I was convinced it was a sign. Of all the people to run into, I run into this guy! By the time I drove into the parking lot at NTW, I had convinced myself that leaving this company was a big mistake! I would stay, put in my time, and one day retire from NTW. The phone was ringing on my desk as I walked into the office. It was John, asking what the reaction was when I handed my boss the letter of resignation. I told John about meeting my old friend at McDonald's and that I had decided to go ahead and stay at NTW. John said "Dad, why do you listen to these people? Why don't you do what you want to do for once?" And with that he hung up in disgust! Five minutes later I received a fax from him. It was a rough cartoon of me being hit over the head with a baseball bat. The bat had the word "Future" written on it. At the bottom of the cartoon in 2-inch letters was the word "COWARD"! That was the push I needed; I went into Loren's office and handed in my letter of resignation! And like they say in the movies "The rest is history!"

We're in Business!

Within a few months and a lot of earth-shattering decisions, Varsity Graphics was in business! Manuel was now my partner in the business and we had our official grand opening on September 6, 1996! What a day that was—one I shall never forget! The shop we rented was in Woodbridge, Virginia. We had all our friends and family there for the opening. The place was packed! We had a ceremony out in the parking lot, and I gave a brief speech. I thanked Dianna for supporting me and gave her flowers. Then I thanked Sheri, telling the story of how Varsity actually got its start, and presented her with flowers. Manuel got up and gave a brief speech, presenting his ninety-six-year-old grandmother with flowers; then she had the honor of cutting the ribbon across the front doors. Before we all went in, a priest blessed the business with holy water. It worked!

The business took off pretty quickly. We were not making millions, but we were able to pay all the bills and still took a little of the money home. A lot of crazy things happened over the next twelve years. I'll highlight some of the most notable.

I became the front man dealing with most of the customers while Manuel became our computer guru. We both shared all the other work. Things were pretty much humming along. I was totally consumed. Dianna would call me most days to see if I was coming home for dinner. When I thought it was about two in the afternoon, it would be six in the evening. After awhile, Dianna quit calling—I got home when I got home.

After a while, things between Manuel and me were not good. I blame no one for our breakup. It was him and it was me, and together things just didn't gel anymore. Money reared its ugly head and we went from being good friends to being good enemies! When we first opened, we had an electrician doing some work for us. As he was getting ready to leave, he said, "This is a great place, you should do well here. Tell me, do you have a partner?" I said "Yes, I do." His reply, "Well, that is your first mistake. If God meant you to have a partner, he would have had one!" It turns out the electrician was right. Manuel and I lasted about a year, and he left after I bought him out. We parted on fairly good terms, but I didn't see him for maybe three years.

I loved having the business on my own. I liked making decisions without having to run it by a partner. I hired some help and things were going great. Business was pouring in at a good pace, and we stayed very busy all the time.

Customers

One day I got a call from a desperate man needing shirts for his church men's retreat. He said he was assigned to get them done and had completely forgotten. He called on a Wednesday and needed them by Friday. I said there was no way we could do them that fast. He begged me, saying that he had already called every shirt business in town and I was his last hope. I finally agreed and we got them done. He was very grateful when he picked them up. He even threw me a bone by having me do some shirts for his part-time company. I got the shirts done the next week. I called him to pick them up, but he never showed up. I called probably five times and still no response. I was really miffed and wrote him a letter. In the letter I said something like "You call yourself a Christian, and you do this to me!

He called as soon as he received the letter, gave me his credit card number, and apologized profusely. He came in a few days later and was still apologizing. He worked for the State Department and he was telling his boss about the great service and goods he had gotten from Varsity. He said "The boss wants you to call him and set up an appointment; he may have some work for you!" Now I'm the one apologizing! If it's not too late to make a long story short, we got the contract to do golf shirts for US Embassies throughout the world, which resulted in a $50,000 contract! Repeat...a $50,000 contract!

Another time, a guy came in from a big company in the area and asked to have a couple of shirts done with his company logo on it. We did the shirts, and he loved them as did everyone in his company, and they all wanted a shirt for themselves. This fluke turned into our biggest customer base and they stayed with us the whole time I owned Varsity. It always amazed me where business came from; you just never knew and that's what I enjoyed so much!

One cold winter day, a homeless-looking guy came into the shop asking for food. He claimed he hadn't eaten in two days. I gave him five bucks and he left. Three days later this same guy came back, and this time he was with an older woman who he introduced to me as his mother. He wanted to get shirts printed with a logo he had designed himself. He was really proud of it, so I thought *Okay, I'll play along with him.* I filled out the order form, figured out the cost, and told him it would cost him $326.00. He turned to his mother and asked for the checkbook. He wrote a check for the full amount, said he would be back in two weeks,

Life Slightly Off Center

and left with his mother trailing behind. I'm thinking *This guy is a little crazy! Two days ago he was in here begging for food and today he's writing me a check for T-shirts*. I called the bank the check was written from and asked if this check could possibly be good. The teller said "Oh yes, that check is very good; believe me, you have nothing to worry about!" We did the shirts; he was back in two weeks and was very happy with the end product. He even gave me a $10 tip!

Another customer wanted shirts with his boat's name on them. It was a four-color job and the shirts came out great. He came to pick them up and accompanying him was a very sexy women. He introduced her as his girlfriend. He was thrilled with the shirts and so was his girlfriend. She said "Oh, honey, can I have one?" He said "Sure, baby, try one on!" She was dressed in a bikini top and wraparound skirt. She whipped off her top and stood there in my showroom with nothing on but her nipple rings! I was floored and couldn't stop staring. Meanwhile the customer is saying to me "Jack, Jack, hello, Jack, how much do I owe you?" They left with her giggling and him telling her how sexy she looked in the new shirt. Me, I am still standing there stunned and may have had a little bit of drool running down my chin! I called Dianna to tell her what had happened. She was also shocked and asked "Was she young?" I said "I don't know how young she was, but she was perky!" Ahhh, another great perk of the shirt business! I cannot understand why everyone doesn't do this for a living!

I Was Never There

We were on the roof of Wild Wings, a local Charlottesville restaurant. We were celebrating Steven's 25th birthday. Steven was surrounded by family and friends and having a great time. I just happened to be sitting at his table. He was deep in conversation with a very attractive girl. I overheard him say "I was pretty much raised by my mother and my sister, Sheri, because my dad was never around." I was totally shocked and hurt to hear him say that. I interrupted him and said "What are you talking about? I was always there! Who ran you all over the place, went to all your soccer games, your school events, and your"...Steven interrupted my tirade and said "Dad, I was just kidding, take it easy! I just said that because I knew you were listening to me."

Driving home that evening, I was telling Dianna what Steven had said and how much it hurt me. She said "He was just joking with you. You know how you joke with everyone. Why is it okay for you to joke around and not okay for your son to do it? You just can't take it, can you?" I was awake all that night, trying to figure out what I wasn't there for, and it just bugged the hell out of me. I thought I was a great dad, but hey, maybe not.

It still bothered me when I went into Varsity on Monday morning. I discussed the whole episode with Benji, the kid that worked for me. Well, I had to get on with my day and would worry about this later. I had errands to run and left Benji to run the shop. When I got back several hours later, Benji said "Jack, Steven called while you were out, and I told him you weren't here and that you are pretty much never here." Steven said he understood totally and would try again later.

Life Slightly Off Center

The Bad Grandfather

Soon after that incident, this happened. I got a phone call at the shop from our son John. He asked if I would be coming to Carson's first T-Ball game the next Tuesday. I explained to him that I couldn't get away; as usual, I was too busy. His reply: "Okay, great, I'll tell Carson his Bad Grandfather cannot make it." John explained that that was what his kids called me, while Dick, his wife's dad, was known as the Good Grandfather.

In my defense, I reminded John that Dick was retired and lived 5 minutes from John's house. I, on the other hand, was running a business with all kinds of deadlines and lived 2 hours away. He didn't buy it, and we hung up with him a little miffed and me feeling guilty and a little hurt.

Steven called soon after that, and I related the conversation I had just had with his brother. He said "Oh boy, Dad, I have the perfect song for you—this will be your theme song from now on." He then proceeded to sing a few lines of "Cat in the Cradle!"

September 11, 2001

September 11, 2001, is the day most Americans can tell exactly where they were and what they were doing. Me, I was heading to our shirt distributor in Manassas, Virginia, to pick up an order of shirts. I was listening to the Howard Stern's radio show and just enjoying the beautiful day. That's when Howard suddenly announced that a plane had flown into the World Trade Center! I along with most people assumed it was small plane and a tragic accident. When it was announced that a second plane had hit the other tower, all hell broke loose. This day would change most people's lives in one way or the other.

When I arrived back at the shop, Benji came running out, panicked, and shouting "Jack, a plane just hit the Pentagon! What will we do, what is going on?" At about that time, a fleet of jets flew overhead. I suggested we just go ahead and get to work and see how this plays out.

We started running shirts while the radio blasted more reports. A plane went down in Pennsylvania, the mall in Washington was hit, and on and on. Some of the reports were totally false, which added to the general feeling of panic. They announced that all government employees were being sent home and the highways in and around DC would be for outbound traffic only. This is about the time I figured it was time to shut things down. I said "Benji, I don't think we want to be running shirts if something happens, so maybe we better head home! "Benji agreed wholeheartedly, and we were out of there!

The rest is history. After things got back to a sort of normal and we were back to work, the phone rang incessantly with people asking for 9-11 shirts, shirts with US flags, anything remotely connected with the tragedy. We did not have them, and I refused to make any. I felt it was wrong to turn this tragedy into a money-making deal. I had guys from my business exchange group calling me, wanting to order shirts by the hundreds to give to their customers. I still refused. Then Benji came up with a great idea. He had heard on the radio that Giant Foods grocery store offered to match any donation they received and it would be given to the Red Cross in connection with the 9-11 disaster. That was it! We would print shirts and donate all the profit.

We had a design on a screen within the hour. It was an American flag with the words "Proud to be an American" above flag and "United We Stand" under the flag. We were hard-pressed to keep up with the orders. There was a line going out the door—the shirts would sell as soon as they dropped out of the dryer. The shirts were still warm when the customers got them! Word got out about what we were doing, and some customers paid twice the asking price for the shirts! We wound up with our story on the radio and the front page of the *Potomac News,* and I was even interviewed on TV. All other work at Varsity stopped for about two weeks while we ran only flag shirts. Our regular customers were very supportive and told us to go ahead and they would wait for their shirts.

It was a great time! Our donation turned out to be $10,000! This was matched by Giant Foods, making our combined donation $20,000! This was something everyone associated with Varsity Graphics was very proud of.

Talking and More Talking

Through the years I have talked to hundreds of customers. It was amazing how many people would come into my shop just to shoot the breeze.

One guy, after a long conversation, said, "The only thing Varsity was lacking was beer on tap!" People told me their troubles, shared their concerns about their families, showed me photos of their kids—we solved the problems of the world, and soon customers turned into friends!

It was a good time for me and is one of the things I miss most about the business. The mailman even used Varsity Graphics as the official place to take his morning break. We would have a cup of coffee together, and if he delivered goodies from my sister Kathy, we would share them.

My Helper, Kathy

Speaking of Kathy, there was nothing that she enjoyed more on her visits East than coming to work with me. She would do whatever I asked and then say "What do you want me to do now?" It was hard to keep up with her and still do everything that I had to get done.

One day I suggested she have a shirt sale out in front of the shop. We had bunches of shirts that either we had screwed up or that had never been picked up. We set up a long table out in front, folded the shirts, and made signs that read "T-Shirts $1.00 Each." I was busy inside and Kathy was outside doing a good business. At one point she came in and said that most of her customers were Hispanic and down on their luck, and would I mind if she gave them a break on the shirts? I said "Sure, do whatever you want." She was busy making new signs and selling shirts like crazy.

I went out to check on her and couldn't believe what she had done. Kathy had made new signs that read "3 Shirts for $5.00" and had a line of people wanting to get in on this great deal! I said "I thought you wanted to give these people a good deal?" Kathy said "I did, so I'm giving them three shirts for the low price of $5.00!" "Oh, so instead of paying $1.00 per shirt or five shirts for $5.00 like we had originally planned, you're charging $5.00 for only three shirts? So, how is this helping them?" I asked. Kathy thought about what she had done, got embarrassed, and said "You're right. I am so stupid, but there is still a line of people thinking three shirts for $5.00 is a great deal!" From that point on, Kathy would throw in two extra shirts with every purchase! She sold everything we had!

Fernando

Fast forward twelve years and Fernando walked into Varsity Graphics. I had gotten a call from a friend of mine, asking if it would be alright if a guy by the name of Fernando came by to check out our operation. He was looking to go into business and thought maybe the shirt business would be a good fit for him. I had never met Fernando before this day, but he was one of those people you liked right away. I gave Fernando free run of the whole place. He studied our operation, got a feel for the customers we had, and on his second day at the shop, he announced that he thought he wanted to buy Varsity Graphics! I was shocked and said, "Sorry, buddy, but Varsity is not for sale."

At that time I had no intention of selling. I was happy with the business, happy with my life, and still enjoying chasing a buck. Dianna happened to be there the day Fernando wrote a figure on a slip of paper and asked, "If I paid you this much, would your business be for sale?" Dianna grabbed me by the shoulders, looked me straight in the eyes, and said, "Jack, sell the damn place!"

It killed me, but I finally admitted that maybe it was time. I was getting tired of the work, and some of the customers were starting to bug me. I just was not as patient as I used to be. Maybe it was time to move on to bigger and better things. So Fernando, my new best friend, and I came up with an agreement, signed the papers, and my baby now belonged to him!

Life Slightly Off Center

The Truck

Included in the sale of Varsity Graphics was my truck. I can't live without a truck so the hunt was on for a new one. Our son John heard I was in the market and offered me his truck since he was getting ready to buy a new one. It was an 1999 Dodge Ram with an extended cab. It was in great condition and had about 90,000 miles on it. He was willing to let it go for $4,000. I jumped at the offer. Such a deal!

A few weeks later, I took my '75 Olds to Kim's Auto Upholstery Shop to get the front seat recovered. I dropped the car off and asked Mr. Kim if he could give me a ride back to my shop. Mr. Kim was a great guy whom I had done business with for years. He was Korean and talked with a distinct accent. He said "Sure, I take you to office; I get truck." I was waiting out in front when he pulled around in a brand new Toyota truck. I mean this thing was loaded. It was a beauty! I climbed in and was telling him how much I liked his truck. He said "Son give me this truck for gift." I said "You've got to be kidding; your son gave you this truck?" He said "Oh yes, he give me; he a very good son." I was astounded and asked if his son had given the truck in gratitude for your paying for a great education for him. Mr. Kim said "Oh no, son go to Air Force Academy, education free! Son gives me truck because he is good son!" I told Mr. Kim I had just bought a used truck from my son and paid $4,000 for it. He looked at me with a puzzled look on his face and said "No, no, no, you no buy truck from son; son supposed to give you truck as gift!"

I think the Koreans have a great custom there, but I don't think it will ever catch on in the United States. At least not in my family!

John did volunteer to go online and get me new license plates for the truck. The day they arrived, Pete and I were sitting out on the back deck having a beer. I opened the package and I though ole Pete was going to wet himself. He wound up doubled over in hysterics, saying "That is the funniest thing I have ever seen!" The plates read ...

JON RULZ

Out to Pasture

I decided we needed a big retirement party for me and a welcome-aboard party for Fernando. The invitation I sent out to customers and friends read as follows:

BREAKING NEWS!!!
JACK RAYMOND ANNOUNCES HIS
RETIREMENT FROM VARSITY GRAPHICS!

After 12 years as owner and operator of Varsity Graphics,
Jack Raymond has decided to lay down his squeegee!
From its humble beginnings in his garage,
Jack has successfully made Varsity Graphics a
Household name and a silk-screening empire!
Jack has earned the love, respect, and adoration
of his clients, employees, and business associates
with his sharp wit and top-notch products.
Join us as we send "our buddy Jack" off to his new adventure
and welcome the new owner, Fernando DaSilva, to the helm.

HAPPY HOUR FRIDAY, JUNE 1ST …5:30 PM to 8:00 PM at 1312 Horner Road.

Life Slightly Off Center

What a great party it was! There was standing room only. Good food, good wine, and a fantastic mix of family, friends, customers, associates, and employees, both past and present, made for an evening I will never forget. Even Manuel, my old partner, showed up and gave a little speech. Sheri, the one who was instrumental in getting this whole Varsity Graphics thing going, concluded the festivities fittingly with the following speech that brought a tear to everyone's eyes:

> So much has happen in twelve years. In 1995 my brother John was 26 and a very single bachelor with not much more to worry about than whether there was enough beer in the fridge and if the Rams would cover the spread. Now he is married with three boys under the age of seven, has helped to start a new business, and calls it a rare pleasure to actually watch a whole football game without a diaper change or an important Thomas the Tank Engine disagreement to referee. My other brother Steven has a similar timeline, but his football games are interrupted by tea parties with his little girl Emerson.
>
> In 1995, I received my first actual Christmas bonus and had no idea what to do with the whopping sum of $500! So I turned it into $1.00 bills, stuffed it into a cigar box, and gave it to Dad as seed money to get Varsity Graphics started. In twelve short years so much has happened!
>
> I can remember the grand opening right here in this location. Much like today, we all had high hopes for what the future offered. I think my dad had a good idea of what he hoped to do with Varsity Graphics...run his own shop, be his own boss, and support the glamorous and luxurious lifestyle my mom has gotten used to in the Air Force as a master sergeant's wife. What I don't think Dad was prepared for were the actual people he would be in touch with on a regular basis...the depth of their friendships and camaraderie making this little business bustle. I know Dad enjoyed the hard work and the sense of ownership, but more that all that, I know he loved the people that he worked with in the shop, as well as the customers and business associates.
>
> You know it must be a good environment to work in when most of his Varsity Graphics stories start out like a bar joke..." So today a Puerto Rican, a Nun, and a Mormon walk into the shop..." "So today a bald kid selling everlasting light bulbs walked into my shop..."
>
> One of the biggest business people of our time, Malcolm Forbes, said "Many of the most successful men I have ever known have never grown up. They have retained bubbling-over boyishness. They have relished wit,

they have indulged humor; they have not allowed 'dignity' to depress them into moroseness. Youthfulness of spirit is the twin brother of optimism, and optimism is the stuff of which American business success is fashioned. Resist growing up!" Now I didn't know my dad was friends with the likes of Mr. Forbes, but Mr. Forbes obviously knew my Dad!

So now, twelve years down the road, it is time for my very youthful, witty, optimistic, and—I know he would like me to add—handsome dad to turn the page onto the next chapter of life and see who else will fall into his path and be delighted by his bubbling-over boyishness. Raise your glasses and toast with me the success and friendships Varsity Graphics has brought to our family and wish my dad and your friend an exciting, relaxing, enjoyable, satisfying retirement. God help Mom!

Needless to say, I left the party with a tear in my eye and a lump in my throat. It had been a great run!

CHAPTER 13

Funny Stories from Family, Friends and Me

Out for a Walk

Our friends Tina and Roger were out for a walk with their four-year-old son Jeffery. They passed a Catholic Church with a large crucifix standing out front. Jeffery asked, "What's that, Mommy?" pointing to the crucifix. His mother explained that was Jesus nailed on the cross, and told a brief story of Christ. Jeffery's lips began to quiver, his little eyes teared up, and he said, "Jeeeez, Mom, you'd think they could have used glue!"

Life Slightly Off Center

The Tag!

My sister Kathy was about to give a speech to a room full of women who were attending a Baptist Mother's Day program. Kathy had her mike on and was ready to go. A girl behind her said, "Kathy, the tag on your dress is out; let me fix it." To which Kathy replied, "If it says size eight or Liz Claiborne, leave it out!" The whole room roared with laughter!

In Uniform

Kathy was always going up to guys in military uniform and thanking them for their service to our country, and while shaking their hand she would say "God bless you." She was telling me that the other day she was stopped at a red light when a car with a man in uniform in it pulled up next to hers. She shouted out to him, thanking him for his service to our country and "God bless you." The guy grabbed the front of his jacket and shouted back, "Hey lady, this is my hunting outfit!" Kathy was totally embarrassed and sheepishly wished him good luck on his hunt.

Sally

My sister Sally's son Michael was getting married. The mother of the bride-to-be was throwing a wedding shower for her daughter. After Sally got the invitation, she called to see if she could bring something. The bride's mother, not very attuned to the social graces, said "Sure, honey, how about you bring the cake!" Sally hung up and thought *Me and my big mouth. Now I'm responsible for the cake, which will most likely cost me forty bucks!* She was hoping the response would be more to the tune of a Jello salad.

The Turkey

This past Thanksgiving Sally decided to deep-fry her turkey. Her husband, Jim, eased the turkey into the boiling oil. After about forty minutes, he pulled it out, only to discover a very "horny" turkey. He had forgotten to take the neck out before cooking it. The neck had worked its way down the inside cavity of the turkey and emerged out between its legs. The end result was a golden fried turkey with the appearance of a huge erection! Sally's grandson took one look at it and said "Grammy, I'm not gonna eat that!"

Prom Nite!

A friend told me this story about an old high school buddy. It was prom night, and Chuck was standing on the porch ringing the bell of his date's house. This was to be their first date, and Chuck was nervous. The parents invited him in and ask him to have a seat. He was sitting in a chair that allowed him to get the first look at his date as she descended the stairs. After a few minutes of stiff chit-chat with the parents, Chuck spotted his date coming down the staircase. She looked beautiful. Then suddenly she stepped on the front of her dress, pulling down the front and exposing her breast! To save her the embarrassment of being seen by the whole family, Chuck, being the quick thinker he was, jumped up and yelled "Look out front," as he pointed out the window. He and everyone else were shocked when they spotted two dogs humping away on the front lawn! Chuck walked to the door, said good evening, and drove off into the night, never to be seen again by the girl or her parents.

How to Save a Buck!

We were sitting around one evening when a friend told us this story. I only hope I can do it justice...this is a good one!

There were five young Marine lieutenants renting a house out in California. The house came complete with a pool. One day a couple of the guys were lying around the pool and noticed the palm trees were in bad shape and needed a good trimming. They called a landscaping outfit that came out and gave them an estimate. They felt the suggested price was outrageous and decided that among the five of them they could do the job and save a lot of money.

They rented a chainsaw and an extension ladder, and presto they were in business! They soon found out that the ladder was not tall enough to reach the palm fronds. Marines being resourceful decided the best course of action would be to climb the ladder as high up the tree as possible and at that point tie a rope around the trunk. With the rope secure, the five of them pulled until the tree had a good bend in it and tied the other end to the gazebo at the side of the pool, which was anchored in cement. Next they braced the ladder against the bent trunk and one of them climbed the ladder with the chainsaw in hand.

Now you have got to picture this: The tree was now out over the water. The foot of the ladder was on the deck of the pool. The lieutenant on the top of the ladder now had a clear shot at the palm fronds. He started the chain saw and started trimming. He cut one frond, then a second, while the guys on the ground cheered him on and the fronds were falling. He was about to cut frond four when all hell broke loose. The pressure was so great on the gazebo that it actually pulled out of the concrete and was propelled up and over the house like a missile into the street in front of the house, hitting a passing car. The ladder snapped in half sending the lieutenant and the chainsaw into the pool!

After the dust settled, the five marines had to pay for damages to the car hit by the gazebo, buy a new chainsaw, have the pool drained, cleaned, and refilled, buy a new gazebo and have it installed, and—oh yeah—shoulder the cost of having the palm tree professionally trimmed.

Life Slightly Off Center

The Car Wash

My sister Kathy was telling us the story of taking her Cruiser Convertible to a self car wash. She pulled into the bay and discovered she didn't have enough change. So she went to the change machine and got her change. She went back to the bay and put her money in, pulled out the wand, which was spitting out soapy water, turned around to wash the car, and found she was in the wrong bay. Her car was in the next bay! There she stood, with wand in hand, still shooting out soap and water in an empty bay! She put the wand back in the holder, sheepishly walked back to her dirty car, and drove away.

This story reminds me of my own car-wash experience. It was one sunny afternoon and I was on my way to pick up Dianna from her job at the school. I was in a small station wagon loaded down with boxes of T-shirts along with our dog Lady. We were a little bit early so I decided to get a quick car wash. I pulled in and only realized the back windows were open when the water and soap poured in. I couldn't get to the window cranks, so Lady and I came out of there soaking wet! When Dianna climbed into the car and found me, Lady, and the inside of the car all soaking wet she said "what the hell happened?" I told her I had just found the greatest deal! I was able to get the car washed inside and out, the dog a bath, and me a shower all for the low, low price of $8.00!

Fill It Up!

We were at a wedding and the father of the bride got up to talk about his beautiful daughter and some of the bone-headed things she had done as a young girl. This story really got a huge laugh from everyone. Diane had just gotten her driver's license and was very anxious to drive the car on her own. Her dad gave her permission to take the car out, but told her to first fill up the tank. This would be her first time at a gas station as the driver. She pulled up to the pump like she knew what she was doing. She got out and discovered the gas tank was on the other side of the car. So she got in and drove to the other side. Got out, and damned if the tank wasn't still on the other side! She got in again and drove around, and the same thing. She was totally confused, and walked into the station to get help, only to find a bunch of guys in hysterics!

The Artificial Inseminator

My buddy Ray, from Alaska, had gotten out of the Air Force and was about to start a new career. He was going to be a foreman on a cattle farm in central Virginia. He was off to school to learn all about raising cattle. One of the classes was how to artificially inseminate a cow. He said after a few days of studying how it was done, each student had to try it on his own. The instructor would follow up to make sure you did it correctly. Ray said he was doing great. He had the procedure down pat. He explained you take an injection of bull sperm and insert your arm up to the shoulder into the cow, feel around for her ovaries and give them a squirt of bull semen. After you have finished, the instructor comes behind you and inserts his arm and feels around to make sure you hit your mark. Ray was feeling pretty good about the whole thing. The instructor said to Ray, "You did fine, except for one thing. The next time, it would be a good idea to take your watch off before you insert your arm." At that, the instructor handed Ray back his watch! Ray always ends the story by saying "It was a Timex and after that licking, it was still ticking!"

First Date

I don't remember where I heard this story, but it really bears repeating. We've all been on first dates that just didn't turn out right. After you read this, you'll consider yourself lucky!

This couple had gone skiing for the day on their first date and they were getting ready to head back home. The guy says to the girl, "It's a long ride back to the city, and there are no gas stations or rest stops for quite awhile, so if you need to use the girls' room, you better do it before we start."

She assured him she was fine. They piled into the car and took off. They were driving for awhile and the girl was squirming in her seat. She finally begged the guy to stop the car because she had to pee really badly and just couldn't hold it another second. He pulled over to the side of the road. She jumped out and squatted next to the right side of the car and let go. Her bare butt came in contact with the rear chrome bumper and it stuck! Sort of the same reaction you get when you put your tongue on cold metal.

She was really stuck and couldn't move. The guy came around and didn't know what to do. If he had some hot water, he would have poured it on the problem, but there was no hot water! He came up with a solution and explained to the now-frantic girl and she agreed that if that was the way it had to be, go ahead. So he unzipped his fly and proceeded to pee on the problem, and presto, she was free!

Now, to my way of thinking, this could have gone either way. It could bring you really close on a first date. Something you could laugh about for years, or, it could have the opposite effect. In this case, he dropped her off and they never saw each other again.

That is what I call a rough first date!

New Siding for the House!

I was talking to my friend Matt on the phone. I had called him to see how he and the family were doing. Matt was a young husband and the father of five. He was a stay-at-home dad, while his wife went out and worked. Things were not easy for them, but they had the best outlook on life. I remember the day he called to tell me that Penny was pregnant with number five. I gave him my condolences because I figured the last thing they needed was another baby. Matt was thrilled! He and Penny were ecstatic with the prospect of another child.

The last time I had talked with Matt, he was saying they had just about enough money saved to have the house re-sided. He had said the place was in really bad shape. It was a real blight in their neighborhood. So at this time, I asked him if he had ever gotten his house re-sided. He said "No, we decided to buy a boat instead."

"A boat," I said, "How did that happen?" He said that he and Penny got to discussing about how when the kids grow up, do we think they will have fond memories of a nicely sided house? Can you imagine them saying to each other, "Hey, remember that great siding we had on our house back when we were kids!" So we decided to buy a boat instead so they will have great memories of all the fun we had with our boat! So we now we have the ugliest house in the neighborhood with a beautiful boat parked out in front!"

I love that story—we should all think like that!

Cowboy Boots!

This next story was told to us by some friends we met up in Alaska. Before coming North, they lived in San Antonio, Texas. Barb wanted to buy a pair of cowboy boots and suggested they go shopping the next day for a pair. That night, as Barb undressed to go to bed, she put her thumbs inside the waistband of her undies and pulled the underwear and jeans off in one easy motion. The next morning she got up and put on last night's jeans, a fresh shirt, and she and Mike went off on their shopping trip.

At the shoe store, Barb picked out a pair of expensive boots to try on. The salesman helped her put the boots on, and she walked around the store to give them a try. They felt great, looked great, and she said "We'll take them." The salesman was pulling the boot off of Barb's left foot and along with the boot came last night's underwear! Barb was shocked, the salesman was embarrassed, and Mike gasped, "How did he do that?"

Surprise!

This is another story related to me by friends about their friends, another one that bears repeating.

One Saturday night, a guy named Ted went over to his fiancée Gail's house to spend the evening. They planned a quiet night at home watching TV, while Gail's parents went to the movies. Before Gail's mother left, she asked Gail to listen for the bell on the dryer and take the clothes out before they wrinkle.

Being home alone was a rare treat for this newly engaged couple. One thing led to another and soon Ted and Gail were naked and getting into some serious stuff. The bell sounded on the dryer and Gail said "I'd better run down and take the clothes out." Ted said "Jump on my back, and I'll give you a ride down!" So down they went, giggling all the way, when suddenly the lights were flipped on and there gathered at the bottom of the stairs were her parents, his parents, their friends, and relatives yelling "SURPRISE!!"

The gang was there for a surprise engagement party. Needless to say, *everyone* got a surprise that evening!

JRAYMOND

367

A Picture Is Worth a Thousand Words!

Ray, a good friend of mine, told me this story from his boyhood days. Ray was thirteen years old and had cut out what he thought was a picture of a woman's vagina from his school science book. He carried the picture in his wallet and it was a big hit with his buddies. Whenever things got dull, Ray would pull out his "dirty" picture and pass it around to all the guys.

School was getting ready to close down for the summer and all the books were handed in. Ray's dad was notified that his son's science book was damaged. Someone had apparently cut a picture out of it and the book would have to be paid for. Ray's dad was angry. Things were hard enough trying to raise four kids, without having to lay out money for damaged school books.

"Ray, why in the hell did you cut up that damned school book?" his dad shouted as Ray walked into the house. Ray stammered, mumbled, and turned red, knowing that his dad wouldn't understand why his son was cutting dirty pictures out of his science book.

"Well, son, I'm waiting, and boy, this better be good." demanded his dad. Ray took the picture out of his wallet and with trembling hands showed it to his dad. His dad studied the picture and, puzzled, looks at his son and said "Boy, why the hell would you want a picture of a throat?" *A throat, a throat,* Ray thinks, *I'm going to get a beating over a throat!*

Ray still laughs over the fact that he and his buddies spent an entire school year snickering and whispering over a picture of a damned throat!

Love Thy Neighbor

Steven and Cristi were living down in Florida. They had bought their first house on the outskirts of Orlando. Dianna and I were visiting them there—I was out in working in their yard and soon began meeting their neighbors. After a couple of days of this, Steven said to me "Dad, I can't believe it! We've been here for six months and we don't know any of our neighbors; you've been here two days and know most of them! What's your secret?" I told him that you just have to get out more and be friendly. People love to talk, so just get them into a conversation. This was easier said than done for Steven and Cristi. They were both very shy and uncomfortable with strangers. I explained that it was worth it to put yourself out there. You never know—your best friend may be living right next door.

I said "The thing your mom used to do when we moved into a new neighborhood or someone moved into ours, was bake a batch of chocolate chip cookies and take them over and introduce herself. This practice led to many good friendships. Do me a favor, the next time someone moves into the neighborhood, have Cristi make a batch of cookies, and take them over and introduce yourself." He promised he would give it a try.

A few months later the house across the street was sold. Soon the new people were in the house. Steven convinced Cristi to bake some cookies and after much cajoling got her to agree to join him delivering the cookies to the new neighbor. They knocked on the door very reluctantly. A guy opened the door, and Steve handed him the cookies and said "Hi, we are from across the street and just wanted to welcome you to the neighborhood." The guy said "Hey, thanks, but we're just flipping this house," and with that he took the cookies and closed the door, leaving Steven and Cristi standing there on the steps. It was then that they swore they would never again try this approach to meet the neighbors, nor take any more of Dad's good advice!

Life Slightly Off Center

Three Seeds

You probably remember me telling the story about John asking me to explain sex to him when he was about eight years old. The session ended with John telling me he was going to have two kids because he had two seeds!

Fast forward to the birth of John's third son, Wyatt. When we got to the hospital, Wyatt had already been born. It happened really quickly. In fact, it happened so quickly that we found John's van parked at the emergency entrance of the hospital still running and with both doors open! He said he was racing down the hospital corridors with Jennifer in a wheelchair, yelling for people to get out of his way and that he would name the baby after them if they would just move!

After all the excitement was over, John and I were standing at the nursery window, admiring this beautiful new baby boy. I said "Son, you're doing pretty good for a guy with only two seeds—what happened?" John looked at me, smiled, and said "Dad, it's a miracle!"

Faulty Air Conditioner

One day Sheri called and asked for her mom. I said "Sorry, kid, but your mother is out doing what she does best, saving me money." In our family this meant Dianna was out shopping for bargains.

"So what's up, can I help?" I asked. Sheri said "My air conditioner isn't working, and I figured Mom might have some suggestions." I said "So you can't ask your dad for help?" Sheri sighed and said "Oh, okay, Dad, my air conditioner isn't working—what should I do?" My advice was "Open the windows!" The conversation ended with Sheri saying "Dad, have Mom call me."

Window Treatment

John had just bought his first house in Charlottesville, Virginia. He was showing it off to Dianna, Sheri, and me. As we wandered from room to room, Sheri noticed that all the windows had wooden valances over them. It was a very dated look. Sheri asked "So, John, what do you think about the window treatment?" John had no idea what a window treatment was and answered Sheri by pounding his fist into the palm of his hand and shouting "By God, in this house, the windows will be treated equally as well as the doors!"

Poor Goldfish

On a trip to visit my daughter, Sheri, I noticed something very strange in her bathroom. She had a goldfish bowl sitting on the back tank of the toilet. I thought, *What a strange place to keep a poor goldfish.* I quickly whipped up a sign and taped it to the wall above the fish bowl.

Athletic Supporter

Our friend Barbara told us a story about her son Brian joining a Little League football team. She received a list of things he would need before his first practice. On the list were items such as a mouthpiece, socks, cleats, and a jockstrap. Barbara headed directly to the sporting goods department of K-Mart. She found everything on the list except for the jockstrap. Barbara had no idea what one looked for in a good jockstrap. Barbara was raised in a house full of sisters, and the subject of an athletic supporter never came up.

Needing help, she asked the sales clerk for advice. He asked "What size will you need—small, medium, large, or extra large?" Barb said "Gee, I have no idea." The clerk rolled his eyes and said "Lady, what size is he?" Barbara blushed and said "I don't know; he's only eight years old. I guess he's about this big." (She was holding up her thumb and forefinger about 3 inches apart) The exasperated clerk, again with the rolling eyes, said "No, Lady! I mean what size is his waist?"

Bud Light

Recently my brother and his wife were sitting in a restaurant getting ready to have dinner. Bill spotted a sign on a far wall that read:

BUD LIGHT

69

Bill was amazed at the price. When the waitress came by for their drink order, he said "We'll have two Bud Lights. Boy, that sure is a great price! Wow, sixty-nine cents. What a deal! Is there a special going on?"

The waitress was puzzled and asked Bill what he was talking about. Bill pointed at the sign and said "There, look, Bud Light, sixty-nine cents!" The waitress rolled her eyes and said "Sir, that's the temperature."

A Lesson in Tipping

Dianna, my brother Bill, sister-in-law Reggie, and I were checking into the Omni Hotel in downtown Charlottesville, Virginia. The reason for the trip was to attend our daughter's wedding. Dianna and I had overpacked as usual and needed a valet cart to get everything up to our room. The bellboy insisted on taking our stuff up. I really could have done it myself, but he would not hear of it. I gave him $5.00 for his trouble.

Later that afternoon Bill and I got into a discussion about tipping. He asked how much I had tipped the bellboy. I told him I had given him five bucks. He was astounded and called me a "cheap bastard." He had given the same bellboy ten bucks for doing exactly what he had done for me.

A few days later, we were checking out of the hotel. This time the bellboy was loading our car with luggage. Keeping in mind the conversation I had with Bill, I slipped the bellboy ten bucks. The bellboy looked at the ten dollar bill, looked at me, and in a very British accent said "Why you cheap bastard!" I was shocked. Billy was right there watching the action and went into hysterics. I mean he was doubled over laughing with tears in his eyes. He stopped me before I could lay into this guy, who by now was red-faced and visibly embarrassed. Billy explained that he had given the bellboy twenty bucks to call me a cheap bastard, and he added that it was worth every penny just to see my reaction. He said the bellboy said "No, sir, I cannot do that; please do not ask me to do that. I could be fired for saying something like that to one of the guests." Bill said it took a long time and twenty bucks to convince him to do it. Bill assured him that I was a good guy and would get a big laugh out it. I *did* get a big laugh out of it and especially enjoyed knowing it cost my brother twenty bucks to get me.

CHAPTER 14

Grandkids!

Our Grandkids

Dianna and I have been blessed with wonderful grandchildren! All of them are different, all of them are very special, and some provide their old Pops with great fodder for his stories. We have Cooper, Henry, Carson, Tucker, Wyatt, Jake, and our little princess and our only granddaughter, Emerson.

I include Carson, who will always be our grandson. He just doesn't live here anymore. He was a great little kid who came too early and left too soon. Carson was the grandchild who always came over to me whenever we met, sort of rubbed against me, looked up with those big blue eyes, and said "Hi Pops."

The following stories will give you an idea of these kids. Some are more of characters than others, but they are all GREAT!

Cooper and Quality Time with Pops

Cooper was four years old, and he and I were heading to our favorite place Dunkin' Donuts! I strapped him into his car seat and we were off. Howard Stern was on the radio, and I knew I should have changed the station immediately, but didn't. Old Howard can get pretty racy, but I figured Coop was too young to understand the show's blue humor; I really got a kick out of it. I was driving along and really not paying attention to the radio.

All of a sudden from the back seat, Cooper yells, "Hey, Pops, what's a vagina?" Oh boy, how does one explain a vagina to a four-year-old? I had to think fast! "Cooper," I said, "They said Virginia and you know that Virginia is the state we live in."

Cooper wasn't buying it. He said "Oh no, Pops, they said vagina. What is a vagina, Pops?" I hit the button on the radio and got some good country music going. There on the horizon was Dunkin' Donuts, and the conversation quickly turned to chocolate-covered donuts with sprinkles. Phew!

Cooper and Quality Time with Grandma!

Dianna was driving home one evening with Cooper in the back seat. We were living in a very woodsy subdivision. Dianna spotted a couple of deer and excitedly yelled, "Cooper, did you see the deer we just passed?" Cooper said, "No, Grandma, I missed them."

Dianna turned the car around so he could get a chance to see the deer. She pulled off the road, aimed into the woods, and put on the high beams. There they were, a big buck on top of a delicate doe, doing the big "deer dance"!

Cooper, upon seeing this, exclaimed "Grandma, Grandma, I think those are Siamese deer!

Life Slightly Off Center

Cooper and Quality Time with His Mother!

Sheri had taken Cooper to Dick's Sporting Goods to get a new pair of sneakers. When they got home from their shopping trip, Cooper discovered the sneakers had silver trim and refused to wear them. Sheri agreed to take them back but decided to take them back to a Dick's Sporting Goods on their way to the beach house rather than the one in town. As Cooper and Sheri walked through this store, Coop was saying how much smaller this store was than the one they had been to that morning.

They were able to exchange the sneakers without any problems. As they were walking out of the store, Cooper, in his booming outside voice, asked "Mom, do you like big Dick's or little Dick's?"

Cooper the Athlete

Sheri had dreams of her Cooper being a superstar in all sports. Unfortunately, Cooper didn't cooperate with the dream and actually wasn't crazy about team sports. Sheri tried everything to no avail. Ole Coop would try whatever sport his mom signed him up for, but he was never the star of the team. I laugh when I recall this story that Sheri related to us.

Cooper was on a swim team. He wasn't fast, but he did try hard. During this particular swim meet, all the kids dove into the pool and the race was on.

Cooper was only faster than one other boy. The other kids were so much faster that they were down the length of the pool and out, while Cooper and the other slow kid were still struggling. By the time they got to the other end of the pool and seeing none of the other swimmers, Cooper figured he had won the heat and the other kid thought he had come in second place. Cooper climbed out of the pool and with arms raised in victory, strutted his stuff! Sheri just sort of disappeared into the crowd.

I'm glad to report that Cooper has found his sport. He is a great runner and really enjoys that.

Cooper and President's Day

It was President's Day and Cooper had learned all about President Lincoln at school. His mom picked him up, and on the ride home, Cooper asked "Mom, do you think I will ever get shot?" She was startled at this question and said "Oh Cooper, what are you talking about? Why would you ask a question like that? Of course, you will never, ever get shot. I guarantee it!" Cooper's response: "Yeah, that's probably what Lincoln's mom told him!"

Life Slightly Off Center

Carson

I recall one incident that still makes me laugh whenever I think about it. Carson, Tucker, and Wyatt were at our house for a sleepover. While eating dinner, Carson asked if I would read them some of my book. Since I have been working on this book for many years, all the grandkids were well aware of it. After dinner we all went upstairs, and I had them each pick a story from the piles of them I had stacked all over my office. I was reading the story that Carson had picked out, and he and his brothers were going crazy with laughter.

I read a few more stories, and Carson, through his tears of laughter, said, "Oh, Pops, if this was any funnier, I'd pee my pants!"

Tucker!

Our son John was taking care of his three young sons while his wife, Jennifer, was away on a business trip. They were at McDonald's for lunch. They had finished eating and John was getting the baby bundled up to leave. Tucker, being Tucker, had to poop as usual. John pointed to the men's room door and told him to go ahead in and get started. John said, "I'll be there in a minute to help you." John kept his eye on the door while he continued getting Wyatt ready to go. A few minutes later John walked into the bathroom to find Tucker sitting in a urinal with his legs hanging over the edge just swinging away. John screamed "Tucker! What are you doing?" Tucker replied, "POOPING!"

I laughed so hard when John told me this story. Just to get some clarification, I asked if it was one of those kids' urinals that are lower to the floor. "No," John said. "It was your regular standard-size urinal, one that would require Tucker to have to actually climb up to get into it." Then John muttered something about "damned kids."

Here is one more recent story about Tucker. It was Saturday night before Easter and John was putting the boys to bed. They were all excited about the pending visit by the Easter Bunny and all the candy that was coming their way. John asked them if they knew what Easter was all about. They both agreed Easter was about candy.

John sat down and told them the story of Easter, and the kids were both amazed. Tucker asked John how he knew about this. John replied the story was in the Bible and that it is what Christians believe. Tucker was puzzled and asked "Dad, are we Christians?" John said "Yes, I guess we are Christians." To this Tucker replied "Gee, I thought we were normal."

Wyatt is fast becoming our resident character. Cooper who held this crown for many years has now become a moody teenager. Coop has just grown up and pretty much stopped giving me fodder for stories. Ole Wyatt is now my chief fodder supplier.

Wyatt was sitting on my lap one evening, and we were watching TV during the presidential campaign. He asked "Pops, why did Barack Obama win the race against John McCain?" This question just blew me away, incredible that a three-year-old would not only remember and pronounce these names but to understand they were in a race. In answer to his question, I explained that Obama had more votes than McCain. "Hmmmm," said Wyatt, a little confused, "I thought it was because Obama could run faster."

Wyatt and our dog Katie were rolling around on the living room floor. Wyatt was giggling as Katie licked his face. Ole Wyatt was happiest when he was asking questions, so he asked, "Pops, is Katie a boy dog?" "Katie is a girl dog," I answered. Wyatt asked "Why?" "Because Katie does not have a penis. You know only boy dogs have a penis," I explained.

Then Wyatt asked "Does Katie have a china? Girl dogs have chinas, right, Pops? You know what, Pops, my mom has a china!"

Three-year-old Wyatt was staying at our house for a few days. I happened to be standing at the toilet peeing when Wyatt burst into the bathroom. He was standing behind me and asked "Pops, have you got a big penis like my dad? My dad's penis is really, really big!" "Can I see your penis, Pops?" As I stood there, I told him it was not polite to ask people to see their penis. Wyatt's reply, of course, was typical of a three-year-old: "Why?" "Because you just don't do it, that's why." That was my answer to most of our grandchildren's questions. I said "How would you like it if I asked to see your penis? You wouldn't like it, would you?" At that, Wyatt pulled down his pants to proudly show off his penis to me! What else could I do but yell "Get out of here, you little runt, beat it!"

Footnote: Penis and china are Wyatt's two favorite words and he uses them at every opportunity.

Emerson

Emerson is our only girl and a girly girl she is. Steven, her father, was hoping that she would be at least a bit of an athlete, but it was not to be. He signed her up for T-ball, hoping she would enjoy it. In order to get her at least halfway enthusiastic, he bought her a pink hat and matching pink baseball glove. Most games, if she agreed to play at all, would find her in the dirt between second and third base making a dirt angel!

At five years old, Emerson is a clothes horse, and before school every morning she won't leave the house until everything matches. She has an outfit for every occasion with jewelry to match.

Emerson's biggest struggle in life up to this point has been to deal with her dirty younger brother, Jake, and her four dirty boy cousins!

Talking about Emerson, this story comes to mind. My buddy Pete and I were putting new hardwood floors in our new house when Steven called. He needed someone to babysit Emerson while he and his wife, Cristi, attended a funeral. I told him that his mom was out of town and I was busy installing hardwood floors. He said "Dad, can you help out here? It will only be for a couple of hours." I reluctantly agreed.

Emerson was about three years old and not yet potty-trained. I kept her busy watching her favorite movie *Cinderella* while Pete and I continued with the floors. After the second loop of *Cinderella,* Emerson came into the room where we working. Pete said "Jack, I think Emerson pooped her diapers; maybe you better change her." My reply "She's fine. Her parents will be here any minute and they can take care of it." Pete said "Jack, I can't believe you're going to let her run around in a dirty diaper! Come on, Jack, you've got to change her; it smells really bad." I gagged at the thought of a dirty diaper, but figured I'd better bite the bullet and do it. So I spread a baby blanket on the family-room floor, positioned Emerson in the center of it, and removed the diaper. It was a "doozie," and Emerson was squirming around while I tried to hold her still and clean her up. Pete was standing there, watching with a big grin on his face. I said "Pete, can you give me a hand here?" Pete's reply was "No, I just do family!" I no sooner got the mess cleaned up and a new diaper in place when Steven and Cristi walked in. I guess timing is everything!

Jake the Baby!

Jake is Steven and Cristi's youngest and the baby of the grandchildren. He is two years old and is fast developing into quite a character. I don't have a lot to report on Jake because he is so young. But I'm sure that if there is a book after this one, he will be a star player! As of this moment, Jake just walked by looking for his grandmother, saying "Poop, poop, Jakey pooped!" Oh boy, do I have those kids trained or what?!

I was over at Steven's house the other day, and he proudly announced that Jake was out of diapers! One of the defining moments in any parent's life. At about this time, Jake walked into the kitchen, minus diapers, and proceeded to poop on the floor! Steven was disgusted and gagging as he cleaned up Jake's mess. I said "Well, at least he didn't do it in his diaper; you've got to give him that much credit. Your next lesson with this kid should be teaching him the difference between the kitchen and the bathroom."

Here is a recent story about Jake. Dianna and I had taken Jake and Emerson to Virginia Beach for a long weekend. We were headed home and the kids were in the back in their car seats. I overhead this exchange between Emerson and Jake and almost went off the road!

Jake: "Emmy, you want to play house?"

Emerson: "OK, I'll be the wife, you are the husband, and you've got to call me honey."

Jake: "OK, I'll be the husband and call you honey, and you be the wife and take your clothes off!"

I told Steven about this exchange when we got the kids home. I asked "What the hell is going on at your house?" Steven laughed and said "Well, I do call Cristi honey!"

Henry

I haven't any funny stories about Henry. Henry is Tom's son from his first marriage. I'm sorry to say that we haven't gotten to know Henry as well as we should have. No good excuse except for time and distance. I do know Henry is a smart kid and destined for great things in this crazy world. At thirteen, Henry, like Cooper, has become one of those dreaded moody teenagers. Hopefully, in the next book, I'll be able to write a whole chapter on Henry alone.

Parenting

One evening John and his boys were over at the house for dinner. In an effort to get the boys to eat their vegetables, John said "If you don't clean your plates, there will be no dessert." I said "We don't have anything for dessert anyway." John, by now completely exasperated, yelled at me, "Dad, were you *ever* a parent?"

CHAPTER 15

Looking for a New Home

Earlysville, Virginia

We decided to move to Charlottesville, Virginia, to be near the kids and grandkids. Now we had to find a new house. That was a lot harder than we had ever anticipated. We looked at maybe 60 houses. I lost count after the first 45. Our son Steven acted as our real estate agent, and he was very patient with us.

I fell in love with a house on Lake Monticello. Not so much the house, but I loved the view. The back lawn went right down to the water where there was a dock with a boat. The owners were willing to throw in the boat! How was that for a sweet deal, a house on the lake with a boat! Oh boy, I was so excited! I was like a kid in a candy store! I couldn't sleep at night just thinking about all the fun we could have in this house with the whole gang! There was just one problem, Dianna hated it. It was too far from Charlottesville, the house was too close to the water, and the house was a shack. My argument was that we would be only thirty minutes from Charlottesville, the reason it was called a lake house was because it was on the lake, and we could fix the place up to look great! Well, she didn't want to hear it, and none of the kids were in my corner on this one, so I had to give up the dream.

We continued our search. Dianna fell in love with a little brick rambler right around the corner from John's house. This is the one she wanted. This was the perfect house. The only problem? I hated it! It had no personality, no garage, and more important, no lake! The asking price was totally outrageous. Dianna wanted this house bad enough to make a deal with me. She said "If you put a reasonable bid on this house and it is not accepted, then we will buy the house on the lake." I said "Great, let's do it!" We put a bid on the rambler, and it was not accepted. Dianna was broken-hearted, while I was doing cartwheels! I said "Okay, let's go back to the lake and take another look." Dianna simply said "No, I was just kidding. I am not going to live out at the lake and that is that." So the search continued!

Earlysville, Virginia

I was out wandering around and came upon a house in the town of Earlysville. It was on a beautiful piece of property and sat up on a knoll. The house seemed to have good bones and I could picture how it would look with a little bit of work. I got Steven to make arrangements to take us through the house. It looked great inside—well, maybe not great—it needed work, but basically it was sound. Dianna liked it and I liked it, and we were both exhausted from looking, and Steven was running out of patience. We put a bid in on the house and it was accepted.

Now we both asked each other "What the hell were we thinking?" The little bit of work to fix this house up turned into a lot of work. New roof, new windows, new shutters, complete paint job inside and out, new doors, new carpeting, new hardwood floors, crown molding, and new furnace, and we were still not finished!

The guy was installing additional windows in the bonus room on a beautiful fall day, and we were admiring the view when he said "You should name this place. Places like this usually have a name. If it were mine, I'd call it Whispering Pines." I said "Hmmm, that is a nice name, but I think if I did name this place, I'd call it The Money Pit!" Oh, I forgot, installing the new driveway, fixing the hole in the pool, and doing major landscaping. It has been a huge job, but the place does look beautiful! The house sits on two acres of lawn and trees—mostly pine trees that I have learned to hate. The backyard has a nice pool and backs up to a horse farm. The grandkids love to come over and feed the horses and take a swim. We've been here about two years now and pretty much enjoy it. We still miss the gang from the old neighborhood, but we are adjusting.

The yard is a constant challenge. With two acres, there is always something to clean up, plant, rake, and more raking. I even developed tennis elbow with all the raking I do. The damned pine needles never stop, and I mean *never* stop falling! Every morning I walk out into the yard and look around at all the work that has to be done, and I think to myself "What the hell was I thinking?"

Meeting New People

When we first moved in, I was out in the front raking when a couple walked by and stopped to welcome me to the neighborhood. I love to talk with people and probably kept them longer than they had planned. Finally, the old guy said to me "You know if you didn't live here, we'd have been home an hour ago!"

Like I said, raking up pine needles has become my main occupation since leaving the real world. I rake piles of needles up all over the yard, load them into the back of the truck, and go off to the dump. Recently I got my truck stuck in the front yard. The more I tried, the deeper it sunk into the mud. Finally I gave up; I jumped in the car and went up to the corner to see if the guy that runs the little auto repair shop knew where I could find someone with a wrecker to pull me out. Ted, the owner, is one of those crabby old guys who has been around these parts forever and has little patience for city slickers like me. I asked Ted if he knew of anyone with a wrecker, because my truck was stuck my in my front yard. Ted has this gravelly voice and he said to me "How the hell did you get stuck in your front yard? What's the matter

with you? Why the hell do you want to pay a hundred bucks for a wrecker when I can pull you out with the winch on my truck?" He was all up in my face. I backed away and said "Great; if you can get it out with your truck, that would be great!" As I leaving, I heard Ted mumbling "Damned people, paying a hundred bucks for a wrecker, idiots!"

I went from there to help a neighbor move a new bed into his house. It was a huge bed and it took me, my neighbor, and two delivery guys

Life Slightly Off Center

to get the thing into the house and up the stairs. One of the delivery guys said to me "Did you notice that some idiot got his truck stuck in his front yard down the street. He must have come home loaded last night!" I asked "What color is the truck?" He said "White." I admitted that I was the idiot and that was my truck and I only wished I was drunk when it got stuck! That was the end of that conversation.

In the meantime, Ted had come down and pulled out the truck and had it parked up next to the house. I went down to his shop to pay him for his trouble. I asked, "So, Ted, how much do I owe you?" He said, in that gravelly voice of his, "hundred bucks."

I meet the most interesting people out in my front yard. I think I have met everyone in the neighborhood while I was out dinking around in the yard. One day a woman came by and introduced herself, and we got to talking. She got such a kick out of our conversation that she said she was going to go home and get her husband. She wanted him to meet me. They came back and she introduced us. He was a nice guy, and we talked for awhile. I learned he was a psychiatrist with a practice in Charlottesville. They were getting ready to leave and said they wanted us to come to dinner and would call with a date. I said "great!" Just about this time, Dianna came down the driveway and I introduced her to Ben and Susan. Well, after some more random conversation, Dianna started telling the story about the time we erased our son, John. As she began to tell the story, I said "No, not that story, Dianna, this guy is a psychiatrist!" She ignored me and went on with the story. After she finished, we all had a big laugh, and they wandered away shaking their heads, never to be heard from again!

I almost forgot about another neighbor I met while I was out working in the front yard. Andrea went running by pushing triplets in a three-seat stroller. A Great Dane was tied to the front and helping to propel the stroller down the street. She stopped, and we chatted for a while. I learned she was a rare combination of half German and half Chinese. Her kids were two years old. This is a really interesting girl. She's a Harvard alumnus and met her husband in grad school at UVA. I invited her to bring her husband by for a beer one day and the kids could take a swim in the pool. They did come by, and her husband turned out to be a good guy. Andrea speaks to the children in German, her husband, Jeff, speaks only English, and the kids speak a mix, which comes out as gibberish! The Great Dane obeys commands in German, English, and Gibberish. That is one smart dog!

The neighbors to our right are great people. He was out washing his car one day when I walked up his driveway to introduce myself. He had his shirt off and was built like a brick outhouse! He's a cop and in great shape. Dianna came over and I introduced her to Mike. He apologized for not having his shirt on. I said "No need to apologize; Dianna loves a good body! In fact we are looking for a pool boy if you're looking for a job this summer." This comment didn't go over as I had hoped.

One day I was out watering the lawn and Mike was going by in his police car when he suddenly turned on his light and siren and pulled into my yard. He jumped out of the car and screamed "You have to stop, you are ruining my life!" We had only been in the neighborhood a few months and I didn't know if it was illegal to water the grass. I was startled since I was not used to having a police car pull into my yard with lights flashing and siren blasting. I asked what the problem was. He screamed "You want to know what the problem is, I'll tell you what the problem is! Every time we drive by your house, my wife starts nagging me about why can't our yard look as good as Jack's yard? Every time I sit down, she's on me about getting outside and getting busy on the damned yard! You have got to stop!" Turned out, he was just giving me a hard time and we both had a good laugh!

Chestnut Grove Baptist Church

One beautiful spring day I was out working in the flower beds on either side of the driveway when a young couple came by and stopped to chat. They were saying how beautiful the yard looked. That's all it takes, and I am your friend. We talked for about 45 minutes. This was one of those times when you meet people and automatically like them. These people I liked instantly. I learned their names were Tonya and Lance. During our conversation, I asked, "So, Lance, what do you do for a living?" He told me he was the Baptist minister at Chestnut Grove Baptist Church. He later told me that after he tells someone what he does for a living, the whole conversation takes on a whole different feel. Things really get very stiff and uncomfortable. Lance and Tonya continued their walk, but not before inviting me to their church.

Dianna and I went to the church that Sunday and we loved it—we loved all the people there and totally loved Lance and Tonya. We have always been the types who go to church on Christmas Eve and Easter. We tried to go for the kids' sake, when they were young, but I hated going and always found an excuse not to go. Excuses like, let's go out in the boat, let's sleep late, let's go on a picnic—any excuse would do. Now we find going to church one of the high points of the week!

This chance meeting of Lance and the introduction to the church was one of the greatest things that has happened in our lives! This was especially apparent when our grandson Carson died suddenly of complications from swine flu, and Lance and the Chestnut Grove family were there for us. We have never experienced such an outpouring of love. We were still the new people in the church, but it didn't make any difference. We felt like we had known these people for years. Cards and letters of support and words of encouragement flooded our mailbox everyday for weeks. Lance was always calling to make sure we were alright and if we needed anything. I introduced Lance to my son John and his wife Jennifer. They loved Lance and asked him to do the funeral service for Carson. Lance did a beautiful job! He talked as if he had known Carson his whole life. Lance even wore a green tie while conducting the service, because that was Carson's favorite color. After the service, I had several friends come up to me and ask if Catholics could go to Lance's church.

So, to Lance and Tonya and the people of Chestnut Grove, we say thank you. Thank you for being there when we needed you most!

The Good Samaritan

Since becoming a member of Chestnut Grove, I've developed a conscience mixed with a little guilt. I guess that comes with the religious territory. This was demonstrated in a big way about a month ago.

This particular Sunday the message at church was "loving unlovable people." The teacher of the Sunday school we attended was saying how easy it is to love our family, friends, healthy people, successful people, and beautiful people. The real test of faith is loving the homeless, the sick, the drunks, the druggies, the deformed, and the poor.

That Sunday afternoon, being a beautiful sunny day, I decided to jump in my classic Olds convertible and head for Orange, Virginia, to attend a car show going on there. Orange is about a 40-mile drive from our house. Upon reaching there, I discovered I was a day late for the car show. Since I was already this far, I decided to drive another 20 miles and visit our good friends Benji and Heather and their brand new baby boy.

I was stopped at a red light in downtown Orange when I spotted her. There she was, an old woman sitting on a stone wall with a walker in front of her. As I watched her, she made several attempts to stand up, but just couldn't make it. She was just too weak. Every time she tried to stand, I was with her, cheering her on in my mind. I was thinking *Come on, lady, you can do it!* The lesson I had learned in church that morning kept running through my head. Here was one of those unlovable people they had talked about. Now I was asking myself, *What would Lance do in this situation,* and I knew he'd stop and help her.

The old me would have driven right by her and not given it a second thought. The new me and my newfound sense of guilt turned the car around and pulled up in front of the old lady who was still trying to stand with every ounce of strength she had. I asked if she needed some help. She smiled a toothless grin, and said that yes, she would love some help. I helped her up, got her situated on her walker, and my good deed was done...or so I thought. At this point my new friend Laurie asked me if I could take her to Alexandria? Alexandria, Virginia, is about a 2-hour drive, and I wasn't going to do that. But I offered a ride to her house. Laurie asked if I could give her a ride to the CVS Pharmacy instead of taking her home. I agreed to this request and helped her into the front seat and put her walker in the back seat. At this point Laurie took the sneaker off her left foot to show me her broken toe. We discussed the broken toe for a bit and then she attempted to put her sneaker back on and was really struggling with it. I'm thinking to myself, *Okay, this is where I draw the line. I'm not going to put her sneaker on for her.* She finally managed it on herself and off we went.

Laurie was old, tattered, and lame, had no teeth, and to top it off, had stringy white hair pulled into a knot on top of her head. This woman was the perfect example of an unlovable person. She never stopped talking about me taking her to Alexandria and her cat. Her cat was beautiful, and she had paid $800 for it, and wouldn't I like to come to her place and see her cat. As the wind was whipping through Laurie's hair, she patted it and said she had just paid $65.00 for her hairdo. I'm thinking she was trying to tell me to put the top up. We finally got to the pharmacy and I got Laurie out of the car, back on her walker onto the sidewalk, and my good deed is done! As she hobbles away, she calls out over her shoulder "Jack, can you wait for me?"

Life Slightly Off Center

A lady in the parking lot, observing this whole operation, came over to me and said "You know, you could get a handicapped parking sticker for your car." Well, 30 minutes later, I'm still outside waiting for my new friend and thinking damn Lance, damn church. I now had about an hour invested in this and wanted to be done with it. I went into the store to find Laurie, and there she was, standing in line with a bottle of mouthwash. I asked if she was okay and she wasn't. She wanted me to go and see if they had a smaller bottle of mouthwash. All she could find was the giant size. I went back, found a smaller bottle, paid for it, and gave it to her. She asked "Don't they have this in yellow?" Now I was getting a little crazy. I helped her out of the store and back into the car. This was when my new best friend asked me if I wanted to go to McDonald's. I said "No, Laurie, I have got to get going." And I explained to her about visiting some friends. She then wanted to know who, where, and why and wouldn't I rather go to McDonald's?

About this time I was getting a little tired of my Good Samaritan experience and just wanted to be on my way. I said "Look it, Laurie, you have two choices here: I take you to McDonald's or I take you to your home—your choice!" She opted for a trip to McDonald's. I pulled up in front of the golden arches, got her situated on her walker, helped her through the door, and gave her a couple of bucks to get a milk shake. As I drove away, I was feeling pretty good. I had just done a good job of help-ing a very unlovable person. I had done my duty, and now I was free of any guilt.

As I was heading to Benji's house, I got a phone call from my friend John. I told him the story of Laurie and how I had spent the last hour and a half. I expected him to give me a thumbs-up, a pat on the back, a "great job buddy," but instead I got a lecture. He went on and on about how could I just leave her at McDonald's with no way of getting home. He said "You've got to go back there and help her get home. My God, the poor woman can barely walk and you just leave her!" After hanging up with John, I was feeling bad and thought maybe I should go back. But I didn't; I went ahead to see Benji and Heather. There I explained to them where I had been and what had happen. Benji, being a police officer, told me that Laurie most likely was an alcoholic. He based this on the fact that she wanted mouthwash and that is what they drink because of the high alcohol content. We visited for about an hour, and then I took off and headed for home. John's lecture was still in my head and I thought, *yeah, maybe I better go check on ole Laurie and give her a ride home.* I went by McDonald's and she wasn't there. I asked the girl behind the counter about a woman on a walker. "Oh, yeah, she just left," replied the girl and, pointing, said she was heading that way. So now I was heading that way and low and behold, there was Laurie, hobbling up the street. I pulled up next to her and said "hey, Laurie, need a ride?" She was all smiles and no teeth and said "Jack, you've come back for me!" I said "Come on, I'll give you a ride home." Laurie then proceeded to yell to another old lady sitting on a bench "Come on, Patty, we got us a ride!" So now I was helping Laurie into the front seat, the walker in the back along with Patty. Patty had white hair hanging down to her waist and no teeth and was skinny as a rail. We must have looked like the homeless express. I and my two girls were whisking through Orange with the top down and the white hair flowing. Patty was just in heaven and loving the ride. She said "What a great day for a ride in a convertible!"

Well, I finally got them both home safe and sound. They lived in a shelter and were not too happy to be back. Laurie whispered to me as I was helping her out of the car "Jack, I've got my bags packed and am ready to go. You could take me to the bank, and I could get gas money, and you could drive me to Alexandria." I again declined and said I had to be going. She then asked if I would like to come to her room and see her cat. I got Patty unloaded, and she thanked me for the ride and for buying Laurie the mouthwash and gave me a big God Bless You! As I drove away, I looked in the rearview mirror and watched the two of them waving goodbye.

I learned a good lesson that day: The next time I have the opportunity to love an unlovable person, I won't. I'll just keep driving and live with the guilt!

What's in a Name?

One day we had a chimney sweep clean out our chimney. I was out in the driveway washing the car when he came out to take a break. I said, "How's it going? My name is Jack." I reached to shake his hand. He shook my hand and said "Hello, my name is Kimberly." I then asked, "So, what's your first name?" He said "Kimberly." I said "Kimberly, you have got to be kidding; I can't believe your parents would name their son Kimberly!"

Now this was one big guy and he got right up in my face, looked down at me, and said "You got a problem with my name?" I said "Oh no, not at all; in fact, everyone calls me Jackie. It's good to meet you!"

Life Slightly Off Center

Carrots

Like I said earlier, our house backs up to a horse farm. The grandkids love coming over and getting carrots from Grandma and feeding the horses.

One summer Saturday afternoon we were having a cookout with some friends. Among the guests was our friend Dick. Ole Dick was intrigued by the horses and asked Dianna if she had carrots to feed them. Dianna went into the house and came out with a bunch of carrots and gave them to the eagerly waiting Dick. As she handed them to him, Dick asked "Do you know their names?" Dianna's snappy reply: "We don't usually name our carrots, Dick. Feel free to call them whatever you like!"

My Buddy John

One of the most interesting and funniest people I have met since moving to this part of the world is a guy named John. He and I met by chance at the local gym. We were working out, and he casually asked "How're you doing?

I wasn't doing well at all that day. I had completely forgotten my and Dianna's 48th wedding anniversary. I had come down to breakfast that morning and found several gifts on the kitchen table for me. I asked Dianna "Is it Father's Day?" "No, you jerk, it's our anniversary!" she shot back at me. Not a good way to start the day. I told John the whole story, and I am sure it was more information than he had bargained for. This led to a great conversation about marriage and life in general. At one point John said "I have friends who are divorced and they remember their anniversary!" Then he started bugging me about what I planned do about forgetting my anniversary. He wanted to know how I would make it up to, as he put it, my "poor wife."

We talked like we had known each other for years. Like old friends! This chance meeting led to us working out together. In fact, we meet at the gym every weekday morning at 5:30 AM and work out for an hour. Working out with a friend makes the process so much less painless. We talk, laugh, argue, kid around, and before you known it, our hour is up and we are on our way to McDonald's for breakfast. If there is any truth about daily exercise being the way to extend your life, then I owe John for whatever extension I might enjoy.

John and I meet once in awhile for a couple of beers and while enjoying a lot of laughs, we are able to solve a lot of the world's problems. John has become a great friend.

Bill and Reggie Come to Earlysville

I love it when my brother, Bill, and his wife come down to visit us. Bill and I get lost out in the yard and stay busy all day just dinking around. He has fondly named this place the Pinederosa. I now have a riding lawn mower and a huge leaf sucker-upper, and we are always out messing around with my new toys.

Every day at four in the afternoon when Bill and Reggie are here, we stop and have our cocktail hour. We were sitting out on the back deck, enjoying a beautiful summer afternoon and our gin and tonics. When we noticed about ten buzzards circling overhead, Billy said "My God, do we look that old?" We finished our drinks in the kitchen.

That same evening we were driving home after having dinner out. Dianna, Reg, and I were discussing the pro and cons of condo living. I definitely did not want to end up in a condo, no matter how nice it was. Dianna and Reggie said they would love to live in a nice condo. Billy apparently was not paying any attention to the conversation. When we asked how he felt about it, he replied "Oh, I'm going to be cremated."

397

Me and the Olds in the Big Parade

My classic 1975 Olds and I were in the big Standardsville, Virginia, Christmas Parade. I had two young beauty queens sitting up on the rear seat waving at the crowd. It was cold, dark, and snowing—the perfect evening for a parade. I was feeling great! The Olds and I had finally made it; we were doing what we were meant to do! I was thinking, *Boy, it doesn't get any better than this!*

I was completely oblivious of everything around me and just enjoying the moment. It was about then that I noticed our position in the parade.

We were behind the Roto-Rooter float. The centerpiece on the float was a toilet with water spouting out of it like a fountain. Talk about bringing me back to reality! The Olds and I were bringing up the rear behind a spouting toilet!

Rules of Retirement!

I've learned a few things since entering this wonderful world of retirement. I've discovered that when it comes to household chores, I can do nothing right. Whenever I attempt to help out around the house, I consistently do it wrong. My wife now starts every sentence this way:

"Jack, I really appreciate your helping out, BUT....you have the washing machine on the wrong setting. Why are you washing darks and lights in the same load? Why do you have the dryer on that setting? Jack, when you load the dishwasher, you never put the knives in this section of the silverware basket, and remember the glasses go up here, and the plates go down here, and don't forget if you're doing pots and pans, you put the setting here." Emptying the dishwasher and putting the dishes away is a lost cause. I never get them back in the right place. Dianna says "Forget it, just leave them be; I'll put them away."

I have found making the bed requires an advanced degree in home decorating! Lines must be straight, and the spread must be even on all sides. Comforter is folded just so with the right color turned up. This color is determined by the time of year. You must put light side up in the winter and the dark side up summer. Or is it dark side up in winter?

The biggest lesson I have learned is that the house is Dianna's domain, and if you value your life, you had better stay out of the way! I stay out of the way, by staying out in the yard. In the yard, I can nothing wrong.

There are no rules outside and I love not having rules! Retirement for Dianna and me means that I stay outside and she stays inside. We hook up for lunch and dinner and happily co-exist!

I spend so much time outside that the other day a woman drove by, stopped, rolled down her window, and asked, "Do you ever go into your house?"

Second Marriage?

One evening Dianna and I were sitting around talking about life in general and remembering all the things we've been through after so many years of marriage.

I asked Dianna "If I go before you, will you get married again?" Her reply was a resounding "NO, I would never marry again!" This is where I expected her to say something like: When you've had the BEST, you can never settle for less, and that I was the best thing to ever happen to her, and on and on with great adjectives about me. Instead Dianna said, "No, I would never do this again! You've got me worn out, and I don't have the strength to go through it again. No, sir, one time at this marriage thing is plenty enough for me!"

...And Life Is Good!

It's October 5th, our youngest son's birthday. It is a sunny fall day, about 60 degrees, and perfect sweatshirt weather. It is my favorite time of year. I am in my Dodge Ram pickup with my faithful dog, Katie, asleep by my side. The radio is pumping out country songs, and I am sipping a cup of Dunkin Donut's coffee and thinking this retired life is okay. All is right with the world except for the fact that my writing assignment for the creative writing course I'm taking at UVA is due in two days and I haven't even started. The assignment is to write about a person who has been important or influential in your life. I cannot think of anyone who falls into that category. I keep thinking that if a person were that important to me, they would jump into of my mind. No one has. There has got to be someone; everyone has someone.

I turned the radio up to catch Allen Jackson's big hit "Remember When." The lyrics "Remember when we were young and so in love" took me back to another time and another place. I'm driving my '49 Dodge with my bride of five days at my side, going through the small town of Phoenix, New York. We were headed to our first home. We turned into a winding driveway with a big house at the top of a rise. We would be living in the apartment over the garage, next to the big house.

Forty-eight years have come and gone since the day I carried my bride over the threshold of that little apartment. Forty-eight years of births, deaths, graduations, weddings, new assignments, new homes, new friends—forty-eight years of life! The lyrics of the song ask "Would you do it all again?" You bet, I would do it all again, but this time I would appreciate Dianna every step of the way!

Well, here I was, home again. I pulled into the long winding driveway to our big house on the hill, then it hit me and I smiled, thinking that the most important person, the most influential person in my life, has been here for the past forty-eight years. She was waiting inside. And she is still happy and in love with life!

The song continues "When we turn grey, and the kids grow up and move away, we won't be sad, we'll be glad for all the life we've had." We are now gray—or at least I am; Dianna is blond and pays big bucks to keep it that way—but we are glad for all the life we've had! It has been a great ride and I look forward to the next forty-eight years!

Oh, I had better call Steven and wish him a Happy Birthday!

Christmas Letters

Dear Readers,

For the past 48 years I have been writing a Christmas letter for all of our family and friends to help them keep up with us. I am including the most recent one in this book to give a sense of how we are doing these days. I guess I just want you to all rest easy knowing we are all okay.

Amazingly our children have survived and even flourished in spite of being raised by a mad man. I guess we can credit Dianna for that. What is even more amazing is that Dianna is still hanging around. She is definitely a glutton for punishment. I think it has become a contest for her to see just how long she can last!

Your Friend,
Jack

P.S. Hope you enjoyed the book. Tell your friends about it but don't let them borrow your copy. Let them go buy their own!

Christmas 2011

Dear Family and Friends,

Well, here we are with another year drawing to an end and it's time to update everyone on the activities here at the Raymond Ranch. Not very much excitement going on, just pretty much life.

I guess the most noteworthy event was the wonderful birthday party my kids threw for me to celebrate my big 70th! They went above and beyond anything I could have wished for. The planning took almost a year and culminated in a huge surprise party attended by family and friends from all over the country. I mean there were friends there that I had not seen in years. I was shocked and touched by everyone who was there. I was speechless, and for Jack Raymond to be speechless is really a testament in itself. Turning 70 was a lot less painful with so many friends and family there to wish me well. Colorado, Montana, New York, and Virginia were

Life Slightly Off Center

well represented. In short it was wonderful, and again I thank you all for coming and for all the messages I received from those that could not be attend.

All the kids are doing fine. All busy raising kids and working hard. Everyone is running in a different direction to get everything done.

John and Jen barely have time to think these days...run, run, and more running and somehow they manage to get it all done. Raising their boys Tucker and Wyatt is their main focus. Every season brings on a new sport and they excel in all and also do great in school. Jen is busy going to school and is on the fast track to becoming an official nurse. John stays busy with Grand Classroom, coaching, and the Carson Raymond Foundation (carson-raymondfoundation.com). The foundation is still doing great things in memory of their son Carson. This year among other things, another school field was completed here in Charlottesville with the help of friends and the University of Virginia baseball team. They are such a great bunch of guys.

Steven and Cristi celebrated the end of diapers in their lives. Jake, who is three, is officially potty trained, which is big news in the Raymond clan. He is in preschool and is quite a character. Emerson is six and in the first grade. She is still a "girly girl" and totally a good kid. Both the kids love to come over and go church with Grandma and Pops. Steve is still with Grand Classroom and pretty much enjoying his work there. Cristi is soon to become a force in the marketing department at her company and has European business trips in her future. Between Steve's travels and Cristi's travels, they should have a very interesting year.

Sheri and Tom are busy raising two teenage sons. That in itself is a full-time job. Sheri left the company she was with this year and is concentrating her efforts on doing volunteer work for Blue Sky. She of course still finds time to play lots of tennis, entertain, travel, and keep everyone anywhere near her on a constant run. Her most used statement is "'What do you want to do now?" Tom is able to keep up with her most of the time and still run his vending company. This guy deserves a medal for endurance! The boys are into everything and also great students. Between keeping up with Sheri, studies, and extra activities, they have no time to get into trouble and are pretty much good kids.

Dianna and I are doing great and just pretty much enjoying life here in this little berg. Living in a college town does have its advantages. We find ourselves enjoying a lot of UVA sporting events. Dianna's favorite are the baseball games; I enjoy the football games the most. I especially enjoy the tailgate parties before and after the game. The actual game is just something to do between parties.

We did a little traveling this year. Our big trip was going to Montana to visit my sister Kathy and her family. It was a great trip! We also spent time in Florida and a week at the beach in North Carolina. Even took another mission trip to West Virginia with our church. We joined the church this year and are pretty involved in lots of church activities. All in all, we had a busy year, a good year.

Well, by now I am sure you are into your second yawn, so I will close here. I think this is enough news for this year. I just reread last year's letter and not a lot has changed, but that's alright because life is good and life continues to be good.

Here is wishing you all a Merry Christmas and hoping 2012 is kind to you and yours!

Love,
Dianna and Jack

Carson Raymond Foundation

www.carsonraymondfoundation.com

The Carson Raymond Foundation is dedicated to honoring the life of Steven "Carson" Raymond, who in his nine short years delighted in the simple pleasures of playing sports with his school friends and teammates. He contracted the H1N1 virus in October 2009 and unexpectedly suffered cardiac arrest.

The Carson Raymond Foundation seeks to provide elementary-age children, regardless of sex, race, religion, or economic ability, with opportunities to participate in neighborhood sports programs. With the cooperation of individuals and community partners, the Carson Raymond Foundation builds fields and provides equipment, instruction, and transportation to allow school children to "GO PLAY" in their own neighborhoods.

A special thanks to all those who work tirelessly to make the Carson Raymond Foundation work.

The University of Virginia baseball team players and Coach Brian O'Connor have been instrumental in the great success of the Carson Raymond Foundation. This great organization is always there with the question "What do you want us to do next?"

Visit www.carsonraymondfoundation.com to learn about the ways the Carson Raymond Foundation makes a difference in the lives of young people in Charlottesville, Virginia, and to find out how you can participate.

23480161R00220

Made in the USA
Charleston, SC
26 October 2013